THE NEW BOOK OF KNOWLEDGE ANNUAL

1985

HIGHLIGHTING EVENTS OF 1984

THE NEW BOOK OF KNOWLEDGE ANNUAL

THE YOUNG PEOPLE'S BOOK OF THE YEAR

GROLIER
INCORPORATED
DANBURY, CONN.

Grolier Enterprises, Inc. offers a varied selection of both adult and children's
book racks. For details on ordering, please write:

Grolier Enterprises, Inc.
Sherman Turnpike
Danbury, CT 06816
Attn: Premium Department

STAFF

CONTENTS

CONTRIBUTORS

EISEMAN, Alberta
Author, *Mañana Is Now; From Many Lands; Rebels and Reformers*

HISPANIC AMERICANS

ELIASOPH, Philip
Fairfield University, Chairman, Department of Fine Arts; art critic, *Stamford Advocate* and *Greenwich Times*

FLORENCE

FINCH, Christopher
Author, *Norman Rockwell's America; The Art of Walt Disney; Rainbow; Of Muppets and Men; Image as Language*

NORMAN ROCKWELL

FREEDMAN, Russell
Author, *How Animals Learn; Growing Up Wild; Getting Born; Tooth and Claw; How Animals Defend Their Young; Animal Architects; The Brains of Animals and Man; How Birds Fly; Animal Superstars*

ANIMAL CHAMPIONS

GOLDBERG, Hy
Sports journalist; former co-ordinator of sports information, NBC sports

SPORTS, 1984

HACKER, Jeffrey H.
Author, *Spectator's Guide to the 1984 Olympics; Carl Sandburg; Franklin D. Roosevelt; Government Subsidy to Industry;* editor, *The Olympic Story*

THE 1984 OLYMPIC GAMES
GOLD ON ICE

HAHN, Charless
Stamp Editor, *Chicago Sun-Times*

STAMP COLLECTING

HELMS, Randel
Arizona State University, Professor of English; author, *Tolkien's World; Tolkien and the Silmarils*

J. R. R. TOLKIEN

HESTER, Erwin
East Carolina University (North Carolina), Professor of English

EDGAR ALLAN POE

INAMDAR, Sarla, M.D.
New York Medical College
INAMDAR, Subhash C., M.D.
New York University School of Medicine

CHILD ABUSE

JELLISON, Jerald M.
University of Southern California, Professor of Psychology; author, *I'm Sorry I Didn't Mean To and Other Lies We Love to Tell*

LIES
LIE DETECTION

KALLIR, Jane
Author, *Grandma Moses: The Artist Behind the Myth; Gustav Klimt/Egon Schiele; Austria's Expressionism; The Folk Art Tradition*

GRANDMA MOSES

KURTZ, Henry I.
Author, *John and Sebastian Cabot; Captain John Smith;* co-author, *The Art of the Toy Soldier*

HEROES OF THE WILD WEST
IN SEARCH OF THE GOLDEN KINGDOM

LANKENAU, Walter C.
Managing Editor, *Creative Crafts & Miniatures* magazine
POPULAR CRAFTS

LEMKE, Robert F.
Executive Editor, *Numismatic News;* author, *Standard Catalog of United States Paper Money, 1981; Coin Finder—Consumer Guide, 1980, 1981; How to Get Started in Coin Collecting*
COIN COLLECTING

MILLER, Bryan
Food reporter. *The New York Times*
FOOD SHOPPING

PASCOE, Jean R., M.D.
Internist
HEALTH

SHAW, Arnold
University of Nevada, Las Vegas, Adjunct Professor of Music; author, *A Dictionary of American Pop/Rock; Honkers and Shouters; 52nd St: The Street of Jazz; The Rockin' 50's; The World of Soul*
THE MUSIC SCENE

SILVERSTEIN, Alvin and Virginia
Co-authors, *So You're Getting Braces; Guinea Pigs; Hamsters; Gerbils*
ORTHODONTICS

SKODNICK, Ruth
Statistician
INDEPENDENT NATIONS OF THE WORLD

STADTLER, Bea
Author, *The Holocaust: A History of Courage and Resistance; The Adventures of Gluckel of Hameln*
HOLOCAUST

STEWART, Marjabelle Young
Author, *Stand Up, Shake Hands, Say "How Do You Do"; What to Do When and Why*
ETIQUETTE

TESAR, Jenny
Series Consultant, *Wonders of Wildlife;* author, *Introduction to Animals* (Wonders of Wildlife series); Designer, computer programs
ABC'S OF BODY TALK
MY COMPUTER: WHAT CAN I DO WITH IT?

THOMSON, Susan Ruth
Author, *A Catalogue of the Kate Greenaway Collection,* Rare Book Room, Detroit Public Library
KATE GREENAWAY

TILMAN, Robert O.
North Carolina State University, Dean of the School of Humanities and Social Sciences; author, *Man, State, and Society in Contemporary Southeast Asia; Bureaucratic Transition in Malaya*
BRUNEI

THE WORLD IN 1984

Voters in the United States showed their support of President Ronald Reagan in 1984 by electing him to a second term in office. Reagan, a Republican, defeated Walter F. Mondale, the Democratic candidate, with 59 percent of the popular vote.

THE YEAR IN REVIEW

In his famous novel *1984,* George Orwell painted a gloomy picture of a world controlled by an all-powerful state. As the real year 1984 drew to a close, however, people found the world far better than the one Orwell had described. While there were troubles in many areas during the year, there were also many positive events.

In the United States, a presidential election campaign dominated the news for most of the year. The campaign saw Republican President Ronald Reagan running for re-election against Walter Mondale, a Democrat who had served as vice-president under Jimmy Carter. It ended in a landslide victory for Reagan, who won 59 percent of the popular vote. To many people, the vice-presidential race was just as interesting as the presidential campaign. The Democrats became the first major party to nominate a woman for that post when they chose U.S. Representative Geraldine Ferraro of New York as their candidate. She opposed Vice-President George Bush who, like Reagan, sought and won a second term.

The overwhelming victory of the Reagan-Bush ticket was seen as a sign that U.S. voters were pleased with the general state of affairs in the country, politically and especially economically. The country continued to bounce back from the deep recession of the early 1980's. But the economic picture was far from perfect —many people were troubled by growing trade and budget deficits. As the government continued to spend more than it took in in revenues, federal officials went to work on various plans to cut the budget deficit. They concentrated their efforts on spending cuts and possible reforms in the country's tax laws.

The United States was not the only country to hold major elections during the year. In Canada, Prime Minister Pierre Elliott Trudeau, who had led the country for sixteen years, resigned in June. The Liberal Party chose John Turner as his successor, but Turner himself was swept from power by Progressive Conservative Party leader Brian Mulroney in elections in September. In Israel, the two leading parties formed a coalition government after July elections failed to give either party a majority. The prime minister's term was to be split by Labor Party leader Shimon Peres and Likud leader Yitzhak Shamir.

In El Salvador, José Napoleón Duarte, a moderate, was elected president in May. This was seen by many people as a promising sign for an end to that country's long conflict between right- and left-wing groups. One of Duarte's first acts was to open talks with the leftist rebels who have been battling the government. Late in the year, talks were also held between the United

States, which has supported the Salvadorean Government, and Nicaragua, which has supported the rebels. But relations between the two countries remained tense.

Tragedy struck India during the year. Indira Gandhi, prime minister for fifteen of the preceding eighteen years, was assassinated by two of her own bodyguards. The assassins were members of the Sikh religious group. Their action came after repeated outbreaks of religious violence had caused the Indian Government to take stern measures against the Sikhs. Gandhi's son, Rajiv, was appointed to succeed her, and the country's future seemed uncertain.

Conflict between religious and political groups also continued in Lebanon, and both Israeli and Syrian troops remained in that country throughout the year. Under pressure from Muslims backed by Syria, the Lebanese Government scrapped a troop withdrawal agreement it had reached with Israel in 1983. Israel then dropped a central demand—that Syrian troops leave at the same time its own forces left—and began to negotiate anew. Terrorist attacks also continued; in one, 24 people were killed when a car loaded with explosives was driven into the U.S. embassy near East Beirut.

Elsewhere in the Middle East, the war between Iran and Iraq threatened the world's oil supply when both sides began attacking tankers in the Persian Gulf. But a hopeful sign that the region might one day find peace was seen in September, when Jordan announced that it was resuming diplomatic relations with Egypt. Along with seventeen other Arab countries, Jordan had broken off relations in 1979 after Egypt signed a peace treaty with Israel.

A possible dispute seemed to have been averted when Britain reached agreement with China on the issue of Hong Kong. This British colony stands on land leased from China, most of which is scheduled to return to Chinese control in 1997. The agreement worked out would guarantee most of the rights and freedoms now enjoyed by Hong Kong citizens for 50 years after China's Communist government takes control. China also continued to increase its trade with the West and to allow more free enterprise at home.

While relations between China and the West were cordial, however, relations between the world's two major superpowers —the United States and the Soviet Union—were chilly. Arms-control talks between the two had been broken off in 1983. And in February, Soviet leader Yuri Andropov died and was succeeded by Konstantin Chernenko. A conservative Communist Party official, Chernenko was considered unlikely to make friendly moves toward the West. But in November the two countries agreed in principle that arms-control talks should be held. And they managed to put aside their differences to provide aid to drought-ridden Ethiopia, where Soviet planes helped fly Western food to thousands of starving people. Small as it was, this act of co-operation seemed a promising sign for the future.

JANUARY

1 Brunei became an independent nation called Brunei Darussalam. The tiny country is located on the northern coast of the island of Borneo, in the Pacific Ocean. It had been under British protection for nearly 150 years. Sultan Muda Hassanal Bolkiah continued as the country's leader. (In September, Brunei was admitted to the United Nations as its 159th member.)

In Nigeria, army general Mohammed Buhari announced that he had assumed control of the country. He succeeded President Shehu Shagari, who had been ousted in a military coup the day before. Shagari had been president since 1979.

3 Syria freed U.S. Navy pilot Robert O. Goodman, Jr. Goodman had been taken prisoner on December 4, 1983, after his plane was shot down while carrying out a bombing raid on Syrian positions in Lebanon. On December 29, the Reverend Jesse Jackson, a Democratic presidential candidate, flew to Syria to seek Goodman's release. He made a personal appeal to Syrian President Hafez al-Assad, who later agreed to free Goodman.

10 The United States and the Vatican established full diplomatic relations for the first time in 117 years. This was made possible when Congress voted, in late 1983, to repeal an 1867 law prohibiting such relations. The 19th-century law had been passed as a result of anti-Roman Catholic sentiment and concern for a unified Italy.

At a White House ceremony, President Ronald Reagan greets Navy pilot Robert Goodman. At right is the Reverend Jesse Jackson, who helped secure Goodman's release from Syria.

Johnny Weissmuller, who died at the age of 79, is shown here in one of his many Tarzan movies. Also shown are Jane, Boy, and Cheetah.

17 The U.S. Supreme Court ruled that people who use video recorders at home to tape television programs for their own use do not violate U.S. copyright laws. The ruling was a victory for manufacturers and users of video recorders. It was a defeat for the motion picture industry, which felt that home recording infringed on the rights of people who hold the copyrights for movies and other TV shows. These people normally receive royalties or other payment every time their work is shown.

20 Johnny Weissmuller, the American swimmer and movie actor, died at the age of 79. Weissmuller won a total of five gold medals in swimming events during the 1924 and 1928 Olympics. He also set 67 world records before retiring from sports in 1929. Weissmuller then became famous as a movie star, playing the role of Tarzan in about twenty movies.

22 William French Smith announced that he would resign as U.S. Attorney General. President Ronald Reagan nominated Edwin Meese III to succeed Smith. To become effective, the nomination would have to be confirmed by the Senate. (Questions about Meese's financial dealings delayed Senate action on the nomination for the rest of the year.)

FEBRUARY

7 Following a worsening of internal conditions in Lebanon, President Ronald Reagan ordered the U.S. Marines to withdraw from the country. The Marines were part of an international peace-keeping force that had been in Lebanon since the fall of 1982. (On February 8, Britain withdrew its force. On February 20, Italy completed its evacuation. And on March 31, the French, the last unit of the force, withdrew, ending the 19-month effort to keep peace in Lebanon.)

9 Soviet leader Yuri V. Andropov died at the age of 69. Andropov became general secretary of the Communist Party's Central Committee in November, 1982, after the death of Leonid Brezhnev. This is the most important position in the Soviet Union.

11 The space shuttle *Challenger* ended an eight-day mission by landing at the Kennedy Space Center in Cape Canaveral, Florida. This was the first time that a shuttle had landed at its launching base. The five-man crew included Bruce McCandless II and Robert L. Stewart, whose space walks were the highlight of the mission. The men used jet-propelled backpacks to move around in space. Unlike previous space walkers, they were not connected

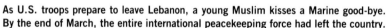

As U.S. troops prepare to leave Lebanon, a young Muslim kisses a Marine good-bye. By the end of March, the entire international peacekeeping force had left the country.

Challenger astronaut Bruce McCandless "rides" the robot arm outside the space shuttle. Foot restraints anchor him to the arm and help him perform tasks in the absence of gravity.

to their ship by safety lines. They truly were "human satellites," orbiting the Earth at the same speed as their spacecraft—17,500 miles (28,000 kilometers) per hour.

13 Konstantin U. Chernenko was chosen to succeed Yuri V. Andropov as general secretary of the Soviet Communist Party's Central Committee. At the age of 72, Chernenko became the oldest person ever chosen to lead the U.S.S.R.

Ricardo de la Espriella, who had been president of Panama since July, 1982, resigned. He was succeeded by Vice-President Jorge Illueca.

15 Ethel Merman, the American musical-comedy star, died at the age of 76. Merman starred in such Broadway shows as *Annie Get Your Gun* and *Gypsy*. Her fourteen movies included *There's No Business Like Show Business, Anything Goes,* and *Call Me Madam.*

29 Prime Minister Pierre Elliott Trudeau of Canada announced that he would resign as head of government and leader of the Liberal Party. Except for a nine-month period in 1979–1980, Trudeau had been prime minister since 1968. Trudeau agreed to remain in office until a successor was chosen at a Liberal Party convention, later in 1984.

MARCH

5 Lebanon canceled its 1983 troop withdrawal agreement with Israel. The U.S.-sponsored pact had called for the simultaneous withdrawal of Israeli, Palestine Liberation Organization (PLO), and Syrian troops from Lebanon. Syria had never accepted the agreement.

16 South Africa and Mozambique signed a non-aggression treaty. It was the first such treaty between white-ruled South Africa and a black-ruled African country.

25 Hawaii's Mauna Loa, the world's largest active volcano, erupted with its biggest outpouring of lava in nearly 35 years. The lava flow threatened the city of Hilo and other populated areas. (On March 30, Mauna Loa's neighbor, Kilauea, also erupted. This was the first time since 1868 that the two volcanoes had erupted at the same time.)

Maryland began celebrating the 350th anniversary of the arrival of its first European settlers. The opening ceremonies took place on St. Clements Island in the Potomac River, where the colonists had landed in March, 1634. A re-enactment of their landing featured a replica of the *Dove,* one of the two small ships that had carried the 140 colonists from England to the New World.

A river of molten lava slides down the slopes of the volcano Mauna Loa. The Hawaiian volcano, which is the largest active volcano in the world, erupted with its biggest outpouring of lava in nearly 35 years.

Tornadoes swept through the Carolinas, killing at least 69 people. Here, a Greenville, North Carolina, resident begins to sort out her belongings from the wreckage.

25 In presidential elections in El Salvador, José Napoleón Duarte of the moderate Christian Democratic Party finished first with 43.4 percent of the vote. Roberto d'Aubuisson of the far-right National Republican Alliance was second with 29.8 percent. Because none of the eight candidates had received at least 50 percent of the vote, a runoff between the two leaders was scheduled. (On May 6, Duarte won the runoff election.)

26 Sékou Touré, president of Guinea and a symbol of African independence, died at the age of 62. Touré had ruled Guinea ever since he led it to independence from France in 1958.

28 At least 69 people were killed and hundreds were injured by tornadoes that swept through North and South Carolina. The tornadoes were part of a huge storm system of near-hurricane strength that resulted from unusual weather conditions. The storm also battered the Northeast with rain and snow and caused widespread flooding in coastal areas of New York, New Jersey, and Connecticut.

3 Rakesh Sharma, a 35-year-old pilot, became India's first person in space. He and two Soviet astronauts were launched aboard a Soyuz T-11 spacecraft for an eight-day visit to the Salyut 7 space station. During the mission, Sharma performed yoga exercises to test yoga's possible effectiveness in combating space sickness.

Members of the armed forces seized power in Guinea. The coup came a week after the death of President Sékou Touré, who had governed Guinea for 26 years. (On April 5, the leader of the coup, Lansana Conté, was named president.)

11 Konstantin U. Chernenko was named president of the Soviet Union by the nation's legislature. This was the second major post he assumed after the death of Yuri Andropov in February. Chernenko had already become general secretary of the Communist Party.

Two giants in different fields died in April: Count Basie, the jazz pianist and band leader .

... and Ansel Adams, the photographer best known for his majestic landscapes of the American West.

13 Astronauts aboard the U.S. space shuttle *Challenger* completed a seven-day mission. The mission's highlight was the first repair of a damaged satellite in space. The astronauts retrieved and repaired Solar Max, a satellite launched in 1980 to study the sun. The satellite had malfunctioned soon after its launch. After the repair work was completed, Solar Max was released back into orbit by the space shuttle's robot arm.

22 Britain broke diplomatic relations with Libya. The step came five days after a gunman in the Libyan embassy in London had opened fire on a group of demonstrators outside, wounding ten and killing a British policewoman. The demonstrators were Libyan exiles protesting the policies of the Libyan Government.

Ansel Adams, the American photographer, died at the age of 82. Adams was best known for his majestic black-and-white landscapes of the American West.

26 Count Basie, the American jazz pianist and band leader, died at the age of 79. His band was one of the most influential groups of the Big Band era in the 1930's and 1940's.

Rashid Karami was named prime minister of Lebanon by the nation's president, Amin Gemayel. Karami replaced Shafik-al-Wazzan, who had resigned in February.

Sultan Mahmood Iskandar became king of Malaysia. He succeeded Sultan Ahmad Shah, who had reigned for five years.

MAY

1 U.S. President Ronald Reagan ended a six-day visit to China. During the trip he met with Chinese officials in an effort to strengthen ties between the two countries.

6 In a run-off presidential election in Ecuador, León Febres Cordero Rivadeneira, leader of the conservative Social Christian Party, was elected president of the nation. He succeeded Osvaldo Hurtado, who had held the position since 1981.

In national elections in Panama, Nicolás Ardito Barletta Vallarina was elected president. The elections were the first to be held since the military had seized power in 1968.

7 The Soviet Union announced that it would not participate in the 1984 Summer Olympic Games in Los Angeles. The Soviets claimed that the United States "does not intend to insure the security of all sportsmen." (All the Warsaw Pact nations, except for Rumania, eventually joined the boycott.)

An ancient Mayan tomb discovered in Guatemala yielded great archeological finds. The most unusual was this ceramic jug with a screwtop lid—the first pre-Columbian twist-open container ever found.

During an annular solar eclipse on May 30, the moon moves across the sky and nearly blocks out the sun. "Annular" means "forming a ring," such as the thin ring of sunlight still seen around the dark moon above.

7   In an out-of-court settlement, seven U.S. chemical companies agreed to set up a $180,000,000 fund for thousands of veterans of the Vietnam War. The chemical companies had manufactured Agent Orange, a plant-killer used by the U.S. military during the war. Agent Orange contained dioxin, a powerful poison. The veterans claimed that exposure to it had caused many of their disabilities.

14   Jeanne Sauvé was installed as governor-general of Canada. She was the first woman ever to be named to the largely ceremonial position.

23   It was announced that archeologists had discovered an ancient Mayan tomb in the Petén jungle of northern Guatemala. The tomb, more than 1,500 years old, was in perfect condition. Its contents included wall paintings, pottery, and the skeleton of a man thought to be a Mayan ruler. Of special interest was a ceramic jar with a screw-top lid. Such a container had never before been found among remains of pre-Columbian cultures.

Richard von Weizsäcker was chosen president of West Germany by the nation's parliament. He succeeded Karl Carstens, who had been president since 1979.

30   A nearly total solar eclipse could be seen in the southeastern United States. In most other parts of the United States and in Canada, a partial eclipse was visible. It was the last major solar eclipse to occur in North America during this century.

JUNE

1 A United Nations Security Council resolution condemned attacks on shipping in the Persian Gulf. The resolution was directed toward Iran, which had been accused by six Persian Gulf nations of carrying out such attacks. The attacks were part of the widening four-year-old war between Iran and Iraq.

3 The *Marques*, a three-masted tall ship from Britain, sank in heavy seas north of Bermuda. Nine crew members were rescued, and nineteen were presumed dead. The *Marques* was one of 42 ships that were participating in a race from Bermuda to Halifax, Nova Scotia.

9 The leaders of seven major industrial nations ended a three-day meeting in London. The countries represented were Britain, Canada, France, West Germany, Italy, Japan, and the United States. The talks focused on economic and political issues.

16 Leaders of Canada's ruling Liberal Party selected John N. Turner to be the party's head. (On June 30, Turner became prime minister, replacing Pierre Elliott Trudeau. Trudeau had announced his resignation as head of government and Liberal Party leader in February.)

14–18 Citizens of the ten countries that make up the European Economic Community (the Common Market) elected representatives to the European Parliament. The European Parliament is an advisory body for the European Economic Community. The elections, the first since 1979, were dominated by domestic issues rather than by the issue of European unity. Except in Greece, the elections were viewed as defeats for the parties holding power in national governments and as victories for extremist and marginal parties.

26 The maiden flight of the U.S. space shuttle *Discovery* was canceled just four seconds before liftoff. The cancellation occurred after computers detected an apparent valve failure in one of the shuttle's engines.

30 Lillian Hellman, the American playwright, died at the age of 79. Among her plays are *The Children's Hour, The Little Foxes,* and *Watch on the Rhine.* Hellman also wrote three volumes of memoirs, including *Scoundrel Time,* in which she recalled the events in the 1950's that led to her being blacklisted in Hollywood for her leftist politics.

Balloons, firecrackers, and dancing dragons welcomed back San Francisco's cable cars, after 20 months of restoration work. The system, which is more than 100 years old, is the last running cable car line in the United States.

5 It was announced that *Seascape: Folkstone,* a painting by the British artist J. M. W. Turner (1775–1851), had been sold for $10,023,200. The price set a world record as the highest ever paid at auction.

14 In national elections in New Zealand, the liberal Labor Party won a majority in parliament. David Lange, head of the party, thus became prime minister. He succeeded Robert Muldoon of the conservative National Party, who had served since 1975.

17 In France, Premier Pierre Mauroy resigned. French President François Mitterrand appointed Laurent Fabius to succeed Mauroy, who had been premier since 1981.

19 At its national convention in San Francisco, the Democratic Party nominated Representative Geraldine A. Ferraro for Vice President. She was the first woman in U.S. history to be the vice-presidential candidate of a major party.

23 In national elections in Israel, no party won enough seats in parliament to form a government. Who would become prime minister would depend on who could form a majority coalition. (On September 14, parliament approved a new government based on a power-sharing agreement between the two major political parties. Labor leader Shimon Peres would serve as prime minister for the first half of the term. And Yitzhak Shamir, the Likud leader, would serve as prime minister for the second half of the term.)

25 In elections in St. Vincent and the Grenadines, the New Democratic Party won a majority of seats in parliament. James Mitchell, head of the party, thus became prime minister. He succeeded Milton Cato, who had held the position since the nation's independence in 1979.

A Soviet astronaut, Svetlana Savitskaya, became the first woman to walk in space. Savitskaya spent more than three hours outside the space station Salyut 7.

26 George H. Gallup, the American who developed the Gallup Poll, died at the age of 82. Gallup developed the methods of public opinion polling that are used by newspapers, governments, advertisers, and other groups throughout the world.

27 James Mason, the British-born actor, died at the age of 75. Mason starred in more than 100 movies, including *A Star Is Born, Georgy Girl,* and *The Verdict.*

On July 4, the torch atop the 98-year-old Statue of Liberty was removed. It will be replaced by a new torch as part of an extensive, two-year renovation of the entire statue, which stands at the entrance to New York Harbor. The reconstruction will culminate in a gala 100th birthday celebration on October 28, 1986.

AUGUST

4 The West African country of Upper Volta changed its name to Burkina Faso. The name change marked the first anniversary of a coup that had set up the current military government. (The name means "land of incorruptible men.") The country also adopted a new flag and national anthem.

5 Richard Burton, the British actor, died at the age of 58. His more than 40 movies included *Cleopatra, Who's Afraid of Virginia Woolf?,* and *The Spy Who Came in From the Cold.* He was also a noted stage actor, especially famed for his roles in Shakespearean plays.

13 Morocco and Libya signed a treaty establishing a "union of states." The treaty was designed to strengthen political and economic ties between the two nations and to provide for mutual defense.

14 The United Nations' second International Conference on Population ended. At the nine-day meeting in Mexico City, delegates from 149 nations approved a declaration that dealt with concerns

British actor Richard Burton died at the age of 58. He is shown here in the movie *Becket.*

This odd-looking vehicle became the first solar-powered car to complete a trip across the United States.

about population growth. The declaration included recommendations to update the program adopted at the first conference, in 1974.

14 J. B. Priestley, the British author, died at the age of 89. Most of his novels and plays dealt with the lives and characters of the British, and they mixed humor with social and political comment.

23 Dzhambiin Batmunkh became head of the Communist Party in Mongolia. He succeeded Yumzhagiyn Tsedenbal, who resigned after having held the post since 1952.

25 Truman Capote, the American writer, died at the age of 59. Capote's works included *Other Voices, Other Rooms; Breakfast at Tiffany's;* and *In Cold Blood.*

29 A solar-powered car completed a trip from California to Florida, becoming the first such vehicle to cross the United States. Built by students at Crowder College in Neosho, Missouri, the car got all its power from sixteen solar panels.

31 During the last week of August, more than a dozen major fires raged across Montana. Almost 250,000 acres of forest and rangeland were scorched, and countless wild animals were killed. Professional and volunteer fire fighters from seven Western states were called in to combat the wind-driven fires. (By week's end, heavy rains helped them put out the flames.)

SEPTEMBER

2 Typhoon Ike hit the Philippines with winds of 137 miles (220 kilometers) per hour. It was the country's worst storm in this century. More than 1,300 people lost their lives.

4 In national elections in Canada, the Progressive Conservative Party won 211 of the 282 seats in parliament—the most seats won by any party in Canadian history. The party's leader, Brian Mulroney, thus became prime minister, effective September 17. He succeeded John Turner of the Liberal Party, who had held the position since June 30.

5 The U.S. space shuttle *Discovery* completed its maiden flight. The six-member crew spent six days in space. The mission's highlight was the launching of three communications satellites.

14 Janet Gaynor, the American film actress, died at the age of 77. In 1928, the first year that Academy Awards were presented, Gaynor received the best actress award.

15 Diana, Princess of Wales, gave birth to her second son, who was named Prince Henry. The baby is third in line for the British crown after his father, Prince Charles, and his brother, Prince William.

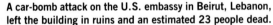

A car-bomb attack on the U.S. embassy in Beirut, Lebanon, left the building in ruins and an estimated 23 people dead.

18 Joe Kittinger, a 56-year-old American, crash-landed his 10-story-tall balloon in northwestern Italy, ending a 3,535-mile (5,688-kilometer) trip that began September 14 in Maine. Kittinger thus became the first person to complete a solo balloon crossing of the Atlantic. He also set a world distance record for a solo balloon flight.

The 39th regular session of the United Nations General Assembly opened at U.N. headquarters in New York City. Paul John Firmino Lusaka of Zambia was elected to serve as assembly president for one year.

20 A car loaded with explosives was driven past guards and exploded in front of the U.S. embassy in Beirut, Lebanon. An estimated 23 people were killed, including two Americans. A pro-Iranian extremist group claimed responsibility for the attack.

25 Jordan announced that it was restoring diplomatic relations with Egypt. Jordan was one of seventeen Arab nations that had broken diplomatic relations with Egypt in 1979, after Egypt had signed a peace treaty with Israel. It became the first of these nations to resume diplomatic ties.

30 A deadly bacterial disease called citrus canker was found to have infected orange, grapefruit, and tangerine trees in Florida. With no known cure for the canker, infected trees had to be cut down and burned to prevent the disease from spreading. By the end of September, more than a million trees had been burned. And all shipments of Florida citrus plants and fruits had been banned.

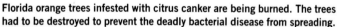

Florida orange trees infested with citrus canker are being burned. The trees had to be destroyed to prevent the deadly bacterial disease from spreading.

OCTOBER

1   U.S. Labor Secretary Raymond Donovan was indicted by a New York grand jury in connection with his past business dealings. He was the first incumbent cabinet officer ever to be indicted. Donovan took a leave of absence from his cabinet post while waiting for the outcome of the case.

2   Three Soviet astronauts returned to Earth after spending 237 days in space. The astronauts completed the longest space flight in history.

12   British Prime Minister Margaret Thatcher narrowly escaped injury when a bomb exploded at the hotel in Brighton, England, where she and her cabinet were staying. The blast killed four people and wounded 32 others. The Provisional Irish Republican Army (IRA) claimed responsibility for the act.

13   The U.S. space shuttle *Challenger* completed an eight-day mission. The seven-member crew included two women and Cana-

Bishop Desmond Tutu of South Africa (shown here with his wife, Leah) won the 1984 Nobel peace prize for his nonviolent efforts to end that country's policy of apartheid.

da's first astronaut, Marc Garneau. Kathryn D. Sullivan became the first American woman to walk in space as she and David C. Leestma tested a system for refueling satellites.

26 Surgeons at Loma Linda University Medical Center in California transplanted a baboon heart into a baby girl called Baby Fae. (Her real name was not made public.) Four days later she became the longest surviving human recipient of an animal heart. Only four ape-to-human heart transplants had been performed previously, all in adults. The longest living of those recipients had died three-and-one-half days after the operation. (On November 15, Baby Fae died of complications that developed when her body rejected the transplanted heart.)

31 India's Prime Minister Indira Gandhi was assassinated by two gunmen who were members of her bodyguard. She was 66 years old. Her son, Rajiv, was chosen as her successor, thereby continuing a political dynasty that began with his grandfather Jawaharlal Nehru. Nehru was prime minister during India's first seventeen years of independence from Britain. Gandhi served as her father's official hostess and close political ally. Following his death in 1964, she was elected to parliament and in 1966 became prime minister. Except for three years (1977–1980), she held the position until her death. (Gandhi's assassination touched off a major wave of violence, and some 1,000 people, mostly Sikhs, were killed.)

THE 1984 NOBEL PRIZES

Chemistry: R. Bruce Merrifield of the United States, for developing a simple, rapid method for making proteins.

Economics: Sir Richard Stone of Britain, for creating a widely used accounting system that measures the performance of national economies.

Literature: Jaroslav Seifert of Czechoslovakia, for his poetry, which "provides a liberating image of the indomitable spirit and versatility of man."

Peace: Bishop Desmond Tutu of South Africa, for his nonviolent leadership in the campaign to end that country's policy of apartheid (racial segregation).

Physics: Carlo Rubbia of Italy and Simon van der Meer of the Netherlands, for their roles in discovering three subatomic particles—two W particles (one electrically positive and one negative) and the neutral Z particle.

Physiology or Medicine: Cesar Milstein, an Argentine-born Britain; Georges J. F. Köhler of West Germany; and Niels K. Jerne, a British-born Dane, for their studies in immunology, which have led to promising new treatments for a wide range of diseases.

NOVEMBER

4 In national elections in Nicaragua, the Sandinista candidate, Daniel Ortega Saavedra, was elected president. The elections were the first to be held since 1974. (The leftist Sandinistas had taken control of the country in a 1979 revolution.)

6 In U.S. elections, Republicans Ronald W. Reagan and George H. Bush were re-elected president and vice-president. They defeated the Democratic candidates, Walter F. Mondale and Geraldine A. Ferraro. The Republicans lost two seats in the Senate but retained a majority in that chamber. They gained fourteen seats in the House of Representatives, where the Democrats kept their majority.

8 U.S. Secretary of Education Terrel H. Bell announced that he would resign as of December 31.

11 The Vietnam Veterans Memorial in Washington, D.C., officially became a national monument, following three days of ceremonies. A bronze statue called *Three Servicemen* was dedicated at the site. It stands near the V-shaped memorial wall, completed in 1982, that bears the names of the 58,000 Americans who were killed or missing in action during the Vietnam War.

Three Servicemen, a bronze statue, was dedicated at the site of the Vietnam Veterans Memorial in Washington, D.C. The Memorial officially became a national monument in November.

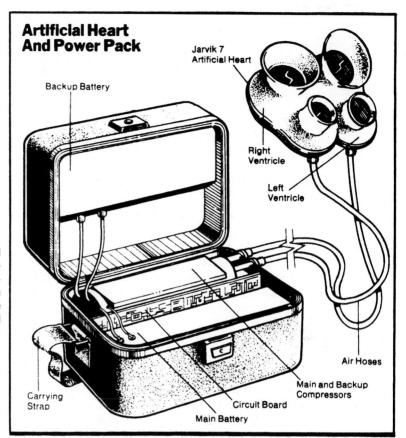

Artificial Heart And Power Pack

Jarvik 7 Artificial Heart

Backup Battery

Right Ventricle

Left Ventricle

William Schroeder's plastic and metal heart was at times connected to a portable, battery-powered unit. Air was pumped through two hoses that attached to the heart. The air forced blood in and out of the heart.

Air Hoses

Main and Backup Compressors

Carrying Strap

Circuit Board

Main Battery

16 Astronauts aboard the space shuttle *Discovery* completed an eight-day mission. The five-member crew retrieved two communications satellites that had misfired into useless orbits after their launch in February. The satellites were brought back to Earth in *Discovery*'s cargo bay.

19 A natural gas plant north of Mexico City exploded, turning a nearby suburb into an inferno. More than 450 people were killed, and about 4,000 were injured.

25 Surgeons at the Humana Heart Institute International in Louisville, Kentucky, removed the diseased heart of a 52-year-old man and replaced it with a permanent artificial heart. This was only the second time that such an operation had been performed. The patient, William J. Schroeder, made steady progress following the operation, taking his first steps only four days later. His new plastic and metal heart was connected, via air hoses, to one of two external power sources—a large, stationary machine or a small, battery-powered unit no larger than a camera bag.

National elections were held in Uruguay for the first time since 1971. Julio María Sanguinetti, leader of the centrist Colorado Party, was elected president effective March, 1985. The elections ended eleven years of military rule.

DECEMBER

3 Poison gas leaking from a pesticide plant in Bhopal, India, killed more than 2,000 people. The gas, methyl isocyanate, also caused eye and respiratory injuries in tens of thousands of others. The accident was the worst industrial disaster on record. The pesticide plant was jointly owned by Union Carbide, a large U.S. corporation, and by Indian investors. The plant was constructed and operated by Indians.

In national elections in Grenada, the centrist New National Party won a majority of seats in parliament. Herbert A. Blaize, the party's head, thus became prime minister. The elections followed eight years of political upheaval, including an American-led invasion in 1983.

4 Scientists announced the discovery and excavation of a ship that sank in the eastern Mediterranean Sea some 3,400 years ago. It was the earliest shipwreck ever excavated. The ship was a treasure trove of Bronze Age artifacts, including gold objects, beads, medallions, pottery, and copper and tin ingots (the metals that are used to make bronze). The discovery was expected to greatly increase our knowledge of Bronze Age trading, seafaring, and shipbuilding practices.

Archeologists map the wreck of a ship that sank off the southern coast of Turkey about 3,400 years ago. It was the earliest shipwreck ever excavated.

A drawing by 8-year-old Danny La Boccetta of New York City was pictured on a 1984 Christmas stamp issued by the U.S. Postal Service. Danny's design was chosen from more than 500,000 designs submitted by young people.

9 Iranian security men stormed a hijacked Kuwaiti airplane at Teheran airport, capturing four Arab hijackers and freeing their last nine hostages. The hijackers had seized the plane on December 3, shortly after its takeoff from Dubai. During the following days they released 153 of the plane's passengers. But they killed two Americans and tortured other passengers who were aboard the plane.

10 American astronomers announced the discovery of what they believe is the first planet to be detected outside our solar system. The planetlike object, estimated to be nearly the size of Jupiter, orbits Van Biesbroeck 8, a star in the constellation Ophiuchus. The star and the newly sighted object (called Van Biesbroeck 8B) are about 21 light years from Earth. A light year is the distance light travels in one year—about 5,878,000,000 (billion) miles.

12 Mauritania's president, Mohammed Khouna Ould Haidalla, was ousted in a coup. The leader of the coup, army chief of staff Maouya Ould Sidi Ahmed Taya, assumed the presidency.

14 In national elections in Belize, the conservative United Democratic Party won a majority of seats in the National Assembly. Manuel Esquivel, the party's leader, thus became prime minister. He succeeded George Price, who had been the dominant political figure in Belize for more than twenty years. The elections were the first to be held since this Central American country became independent in 1981.

George and Barbara Bush, and Nancy and Ronald Reagan. President Reagan and Vice-President Bush were re-elected to a second term of office in a landslide victory.

THE U.S. PRESIDENTIAL ELECTION

Ronald Reagan proved himself one of the most popular presidents in United States history in 1984, winning a second four-year term in a vote that was widely termed a landslide. Reagan carried 49 states in the election. The Democratic candidate, former vice-president Walter F. Mondale, won only his home state of Minnesota and the District of Columbia.

The election came at the end of a long and hard campaign that included a historic first: Geraldine Ferraro, a U.S. representative from New York City, was the Democratic vice-presidential candidate. She was the first woman to be nominated for that post by one of the major parties.

The campaign was also highlighted by important differences in philosophy between the two parties. But in the end, most analysts agreed that when Reagan and his running mate, Vice-President George Bush, defeated Mondale and Ferraro, it was the president's personal popularity that carried the day.

CHOOSING THE CANDIDATES

Both parties chose their candidates in the same way. In each state, they held primaries (direct elections) or caucuses (party meetings) to choose delegates to go to a national party convention. The delegates were pledged to support one candidate or another at the convention.

Reagan announced on January 29, 1984, that he and Bush would seek a second term. From that point on, there were no serious challenges to his nomination. The Republican primaries and caucuses were largely formalities. They confirmed support for Reagan, who before his election in 1980 had served as governor of California and had also been a movie star.

But the Democratic nominations were by no means as certain. Early in the year, Mondale was clearly the front-runner. He had served twelve years as a senator from Minnesota and was vice-president under President Jimmy Carter from 1977 through 1980. But seven other Democrats also sought the presidential nomination. They were former governor Reubin Askew of Florida; Senator Alan Cranston of California; Senator John Glenn of Ohio, a former astronaut; Senator Gary Hart of Colorado; Senator Ernest F. Hollings of South Carolina; Jesse Jackson, a minister who was president of People United to Save Humanity (PUSH), a social action group; and former senator George McGovern of South Dakota.

Mondale took an early lead by winning the Iowa caucuses in February. But at the end of the month, Hart scored a stunning upset by winning the New Hampshire primary. Hart went on to sweep the New England primaries, and he also did well in some western states. Mondale was strongest in the Midwest and the South.

Gradually most of the other candidates dropped out, leaving a three-way race between Mondale, Hart, and Jackson. Jackson, the first serious black presidential contender, did best among black voters. He tried to broaden his appeal to all minority groups, calling his supporters the Rainbow Coalition. And he made headlines with two trips abroad—to Syria, where he arranged the release of a captured U.S. Navy pilot, and to Cuba, where he arranged the release of a group of American prisoners. But his efforts weren't enough to catch Mondale and Hart.

The outcome of the race wasn't clear until the last Democratic primaries were held, on June 5—and Mondale won just barely enough delegates to assure him the nomination.

At the party convention, held in San Francisco, California, from July 16 through July 19, attention focused on the party platform and on the choice of a vice-presidential candidate. Since 1892, some 21 women had been vice-presidential candidates, but always for minor parties. Mondale's choice of Geraldine Ferraro, confirmed by the convention, was thus an important first.

The Republican Party's convention was held in Dallas, Texas, from August 20 through August 23. There, too, the party platform was a major concern. Different planks, or statements of policy, were supported by conservative and liberal Republicans. In the end, the conservatives won out, and the platform that was adopted reflected most of their positions.

THE ISSUES

The candidates offered voters two different views of the United States. In his campaign speeches, Reagan stressed recent improvements in the economy. He said that Americans had been better off under his administration than they had been for many years, and that they could once again be proud of their country's status abroad.

Mondale said that Reagan's policies had made life better for the rich, but that the poor were worse off. He said that the United States should be a country where people cared about those less fortunate than themselves. He also said that Reagan's foreign policies were pushing the country toward war.

The Democratic candidates were former vice-president Walter F. Mondale and Geraldine Ferraro, the first woman to be nominated for vice-president by a major party. They won only the state of Minnesota and the District of Columbia.

The candidates and their platforms also differed sharply on some specific issues:

• **Taxes and Budget Deficits.** Mondale proposed a specific plan to reduce the federal government's enormous deficits. It included raising taxes, especially for the wealthy, and reducing government spending. Reagan didn't offer a specific plan. He said that he wouldn't raise taxes, but he supported a tax reform plan that would equalize tax rates. (Under present tax law, wealthy people are taxed at higher rates than people who earn less.)

• **The Military.** The Republican platform called for the United States to be stronger militarily than any potential adversary. Reagan continued to support the military buildup he had begun in his first term. Mondale criticized the buildup, saying it had been done at the expense of needed social programs. His platform called for less emphasis on military strength in foreign relations.

• **Arms Control.** The Democratic platform supported a mutual and verifiable nuclear freeze—an end to the nuclear arms race with the Soviet Union. Mondale criticized Reagan for being the first president not to make progress in arms control. Reagan defended his record, blaming the Soviets for the lack of progress. He said arms control would be a major goal of his second term.

Senator Gary Hart of Colorado proved to be an unexpectedly strong contender for the Democratic presidential nomination. He swept the primaries in the New England states and also did well in some western states.

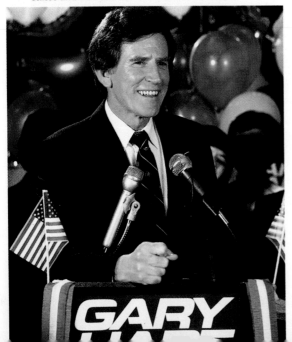

• **Equal Rights.** Both parties said they opposed discrimination against minorities. The Republican platform made no mention of women's rights, and it opposed busing to achieve racial integration in schools. The Democrats criticized Reagan's record on civil rights. They supported affirmative action to end discrimination, and they backed a constitutional amendment assuring equal rights for women.

• **Social Programs.** The Democrats called for more government-supported job training programs and more aid to education. The Republicans said that job opportunities would increase as the economy improved and that education should be under local control.

There were other issues in the campaign, too. The finances of both vice-presidential candidates were criticized. And the Democrats criticized the Republicans for their ties to fundamentalist Christian groups, saying that these groups would influence government decisions such as the appointment of Supreme Court justices. Reagan denied that this would happen. He said that allowing prayer in public schools, which he supported, would promote religious freedom rather than mix politics and religion.

THE CAMPAIGN

From the start of the final campaign, in September, public opinion polls showed Reagan heavily in the lead. Support for Mondale was strongest among minorities and labor groups. The Democrats hoped that having Ferraro on the ticket would increase their support from women, which was already strong. But Reagan had a wide base of popularity in most parts of the country.

The high point of Mondale's campaign came on October 7, in the first of two televised debates between the presidential candidates. He made a strong showing, while to many viewers Reagan seemed less sharp. This raised a new issue—whether Reagan, at 73, was too old for the job of president.

Mondale's supporters began to hope that their candidate might gather enough support to win. But Reagan presented himself better during the second debate, and he seemed to quickly regain the ground he had lost after the first one. (The two vice-presidential can-

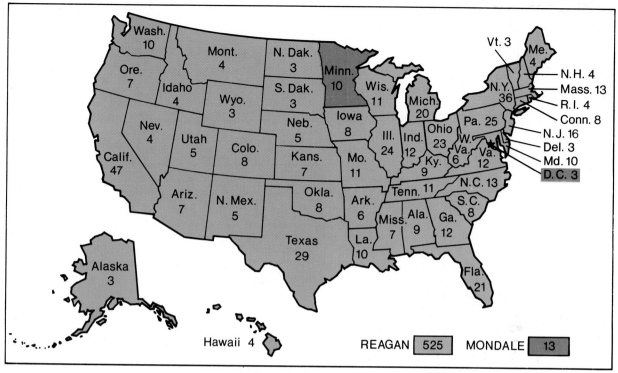

HOW THE COUNTRY VOTED
(The numbers are each state's electoral college votes—270 were needed to win.)

didates also debated on television.) Republicans began to talk of winning all 50 states. They also hoped to gain more than 25 seats in the House of Representatives—enough to be assured of support for their policies. (They already had a majority in the Senate.)

THE ELECTION

In the election on November 6, Reagan won 59 percent of the popular vote. His 49-state sweep gave him 525 electoral votes, compared to 13 for Mondale. Almost 52 percent of eligible voters had cast ballots. This was up slightly from the 1980 election, which had had the lowest turnout since 1948. Reagan drew his strongest support from whites in the middle and upper classes. Mondale got many votes from blacks and low-income groups. More women supported Mondale than did men, but Reagan still took 57 percent of the women's vote.

After the election, Mondale said that he would retire from politics. He laid the failure of his campaign to his lack of appeal on television and the fact that he had bluntly stated that he would raise taxes. The Democrats found some silver linings in the election, though. Jesse Jackson's primary campaign had succeeded in registering many new black voters. And while Ferraro hadn't drawn enormous support from women, she had broken new ground.

Reagan received more electoral college votes than any candidate in the nation's history. But the Republicans didn't make the gains in Congress that they had hoped for. They lost two seats in the Senate, although they kept their majority. And they picked up just fourteen seats in the House. This meant that rather than getting automatic support for his programs, Reagan would have to work with a divided Congress in his second term. And state and local governments were still dominated by Democrats. In most races, the incumbents—the people who were already in office—won.

For this reason, many analysts felt that the election didn't reflect wide support of the conservative policies outlined in the Republican platform. While the United States had become somewhat more conservative, the vote more accurately seemed to show that the people liked Reagan, and that they were happy with the state of the country in 1984.

41

CHOOSING A PRESIDENT—U.S. STYLE

The U.S. presidential election has four main steps. In the preliminary campaigns, would-be candidates from each political party bid for support from party members. At the party nominating conventions, the parties choose their candidates for president and vice-president. Finally come the presidential campaign and the election itself. Here are some of the terms you're likely to hear during each of the steps.

THE PRELIMINARIES

Primary: Primary elections are the main method of choosing delegates to the party nominating convention. Rules vary from state to state, but generally voters cast ballots either for candidates themselves or for delegates who say they will support those candidates. But some delegates are uncommitted—they don't have to say whom they'll support.

Write-ins: A few states allow voters to write in the names of candidates who are not actually entered in the primary.

Caucus: In some states, delegates to the party nominating convention are chosen in caucuses. Party members meet in local groups, and each presidential hopeful tries to get their support. The party members choose delegates who will support the candidate they like best.

Favorite son candidate: A favorite son candidate is usually an important figure—a governor, perhaps—in one state. He or she has the support of the state's delegates. The favorite son isn't expected to win, but this way the delegates aren't committed to any of the major candidates until the nominating convention actually begins.

Dark horse candidate: An unknown candidate who is given little chance of succeeding is sometimes called a dark horse.

Bandwagon movement: A candidate tries to create the impression that he or she is drawing wide support and is certain to win. This encourages party members to support the candidate, for fear they will be left out when the victory is won.

THE PARTY CONVENTIONS

Keynote address: At the start of the convention, a party leader gives the keynote address. It sets the tone for the campaign that will follow.

Platform: The party also decides on its platform—a statement of its goals and positions.

Ballot: At the convention, the delegates cast ballots to decide who will get the nomination. A simple majority is enough to win. Usually the chosen presidential candidate then picks the vice-presidential candidate, and the delegates confirm the choice in another vote.

Deadlock: If no candidate gets a majority after several ballots have been cast, the convention is deadlocked. This is rare. The last true deadlock occurred in 1924, when the Democrats cast 103 ballots before picking John Davis as their candidate.

THE CAMPAIGN

Kickoff: The kickoff, or start, of each party's campaign has traditionally been a major speech given by the candidate sometime around Labor Day. But in recent elections most candidates have started their campaigns months—and perhaps years—before this.

Public opinion polls: Polls attempt to find out how people will vote. They are taken by the parties and also by independent organizations throughout the campaign, to find out who is ahead. Candidates may adjust their strategies if the polls show they are falling behind.

Television debates: Television debates between the major candidates have become an important part of presidential campaigns. The formats for such debates vary, but usually each candidate is given a chance to answer certain questions and discuss certain issues.

THE ELECTION

Election Day: Voters go to the polls on Election Day—the Tuesday that follows the first Monday in November. In 1984, this was November 6.

Electors: These people actually choose the president. Each state is allotted a certain number of electors. The candidate who wins the most votes in the state's election wins the support of *all* of that state's electors. The electors meet and cast their vote in December. In this system, a candidate can win a majority of the popular vote and still lose the election because he or she doesn't control enough electoral votes.

A NEW DIRECTION FOR CANADA

The election of a new leader set Canada on a fresh course in 1984. In nationwide parliamentary elections on September 4, the Progressive Conservative (PC) Party won the largest majority in Canadian history. PC leader Martin Brian Mulroney thus became prime minister, replacing Liberal Party leader John N. Turner.

The vote marked the end of a half-century of Liberal Party leadership—the Liberals had held power for all but seven of the preceding 50 years. Clearly, the election results seemed to say, Canadians were ready for a change.

THE CANDIDATES

By the time of the election, John Turner had been in office barely two months. A 55-year-old corporate lawyer from Ottawa, he had first been elected to Parliament in 1962. In 1968 he had sought the Liberal Party leadership but had lost to Pierre Elliott Trudeau.

Trudeau served as prime minister until 1984, except for nine months in 1979–80. Turner served as finance minister under him but, in 1975, resigned in a dispute. For the next nine years, he stayed away from politics. But when Trudeau announced his retirement early in 1984, Turner once again sought the party leadership. He won it, defeating energy minister Jean Chrétien, at a party convention in June. And on June 30, Turner was sworn in as prime minister.

Brian Mulroney, who was born in Quebec, was a newcomer to Canadian government. At 45, he had had a highly successful career as a labor lawyer and businessman. He had never run for office, but during the 1970's he had become active in the PC Party. In 1979 he made a bid for the party leadership but lost to Joe Clark, who then served briefly as prime minister. But in June, 1983, Mulroney was chosen party leader.

THE CAMPAIGN

Almost as soon as he took office, Turner called for an election, to confirm popular support for his government. And if the election had been held right away, the Liberals might have won it—polls taken in early July showed the Liberals leading by eleven percentage points. But in the two-month campaign, the picture changed dramatically.

For both of the major parties, the key to the election was to gain more votes in areas where they had traditionally been weak. The Liberals had always been strongest in Quebec and the rest of eastern Canada, while the PC party traditionally drew most of its support from the west. To win a majority, each party would have to draw votes from the other's stronghold.

Brian Mulroney of the Progressive Conservative Party became prime minister of Canada in 1984. In doing so, he ended nearly 50 years of Liberal Party leadership.

The PC Party was able to accomplish its goal with Mulroney, a native of Quebec who spoke French fluently. An engaging television personality, Mulroney presented himself not as strongly conservative but rather as a moderate. He promised to increase military spending, maintain Canada's social welfare programs, and cut the government's budget deficit, largely by increasing taxes for the wealthy. He also said he would improve relations with the United States. In all his campaign statements he stressed his differences from Trudeau and the other Liberals.

Turner's positions were generally not quite as liberal as Trudeau's had been. In fact, they were not markedly different from Mulroney's. He also promised to cut the deficit and increase investment. And he, too, stressed that his government would be different from Liberal governments of the past. But he maintained the Liberal Party's stands in favor of nuclear disarmament and social welfare programs, and he kept many areas of Trudeau's government intact. For example, one of his first acts during his short term as prime minister was to appoint a number of officials who had been recommended by Trudeau.

THE ELECTION

As September 4 drew nearer, polls showed the Liberals losing ground. Turner's campaign was plagued with internal divisions, and he failed to convince people in the west that he had their interests in mind. He also seemed to be losing support in one of the most crucial areas of the campaign—women's issues.

Canadian women make up 52 percent of the country's voters, and they traditionally have voted Liberal. This time both candidates said they supported more financing for day care, increased hiring of women for government jobs, and other steps to solve problems women faced. The women voters apparently thought Mulroney was more sincere, and he gained support among them.

Still, the key issues of the election were economic ones. Canada's economy had grown rapidly during the 1960's and 1970's. But since 1980 it had been in a recession, and it lagged behind the United States in recovery. Unemployment was over 11 percent overall and over 20 percent for young people. People seemed to think that a fresh government might be able to revive the economy.

The voters gave the PC party a resounding victory—50 percent of the popular vote. The Liberals, by contrast, took 28 percent, while the smaller New Democratic Party took 19 percent. The PC party won 211 of the 282 seats in Parliament, a gain of 111 seats. The Liberals held just 40, their lowest number ever.

On September 17, Mulroney was sworn into office as prime minister. Just where Canada's new course would lead remained unknown. But the voters had clearly called for a change.

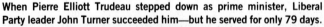

When Pierre Elliott Trudeau stepped down as prime minister, Liberal Party leader John Turner succeeded him—but he served for only 79 days.

THE END OF THE TRUDEAU ERA

Pierre Elliott Trudeau led Canada for sixteen years. When he resigned his post as prime minister in 1984, it was the end of an era for the country. He had held his office longer than any other Canadian prime minister except William Lyon Mackenzie King. (Mackenzie King served for 22 years from the 1920's through the 1940's.) Trudeau's period of leadership was marked by important changes in Canada and also by his dashing personal style, which made him famous around the world.

Trudeau was born to a wealthy family in Montreal, Quebec, on October 18, 1919. He grew up speaking both French and English. After graduating with a degree in law from the University of Montreal, he studied and traveled abroad. Then he began to practice law in Montreal. In 1961, he joined the law faculty at the University of Montreal.

Trudeau became known as a champion of liberal issues and a supporter of civil rights. This was a time when many French-speaking Canadians were struggling against discrimination. Some wanted the province of Quebec to secede and become a separate country. Trudeau believed strongly in equal rights, but he also believed that Canada should remain unified.

Because he wanted to show that French-speaking Canadians could play an important part in government, Trudeau entered politics in 1965. He was elected to the Canadian Parliament as a member of the Liberal Party. Two years later he was appointed minister of justice and attorney general. And in 1968, he became the leader of the Liberal Party. Because the Liberals then had the most seats in Parliament, he automatically became prime minister. But to solidify his position, he called an election.

Trudeau appealed to many voters, not only with his political views but also with his style. He seemed different from traditional politicians. He often wore flashy clothes and sported a flower in his lapel. He could quote literature on the spur of the moment, and he enjoyed skiing, skin diving, and fast cars. "Trudeaumania" swept the country, and the Liberals won a majority in the election.

Trudeau's popularity later fell somewhat, but he remained in power until May, 1979, when the Progressive Conservative Party won an election. He then resigned as Liberal leader. But the new government lasted less than a year, and Trudeau again led his party to victory in February, 1980.

In office, Trudeau worked for equal rights for all Canadians. There were new social programs.

French, together with English, became an official language of the country. But in 1970, when Quebec separatists began a terrorism campaign, Trudeau was quick to call out troops and order arrests.

Canada's French-speaking minority was not the only group to gain in civil rights under Trudeau— he was the driving force behind a new Canadian constitution, which included a charter of rights. The adoption of the constitution in 1982 marked the end of Canada's last colonial ties to Britain.

Trudeau also tried to expand Canada's relations with foreign countries and make the country less economically tied to the United States. He established diplomatic relations with China in 1970, and he increased trade with the Soviet Union. He called for negotiations between rich and poor countries and between East and West. In his last year in office, he traveled to major world capitals and to the United Nations, urging talks on disarmament.

The Trudeau era officially ended on June 14, 1984. In his farewell speech, he said, "Our dreams for this beautiful country will never die."

CHINA AND THE WEST

The year 1984 marked the fifth anniversary of the start of formal diplomatic relations between the United States and the Communist government of the People's Republic of China. And there was much contact between the two nations during the year. U.S. President Ronald Reagan visited China, and high-level Chinese officials traveled to the United States, as well as to Canada, Japan, and countries in Western Europe.

Once bitterly opposed to each other, China and the United States could see much progress in their relations. In particular, trade between China and the United States and other Western countries had increased dramatically. But China and the West still had different views on many aspects of international affairs, and there were still many areas of strain. One area of disagreement involved Taiwan (the Republic of China).

ECONOMIC TIES

In 1949, when the Communists took control of mainland China, the Nationalist Chinese fled to the island of Taiwan, some 90 miles (145 kilometers) off the Chinese coast. Since then, the Nationalists have continued to assert that they are the true leaders of all China. For 30 years the United States supported their claim. But that changed in 1979, when the United States established full diplomatic relations with mainland China and ended its formal ties with the Nationalists on Taiwan.

China at that time was eager to modernize its industries and expand trade with the West. It had high hopes that starting relations with the United States would bring an influx of new technology and modern equipment. The influx didn't come, largely because the United States placed restrictions on the export of technology to Communist countries. But there was a great increase in trade. At the same time, China began to reform its state-controlled economic system, allowing more free enterprise. And as a result of trade and reform, the Chinese economy began to grow rapidly.

In China, billboards that once proclaimed the political sayings of Chairman Mao Zedong now advertise an array of foreign goods. In recent years, China has modernized its industries and expanded both trade and contact with the West.

In April, 1984, U.S. President Ronald Reagan and his wife, Nancy, visited China and combined business with pleasure. Reagan signed agreements on investments and cultural exchanges and agreed to help China build nuclear reactors.

In 1983, the United States decided that in trade, it would treat China as a friendly non-aligned country rather than as a Communist country. This loosened the restrictions. And in 1984, China announced that it planned to sign contracts for $1,000,000,000 (billion) worth of Western equipment.

Chinese Premier Zhao Ziyang visited Washington, D.C., in January and signed a new industrial co-operation treaty. Later in the year, Chinese and U.S. officials announced that the United States had agreed to sell military equipment to China. Chinese officials also traveled to several other Western countries, buying industrial and military equipment.

In April, President Reagan visited China and signed agreements on investments and cultural exchanges. He also agreed to help China build nuclear reactors. Such an agreement had been blocked by fears that China would use the nuclear material to make weapons. China had had nuclear weapons for about twenty years. It had refused to sign a nuclear nonproliferation treaty, which would ban the spread of nuclear arms, and it had been accused of passing nuclear technology to Pakistan and other countries. But this time the United States was satisfied with a statement that China wouldn't use the material to make weapons or to help other countries do so.

The growing trade between China and the West was seen by many people as an encouraging sign. But there were still enormous differences between China's Communist beliefs and the democratic ideals of Western countries.

CHINA AND HONG KONG

Hong Kong, on the southern coast of China, has been a British colony since 1842. It consists of a group of islands and a small piece of mainland territory. The land was ceded to Britain under several treaties, but most of it is leased from China under an agreement that will expire in 1997.

The Chinese Government had long made it clear that it intended to resume control over Hong Kong on that date. But many peo-

The British colony of Hong Kong is a bustling industrial center, whose people enjoy political and economic freedom. In 1984, Britain and China announced a plan under which Hong Kong would become a self-governing province of China after 1997. Many people were concerned that China would try to run Hong Kong along Communist lines.

ple were concerned that this would mean enormous changes for the people of the colony. Hong Kong is a center of commerce, manufacturing, and banking. Its people enjoy political and economic freedom. A change to Communist rule, with its tight political restrictions and state-run economy, would end that. So to help ease the transition and guarantee some of the rights of Hong Kong's citizens, the British began to negotiate with the Chinese over what path Hong Kong's future would take.

The negotiations started in 1982 and dragged on for two years, but on August 1, 1984, Britain and China announced an agreement. Under this plan, Hong Kong would become a self-governing province of China after 1997. In that year British troops would withdraw, and China would take responsibility for Hong Kong's defense. But for at least 50 years, Hong Kong would retain its legal system, its free port status, its currency, and its tax system. Its people would be free to come and go. A joint Chinese-British liaison group would oversee the transition.

People in Hong Kong were on the whole satisfied with the agreement. But many wondered if, once the British left in 1997, the Chinese would in fact try to run Hong Kong along Communist lines. The uncertainty had a harmful effect on Hong Kong's economy —several important business firms left, and others considered doing so as the date of transfer drew closer.

CHINA AND TAIWAN

The negotiations on Hong Kong were watched closely by people on Taiwan because Communist China also continued to press its claim to that island during 1984. China had repeatedly proposed re-unification plans that would bring Taiwan under the control of the mainland government. Like Hong Kong, Taiwan had prospered with a free-enterprise economy. The Communists promised that Taiwan would be self-governing and that its economic system and way of life wouldn't change.

The Nationalist Government, which continued to claim to be the true government of all China, distrusted these proposals. The Nationalists pointed out that in 1950 China had taken control of Tibet and promised that it would be self-governing, but that in 1959 the Tibetan Government had been dissolved and the Communists had imposed their own system. They said that Hong Kong would likewise be betrayed.

China and Taiwan were not completely cut off from each other. Many families had members in both areas, and there was a considerable amount of trade and other contact through unofficial channels. But over the 35 years of separation, these ties had grown weaker. Many Taiwanese were curious about the mainland and interested in increasing contacts. They seemed, however, more interested in continuing their prosperous way of life than in rejoining the rest of China. They were leery of the changes that Communist rule might bring.

The Chinese said that the question of Taiwan was the biggest block to improvements in U.S.-Chinese relations. While the United States had ended formal diplomatic ties to Taiwan, it continued to support the Nationalist Government there and kept up unofficial ties. President Reagan especially was a strong supporter of Taiwan. And the Chinese were particularly annoyed by U.S. arms sales to the Nationalist Government, which had continued even after diplomatic recognition ended. In 1982, the United States had agreed to gradually reduce such sales, but the Chinese said that the reductions that had been made weren't large enough.

But while China continued to have these and other disagreements with the West, it showed no signs of moving closer to other Communist countries. Relations with the Soviet Union remained cool. And there were border clashes with Vietnam, a Soviet ally, in 1984, as there had been in past years. It seemed likely that China would continue to steer its own course in its dealings with other countries.

In Communist China, this sign urges re-unification with Taiwan. It reads, "Missing home and looking forward to re-unification—one family on two shores." China has repeatedly pressed its claim to the island. But Taiwan, like Hong Kong, has a free-enterprise economy and is afraid of the changes that Communist rule might bring.

THE THREATENING DEFICITS

The year 1984 was a sunny one for the United States economy. The country seemed to be bouncing back from the recession that had affected most of the world's countries in the early 1980's. The gross national product (the total value of goods and services produced in the country during the year) was growing rapidly. But prices were rising more slowly—at a rate of 4 percent, rather than the 1980 rate of 12.4 percent. And by mid-year, unemployment had fallen to 7 percent from nearly 12 percent during the recession.

Nearly everyone was pleased with these trends. But there were also some clouds on the economic horizon. Some people worried that the recovery might be too much of a good thing—that as people began to spend money more freely, high inflation would take hold again. Of even more concern were two enormous deficits—the trade deficit and the federal budget deficit.

THE TRADE DEFICIT

Until the 1970's, the United States nearly always managed to earn more on exports than it spent on imports each year. More money came into the country than left it. One big reason was that the United States was a leader in manufacturing and technology, and U.S. products were in demand.

In the 1970's the United States began to fall behind in technology. Manufacturers were running outmoded, inefficient plants, and their labor costs were high. To cover their costs, they had to charge more for their products. People began to buy less expensive products from other countries. At the same time, the cost of imported oil rose sharply.

The United States began to spend more on imports than it earned on exports, and the trade deficit soon became enormous. It was expected to be $70,000,000,000 (billion) or more in 1984. That meant that a tremendous amount of money was being drained from the country.

Some people thought that the problem could be solved by placing restrictions on imports. For example, the United States could set tight limits on the number of shoes that were imported each year. With fewer foreign shoes in stores, people would have to buy American shoes. Or the government

The United States now buys from other countries (imports) more goods than it sells (exports)—thus causing a trade deficit. This means that a tremendous amount of money is being drained from the country.

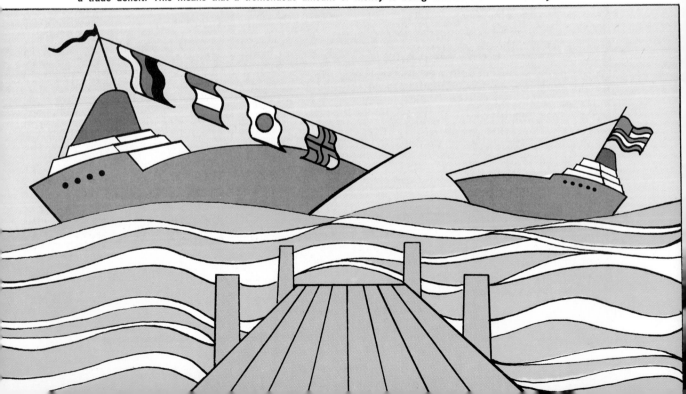

could charge a high tariff or import duty on imported shoes. This would raise the price of the imported shoes, and people would no longer want to buy them. As the trade deficit grew larger in the 1980's, such restrictions were placed on imported cars, textiles, sugar, motorcycles, and steel.

Many people thought this was a bad solution. Restrictions would raise prices and give consumers fewer products to choose from. A better solution, these people said, would be for U.S. industries to become more efficient, so that they could compete internationally. But this wasn't easy. The industries would have to modernize their plants, and to do that they would have to borrow money. And interest rates on loans were very high in 1984—largely because of the enormous federal budget deficit.

THE BUDGET DEFICIT

Each year since the 1940's, the federal government has regularly spent more money than it has taken in, in taxes and other revenues. During the 1950's, the budget deficits were small. But they grew, and in the 1980's they took off. By mid-1984, the 1985 deficit was expected to be $180,000,000,000 (billion). For the year 2000, the deficit is expected to be $1,500,000,000,000 (trillion).

There were several reasons for the enormous increases. The government had cut some taxes, reducing revenues. Military spending was increasing dramatically. Some social programs, such as welfare, had been cut back, but overall spending on these programs was increasing, too. And because the government had to borrow money each year to cover its costs, it had to pay an increasing amount of interest on its outstanding loans.

The government had two methods of reducing the deficit—raise taxes and cut spending. Doing either wasn't easy. If taxes became too high, people would have less money to spend, and that might set off another recession. But if government spending were cut too much, the country would be harmed. Perhaps it would be unable to defend itself in a war. Or people who received welfare or other social benefits might suffer. A Congressional study showed that more than 550,000 people had already been made poor by cuts in federal programs.

In June, Congress approved a "down payment" on the deficit—$50,000,000,000 (billion) in tax increases through 1987, and spending cuts of $13,000,000,000 (billion). This would reduce the deficit by a bit more than a third. Meanwhile, lawmakers continued to debate various ways of reducing future deficits. And the government continued to borrow money to cover its costs.

More government borrowing meant that less money was available for private individuals and industries to borrow, and this helped keep interest rates high. People worried that if interest rates became too high, that, too, could bring back high inflation and end the recovery.

Concern about the high U.S. interest rates and trade and budget deficits was shared by many people around the world. Other countries didn't want the United States to impose import restrictions—exports to the United States were helping to fuel their own recoveries. Developing countries were deeply in debt and couldn't pay high interest rates. And the United States was leading the world in recovering from recession. If it lapsed back into recession, other countries might follow.

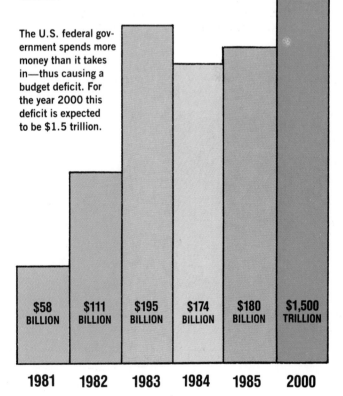

The U.S. federal government spends more money than it takes in—thus causing a budget deficit. For the year 2000 this deficit is expected to be $1.5 trillion.

$58 BILLION	$111 BILLION	$195 BILLION	$174 BILLION	$180 BILLION	$1,500 TRILLION
1981	1982	1983	1984	1985	2000

THE MIDDLE EAST

Long-running conflicts continued to trouble the Middle East in 1984. The region's problems drew worldwide attention because of its importance—the Middle East is at the crossroads of three continents (Africa, Asia, and Europe) and produces much of the world's oil.

During the year fighting between Iran and Iraq threatened shipping in the Persian Gulf, through which tankers carry oil at the rate of over 7,000,000 barrels a day. Lebanon, torn by civil war since the 1970's, continued to see violence and disputes among its many different religious and political groups. Israel had its second change of government in less than a year. And terrorist attacks continued to take a toll of lives throughout the region. But there was also a new glimmer of hope for peace in the area of Palestine.

THE PERSIAN GULF

The war between Iran and Iraq began as a border dispute in 1980—both countries claimed a waterway called the Shatt al Arab, which leads into the Persian Gulf. Iraq at first made great gains, seizing large areas of Iranian territory. But Iran refused to surrender. Its Shi'ite Muslim rulers, who came to power in a revolution in 1979, said their goal was to topple Iraq's government. And by 1982, the Iranians had pushed the Iraqis back. The fighting continued in a stalemate. Losses on both sides were staggering—hundreds of thousands of soldiers killed, and millions of dollars lost in reduced oil exports.

Early in 1984, Iran announced that it was gathering its forces for a final offensive that would bring Iraq to its knees. But the offensive fizzled out. Instead, in April and May, the Iraqis began to attack tankers that called at Iranian ports to pick up oil. Tankers began to avoid these ports, and Iran's oil exports fell off even more than they had before.

The Iranians responded with attacks on ships *anywhere* in the Gulf. The attacks raised serious concern—if the Persian Gulf became unsafe for shipping, a large part of the world's petroleum supply would be cut

During 1984, fighting between Iran and Iraq threatened shipping in the Persian Gulf, through which tankers carry oil at the rate of over 7,000,000 barrels a day. Here, a Saudi tanker is set ablaze during an Iraqi air attack.

off. There were also fears that Iran intended to widen the war by attacking Saudi Arabia and other countries not directly involved in the dispute.

Diplomatic efforts didn't stop the attacks, and the United States offered to support the neutral Gulf countries in any confrontation with Iran. In May, the United States sent a shipment of anti-aircraft missiles to the Saudis, to help protect shipping.

Most of the Gulf countries were concerned about what might happen if Iran won the war. Iran had openly advised Shi'ite Muslims in several Arab countries to stage revolutions of their own. For this reason Kuwait, which has a large Shi'ite population and is geographically close to the war, had long supported Iraq with economic aid. And the effect of the new attacks on shipping was to bring other Gulf states somewhat closer to the Iraqi side. In June, the Saudis became directly involved, shooting down two Iranian jet fighters that were preparing to attack tankers in Saudi territory.

When Iran continued to attack tankers after that incident, the Saudis announced that they would send jets beyond their territorial limits to protect shipping in the Gulf. This produced a brief lull in the conflict. But from July through the end of the year, there continued to be occasional attacks on tankers. And the war between Iran and Iraq dragged on, just as much a stalemate as ever.

LEBANON

As 1984 began, the Lebanese Government was trying desperately to establish control over the central part of the country. The north and east were controlled by Syrian troops, who had first arrived in 1976 as a result of Lebanon's civil war. The south was controlled by Israel, which had invaded Lebanon in 1982.

The Israelis' goal had been to drive out fighters of the Palestine Liberation Organization (PLO), who were attacking Israel from bases in Lebanon. After they had succeeded, the Lebanese and Israeli governments had agreed that the Israeli troops would gradually pull back to the south but would leave the country only if the Syrians did. The Syrians refused to leave, so both foreign armies remained in place.

The Lebanese Government was supported by an international peacekeeping force, made up of troops from the United States, Britain, France, and Italy. Most of these troops were stationed in and around Beirut, the capital. But despite their support, the government was unable to stop outbreaks of fighting between Christian, Islamic, and various political groups. And in February the Lebanese cabinet resigned, under pressure from Arab groups who opposed the government's policies. These groups, backed by Syria, also demanded that Lebanese President Amin Gemayel resign. And they quickly seized key bases in Beirut from the Lebanese Army.

Unable to prevent the situation from deteriorating, the international peacekeeping force began to withdraw. The British left first, in early February, followed by the Italians and the Americans. The French were the last to go, in March. Meanwhile, Gemayel reached an understanding with his opponents. They agreed that Lebanon would drop its accord with Israel and negotiate instead with Syria. A new government, giving greater power to Arab and Muslim groups, would be formed.

A new cabinet took office April 30, but it didn't immediately end disputes between the various factions. The ministers couldn't agree on who should control the army or how Israel and Syria should be dealt with. Fighting continued. In July, however, the army took over control of most of Beirut, and crossing points between Muslim and Christian sections of the city were opened. The airport, closed for five months, was also reopened.

But the country's problems were by no means over. Sections of the countryside were still controlled by Christian and Muslim militias. Syria was still entrenched in the north, and Israel in the south. But Israel said it would drop its demand that the Syrian troops withdraw at the same time the Israeli troops did. And in November, Israel and Lebanon began to negotiate a new troop withdrawal agreement.

Terrorist attacks also continued. On September 20, a car loaded with explosives drove up to the U.S. embassy near East Beirut and exploded, killing two Americans and

U.S. troops and civilians leave Beirut, Lebanon, in February, 1984. The U.S. troops were part of an international peacekeeping force. But the force was unable to help the tense political situation there, and all the troops withdrew from the country by the end of March.

21 other people as well as the driver. Such suicide terrorist missions had occurred before. In 1983, similar car bombs had hit an earlier U.S. embassy, the French and U.S. military compounds in Beirut, and the Israeli headquarters in southern Lebanon, killing a total of more than 400 people. Various Islamic terrorist groups were blamed for these attacks.

EGYPT AND JORDAN

On September 25, Jordan announced that it was resuming diplomatic relations with Egypt. Jordan was one of seventeen Arab countries that had broken relations with Egypt in 1979. They did this because Egypt had become the first Arab country to recognize Israel and to sign a peace treaty, the Camp David accord, with that country.

Some other Arab countries, especially Syria, criticized Jordan. But elsewhere the event was welcomed. One of the thorniest issues in the Middle East has been the question of a homeland for the Arabs of Palestine (the area that is now Israel). One possible site for this homeland would be the West Bank, an area that Israel seized from Jordan in 1967. Egypt and Israel had tried to work

out plans for setting up such a state. They failed, partly because both Jordan and the leading Palestinian group, the PLO, wouldn't take part in the talks. But in 1984 the PLO was split, and its more moderate members agreed to recognize Egypt. When Jordan also resumed ties with Egypt, there were new hopes that a solution to the West Bank problem would be found.

In November, Yasir Arafat, the PLO leader backed by the moderates, called a convention in Jordan. The militant faction boycotted the meeting, but enough members came to show support for Arafat. The convention called for new efforts to establish an independent Palestinian state but didn't come up with a firm plan for doing so.

ISRAEL

Israel's Prime Minister Yitzhak Shamir had taken office in the fall of 1983. He had succeeded Menachem Begin, who had retired, as head of the Likud, a coalition of right-wing parties. And in mid-1984, he faced an election that he hoped would confirm popular support for his government.

Shamir's chief opponent was Shimon Peres, head of the Labor Party. He urged better treatment for the Arabs of Israel and greater compromise on the issue of the West Bank. Another key issue in the election was the economy—inflation was running at 400 percent a year.

In the voting on July 23, no party won a majority. Labor won 44 seats in parliament, while the Likud won 41. The remaining 35 seats were split among 13 minor parties. Both Labor and the Likud then tried to persuade some of the minor parties to join them, to form a majority. But neither had success.

In the end, Labor and the Likud decided to form a coalition of their own. After long negotiations, they agreed that Peres would serve as prime minister for 25 months and then step down to let Shamir serve the second half of the term. The new government took office in mid-September.

THE RED SEA

In July, mysterious explosions began to damage ships in the Red Sea, which lies between Africa and the Arabian peninsula. The Red Sea leads to the Suez Canal and is a major route for oil tankers and other ships. Egypt, which controls the canal, suspected that areas of the Red Sea had been mined by terrorists. Suspicion fell on Libya, which has been involved in terrorism in the past.

An international force of minesweepers began to comb the Red Sea in August. The force included ships and helicopters from the United States, Britain, France, and Italy, as well as countries in the area. They hoped that finding the mines would not only protect ships from further damage but also provide clues to who had planted them. In October the British found a Soviet-made mine. The Soviet Union supplies Libya with arms, and a Libyan cargo ship had cruised the area just before the explosions began.

The Red Sea mines were another example of the unpredictable violence that often colors events in the Middle East. While people everywhere hoped the region would soon find peace, the outlook at the end of 1984 was still unclear.

In national elections in Israel, no party won enough seats in parliament to form a government. After long negotiations, the two major parties formed a coalition. They agreed that Labor leader Shimon Peres (*left*) would serve as prime minister for 25 months, and that Likud leader Yitzhak Shamir (*right*) would serve for the second half of the term.

AROUND THE WORLD

Religious strife and assassination in India, hope for peace in Central America, and new leadership in the Soviet Union were some of the events that made newspaper headlines in 1984. A run-down of these and other important developments around the world follows.

INDIA

India, the world's largest democracy, is home to a wide variety of religious and ethnic groups. And over the years, these groups have clashed many times. Often the violence has centered in the Punjab, a region that was divided between Pakistan and India when their boundaries were drawn in 1947. Some 250,000 Indians were killed in religious riots then, with Muslims eventually withdrawing to Pakistan, and Hindus to India. The Sikhs, a third religious group, were often caught in

India's many religious groups have clashed repeatedly over the years. This violence ultimately led to the assassination of Prime Minister Indira Gandhi in 1984.

the middle. The Sikhs make up about 2 percent of the population. They split from the Hindus about A.D. 1500, and their religion is based on belief in one god. (Hindus believe in many gods.)

In 1983, fighting between Muslims and Hindus led to more than 1,500 deaths in the northeastern state of Assam. In 1984, there were more Hindu-Muslim killings in Bombay. And the Sikhs, who had long sought more political and religious freedom, turned increasingly to violence. This violence ultimately led to the assassination of Indian Prime Minister Indira Gandhi.

The Sikhs felt that the government had discriminated against them. Some Sikhs said that their goals could only be gained through violence, and they began a terrorist campaign. Their base was the chief Sikh shrine, the Golden Temple at Amritsar, which was considered off limits to government troops. But in June, as terrorism in the region increased, Indira Gandhi ordered government forces to storm the temple. At least 600 people, mostly Sikhs, were killed.

Many Sikhs were outraged, and there were fears that violence might spread. The Indian army took over to maintain security in the Punjab. There were several other outbreaks, but for the most part the violence didn't spread. Most of the Sikh extremists were arrested, and the government turned the temple back to the religious group in late September. But there seemed to be little progress in working out the disputes that had caused the violence to begin with. And many moderate Sikhs had hardened their antigovernment position.

Then, on October 31, Gandhi was shot dead outside her home. The assassins were two of her bodyguards, both Sikhs. Other bodyguards opened fire, killing one of the two and wounding the other. There was some speculation that the assassination was part of a wider Sikh plot to kill other Indian leaders.

Gandhi's son, Rajiv, was appointed to succeed her. Her death was widely mourned, and in some areas riots broke out. At least 1,000 Sikhs were killed, and the army was called out to control the attacks.

Indira Gandhi was assassinated by two of her bodyguards, who were Sikhs. Earlier in the year government troops had tried to stop a Sikh terrorist campaign by storming the group's holiest shrine, the Golden Temple at Amritsar (*above*). At least 600 people, mostly Sikhs, had been killed.

Gandhi had led India for fifteen of the preceding eighteen years. Her family had long been important in Indian politics—her father, Jawaharlal Nehru, had been prime minister from 1947 to his death in 1964. Gandhi had accomplished much during her years in office. She made India a nuclear power, helped hold its many groups together, and fought the country's major problems, hunger and poverty. She was also a controversial leader, having at times jailed her opponents and censored the press. After her death, India's future seemed unclear. Prime Minister Rajiv Gandhi called for national elections in December.

CENTRAL AMERICA

There were encouraging signs for peace in Central America, which has long been torn by civil wars. In El Salvador, leftist rebels have been fighting the government, which has mostly been controlled by conservative, right-wing groups. Some of these groups have been linked to kidnapping and murders, and they have been strongly opposed to negotiating with the rebels.

In 1984 a new government came to power. In presidential elections held in March, none of the eight candidates won a clear majority. But in a run-off vote held in May, José Napoleón Duarte, a moderate, defeated Roberto d'Aubuisson, a candidate of the far right.

Duarte moved quickly to end the actions of the right-wing "death squads." Some of the people thought to be responsible were demoted, and five soldiers were convicted of the 1980 murder of four U.S. nuns. Soon there were fewer reports of kidnappings and murders. This and Duarte's moderate outlook were welcomed in the United States, and he was able to get more U.S. aid for his country.

Then, in October, Duarte announced that he was ready to begin negotiations with the rebels. The rebels replied that they were also willing to talk. The two sides met on October 15 and agreed to form a joint commission that would seek an end to the civil war. They met again later in the year.

There was also hope for peace in Nicaragua, where leftists came to power in a 1979 revolution. Since then, the Nicaraguan Government had supported the Salvadorean rebels. The United States had cut off aid to Nicaragua, and it had begun to support guerrilla bands who opposed the leftist government. In an effort to stop arms shipments from Cuba that were being sent through Nicaragua to the Salvadorean rebels, the United States helped some of these groups place mines in Nicaraguan coastal waters. The mining was widely condemned. In May, the World Court ruled that it should be stopped. The United States replied that the mining had already ended and wouldn't be resumed.

On November 4, the Nicaraguan Government held elections. But because the ruling Sandinista Party controlled the press and made campaigning difficult, key opposition groups wouldn't take part, and a Sandanista victory was assured. During the year, the government also announced that it was willing to agree to a treaty that had been drawn up by the Contadora countries—a group made up of Venezuela, Colombia, Panama, and Mexico. These countries have been attempting to work out a peace agreement for the region.

The treaty called for the withdrawal of all foreign troops and advisers from Central American countries, an end to support for rebel groups, free elections, and amnesty for political prisoners. Honduras, Guatemala, Costa Rica, and El Salvador had previously said that they were willing to sign. The United States, however, said it had reservations about the treaty, particularly about how it would be enforced.

Late in the year there were new tensions between Nicaragua and the United States. The United States said that Nicaragua was importing Soviet fighter planes. Nicaragua denied this but also said that it feared a U.S. invasion.

THE SOVIET UNION

Soviet leader Yuri V. Andropov died on February 9, 1984, at the age of 69. He had succeeded Leonid Brezhnev as general secretary of the Soviet Communist Party less than fifteen months earlier. Andropov's place was taken by Konstantin U. Chernenko, a long-time Party official with a reputation as a conservative. This seemed to signal the end of various economic reforms that Andropov had started—at 72, Chernenko seemed unlikely to make major changes in the system. In fact, by the end of the year there were rumors that his own

In Nicaragua, a billboard proclaims: "We are defending the country for the future of the children." In 1984 the Sandinista government built up its defenses, saying that it feared a U.S. invasion. The United States denied that this would happen.

health was failing. Meanwhile, Soviet troops remained bogged down in fighting in Afghanistan. And relations with the United States continued to be cool. But late in the year, the two powers agreed to hold arms-control talks. (Earlier talks had been broken off in 1983.)

AFRICA

Agreements designed to end several long-running conflicts were drawn up in 1984. For years Mozambique had supported rebels in South Africa, and South Africa had backed guerrilla fighters in Mozambique. But in March the two countries signed a non-aggression treaty and agreed to end this support. It was the first such pact between white-ruled South Africa and a black southern African nation. And in October, Mozambique signed a truce with its rebels, and South Africa agreed to monitor the truce.

There were hopes that the agreement might become part of a wider peace. South Africa was also supporting rebels and staging raids in Angola, while Angola backed fighters in the South-African controlled territory of Namibia. Early in 1984, South Africa and Angola declared a cease-fire and began to withdraw. Many issues remained to

be resolved, mostly involving Namibia. South Africa controlled that territory in defiance of the United Nations, which wanted it to become independent. But the cease-fire seemed to be an encouraging sign.

In northern Africa, Libya and France agreed to withdraw their troops from Chad. Libya was fighting in support of rebels who wanted to overthrow the Chadian Government. The government had asked the French troops to come to its aid in August of 1983. The French helped maintain an unofficial cease-fire line that divided the rebel-held north of the country from the government-controlled south. And in September, France announced the withdrawal agreement with Libya. By the end of November the French troops had withdrawn, but the Libyan troops remained. This caused some embarrassment for the French Government.

Many African countries, especially Ethiopia, continued to suffer severe drought in 1984. Throughout the Sahel (the region just south of the Sahara) crops failed, livestock died, and tens of thousands of people were starving to death as a result. Governments and people around the world mounted a major relief effort to send food and other supplies to the region.

In northern Africa, Libya and France agreed to withdraw their troops from Chad. The French had been supporting the government, and the Libyans had been supporting rebels trying to overthrow the government. But by the end of November, only the French troops had pulled out *(below)*.

NEWSMAKERS

Jeanne Benoit Sauvé is the first woman to hold the post of governor-general of Canada. She was born on April 26, 1922, in a small town in Saskatchewan, and she grew up in Ottawa. She first came to national attention as a television journalist. But in 1972, as a member of the Labor Party, she was elected to parliament. She later held various cabinet posts and served as speaker of the House of Commons. She was appointed governor-general to succeed Edward R. Schreyer, who completed his five-year term in January, 1984. The governor-general of Canada is the head of state, but the post is largely ceremonial.

After a close election, **Shimon Peres** was chosen to form a new Israeli government in 1984. Peres, head of the Labor Party, ended up forming a coalition with the other major vote winner in the election, Prime Minister Yitzhak Shamir of the Likud. The two leaders decided to split the term of office between them, and Peres took office as prime minister first. Born in Poland on August 16, 1923, Peres had emigrated to Palestine in 1934. He had a long career in politics and government and served as defense minister in the 1970's. Peres became head of the Labor Party in 1977 but lost the national elections in 1981 to Menachem Begin, who was then the Likud leader.

When **José Napoleón Duarte** became president of El Salvador in the spring of 1984, it marked the first time that an elected civilian had legally come to power there since 1931. But it was the third time that Duarte, 57, had been chosen to lead the country, with its long history of civil war and struggle between right- and left-wing groups. Known as a moderate, he was first elected president in 1972. But right-wing army groups took power, and he spent more than seven years in exile. Then, from 1980 to 1982, he headed a military-civilian junta that governed the country. In 1984, one of his first acts in office was to begin talks with El Salvador's leftist rebels.

Rajiv Gandhi, 40, was appointed prime minister of India when his mother, Indira Gandhi, was assassinated on October 31, 1984. He was something of a newcomer to government—he had enjoyed a career as a pilot while his younger brother, Sanjay, had become involved in politics. But after Sanjay died in a plane crash in 1980, Rajiv was elected to fill his seat in parliament. His efforts to end corruption in government earned him the nickname Mr. Clean, and he became one of his mother's closest aides. Rajiv's first task after taking office as prime minister was to end the rioting that had followed his mother's death.

A new member of the British royal family arrived on September 15, 1984—**Prince Henry Charles Albert David** (or just plain Harry, to his friends). Prince Harry is shown here with his mother, Princess Diana. He is third in the line of succession for the British throne, behind his father, Prince Charles, and his 2-year-old brother, Prince William. His birth was greeted with pealing church bells and 41-gun salutes.

In February, **Konstantin Ustinovich Chernenko** became head of the Soviet Communist Party—the most powerful man in the Soviet Union. He succeeded Yuri Andropov, who had died. Chernenko, 72, had long been a member of the party's Central Committee. He was born in Siberia to a peasant family and worked his way up through the party ranks. Known as a conservative who was loyal to the party's doctrine, he was the oldest person ever chosen for the position.

John Napier Turner, 55, led Canada from late June to mid-September of 1984—the second shortest term of any Canadian prime minister. Turner was chosen to succeed Pierre Elliott Trudeau, who had retired, as Liberal Party leader. But he lost the national elections held in September to Brian Mulroney, head of the Progressive Conservative Party. Turner, a businessman, had been elected to Parliament in 1962 and first tried for the party leadership in 1968.

Geraldine Anne Ferraro was the Democratic candidate for vice-president of the United States in 1984—the first woman nominated for the post by a major party. Born in 1935 in Newburgh, New York, she had previously been a teacher, a lawyer, and an assistant district attorney. In 1978 she was elected to the U.S. House of Representatives from Queens, New York. Although her ticket lost in the 1984 election, her campaign was seen as an important step for women.

ANIMALS

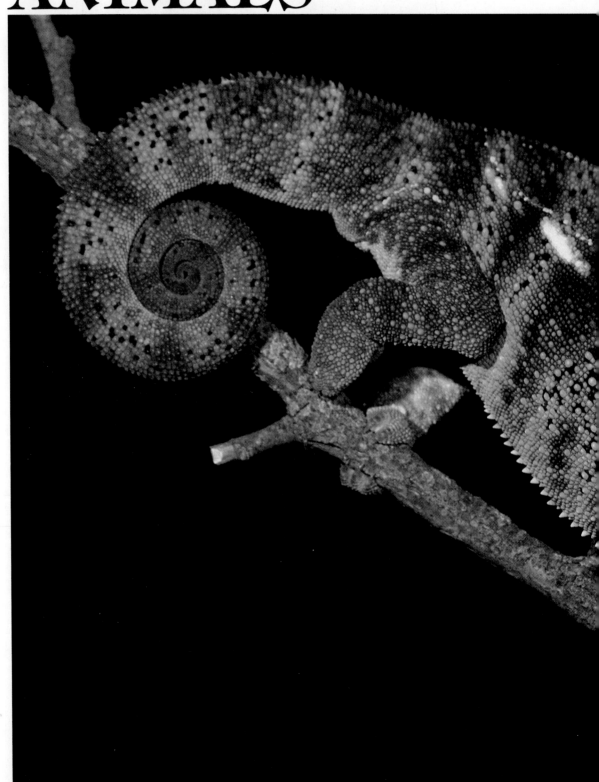

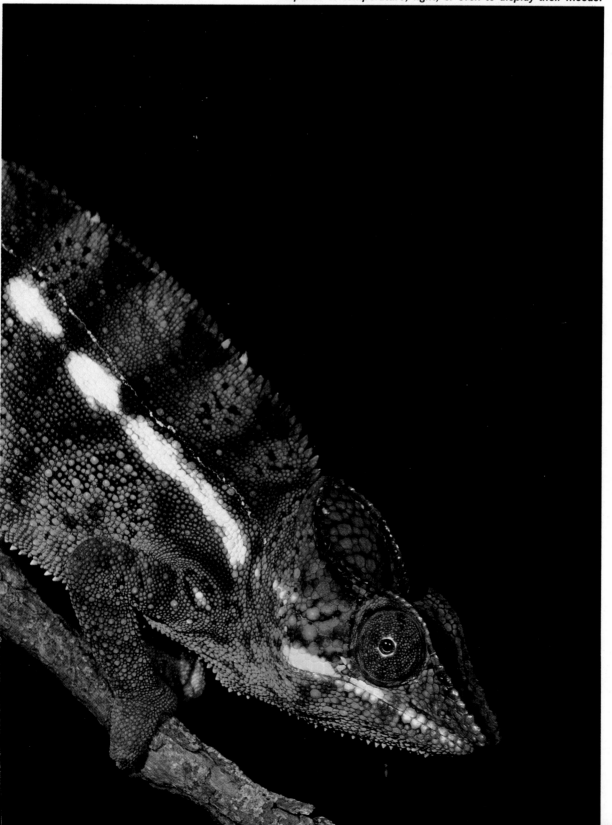

Sporting shades of green that will blend with nearby foliage, a chameleon waits for its prey—an insect—to come along. These little lizards are famous for their ability to change color, in response to temperature, light, or even to display their moods.

The chameleon, a lizard whose name means "little lion," is best known for its ability to change colors.

QUICK-CHANGE ARTISTS

A small brown chameleon sits on a shady branch. Only an alert observer would spot it. Later, that same chameleon moves through sunlit leaves. Within seconds its skin turns a bright green. Once again it blends into its environment, becoming invisible to its enemies and to the insects it hopes to catch.

The chameleon's ability to change color is probably its best-known feature. But contrary to what many people believe, a chameleon doesn't change color just to match its surroundings. More often, changes occur in response to temperature, light, and the animal's mood. In the warm, bright light of day, chameleons generally display vivid colors. At night, when it's comparatively cool, they fade to a pale color. If a chameleon is frightened, it will change colors, becoming very noticeable. It will turn pale when it is ill. And a female chameleon may become brightly colored just before she begins to lay eggs.

The colors a chameleon can change into vary from species to species. Generally they include shades of yellow, green, and brown. Blues, reds, and black may also be present. The color may be uniform over the chameleon's body. Or there may be colored patterns of spots or stripes.

Chameleons are able to change their body color because of special color cells, called chromatophores, in their skin. These cells contain all the color pigments that an individual chameleon has. One of these pigments is melanin, a dark-colored substance that moves around the cells and plays a major role in the lizard's color changes. As a chameleon responds to a situation, nerve impulses are sent to the chromatophores. And the melanin there moves according to the commands sent by the impulses. For example, if a chameleon moves among bright green leaves, the melanin contracts into a small area of each cell, allowing the green pigment to dominate. When the animal moves onto a dark branch, the melanin spreads throughout each cell, masking the green and other bright pigments.

"LITTLE LIONS"

There are about 90 species of chameleons. They belong to the lizard family *Chamaeleontidae*. Most live in southern Africa or Madagascar, but a few can be found along the Mediterranean and in Asia. None are natives of the Americas—although many people incorrectly call the American anole lizard a chameleon.

Chameleons have massive heads and flat, scaly bodies. Their bulging eyes are almost completely covered by scaly lids. Some species have horns on the head, and many have a crest along the back or under the throat. Most chameleons grow to about a foot (30 centimeters) in length. But some pigmy chameleons are only 2 inches (5 centimeters) long, and the largest chameleons measure nearly 2 feet (60 centimeters) from snout to tail.

Although some species of chameleons make their homes on the ground, most live in trees and bushes. They are amazingly well-adapted to life in the trees. They have feet that grip like hands, and they are the only lizards that have gripping tails. Chameleons are so perfectly suited to tree life that they rarely venture down. Usually they do so only to move to another tree or to bury eggs—the females of some species dig nests in the ground for the eggs they lay. (Other species give birth to live young.)

Looking like a harmless leaf or part of a branch, a chameleon spends most of its time just lying in wait for prey. Chameleons are extremely good hunters. In fact, they have been named for their hunting skills: The word "chameleon" comes from a Greek word meaning "little lion." In addition to using color changes, the chameleon has two other adaptations that aid in hunting—its eyes and its tongue.

A chameleon's large, bulging eyes can look in two directions at once. One eye can look forward while the other swivels around to see what's behind. This means that the lizard can check out the entire neighborhood without moving and without giving itself away. But once an insect comes into view, the chameleon focuses both eyes on it. Slowly the chameleon creeps toward the prey. Once in range, it is ready to use its special weapon—its tongue.

Fully extended, a chameleon's tongue may be longer than its body, and it can be shot forward with lightning speed. The tip is covered with a sticky substance that catches and holds its prey. Powerful muscles controlling the tongue draw it back with the fresh meal attached. The prehistoric-looking little lizard will then quietly lie in wait until another unsuspecting victim comes along!

When a hungry chameleon wants to dine, it catches the prey with a special weapon—its tongue.

PARTNERS— PETS AND PEOPLE

You can probably think of lots of ways in which animals help people. There are guide dogs for the blind, companion dogs that help the deaf, and monkeys that help disabled people. Other animals are trained for special jobs, too—horses that pull wagons and dogs that help the police, for example. In Germany, short-legged dachshunds even help the telephone company, by pulling phone cables through narrow spaces.

But did you know that a pet—any pet— can make you a happier, healthier person?

HOW PETS HELP PEOPLE

In recent years, a number of scientists have studied the relationship between pets and people. Here are some of the surprising things they've found:

• Being around a pet can lower your blood pressure. More than 50 years ago, scientists learned that a dog's blood pressure goes down when it's petted. Now they've found that the same thing happens to the petter. And other studies have shown that blood pressure drops when people simply talk to pet birds or watch tropical fish.

Lower blood pressure can mean a longer, healthier life. One study of heart-attack patients showed that the patients who owned pets lived longer. At first the researchers thought the reason might be that patients who owned dogs were forced to exercise by walking their pets, and exercise is good for the heart. But even when the dog owners were excluded from the study, the results showed that people who owned other kinds of pets—cats, birds, fish, even lizards— lived longer.

• Pets may help sick people recover faster. Researchers haven't yet done detailed studies on this subject. But many doctors have stories of pets who snapped patients out of the blues and helped them get up and around faster. As one researcher described it, "We're beginning to think that it helps many sick people just to have something that is alive. The presence of other life seems to be a stimulus that we need to find out more about."

• Just as animals help people who are physically ill, they also help people who are having emotional problems. One Florida study involved autistic children, who are usually very withdrawn and rarely speak. The researchers took the children several times to play with dolphins at an aquarium. All the children perked up, and several got interested enough to feed or splash water on the dolphins. One boy even began to speak, answering "Yep" when asked if he wanted to visit the dolphins again.

Other researchers have reported similar successes using dogs, horses, cats, fish, and goats. Contact with animals doesn't replace the usual therapy for people with emotional problems. But when people are very withdrawn and don't want to talk about their problems, a pet can help break the ice.

• Pets can help healthy people, too. People who live alone feel less lonely if they have a pet. Pets are companions—especially pets like cats and dogs because they respond to people and are attentive. Studies show that many people treat their pets just as though the pets were other people. They talk to them, and they feel that the pets sense their moods. Some people even confide their deepest thoughts and feelings to their pets.

• Families are often drawn closer together when a pet is in the house. One researcher studied 60 families and found that many of them became closer after they got pets. They argued less, and they spent more time playing together. One woman even cooled family arguments by saying, "Stop fighting, you're upsetting the dog."

Did you know that a pet—any pet—can make you a happier, healthier person? Most people seem to have a need to love and care for something, and to talk to and touch other living things. Children often find that pets can be special friends because they aren't critical and don't make judgments about people.

LOOKING INTO THE RELATIONSHIP

The fact that pets help people seems to be beyond question. But why is it that pets have all these good effects on people? The researchers don't know for sure, but they've thought of many possible reasons.

One is that people seem to have a need to love and care for something. People also need to talk to and touch other living things. When these needs aren't met, people often become depressed. But a pet is always there to fill these needs. A dog or a cat may greet you at the door, and it will always welcome your words or touch.

For young children, a pet can be a bridge between caring for their parents and caring for people outside the family. Pets also provide a sense of stability—when a family moves to a different area or if it breaks up, pets are friends that stay with you. And training a pet can give young people a sense of importance and satisfaction.

Older children often find that pets can be very special friends because they don't make judgments about people. Your dog doesn't care how you dress. A horse won't mind if you failed your math quiz. Your cat will never be bored or critical of your conversation. You can't win—or lose—a game with a gerbil. So people who are under a lot of social pressure find they can relax with animals because the animals accept them just the way they are.

Pets are loving companions for people who live alone. Dogs in particular provide them with a sense of security. And pets can add a great deal to the lives of people who are retired. When people retire, they sometimes have little to do, and they may feel useless. Feeding and caring for a pet helps

Pets make loving companions for people who are retired. Caring for a pet helps them establish daily routines. Dogs in particular provide a sense of security. And walking a dog provides exercise.

such people establish daily routines in their lives. Walking a dog provides exercise. And, perhaps most important, the fact that the pet depends on them helps them feel useful and needed.

Pets are also social ice-breakers. People you'd normally never meet will come up and talk when you're walking a dog. And pet owners always have something to talk about with each other—their pets.

But most of all, pets are fun. We smile when we see brilliant tropical fish darting around a tank. We laugh at the antics of a parakeet or a puppy. And even the most straight-laced person will get down on the floor to play with a kitten. Pets help us relax, and they help us enjoy life.

MATCHING PETS AND PEOPLE

Because of the link between pets and health, many convalescent homes now keep house pets. Others encourage volunteer groups to bring pets to visit their patients. Schools and hospitals that work with emotionally disturbed people also keep pets. Doctors and psychologists often prescribe pets for their patients. There's even a prison in Ohio where hardened criminals are learning to relate to the world by caring for animals—dogs, geese, parrots, ducks, chickens, fish, deer, and a goat.

Some animal therapy programs combine physical and emotional benefits. For example, there are horseback riding programs for children who are physically and emotionally disabled. Riding helps the children with physical problems gain co-ordination and overcome their disabilities. And contact with the horses seems to help children with emotional problems open up.

Animals are helping people in many ways, it seems. And more and more people—both families and individuals—are choosing pets. In the United States alone there are about 45,000,000 dogs, 35,000,000 cats, and 8,500,000 horses.

But researchers caution that good things don't happen every time pets and people get together. For good to come out of the relationship, the pet and the person have to be suited to each other. Some situations don't work—a nervous, excitable dog, for example, living with a nervous, excitable person in a small city apartment.

Another important factor is how deeply the person is attached to the pet. When people have to take care of a pet they don't really like, the pet can actually add stress and tension to their lives. Sometimes they end up giving the pet away or abandoning it.

For these reasons, people should choose their pets very carefully. If you're going to get a pet, think about what the animal will need in terms of care, space, and exercise. If you live in a small apartment, choose a small pet. If you're away from home much of the day, consider a bird, a hamster, or fish—none of which will have to be walked several times a day. Remember that any animal can be a helpful partner, if you love and care for it.

Pets are social ice-breakers. People you'd normally never meet will come up and talk when you're walking your dog.

Snout beetle

Diamond beetle

Scarab beetle

BEETLE-MANIA

A glimpse at the photos on these pages shows that the variety found among beetles is truly extraordinary. And no wonder. There are some 300,000 known species, or kinds, of beetles. In fact, almost one out of every three species of insects is a beetle. They live in nearly every part of the world.

Beetles belong to the scientific order *Coleoptera,* which means "sheath-winged insects." And this term describes perfectly how beetles differ from other insects: They have a pair of thick, leathery front wings that act as sheaths, or shields, and protect the delicate underwings used for flying.

Beetles range in size from the tiny fungus beetle, which is only 0.01 inch (0.25 millimeter) long, to the Hercules beetle, which may be more than 7 inches (18 centimeters) long. They also vary greatly in shape. They may be long and slender or almost circular. Some are sturdily built, while others are delicate. Some are boxlike, and some are flat, almost paper thin. Beetles also have a remarkable range of colors and patterns. Among the best-known beetles are the ladybug, the June bug, and the firefly.

Every species of beetle has its own scientific name. But many are best known by their common names, which are usually based on the insect's appearance, feeding habits, or habitat. Giraffe beetles, for example, look like odd, six-legged giraffes sporting long antennas. And diamond beetles look as if they are studded with glittering jewels.

Snout beetles, as you might guess, have very long snouts, or beaks. The snout is used for making holes in seeds, fruit, or stems. The female snout beetle lays her eggs in these holes.

Tortoise beetles have the kind of broadened shape and distinctive markings that make them resemble box turtles. Another good common name for these insects might be chameleon beetles, for they can quickly change their color to better blend with the environment.

Leaf beetles are often flamboyantly colored, with brilliant, iridescent patterns. But the names of these beetles come from the fact that they dine primarily on leaves. Many are serious agricultural pests. One of the most notorious is the Colorado potato beetle, which has caused severe famines in many parts of the world.

Some of the best-known of all beetles are the scarab beetles, Most famous is the sacred scarab, which the ancient Egyptians considered to be a symbol of eternal life. Images of this beetle are often carved on emeralds and other precious stones and are worn as rings or necklaces. These scarabs are believed to protect the wearer against evil.

Tortoise beetle

Leaf beetle

Giraffe beetles

ANIMAL CHAMPIONS

How far can a kangaroo jump? How fast can a falcon fly? How strong is an elephant?

Experts don't always agree on how far an animal can leap, how fast it can move, how strong or smart it may be. It's difficult to test the performance of animals in the wild. And it's hard to measure qualities like strength and intelligence.

Even so, animal-watchers have come up with plenty of facts and figures about the amazing abilities of animals and how they measure up to humans.

Swimming Champs. In the Olympic Games, a champion swimmer can reach a top speed of about 5 miles an hour. At that rate, the swimming champ would be left far behind by most creatures that live in the sea.

A sea otter can swim twice as fast as an Olympic champion, a walrus three times as fast. Sea turtles paddle along at 22 miles an hour. Dolphins reach 25 miles an hour.

Penguins are the best swimmers among birds. They use their wings as flippers and their feet as rudders as they zip through the water at speeds of up to 30 miles an hour.

Sharks have been timed at 40 miles an hour, marlins at 50, and swordfish at 58. But the fastest swimmer in the sea is the sailfish. A sailfish has been clocked at the record-breaking speed of 68 miles an hour—about twice the speed of a nuclear submarine.

Running Champs. The top speed ever recorded for an Olympic runner is 27 miles an hour. That's faster than a charging elephant (24 miles an hour), but not quite as fast as a charging rhinoceros (28 miles an hour).

Grizzly bears have been clocked at 30 miles an hour as they galloped on all fours. A house cat chasing a mouse reaches about the same speed as a grizzly. Wolves and coyotes can approach 40 miles an hour.

The fastest member of the dog family is the greyhound, with a record speed of 41.7 miles an hour. The top speed for a racehorse is 43.3 miles an hour. That's fast, but it's not quite as fast as an ostrich can run. In Africa, an ostrich was timed at 43.5 miles an hour. It's the fastest bird on two legs.

Deer and antelope can top 50 miles an hour when they're running for their lives. A pronghorn antelope has been timed at 61 miles an hour. The only animal that can run faster is the swift, sleek cheetah. In one speed test, a cheetah was clocked by a speeding automobile. It covered 700 yards in 20 seconds, averaging just over 71 miles an hour. That makes the cheetah the fastest creature on land.

Flying Champs. Scientists have used many methods to measure the flying speeds of birds. Birds have been timed from the ground by observers armed with binoculars and stopwatches. They've been followed in airplanes, tracked by radar, and tested in special wind tunnels.

The wandering albatross—which has the longest wings of any bird—has been clocked at 77 miles an hour. Golden eagles reach 80 miles an hour. Racing pigeons have been timed at top speeds of 90 miles an hour.

The fastest birds are swifts and falcons. They have swept-back pointed wings like those of a jet plane. Swifts can easily top 100 miles an hour in level flight. In the Soviet Union, a spine-tail swift was clocked at 106 miles an hour.

Falcons can also top 100 miles an hour in level flight. And when these powerful bullet-headed birds swoop down and dive after prey, they may travel at twice that speed or more. To find out how much more, two scientists trained a peregrine falcon to fly in a special wind tunnel. They estimated that the

Swimming champs: Using their wings as flippers and feet as rudders, penguins are the best swimmers among birds.

falcon's top speed during its power dive was 325 feet a second—about 240 miles an hour. That's the fastest speed ever recorded for any animal moving under its own power.

Jumping Champs. An impala can cover a distance of 35 feet in a single leap. A mountain lion can jump as far as 39 feet. But the champion jumper is the kangaroo.

Normally, a kangaroo walks about on all fours. As it speeds up, it starts hopping on its powerful hind legs. A kangaroo in a hurry can hop along at 30 miles an hour. And it can cover 30 feet or more with each hop. The longest jump ever recorded for a kangaroo is 42 feet.

Kangaroos can jump farther than any other animal, but they're not the best jumpers for their size. At most, a kangaroo can jump about 8 times the length of its body. A frightened jack rabbit can jump 11 times the length of its body. And a jumping mouse, less than 4 inches long, can cover 10 to 12 feet at a single bound—more than 30 times the length of its body.

The best jumper for its size is an insect— the common flea. A flea can jump as far as 13 inches. Compared to the mighty 42-foot leap of a kangaroo, a 13-inch jump might not seem like much. And yet that's 200 times the length of a flea's body! If Olympic champions had the jumping power of a flea, they could sail over five city blocks with a single easy leap.

Flying champs: A swift is one of the fastest flying birds. Swifts have swept-back, pointed wings like those of a jet plane, and they can top 100 miles an hour in level flight.

Running champs: The sleek cheetah is the fastest creature on land. In one test, it averaged 71 miles an hour.

Jumping champs: The kangaroo is the champion jumper. It has been known to cover 42 feet in a single leap.

Diving Champs. When a duck dives for its dinner, it may reach a depth of 200 feet below the surface. Another diving bird, the loon, has been known to dive as deep as 240 feet. The best divers among birds are penguins. One penguin, observed through the window of a diving bell, reached a depth of 885 feet. The deepest dive ever recorded for a human scuba diver is 437 feet.

Some seals and whales regularly dive 1,000 feet or more as they hunt for food. They may stay under water for one to two hours before coming up for air. A finback whale has been recorded at a depth of 1,150 feet, and a Weddell seal at a depth of 2,000 feet.

The deepest dive ever recorded for a free-swimming, air-breathing animal was made by a 47-foot sperm whale in the Pacific Ocean off the coast of South America. The whale reached a depth of 3,720 feet below the surface, where it became entangled with a submarine cable on the ocean floor.

Champion Travelers. Few animals, if any, can outwalk the caribou. Caribou spend the winter in the forests of Canada. In spring they head north, traveling in great herds. They walk through melting snows past the timberline and across the tundra to the shores of the Arctic Ocean. They spend the summer grazing in the tundra. Then they turn around and head back to their forests, a round-trip walk of more than 1,000 miles.

Every fall, monarch butterflies migrate from Canada and the northern United States to the Gulf of Mexico and other southern areas. Fluttering along at 10 miles an hour, resting at night on bushes and trees, these frail insects fly 2,000 miles or more to their winter homes. In spring, their descendants make the trip back north.

The longest journeys at sea are made by gray whales. During the winter they live in warm lagoons along the coast of Mexico. As winter ends, they travel north to the Arctic Ocean, a trip that takes three months of steady swimming and covers between 4,000 and 6,000 miles. All summer long the whales gorge themselves on arctic plankton. Then they spend three more months swimming another 4,000 to 6,000 miles on their way back to Mexico.

Some birds cross the equator twice yearly as they migrate between their summer and winter homes. White storks spend the summer in northern Europe and the winter in southern Africa—a one-way trip of 8,000 miles. And golden plovers fly 10,000 miles from their summer nesting grounds in the arctic to their winter quarters in Argentina.

The champion long-distance traveler is the arctic tern, a relative of the sea gull. During the warm summer months, these birds hatch their eggs and raise their young along the ice-free shores of the Arctic Ocean, close to the North Pole. As summer ends, the terns head south. They fly from the Arctic Circle to the seas of Antarctica, a one-way trip of about 12,000 miles and the longest continuous journey made by any living creature.

The Strongest Animals. In official competition, a champion weightlifter can lift about four times his own body weight. A chimpanzee has been known to lift six times its body weight. Chimps are smaller than humans, but they're much stronger.

According to Jane Goodall, an expert on chimpanzees, the average chimp is about three times stronger than the average person. When Goodall studied wild chimpanzees in Africa, she coaxed them into her research camp by leaving bananas out for them. Extra bananas were kept locked away in metal strongboxes, to be used when needed. Two chimps were smart enough to figure out how to get into the strongboxes. And they were strong enough to do it. They broke into the boxes by snapping steel cables with their bare hands.

Gorillas are a lot bigger than chimps. It's hard to tell how much stronger they may be because they don't often display their strength. Scientist George Schaller, who studied wild gorillas, believes that a full-grown male gorilla has "the strength of several men." Schaller has seen gorillas reach into a tree and rip down branches thicker than a muscle-builder's arms.

The American Indians regarded the grizzly bear as the most powerful creature on Earth. When a grizzly searches for insects to eat, it can flip boulders over like cardboard boxes. When it hunts for bigger game, it can break the neck of an elk or moose with a single blow of its paw. It can pick up an elk carcass weighing the better part of a ton and carry it off to a hiding place.

In the teak forests of Southeast Asia, a trained work elephant can lift a ton of logs with its trunk. And it can drag a load of logs weighing 10 tons. As the biggest of all land animals, elephants are also the most powerful. But they're not the strongest animals for their size.

The strongest animals for their size are insects. An ant can pick up a stone more than 50 times its own weight. It can carry that stone up a long underground tunnel and drop it outside its nest. If a big elephant had that much strength, it could lift at least 300 tons of logs with its trunk and carry them hundreds of yards up a steep hill.

Ants aren't as strong as some beetles. Scientists tested beetles for their lifting ability by placing them in little harnesses with weights attached. In these tests, beetles were able to lift 850 times their own weight. A 200-pound man that strong would be able to lift a weight equal to 14 full-grown elephants. And if an elephant were as strong as a beetle, it could lift a Navy destroyer.

The Brainiest Animals. The brainiest creatures on Earth are the great whales. A cap-

Champion travelers: Every fall, the frail monarch butterfly migrates 2,000 miles from Canada to the Gulf of Mexico.

The strongest animals: Despite its lumbering gait, the grizzly bear is one of the most powerful creatures on Earth.

tured blue whale had a brain that weighed in at about 15 pounds. A sperm whale had a brain that weighed just over 20 pounds. That's the biggest brain ever recorded.

Next to the whales, elephants have the biggest brains. An elephant's brain averages about 11 pounds, but the largest elephants have brains that weigh 13 pounds or more.

An average human brain weighs about 3¼ pounds—not much compared to elephants and whales. And yet no one believes that elephants or whales are smarter than humans. A giant brain doesn't always mean a giant I.Q. Brain size is important, but it doesn't tell the whole story about an animal's intelligence. Even more important is the size of an animal's brain compared to the size of its body.

Humans have the biggest brains for their size. An average person has about one pound of brain for each 50 pounds of body weight. An elephant has only one pound of brain for each 1,000 pounds of body weight. A large part of an elephant's brain is devoted to controlling the movement of its big body.

Even so, elephants have plenty of brain power left over for intelligent behavior. The ancient Greeks regarded the elephant as the smartest of all animals. Today, scientists still rank elephants near the top when it comes to measuring animal I.Q.'s. Elephants learn fast, and they have long memories. A trained work elephant can remember the meanings of more than 200 commands. Experienced work elephants will often perform the right act even before they hear a command.

Apes seem to be smarter than elephants. Chimpanzees, gorillas, and orangutans all have big brains for their size. Often, they are able to solve problems that require real understanding.

In one problem-solving experiment, a hungry chimp was placed in a room. A banana was hanging from the ceiling, out of reach. Boxes were scattered across the floor. The chimp looked around, grabbed a box, placed it beneath the banana, and climbed on top. The banana was still out of reach, so the chimp piled a second box on top of the first one. After piling up five boxes, the chimp was able to grab the banana.

In another hanging-banana experiment, a scientist scattered both boxes and sticks across the floor. Would the chimp pile up the boxes to reach the banana? Or would he find the longest stick and knock the banana down? The chimp did neither. Instead, he took the scientist by the hand, pulled him to the center of the room beneath the banana, climbed up on his shoulders, and grabbed the banana. That was one solution the scientist hadn't thought of.

The strongest animals: Insects are the strongest animals for their size. An ant, for example, can lift an object more than 50 times its own weight. Here, an ant is pushing a captured snail.

The brainiest animals: Chimpanzees have big brains for their size and are often able to solve problems that require real understanding. Here, a chimp is being taught sign language.

At one time, chimpanzees were considered the smartest of the apes, followed by gorillas and orangutans. But in recent tests, all these apes achieved similar scores. And in some I.Q. tests, orangutans scored higher than gorillas or chimps. So until further research is done, it's hard to say which ape is the most intelligent.

One animal, the dolphin, may be smarter than any ape. Next to humans, dolphins have the biggest brain for their size—about one pound of brain for each 85 pounds of body weight. A chimpanzee, by comparison, has about one pound of brain for each 150 pounds of body weight.

Bottle-nosed dolphins have become famous as star performers at seaquariums. They seem to enjoy learning, and they can master a wide variety of difficult tricks and stunts. Dolphins catch on quickly. Often they learn a trick simply by watching other dolphins perform. Trainers say that they learn faster and remember longer than any other animal.

Everyone who has studied dolphins or has worked with them agrees that they're very smart animals. But no one knows exactly how smart they really are. It's difficult enough to test the intelligence of our fellow humans. It's even more difficult to understand the minds of creatures such as dolphins. Their lives are so different from our own lives, and their brains work differently too.

Humans live in a world of sight. Our eyes tell us much of what we know about the world. A big part of the human brain is devoted to seeing. Dolphins live in a world of underwater sounds. While it's not possible to see very far under the water, sounds travel clearly through the water. A dolphin gets most of its information through its ears, not its eyes. It has a much larger part of its brain devoted to hearing than a human has. And its brain differs from the human brain in other ways as well.

Since each animal has a different kind of brain and lives in a world of its own, it's very tricky to compare animals by means of intelligence tests. A test that's fair to a dog, for instance, might not be fair to a cat.

Suppose that a dog wanted to test the intelligence of a human. A dog lives in a world of smells. It gets most of its information through its nose. A large part of a dog's brain is in charge of analyzing and identifying odors. So if a dog could set up an I.Q. test for humans, it might ask a person to follow a scent-trail through a forest. The dog in charge of this test would have to conclude that we humans are pretty stupid!

RUSSELL FREEDMAN
Author, *How Animals Learn*

Sea otter

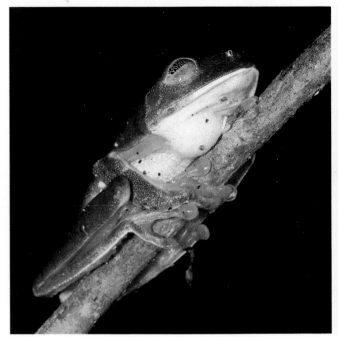

Tree frog

Koala

DO NOT DISTURB

If you're like most people, you spend at least a third of every day sleeping. During sleep, muscles relax, heartbeat and breathing slow down, and you gradually lose awareness of your surroundings. Sleep lets your body rebuild energy after a busy day.

Just like you, most animals need periods of sleep each day. But you might find some of their sleeping habits—and their bedrooms —surprising. A tree frog, for example, will fall asleep in the middle of the day, right in the branches of a tree. Like most amphibians, the tree frog sleeps very lightly and doesn't dream. The slightest noise will awaken it. Birds and mammals sleep more deeply. Mammals dream, and scientists think that birds may have very short dreams, too.

Some animals can sleep almost anywhere. Sea lions stretch out and doze off on a bed of hard rocks. Another ocean-loving animal, the sea otter, likes to float lazily on its back and be rocked to sleep by the waves. Before it goes to sleep, a sea otter will wrap strands of seaweed called kelp around its body. The kelp looks like it's being used as a blanket, but it's not. It acts as an anchor that keeps the sea otter from drifting away with the ocean currents.

Many birds fall asleep while firmly grasping a tree branch, often with one leg. Most birds are active during the day and doze in the trees at night. But some birds, such as owls, are nocturnal—they sleep during the day and hunt for food at night.

The koala also sleeps during the day, cradled in the branches of a eucalyptus tree. This tree provides the koala not only with a bed but also with dinner—its leaves are the Australian animal's only food.

Some animals are super sleepers—they hibernate during the cold winter months. Hibernation is different from true sleep. The animal's heartbeat and breathing slow down much more than they do in sleep, and its body temperature drops. This means that the animal uses much less energy, and it can live for months on fat stored in its body.

The dormouse is a famous hibernator—in fact, its name is thought to come from the French word *dormir,* which means "to sleep." The dormouse prepares for winter by eating as much as it can and getting fat. Then it curls up in a snug den and snoozes the winter away. When it wakes up in the spring, it may weigh only half what it weighed in the fall.

A famous literary dormouse was a guest at the Mad Hatter's tea party in *Alice's Adventures in Wonderland.* And, as you may have guessed, it spent most of the time dozing over its teacup!

Sea lions

Saw-whet owl

Dormouse

ANIMALS IN THE NEWS

This newborn foal is truly a horse of a different color—the first zebra to be born to a horse. Veterinarians accomplished the feat by taking a ten-day-old embryo from a zebra at the Louisville Zoo and then implanting it in a Kentucky quarter horse mare. A year later Kelly, seen here grazing in the background, gave birth to the baby zebra, who weighed in at 70 pounds. This marked the first successful embryo transfer between two different equine species. Scientists now hope to use the technique to breed more animals of species that are endangered, such as Grevy's zebra.

After Lucky, a 350-pound loggerhead sea turtle, lost both front flippers to a shark, doctors came to the rescue. A team of surgeons equipped the turtle with a pair of custom-designed rubber flippers, with the hope that she would then be able to return to the ocean. (Lucky is shown here during her first swim with the new flippers.) But the surgeons' efforts were unsuccessful—the turtle's bones weren't strong enough to hold the artificial flippers. Although Lucky won't be able to return to the sea, she will be well taken care of at her new home in the Theatre of the Sea in Islamorada, Florida.

Is it a miniature walrus? A sausage with tiny teeth? Neither. This little animal is a naked mole rat, an African rodent that lives in underground colonies. Scientists are studying the mole rat (which is neither a mole nor a rat) not for its looks but for its behavior. Mole rats, it seems, act just like some species of bees and termites. One female is the queen of the colony and produces all the young. Each of the other mole rats has a specific job to perform, such as gathering food or digging tunnels. The mole rats are the only mammals known to behave in this way.

On east and west coasts alike, some of the most popular entertainers of 1984 were whales. "Whale watch" cruises, offering (but not promising) a sight of the giant ocean mammals, were sellouts at $20 a ride. Why do people find whales so appealing? Their size, grace, intelligence, and mystery have all been offered as reasons. At any rate, scientists agree that watching whales is much better than killing them. Many species of whales were driven to near extinction by whaling ships in the past. Now the new interest in whales is helping scientists learn more about how these fascinating giants live.

Question: What can defeat the entire U.S. Air Force without firing a shot? Answer: The Guam rail, a tiny flightless bird that lives only on the Pacific island of Guam. The bird and the military came face to face when the Air Force decided to clear some trees and brush around its facilities on the island. The idea was to make it harder for saboteurs to sneak up on buildings where nuclear weapons were stored. But the woody area turned out to be the chief habitat of the rails. In 1968, there were about 80,000 of the birds. But by 1984, for unclear reasons, the number had shrunk to 50. People protested that if the brush were cleared, the last Guam rails might die. And the Air Force dropped its plan.

The Louisville Zoo's zebra wasn't the only animal to be born to a surrogate mother in 1984. At the Cincinnati Zoo, this rare antelope, called a bongo, was born to an eland antelope mother. Veterinarians used the same technique as that used in Kentucky. But this time the bongo that supplied the embryos was in Los Angeles. The scientists flew from California to Ohio with seven embryos in vials taped under their arms, to keep them near body temperature. ("Little did the people on the plane know they had a herd of bongos riding with them," said one zoo official.) In the future, scientists hope to fly embryos of rare species from Africa to surrogate mothers elsewhere, rather than shipping full-grown animals.

The Cincinnati Zoo celebrated another blessed event in 1984—the birth of five rare white tiger cubs. In the wild, white tigers are scarce because their color makes them an easy mark for predators. Today only 70 of these creatures are known to exist, and the zoo has bred 30 of them. The cubs born in 1984 were to be sold to zoos around the world, at prices up to $60,000.

Look! Up in the sky! It's a bird . . . it's a plane . . . No, it's a bee—the world's largest. The female *Chalicodoma pluto* measures 1¾ inches long, and it is shown here alongside a normal bee. Long thought to be extinct, *C. pluto* is native to Indonesia. It was sighted in 1859 by Alfred Russel Wallace, a British biologist. But no one else ever found the bee—it was so rare that even people who lived on the island didn't see it. Then, 122 years after Wallace's sighting, a U.S. biologist rediscovered the bee. And he found something that Wallace hadn't: the bees' nests. *C. pluto* builds its nests inside the nests of tree-dwelling termites. The bees wall off their quarters with tree resin, which the females carry to the nest in their enormous plier-shaped jaws.

DINOSAUR DILEMMAS

Dinosaurs ruled the Earth for more than 150,000,000 years. Then, about 65,000,000 years ago, they became extinct. How do we know this, since no human being has ever seen a living dinosaur? We know of these reptiles only by their remains—fossilized bones and teeth, footprints in rock, and fossilized nests and eggs. Paleontologists (scientists who study fossils) have long been trying to find answers to some of the puzzling questions about dinosaurs. And recently, fascinating information has come to light about these creatures of long ago.

• People used to believe that all dinosaurs were huge animals. And, indeed, many were enormous. The largest known dinosaur, *Ultrasaurus,* weighed 80 tons and stood as tall as a six-story building. But at the other end of the scale were dinosaurs no larger than chickens. Paleontologists are still discovering new species, or kinds, of dinosaurs. In the past 15 years, in fact, at least 50 new species have been identified.

• From fossilized dinosaur nests discovered in Montana, we have also learned more about how some dinosaurs lived. The nests contained the remains of eggs, baby dinosaurs, and juveniles ranging from 3 to 5 feet (90 to 150 centimeters) in length. They appear to be the remains of duckbill dinosaurs —plant-eating creatures with broad, ducklike bills. Scientists believe that the nests are evidence that adult duckbills cared for their young for at least a few months after they hatched, bringing them food and protecting them from enemies. The young didn't leave the nests until they were several feet long and able to join their parents in the search for food.

• The discovery of the nests added to one of the major controversies concerning dinosaurs: Were they cold-blooded, inactive animals—like all modern reptiles? Or were they warm-blooded, lively animals—like people and other mammals? For many years, it was believed that all dinosaurs were sluggish, cold-blooded creatures. But there is increasing evidence that at least some dinosaurs were warm-blooded. The duckbills, for example, apparently grew very quickly, unlike modern reptiles. Rapid growth implies rapid metabolism—and this is a characteristic of warm-bloodedness. (*Metabolism* refers to all the chemical changes that take place in a plant or animal to keep it alive.)

Another argument for warm-bloodedness is the way in which some dinosaurs were built. The reptiles of today are sprawlers. Their bodies are close to the ground and their legs stick out to the side. In contrast, many dinosaurs stood erect and walked on two legs. Their heads, like ours, were well above their hearts. To pump blood upward requires a high-blood-pressure circulatory system. Today, only warm-blooded animals have metabolism rates that are high enough to support this type of circulatory system.

Warm-bloodedness, however, requires huge amounts of energy—the body temperature must remain high even when the environment turns chilly. A 40-ton animal would have to eat as much as a ton of food a day to maintain a constant, warm body temperature. For this reason, some scientists believe that at least the large, sluggish dinosaurs, such as *Brontosaurus,* were cold-blooded.

• What happened on Earth 65,000,000 years ago that doomed the dinosaurs? This is the question about dinosaurs that most intrigues people. Many theories have been proposed. Some scientists believe that the climate turned colder, killing off the dinosaurs' food supplies. Others insist that the climate turned warmer, making it too warm for dinosaur eggs to hatch. Still another theory is that changes in the Earth's magnetic field at that time increased the amount of deadly radiation that hit the Earth from outer space.

One of the more popular theories puts the blame on a huge asteroid that, some experts say, crashed into Earth about 65,000,000 years ago. The collision caused giant earthquakes and tidal waves. More importantly, it filled the atmosphere with so much dust and other debris that sunlight couldn't reach the Earth's surface. For three years, the Earth was dark. Without enough light, the plants died. Then the animals that fed on the plants starved to death. Finally, the meat-eating animals died.

According to this theory, the dinosaurs had no way to survive such a catastrophe. Nor did many other kinds of animals and plants. But some species were able to deal with the darkness. Seed-producing plants died but their seeds remained in the soil, ready to grow when conditions were right. Tiny mammals—the predecessors of today's mammals—hibernated through the cold, dark years. When conditions returned to normal, these plants and animals thrived.

But the dinosaurs were no more. Their remains slowly sank into the mud, becoming fossilized and hidden from view. Today it is those remains that enable us to imagine what the Earth and its inhabitants were like so very, very long ago.

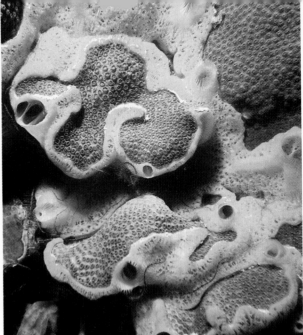

STRANGE
WATER DWELLERS

Sponges are some of the most unusual creatures in the animal kingdom. For centuries, in fact, many people thought that these strange water dwellers were plants—they are motionless and seem to be rooted in place, and if you touch one, there is no apparent reaction.

Sponges are among the most primitive of the many-celled animals. They have no hearts, lungs, brains, sense organs, or nervous systems. More than 5,000 different kinds, or species, of sponges are known. Most species live in oceans. A few live in lakes and other bodies of fresh water. Sponges can be found at great depths, but most live in shallow coastal waters. They live attached to rocks, wharf pilings, and other underwater objects. Many live singly; others live in colonies.

Sponges come in many sizes, shapes, and colors. Some are no larger than a grain of rice. Others are more than 6 feet (2 meters) in diameter and weigh as much as 100 pounds (45 kilograms). Sponges may be shaped like fans, vases, bowls, or trumpets. Some are rounded masses, while others branch out like trees. Many are dull beige or

brown in color. But some are beautifully colored in vivid shades of green, red, orange, or violet.

Although they may vary in appearance, all sponges have the same simple structure. The body consists of several layers of cells surrounding a central cavity. The surface of the body is punctured by tiny pores. It is these pores that give sponges their scientific name, Porifera, or "pore-bearers." Water flows through the pores into the central cavity, bringing the sponge food and oxygen.

Some of the sponge's cells produce a skeleton of sorts, which gives the animal shape and prevents the body from collapsing. In most cases, the skeleton consists of tiny needlelike structures called spicules (from the Latin word *spiculum,* which means spine). Depending on the species, the spicules are made either of limestone or glass.

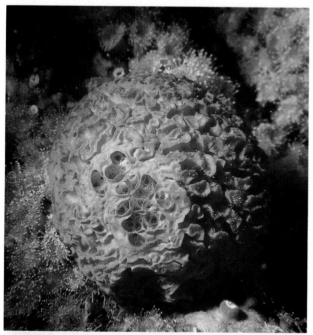

Sponges don't have many natural enemies, probably because they don't taste very good. Some crabs make use of this fact— they attach small pieces of sponge to their shells. As the unappetizing sponge grows, it conceals the crab from predators.

Some small sea animals escape from predators by hiding in sponges. In the western Pacific, young shrimp frequently seek shelter in a delicate sponge called Venus's-flower-basket. Often, both a male and a female shrimp are found in the same sponge. As the two shrimp grow, they become trapped inside the sponge and spend their entire lives there. Natives of the area believe that this symbolizes fidelity in marriage, and they often give a Venus's-flower-basket as a present to newly married couples.

The only sponges of economic importance are the bath sponges. When alive, these sponges are dark brown or black in color. But when they have been dried and bleached, they turn a pale yellow-brown. Bath sponges are soft because they don't have spicules. Instead, their skeletons consist of a fibrous network of a substance called spongin. When dried, these sponges are able to absorb huge amounts of water. This ability to absorb liquid has been put to use by people for thousands of years. Wall paintings on the Greek island of Crete show that sponges were used as paint rollers some 4,000 years ago!

SCIENCE

Floating free 175 miles above the Earth, astronaut Bruce McCandless II tests a new jet-propelled Manned Maneuvering Unit (MMU). McCandless was a mission specialist on the February flight of the U.S. space shuttle Challenger. The MMU, which looks like an oversize backpack, enabled him to become a human satellite—the first person to move freely in space without any lines tethering him to the spacecraft.

SPACE BRIEFS

The dazzling achievements of science and technology are nowhere more evident than in space. The year 1984 saw the first "human satellites" . . . the first filling station in outer space . . . the first space performance of yoga exercises. But more important than these "firsts" were advances in the uses of space. The use of satellites for communications has become a multi-billion-dollar-a-year business. And experiments conducted by satellites and spaceships are greatly extending our knowledge of Earth and the universe in which we live.

THE U.S. SPACE SHUTTLES

The first flight of a re-usable shuttle took place in 1981. By the end of 1984, fourteen missions had been completed. Each mission built on the knowledge gained in previous missions, and each extended the shuttles' capabilities. Five missions were completed in 1984. Here are the highlights:

During *Discovery*'s maiden flight, an extendable solar-energy panel (for use on space stations) was tested.

Mission 10. On February 11, *Challenger* completed an eight-day mission with a perfect landing at Cape Canaveral, Florida—the first time that a shuttle had landed at its launching base. (Landing shuttles at their launching base reduces the cost and time required to get them ready to fly again.) Aboard *Challenger* were Vance D. Brand, Robert L. Gibson, Bruce McCandless II, Ronald E. McNair, and Robert L. Stewart.

Two communications satellites were launched by the crew. But their rocket boosters misfired, sending the satellites off course and into useless orbits. Another problem arose when the shuttle's robot arm failed to work properly. These failures, however, were overshadowed by the triumphs of two free-flying excursions outside the spaceship by McCandless and Stewart. Previously, astronauts who ventured outside a spacecraft remained attached to the craft by safety lines. But McCandless and Stewart were, in effect, human satellites. They wore jet-propelled backpacks known as Manned Maneuvering Units. Each unit had 24 tiny jet thrusters. "Controllers" extending forward from the pack enabled the astronaut to move in any direction.

Mission 11. On April 6, *Challenger* began a seven-day flight. Aboard were Robert L. Crippen, Terry J. Hart, George D. Nelson, Francis R. Scobee, and James D. Van Hoften. They succeeded in their primary objective—retrieving and repairing Solar Max. This satellite had been launched in February, 1980, to study the outer surface of the sun. Within a year of its launching, several important components had failed. As a result, Solar Max couldn't be sufficiently stabilized to perform its scientific observations.

The astronauts used *Challenger*'s robot arm to catch Solar Max and place it in the space shuttle's cargo bay. There, the astronauts succeeded in replacing the defective parts. The robot arm then picked up Solar Max and released it back into orbit.

The tools used by astronauts in space are specially designed for the weightless environment. Consider, for example, the wrench used during the repair of Solar Max. Because

Mission 13's record crew of seven. During the October mission, Kathryn Sullivan (*left*) became the first American woman to walk in space as she and David Leestma (*center right*) tested a system for refueling satellites in space.

of the lack of gravity in space, an astronaut trying to use a regular wrench would turn in circles—while the bolts remained unmoved. So a special battery-powered wrench was designed that would turn the bolts instead of the astronaut.

The Mission 11 crew also deployed an enormous satellite carrying 57 experiments designed by U.S., Canadian, and Western European scientists. The experiments are designed to show how certain materials and processes are affected by the harsh environment of space. The satellite and its experiments will be picked up and returned to Earth in 1985.

"How does space travel affect living things?" is a frequently asked question. Mission 11 added to our knowledge in this area, for it carried aloft a colony of honeybees. The bees were able to build a nearly geometrically perfect honeycomb, despite the absence of gravity. The colony's queen even laid 35 eggs during the flight.

Mission 12. *Discovery*, the third of the U.S. space shuttles, began its maiden flight on August 30. Aboard the six-day flight were Henry W. Hartsfield, Jr., Michael L. Coats. Steven A. Hawley, Richard M. Mullane, Judith A. Resnik, and Charles D. Walker. Resnik was the second American woman to travel in space; Walker was the first commercial passenger, or non-astronaut, on a shuttle.

The crew successfully launched three communications satellites. They also tested a long, extendable solar-energy panel. The panel was a prototype for devices that may be erected on future space stations, to gather energy in space. And using *Discovery*'s long robot arm, the crew knocked a chunk of ice off the side of the shuttle. The ice had blocked the shuttle's waste water outlet and could have damaged the spaceship during its re-entry into Earth's atmosphere.

Mission 13. In October, *Challenger* returned to space with a record crew of seven: Robert L. Crippen, David C. Leestma, Jon A. McBride, Sally K. Ride, Paul Scully-Power, Kathryn D. Sullivan, and Marc Garneau—the first Canadian to fly in space. During the eight-day mission, Sullivan became the first American woman to walk in space as she and Leestma tested a system for refueling satellites in space. Their work opened the way for routine servicing of satellites that have run out of fuel.

Another important objective of the astronauts was to conduct surveys of the Earth's surface. They used an imaging radar system and a large-film camera to record detailed images of Earth. Among the events they monitored was Hurricane Josephine, an Atlantic storm that for a while threatened to delay or move the shuttle's landing.

Mission 14. In November, *Discovery* went aloft on an eight-day mission. It had a crew

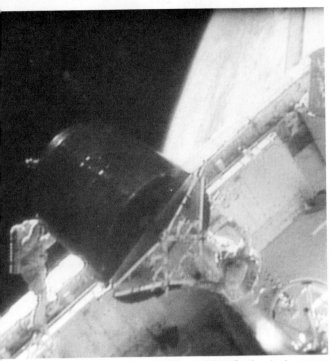

Mission 14: Joseph Allen and Dale Gardner try to maneuver the retrieved Palapa satellite into the cargo bay.

On October 2, a capsule carrying 3 Soviet astronauts floated to Earth—setting a new space-endurance record.

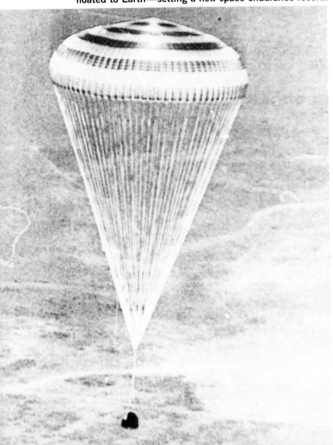

of five: Frederick H. Hauck, Joseph P. Allen, Dale A. Gardner, David M. Walker, and Anna L. Fisher—the first mother to travel in space. The astronauts deployed two communications satellites. Then, in spectacular space walks, they retrieved Palapa B-2 and Westar 6, the two satellites that had misfired after being launched by Mission 10 in February. *Discovery* caught up with Palapa first. Allen left the spacecraft. Propelled by thrusters in his Manned Maneuvering Unit, he moved toward Palapa. Allen carried a long probe, called a stinger, which he locked onto the satellite to bring it under control. Fisher, at the shuttle's controls, used the robot arm to grasp the stinger and pull both the satellite and Allen toward the shuttle's cargo bay. The next step was to attach a special device to Palapa so that the robot arm could lower the satellite into the cargo bay. But a small fixture protruding from the satellite made it impossible to attach the device. For 90 minutes Allen and Gardner struggled with Palapa and manually maneuvered it into the cargo bay.

Two days later, *Discovery* caught up with Westar. This time it was Gardner who flew out to the satellite and inserted the stinger. Again Fisher extended the robot arm—but it wasn't used to grab the stinger. Instead, Allen was secured to the end of the arm, and he grabbed hold of an antenna atop Westar. He held on tightly while Fisher hauled back the arm, bringing Westar close to the cargo bay. Then Gardner successfully attached a device, and the satellite was lowered into the bay.

After the two satellites were brought back to Earth, they were examined and declared to be in sound shape. Both were scheduled to be relaunched.

THE SOVIET PROGRAM

The Soviet Union's space program continued to emphasize lengthy stays in space aboard the Earth-orbiting space station Salyut 7. On February 8, 1984, three astronauts were sent aloft in a Soyuz T-10 craft. They were Leonid D. Kizim, Vladimir A. Solovyev, and Oleg Y. Atkov, a heart specialist. The men docked with Salyut 7 and stayed there for 237 days before returning to Earth —completing the longest space flight in his-

In July, Soviet astronaut Svetlana Savitskaya left the Salyut 7 space station and became the first woman to walk in space. She was also the first woman to make two space flights.

tory. During their mission aboard Salyut 7, the astronauts were visited by two other Soviet space crews.

One of the visitors was Rakesh Sharma, India's first man in space. He and two Soviet astronauts spent eight days aboard Salyut 7 in April. Sharma performed yoga exercises several times daily. This was part of a study of the effects of space flight on the human body. One of the things scientists hoped to learn was whether yoga might be effective in combating space sickness, which often bothers astronauts.

In July, one of the three visitors to Salyut 7 was Svetlana Savitskaya—the first woman to make two space flights. On July 25, Savitskaya became the first woman to walk in space. During her 3 hours and 35 minutes outside the space station, she performed a variety of welding and soldering operations.

The Soviet Union may soon have a space shuttle of its own, or a new and larger space station. Photographs taken by U.S. satellites show that the U.S.S.R. is developing a booster rocket for a space shuttle, as well as large rockets similar to those used by the United States in the Apollo moon program. All these new rockets are designed to use liquid hydrogen, which has never been used before in the Soviet space program. Current Soviet rockets use a mixture of kerosene and liquid oxygen. But liquid hydrogen is needed if heavy payloads are to be efficiently lifted into space.

PREPARING FOR HALLEY

Every 76 years, Earth is visited by a famous celestial wanderer: Halley's comet. It will visit us in 1985–86, and scientists around the world are getting ready for its arrival. Halley will be the most intensively studied comet ever. Most of the world's telescopes will be focused on it. Four spacecraft will approach it to collect data on its nucleus and its long tail of dust and gases. Aircraft will go aloft in efforts to gather some of the comet's dust. These efforts are being co-ordinated by a worldwide organization known as International Halley Watch. More than 800 astronomers from 47 countries are participating in Halley Watch. In addition, thousands of amateur astronomers are expected to share their observations with the group.

In 1984, as a rehearsal for the big event, astronomers set their sights on comet Crommelin. Crommelin, which orbits the sun every 27 years, came within 72,000,000 miles of Earth on March 17. It is smaller than Halley's comet and has either a very small tail or no tail at all. But it passed Earth at about the same distance and in the same position as will Halley in March, 1986.

95

SUIT YOURSELF!

As people flew higher and higher into the atmosphere and, eventually, into outer space, they found that they needed special clothing. On these pages are three spacesuit ideas that didn't work—and one that did.

The fancy suit with its own solar-power headpiece (**A**) had hundreds of small metal "scales" designed to reflect heat. This was to prevent a moon explorer from being harmed by the sun's heat.

The suit that looks like a giant peanut (**B**) was designed for people who flew in high-altitude airplanes. The suit has a robot arm and hand. But the person wearing this suit could use only one hand—and no feet.

The "five-legged" tin can (**C**) was designed to let a moon explorer rest his legs a bit. After extending the tripod to the moon's surface, the astronaut could curl up on a built-in seat and eat his lunch or take a nap. Then he could re-insert his legs into the suit's trousers, retract the tripod legs, and resume his chores.

Unlike the suits on this page, the one on the following page is very practical. This suit, with a jet-propelled backpack attached, was used by astronauts in 1984 when they left their space shuttle to repair a satellite in space. For the first time, astronauts were not connected to their craft by safety lines.

A

B

C

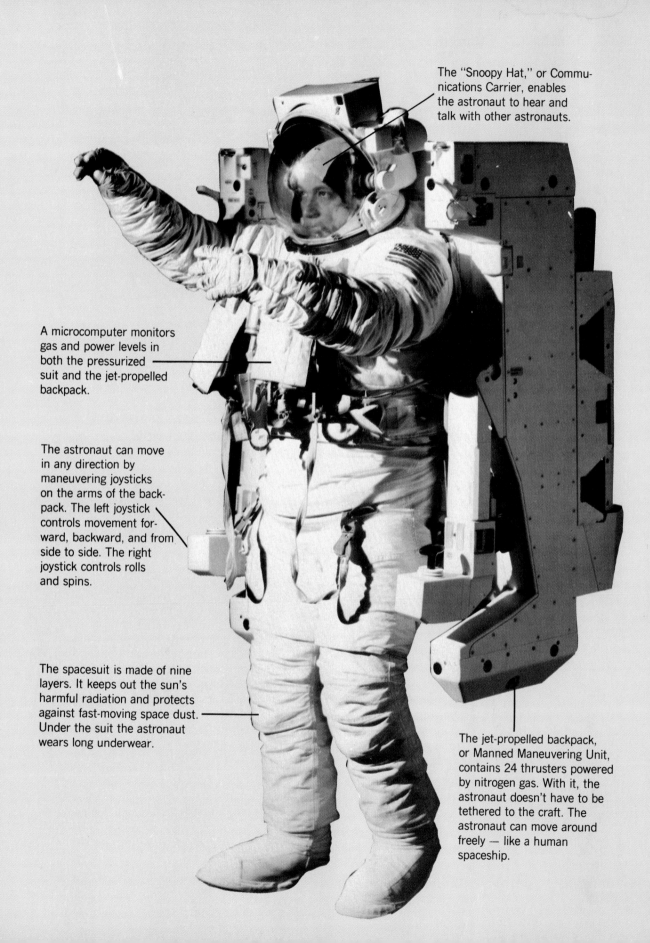

The "Snoopy Hat," or Communications Carrier, enables the astronaut to hear and talk with other astronauts.

A microcomputer monitors gas and power levels in both the pressurized suit and the jet-propelled backpack.

The astronaut can move in any direction by maneuvering joysticks on the arms of the backpack. The left joystick controls movement forward, backward, and from side to side. The right joystick controls rolls and spins.

The spacesuit is made of nine layers. It keeps out the sun's harmful radiation and protects against fast-moving space dust. Under the suit the astronaut wears long underwear.

The jet-propelled backpack, or Manned Maneuvering Unit, contains 24 thrusters powered by nitrogen gas. With it, the astronaut doesn't have to be tethered to the craft. The astronaut can move around freely — like a human spaceship.

ABC'S OF BODY TALK

A frog in your throat . . . butterflies in your stomach . . . goose bumps on your arms . . . sand in your eyes. What is your body saying?

Your body constantly reacts, or talks back, to the world in which it lives. It talks back to germs that try to invade it. It talks back to embarrassing stories, to chilly weather, to sleepless nights.

Which of the following are part of your body talk?

Black and Blue Marks. Sometimes you bang a part of your body against a hard object. Your skin doesn't break. But there's damage, and your skin turns "black and blue." What happened? When you bump yourself, small blood vessels just under the skin's surface are broken, and blood seeps out of the vessels. Your body stops this bleeding in the same way that it stops bleeding from a cut— the blood thickens and forms a clot. Blood that clots under the skin appears a dark purple. As fluids in your body break down the clot, the color changes to blue, then green, then yellow. Finally, the black and blue mark disappears.

Blushing. Someone embarrasses you—and your face turns bright pink. Why? When you are embarrassed, you get excited. Your brain tells your heart to pump faster. It also tells the capillaries (tiny blood vessels) in your body to get wider, so they can carry the extra blood being pumped out of the heart. You usually don't notice the extra blood that rushes to your arms or legs. But you do notice it in your face. And so does everyone else—the rushing blood makes the skin of your face flush with color.

Burps. Burps are your body's way of releasing air you have swallowed. As you eat and drink, you swallow air. You also swallow air that is trapped in food and drinks, such as in sodas. As more and more air fills your stomach, more and more pressure builds up. When there is enough pressure, the air pushes its way up and out. It goes up through the esophagus (the tube that leads from your stomach to your mouth). When it reaches the top of the esophagus, it rushes out with a funny noise—a burp.

Butterflies in Your Stomach. Your stomach is constantly moving, churning the food you've eaten and pushing it slowly toward the small intestine. If you are upset about something, your brain may tell your stomach muscles to stop working in order to save energy. It does this so that other muscles in your body will have enough energy to deal with whatever is upsetting you. When the smooth movement of the stomach is suddenly disrupted, it feels as if a bunch of butterflies were doing flip flops inside you.

Circles Under Your Eyes. The skin below your eyes is very thin and filled with hundreds of tiny blood vessels. Usually, the blood in these vessels is rich in oxygen and red in color. But when you're very tired or when you don't sleep well, your blood doesn't circulate at its usual speed. Old blood, low in oxygen and bluish in color, collects in the vessels, forming dark rings below your eyes.

Frog in Your Throat. Sometimes your vocal cords may be sore, either from using your voice too much or from an infection. When this happens, you sound hoarse, or as though

you have a "frog" in your throat. As soon as your vocal cords heal, the frog disappears.

Goose Bumps. Almost every part of your body is covered with tiny, often invisible hairs. At the base of most hairs is a tiny muscle. When your skin gets cold, these muscles tighten in an effort to help stop the loss of heat. This makes the hairs stand up, forming little bumps. You can also get goose bumps when you're under stress or frightened. When you get nervous, glands in your body may secrete a chemical called adrenaline. Adrenaline helps your body deal with emergencies. Among other things, adrenaline tightens the tiny hair muscles, causing goose bumps.

Hiccups. Hiccups can be annoying. They seem to start up for no reason, and they can be hard to stop. Hiccups occur when something goes wrong with your diaphragm (a flat, sheetlike muscle between your chest and abdomen that helps you breathe). Usually the diaphragm contracts and expands smoothly and regularly, and breathing is normal. But sometimes, and no one is quite sure why, the diaphragm becomes irritated and starts to make abrupt little contractions, or

Sand in Your Eyes. Tears are a fluid that contains salt and other chemicals. This fluid is constantly secreted by glands behind your eyelids. At night when you are asleep, the tears collect in the corners of your eyes. Gradually the fluid dries out, leaving behind the chemicals. These form the crusty, sticky "sand" that you rub from your eyes when you awaken in the morning.

Shriveled Skin. If you spend too much time relaxing in a hot bath, your hands and feet may look like wrinkled prunes. This doesn't happen to the skin on other parts of your body because that skin contains sebaceous glands. These glands secrete an oily substance that coats the skin and lessens the amount of water leaving the body. But the skin on your hands and feet doesn't contain sebaceous glands. Thus water inside your skin slowly oozes out into the bathwater. Your skin is actually drying from the inside out. If your skin loses too much water, some of its cells collapse, causing the skin to shrivel.

Snoring. If you breathe through your mouth when you sleep, you may be snoring. As air rushes in and out of your mouth, the soft palate (soft tissue in the roof of the mouth

jerks. This disrupts the smooth intake of air into the lungs and produces a noise that sounds like "hiccup." Hiccups are most likely to happen when you eat or drink too quickly, when someone tickles you, or when you laugh a lot.

Lump in Your Throat. You worry about something, and the muscles in your body tighten. Even the muscles in your throat may tense up. And this is what makes you feel as if you have a "lump" in your throat and can't swallow. The problem quickly disappears when you calm down.

Mouth Watering. You smell cookies baking, or you think about your favorite pizza. Your brain automatically remembers that cookies and pizza are foods you like to eat. So it prepares your body for eating by telling glands near your mouth to start giving off saliva—thus making your mouth water. (Saliva is a fluid that moistens food and makes it easier to swallow. It also contains chemicals that help digest food.)

near the throat) vibrates. This vibration produces the rough, sawing sound of snoring. Nearly everyone snores sometimes. But you'll be most likely to snore if your nose is stuffed up from a cold or if you sleep on your back.

Spots Before Your Eyes. If someone takes your picture with a flashbulb, you may see spots for a few seconds after the flash goes off. Why? When light enters your eyes, it hits the cells in the retina (the thin inner coat of the eyeball). Chemical changes occur in these cells, and this causes messages to be sent to the brain about what you are seeing. But if you look at a very bright light, such as a camera flashbulb, you expose the cells to too much light. The overexposed cells create the spots before your eyes.

Sweat. You're playing tennis on a hot summer day, and you're drenched in perspiration. What's happening? Your body is sweating to help you cool off. Sweat is a salty liquid that is produced by glands in the skin. It moves through the narrow glands to openings, or pores, in the surface of the skin. The sweat spreads over the warm skin. As it evaporates, it takes heat away from the skin. On a hot day, an adult will sweat about a quart (.9 liter) of liquid.

Tears. Do you think of tears as something your eyes produce when you are sad? Actually, you have tears in your eyes 24 hours a day. Tears are a fluid containing salts and other chemicals. They are constantly secreted by glands behind the eyelids, and they moisten and protect the eyes. If a speck of dirt, for example, gets in your eyes, tears wash it away. But when you're very unhappy, the muscles around the tear glands tighten. This squeezes a great deal of fluid out of the glands. The fluid collects in your eyes until there is so much of it that the tears run down your face. The same thing may happen when you laugh very hard.

Tickle in Your Throat. A thick, sticky substance called mucus keeps your throat moist. But if you breathe in dust or if the air is very dry, part of your throat may dry out. This creates an irritation, or a "tickle." You usually react by coughing. If that doesn't work, a drink of water should do the trick.

Yawning. When you're tired, or bored, or even just very relaxed, your body ceases to

be alert. Your breathing and heartbeat slow down. As a result, there's less oxygen in your bloodstream. Your brain reacts by forcing a yawn. Yawning opens up the air sacs in your lungs, so that more oxygen can enter the blood. But scientists can't explain everything about yawning. For instance, they don't know why yawning is contagious—why people sometimes yawn just because they see someone else yawning. And do you *pandiculate* when you yawn? In plainer English, this asks if you stretch your arms when you yawn. Lots of people do!

JENNY TESAR
Series Consultant, *Wonders of Wildlife*

THE 1984 WORLD'S FAIR

Louisiana is Cajun country, a land of moss-draped bayous, spicy foods, exciting music, and warm hospitality. The Cajuns are descendants of French Canadians who settled in Louisiana over 200 years ago. When work is done and partying begins, they shout "*Laissez le bon temps rouler!* (Let the good times roll!)"

It was with these words that Governor Edwin Edwards opened the 1984 Louisiana World Exposition—the first world's fair named after a state rather than a city. Set on the Mississippi River in downtown New Orleans, the fair opened in May, 1984, and ran for six months. Millions of visitors enjoyed exhibitions from some 25 nations and from many U.S. states and corporations. The exposition was a wonderland of science and technology, education and entertainment, fantasy and fun.

The fair's theme was "The World of Rivers . . . Fresh Water as a Source of Life." This was an appropriate theme for a fair set on the banks of one of the world's greatest rivers. And throughout the fair, the water theme was used with imagination and humor.

In front of the main entrance was a huge sculpture of the sea god Neptune wrestling with an alligator. Two large mermaids and a pelican surrounded the entrance gates. Within the fairgrounds there were sparkling fountains, pools, water sculptures, and winding streams.

One of the most popular water attractions for young visitors was the Kid Wash, which sprayed, rinsed, and dried children in the same way that a car wash launders an automobile. At the Aquacade—a show featuring synchronized water ballet—the spectacular finale consisted of fifteen Olympic divers hitting the water at the same time.

Canada's pavilion featured a film that took viewers on a madcap ride over rapids, falls, and rivers. The film celebrated Canada's claim of having more fresh water than all the rest of the world combined. In the Louisiana Pavilion a boat carried visitors through a sound-and-light show of the state's bayous, swamps, and waterways. The display of a company called America's Energy Electric Exhibits showed how water is used to produce electricity.

The official mascot of the fair was a pelican, the state bird of Louisiana. And a human-size pelican named Seymour D. Fair, complete with top hat, waistcoat, and umbrella, was a regular sight. But the major symbol of the fair was the Wonderwall. This half-mile-long, three-story-high, architectural delight was a colorful mix of temples, towers, archways, fountains, fantasy characters, and whimsical animals. Grecian urns sat among the rooftops, golden cupids blew their horns, and alligator-shaped seats helped weary tourists.

Visitors had a chance to glide across the Mississippi in gleaming cable cars suspended some 370 feet (113 meters) above the river. This offered a bird's-eye view of one of America's largest and busiest ports. Freighters, barges, and tugs could be seen working their way up and down the river. And majestic tall ships were docked along the waterfront.

Most of the restaurants at the fair featured Louisiana food—gumbo, oysters, creole jambalaya, Cajun catfish, and spicy fried chicken. But international fare, from German wursts to Chinese egg rolls, was also available.

Nonstop entertainment featured marching bands, Mardi Gras parades, and carnival-style rides, including the world's largest ferris wheel. There were street performers: clowns, dancers, magicians, jugglers, and acrobats. Of course there was music—especially the jazz, Dixieland, and country Cajun music for which Louisiana is famous. And every evening a fireworks display, choreographed to music, signaled the end of another day at the fair.

Although the fair ended in late 1984, many of its best features have become permanent parts of New Orleans. The cable-car system still carries people across the Mississippi. The renovated brick warehouses have been turned into stores, offices, and apartments. The riverfront promenade is used by walkers, bicyclers, and picnickers. The good times are still rollin' in this exciting city on the banks of the Mississippi.

Kid Wash was one of the fair's most popular attractions. The fair also boasted the world's largest ferris wheel. (You can see the fantasy Wonderwall in the background.)

THE GREAT CHOCOLATE BINGE

Thick, glossy chocolate bars studded with almonds . . . chocolate-coated candies oozing creamy fillings . . . fresh strawberries dipped by hand in tubs of melted chocolate . . . chocolate ice cream, chocolate-chip cookies, chocolate syrup in your milk.

Has the world gone on a chocolate binge? So it seems. In the United States, people are eating more chocolate than ever—on the average, more than 9 pounds (4 kilograms) a year for every man, woman, and child in the country. Europeans eat still more chocolate. The average Belgian, for example, eats 15 pounds (7 kilograms) a year.

Why are people going crazy over chocolate? For the most part, they simply love the taste. But chocolate has also become high fashion. People are paying more than $30 a pound for gourmet chocolates that carry a famous name. Exclusive shops in some cities carry fresh chocolates that are flown in daily from Europe. Others specialize in custom chocolate designs—one such firm will reproduce your portrait in chocolate.

Buttons and T-shirts proclaim the love of chocolate. Resorts hold special chocolate-binge weekends. There are all-chocolate cookbooks. There's even a bimonthly newsletter called *Chocolate News*—which is printed on chocolate-scented paper and brings its readers the latest word on such items as chocolate chili and chocolate dog biscuits. And *Chocolate: The Consuming Passion*, a recent book that pokes fun at the craze, has sold thousands of copies.

THE "FOOD OF THE GODS"

Chocolate has always been considered something of an exclusive treat. In the 1500's, Spanish explorers in South America found Indians drinking a dark liquid made from the beans of the cacao tree. They took some beans back to Spain and added sugar to the drink. For years, chocolate was a secret closely kept by the Spanish nobility. But eventually word of the delicious substance got out. In 1775, the Swedish botanist Carolus Linnaeus gave the cacao tree its scientific name—*Theobroma*, from Greek words meaning "food of the gods." Today most of the world's cacao is grown in West Africa, although South America still grows a substantial amount.

Turning beans into chocolate is a complicated process. It takes about 400 beans to make a pound of chocolate. The beans are first fermented, dried, sorted, and roasted. Then they are shelled, and the soft centers are crushed to form the dark liquid known as chocolate liquor. (Despite its name, it contains no alcohol.) More than 50 percent of the chocolate liquor is made up of fat, called cocoa butter.

Hardened chocolate liquor is sold as unsweetened baking chocolate. To make powdered cocoa, most of the fatty cocoa butter is pressed out of the liquor, and what's left is ground and sifted. To make chocolate candy, extra cocoa butter, sugar, vanilla, and sometimes milk are added to the chocolate liquor. The mixture is placed in a huge tub, where it is blended and smoothed for anywhere from a few hours to several days. Then it is heated to remove fat crystals and molded into its final form. But chocolate makers won't tell the details of their recipes and processes. They consider chocolate making an art.

CHOCOLATE AND HEALTH

Chocolate lovers say that the flavor of their favorite treat just can't be duplicated artificially. And they may be right—chocolate consists of more than 300 chemical substances. But while millions of people are bingeing on chocolate, what's happening to their health? Are some of those substances harmful?

Chocolate has been blamed for helping to cause acne, tooth decay, obesity, and heart disease. Nutritionists agree that chocolate is certainly not a health food. It's high in fat and sugar. That means it's high in calories, so while chocolate is a good source of energy, it can also make you put on weight. But, the nutritionists say, chocolate is no worse than any other sweet. In fact, if you must eat candy, chocolate may be a good choice. It contains small amounts of protein, calcium, and iron, which your body needs.

Cocoa, chocolate syrup, and instant chocolate powders are the most healthful forms of chocolate because they contain the least fat. Two tablespoons of instant powder have about 55 calories. Chocolate candy has much more fat. A typical chocolate bar has 220 calories. But chocolate doesn't contain cholesterol, a fatty substance that's thought to cause heart disease.

A few people are allergic to chocolate— they may get headaches or break out in rashes. But studies have shown that for most people, chocolate doesn't cause acne.

Chocolate does contain small amounts of caffeine, a stimulant. Too much caffeine can make you nervous and keep you awake at night, and it can also harm your health. But chocolate has only about 10 percent of the caffeine found in coffee. Chocolate has larger amounts of another stimulant, theobromine. But because theobromine acts on muscles rather than nerves, it won't make you nervous or keep you awake.

Another chemical in chocolate is phenylethylamine. This chemical is produced naturally in the brain, especially when people are feeling loved and loving. Some doctors have suggested that unhappy people may crave chocolate because they're not producing any phenylethylamine of their own.

What about tooth decay? Rather than causing cavities, some researchers think, chocolate may actually help prevent them. One study found that people who ate a pound of chocolate a week had no more cavities than people who ate no sweets. People who ate other kinds of candy, though, had five times as many cavities.

Of course, any sweet is bad for you if you eat too much of it. The fat and sugar in chocolate can fill you up quickly. Then you won't be hungry for more nutritious foods. But if you're not overweight and you know you're getting all the nutrients your body needs, you can give in to your chocolate craving every now and then. Enjoy!

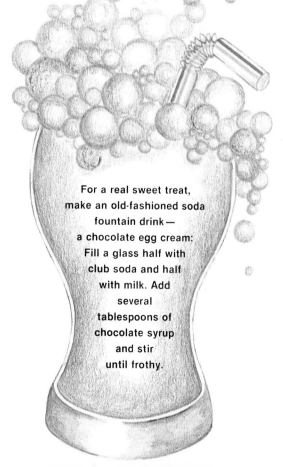

For a real sweet treat, make an old-fashioned soda fountain drink— a chocolate egg cream: Fill a glass half with club soda and half with milk. Add several tablespoons of chocolate syrup and stir until frothy.

THE QUEEN OF FLOWERS

"Of all the flowers, methinks a rose is best."
William Shakespeare

Since ancient times, poets have praised roses as symbols of beauty and love. Songwriters have compared beautiful women to roses. Artists have created magnificent paintings of roses, and roses have served as symbols of royalty. The Greek poet Sappho gave the rose its proper title: the Queen of Flowers. And even today, the rose ranks as the world's most popular flower.

THE ROSE PLANT

There are some 200 species of wild roses —and more than 10,000 garden varieties that have been specially cultivated. All the roses are members of a single genus, *Rosa*. This genus is part of a much larger family, *Rosaceae*, which includes many important trees, shrubs, and herbs. Apple, pear, peach, and cherry trees are members of this family.

While there are many kinds of roses, they all have certain characteristics in common. The plants are mostly shrubby, with woody stems and sharp thorns. Each leaf is composed of an odd number of separate leaflets, usually five to seven. The flowers are rings of soft, fragrant petals, borne singly or in groups.

After the flower's petals drop, its base develops into a small fruit—the rose hip—which contains the plant's seeds. Rose hips look like tiny apples. When they are ripe, they are red, orange, yellow, or brown, depending on the variety.

There are several important differences between wild roses and the garden types. The wild roses are mostly ramblers—they sprawl across the ground. Their white, pink, or red flowers usually have five petals, arranged in a single layer. And most wild roses have a single period of bloom, usually in spring or early summer.

Garden roses, on the other hand, grow in many different ways—upright, as shrubs; climbing over trellises; and even as trees.

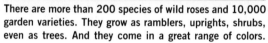

There are more than 200 species of wild roses and 10,000 garden varieties. They grow as ramblers, uprights, shrubs, even as trees. And they come in a great range of colors.

Some kinds bloom twice a year, and many bloom repeatedly from spring to frost. Their flowers have many petals, arranged in several layers. And they come in a great range of colors, including pink, red, white, yellow, peach, and lavender.

ROSES FOR EVERY GARDEN

Special varieties of roses have been grown for gardens since ancient times. Today there are varieties for different climates, different soils, and different uses. These thousands of roses have been developed over centuries by crossing different species and varieties. A cross occurs when the pollen produced by a rose of one plant is transferred to the egg-producing structure of a blossom on another plant. If the egg is fertilized it develops into a seed. The seed contains genetic material from both parents. When it is planted, it develops into a new variety.

Wind and insects are nature's agents of cross-breeding. Even more important are human agents—people who cross existing

rose varieties in the hope of creating ever more perfect plants. The mechanics of cross-breeding are fairly simple, and many amateur gardeners try their hands at it. But only rarely does a cross result in an outstanding new variety.

Here are the major kinds of garden roses:

• **Old-fashioned roses** include some varieties, such as damask and gallica, that have been around since before the time of Christ. Some other old-fashioned roses are moss roses, named for the mosslike fuzz on their stems, and cabbage roses, with flowers that look like little cabbages. Most old-fashioned types have rich, heady fragrances and bloom once a year.

• **Tea roses** were named for their scent, which resembles that of freshly crushed tea leaves. Along with another variety, called China roses, tea roses originated around 1800. They have a long blooming season but are not very hardy.

• **Hybrid teas** are the roses that are usually sold by florists. These varieties were developed by crossing teas with other types in the late 1800's.

• **Polyanthas** were developed at about the same time as the hybrid teas. But while hybrid teas bear flowers on long stems, polyanthas are low-growing plants that produce clusters of small flowers. Like the hybrid teas, though, the plants are everblooming.

• **Floribundas** were created by crossing hybrid teas and polyanthas. They are shrubbier and have larger flowers than the polyanthas. Their name—a Latin word meaning "flowers in abundance"—tells something important about them: Floribundas carry quantities of blossoms from early summer until frost.

• **Grandifloras** resemble both the hybrid teas and the floribundas. The flowers look like those of the hybrid tea, but they're borne in clusters like those of the floribunda.

• **Miniature roses** are dainty plants ranging from 4 to 18 inches (10 to 46 centimeters) in height. Some have flowers no bigger than a penny. Their small size makes them well suited to rock gardens, window boxes, and indoor containers. But their flowers have very little fragrance.

• **Climbing roses** and **ramblers** don't really climb. Instead, they have long trailing stems that can be trained to grow over walls and fences. There are many types of climbing roses. Some have large flowers, and some small; some bloom once a year, and others are everblooming.

• **Tree roses** don't grow naturally—they are created by gardeners. The desired rose variety is grafted onto a tall stout stem, or standard, with healthy roots. The rose plant then gets all its nourishment through the standard. Most rose trees are between 2 and 5 feet (60 to 150 centimeters) tall.

ROSES IN HISTORY AND LEGEND

Since roses have been popular through the ages, they are rich in history and legend. For example, the Greeks had numerous stories concerning the origin of roses. Many had to do with Aphrodite, the goddess of love and beauty. According to one legend, the god-

The roses in French Empress Josephine's garden were painted by artist Pierre Joseph Redouté. His detailed watercolors are still important reference works.

dess Cybele created the first rose. She was jealous of Aphrodite and wanted to be sure that there would be something on earth more beautiful than her rival.

Another legend told how red roses came to be. The goddess Aphrodite learned that her beloved, Adonis, was wounded. As she rushed to him, she ran through a hedge of roses. The thorns pricked her skin, drawing blood that stained the flowers red forever.

To the Egyptians and Romans, roses were symbols of luxury. At Cleopatra's palace in Egypt, the floors were strewn with rose petals. When she entertained Mark Antony, the carpet of petals was knee-deep. The Roman emperor Nero was one of the most extravagant rose-lovers of all time. His guests rested on pillows stuffed with rose petals, while fountains sprayed rose water into the air.

Roses have also been political symbols. In England during the 1400's, two royal groups, the House of York and the House of Lancaster, battled for the crown in what became known as the War of the Roses. York took the white rose as its symbol, and Lancaster used the red rose. The fighting lasted more than 30 years, until 1487. Then Henry VII, a Lancastrian, married Elizabeth of York. The red and white roses were joined in the Tudor Rose, which became the national flower.

Roses found a royal patron in the early 1800's in France. Empress Josephine, the wife of Napoleon I, established one of history's greatest rose collections and did much to popularize rose growing. Her garden contained some 250 different types of roses. Their beauty was recorded by the French artist Pierre Joseph Redouté, whose detailed watercolors are still important reference works.

A PLANT WITH MANY USES

Even in ancient times, people knew that roses could provide more than beauty. The Romans used rose petals and hips to make delicious wines, jellies, and honey. And they turned roses into medicines that were said to cure every imaginable ailment. Belief in the medicinal value of roses continued through the Middle Ages.

The Arabs, on the other hand, simmered rose petals in water and turned them into an important cooking ingredient. Today rose water is also used in colognes and cosmetics.

Another fragrant rose product is rose oil, which is made by putting petals from fresh, fragrant blooms into olive oil. After a day or two, the petals are mashed and the oil is strained. Then the process is repeated, using the same oil, with ten or more batches of petals. The fragrant oil is used in perfumes, scented candles, and other sweet-smelling items.

Roses are no longer used in medicines, but they do have healthful properties. Rose hips have more vitamin C than any other fruit or vegetable—up to 20 times as much as oranges. Hips from plants that haven't been sprayed with pesticides are used to make tea, jelly, and even wine. The Queen of Flowers not only brings beauty, it may bring good health as well.

SAY IT WITH ROSES

Our language and literature are filled with expressions that use roses to make comments about life and people. Here is a small sample of such sayings, together with their meanings:

Gather ye rosebuds while ye may—take advantage of opportunities that exist today because they may not exist tomorrow.

No rose without a thorn—something always detracts from pleasure.

Seek roses in December—search for the impossible. (This expression is from a poem by Byron, written before refrigeration and other modern inventions made it possible to buy roses at any time of year.)

A rose by any other name would smell as sweet—a change of name doesn't change the qualities of a person, object, or idea.

Everything's coming up roses—everything is going along beautifully.

A bed of roses—a soft, comfortable life.

Looking at the world through rose-colored glasses—being overly optimistic and ignoring obvious faults or problems.

Barsamian

CHATTERING TREES

No, this isn't a fairy tale about trees that whisper "Hello!" as you walk by. This is a true story about how trees defend themselves against attacking pests—and how they may even communicate the danger to other trees.

You might think that trees are quite defenseless when caterpillars and other pests are munching on their leaves. But they really aren't. Within hours of an attack by pests, the damaged trees fight back. They change their chemistry by increasing the amount of phenols in their leaves. High levels of this chemical substance make the leaves less tasty and less nutritious, thereby discouraging pests that have come to dine.

In 1983, scientists studying Sitka willows made an exciting observation. They found that when some willows were attacked by pests, other nearby willows also started to increase the amount of phenols in their leaves—as if in preparation for an attack. By the time insects reached these trees, the leaves were filled with phenols. Many scientists now think that trees under attack can somehow communicate the danger to their neighbors.

How do trees communicate? No evidence was found that the roots had carried the message—the root systems of the willows weren't touching one another. It may be that trees give off a chemical substance that travels through the air to other trees. If so, the chemical may be a gas called ethylene. Damaged trees give off more ethylene than undamaged trees.

Another group of scientists tried to find out more about how trees communicate. They worked with seedlings (very young plants) of poplar and sugar maple trees. They grew the seedlings in sealed containers. Each container held several seedlings. But the seedlings were in separate pots, so there was no direct contact between the plants. They shared only the same air.

The scientists played the role of "pest." They tore the leaves of some seedlings. Within 52 hours, the level of phenols had doubled in those seedlings' leaves. This wasn't surprising. The undamaged seedlings, however, had increased their phenols by 58 percent!

The air in the containers was tested, but the scientists weren't able to find ethylene or any other chemical messenger. This didn't mean that such a messenger wasn't there—better equipment may be needed to detect it.

Even if the chemical that acts as the messenger is found, many questions will remain. How do trees produce the chemical messenger? How do neighboring trees detect it? Do all trees give off chemical messengers? As you see, there is still much to learn about the trees that share this planet with us.

THE GREENHOUSE EFFECT

You probably know the story of Chicken Little, who warned everyone: "The sky is falling! The sky is falling!" That alarming warning wasn't true. Today, some people are warning: "The ice caps will melt! The ice caps will melt!" *This* prediction, however, just might come true.

The polar ice caps may melt because the Earth is going to get warmer. Many scientists have predicted this warming trend for a long time. In late 1983, two major reports confirmed the trend—but implied that the warm-up may happen more quickly than expected. One report, in fact, predicted major changes in climate by the end of the century.

This warming trend is known as the "greenhouse effect." It is caused by rising levels of carbon dioxide in the Earth's atmosphere. A greenhouse lets in sunlight and then traps the heat. It's warm inside a greenhouse even on a cold day. Carbon dioxide in the atmosphere acts much like the glass in a greenhouse. It allows sunlight to pass through the air, but it doesn't let the heat escape back into space.

Carbon dioxide makes up only a tiny percentage of the atmosphere. But there's enough of it to keep our planet at an average temperature of about 60°F (15°C). The amount of carbon dioxide in the Earth's atmosphere has been increasing, however. The gas is released into the air by the burning of fossil fuels (oil, gas, and coal), primarily by industries and automobiles. Each year, more than five billion tons of carbon dioxide enter the atmosphere. The gas accumulates, forming a kind of "thermal blanket" around the Earth—and trapping more and more heat. This causes the temperature to rise.

So far, the effects of the thermal blanket have been difficult to measure. But scientists feel that an increase of even a few degrees could have major effects on Earth. Weather patterns could change. Some areas might receive more rain, making the land more fertile. Areas that are now farmlands might turn into deserts. Temperature increases in the polar regions would cause the polar ice caps to melt rapidly. The level of the sea would then rise, resulting in severe flooding of coastal areas.

No one is sure if anything truly catastrophic will actually happen. Most scientists believe that if we can't prevent the greenhouse effect, we can prepare for it—and find ways to deal with the effects.

The "greenhouse effect" is caused by high levels of carbon dioxide in the atmosphere. This accumulation stops the sun's heat from escaping back into space, thus causing the temperature to rise.

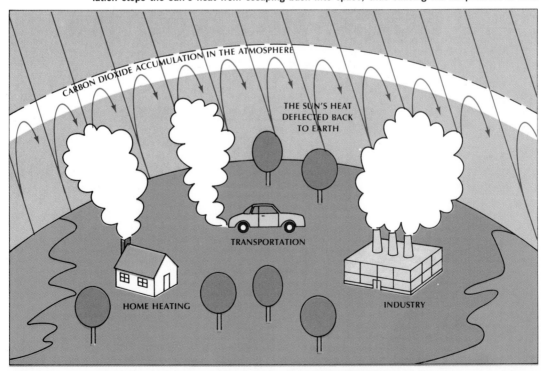

A FROSTED FAIRYLAND

Have you ever woken up on a crisp fall morning to find the world transformed into a glittering fairyland, where diamonds sparkle on every blade of grass? The sparkles aren't diamonds, of course—they're frost, which formed overnight while you slept.

Frost forms in much the same way that dew forms. During the day, sunlight warms everything it touches—grass, leaves, flowers, stones. At night, these objects begin to cool off. When they are cool enough, water vapor in the air condenses on them and forms tiny droplets. This is dew.

If, however, the surfaces of objects cool to freezing or below, the water vapor changes directly to crystals of ice. This is frost, or hoarfrost. There are two basic types of frost crystals. Some are hollow, six-sided columns. Others are flat plates, rather like snowflakes. But unlike snow, frost isn't con-

sidered precipitation. It doesn't fall to earth as precipitation does—it forms there.

Frost is most likely to form on nights that are clear as well as cold. Objects cool off more on such nights because there are no clouds to reflect heat back to the earth's surface. It also helps if there is a lot of moisture in the air that is closest to the surface and if there is very little wind.

After such a night, the first rays of morning sunlight reveal a wonderland. Icy white crystals edge deep green leaves and blades of grass. Bright berries seem to have been dipped in sparkling sugar. Twigs and branches wear armor of ice. And flowers seem to have sprouted extra petals overnight —petals of glittering frost.

If the temperature drops too low, plants can be damaged. But often frost does no harm. This was the case with the damselfly pictured to the right. As the sun warmed the air, the damselfly's diamond-studded coating melted, and it flew away.

Home computers are useful in an amazing number of ways. And with special hardware called peripherals, your computer can do even more tasks. For example, with a printer attached, you can use your computer for school reports and homework.

MY COMPUTER: WHAT CAN I DO WITH IT?

• Mark is planning a trip to Puerto Rico. He uses his home computer to make airplane and hotel reservations . . . and to buy vacation clothes.

• Suzanne uses her computer to learn how to type. First she learned the correct positions for her fingers. Now she is playing a computer game in which giant words fall from the sky. They can be repelled only by typing the same words on the computer keyboard. The better Suzanne types, the faster the words fall and the more exciting the game is.

• Diane covers high school sports for a local newspaper. She writes her articles on a computer. A special attachment that connects the computer to a telephone lets Diane send each article directly from her home to the newspaper.

• Steve has designed a computer game and wants to sell it to other computer owners. He places an ad on an electronic bulletin board and then uses his computer to call the bulletin board for messages.

Millions of people are crazy about their home computers. Why? Because the machines are useful in such an amazing number of ways. They provide fun and entertainment in the form of computer games. And they make a variety of jobs—from writing a report for school to managing a business—easier and more efficient.

To get a computer to do what you want it to do, you must give it a set of instructions. The instructions are called a program, or *software*. (The computer and any machines attached to it are called *hardware*.) You can write software yourself, or you can buy software that has been written by other people. Thousands of commercial software programs are available, and the number increases every day.

For some tasks, you need special hardware called *peripherals*. For example, if you want to use your computer to write letters or school reports, you need a printer attached to the computer. If you want the computer to "talk" with a computer in a distant town, you need to use a *modem*. This device connects the computer to your telephone line.

Your Private Tutor. A computer is an excellent learning tool. People like to learn with computers because they can learn at their own speed. There is also constant interaction between the person and the computer. The computer immediately tells if an answer is correct. And if an answer is wrong, the computer doesn't get angry or make the person feel stupid.

There are educational programs for people of all ages, from preschoolers to adults. Some programs are tutorials—they teach specific subjects such as algebra or computer programming. Others provide drill and practice (the typing game played by Suzanne is an example). Still other educational programs are simulations. That is, they imitate the way things happen in real life. One popular simulation asks you to operate a nuclear power plant. You must try to supply electricity profitably. Otherwise, you'll lose your license to operate the plant.

The Expert Writer. When you write letters or reports, are they filled with erasures and misspellings? Do you often have to rewrite something because you forgot to include information or because you need to make changes? A home computer with a printer and word processing software will help solve these problems. Writing letters, term papers, or even a novel is faster and easier on a computer than by hand.

Let's say that you want to write a letter. As you type on the computer keyboard, the text appears on the screen. If you want to make a change, you move a special flashing mark (the *cursor*) to the place in the text where the change is desired. Press a few keys—and the text is just the way you want it. When you have finished the letter, you can use a spelling checker program. This will point out any spelling errors you may have made and give you the chance to correct them. When the letter is finished, press a few more keys and it will be printed onto paper, with no typographical errors.

Shape Up. Software products designed to help people become healthier are now quite popular. These include nutrition, exercise, and biofeedback programs.

Some nutrition programs keep track of what you eat. This lets you make sure that

Many educational programs for young people teach specific subjects, such as reading and writing.

If you have a modem you can use your computer to hook up to "bulletin boards," which allow you to exchange messages with other computer owners. The computer screen shown above is a bulletin board index. Choosing one option—for example, Ask the Expert—leads to a list of fourteen bulletin boards (below). In each, you can ask questions of an expert in that subject. And the expert will answer you via his or her computer.

you are getting the right amounts of vitamins, proteins, and other nutrients. Other programs help you plan well-balanced meals that are within your budget. One software package provides information on food additives and gives advice on how to improve your eating habits.

There is software that helps you plan personalized exercise programs based on your fitness level. Other software shows you how to do aerobic exercises and keeps track of your progress.

Biofeedback programs train you to relax. When you aren't relaxed, your muscles are tense and the electrical resistance in your skin is comparatively high. By attaching a monitor to your body and connecting it to the computer, you can measure muscle tension or electrical resistance and see how it changes as you do various relaxation exercises. The computer screen usually shows this information in the form of a graph.

Running a Business. Running a business can be very complicated and time-consuming. But software programs can make many business-related chores easier. For example, let's say that you have a small business making fancy salads. You sell the salads to neighbors and to people at school. You can use your computer to keep a list of customers, their addresses, what salads they like, how often they have ordered from you, and how much money they owe. If you want to send the customers an advertisement, you can write the ad on the computer and then print as many copies as you need. You can also ask the computer to use the customer list to produce mailing labels for the ad.

You'll want to keep track of your business expenses and income. This information can be kept in an accounting program. Each time you take in or spend money, type the information into the computer. The computer immediately recalculates all the information you have given it so that it can provide an up-to-the-minute picture of how your business is doing.

Information, Please. If you have a modem, you can use your computer to obtain information from data banks. A data bank is like a library—it is a collection of information (data). Different data banks contain different types of information. For example, a stock market data bank contains current information on stock prices. An airline reservation data bank contains information on flight times, ticket costs, and seating options.

Some computer data banks are interactive. Instead of simply reading what they contain, you can add your own information. For example, an airline data bank may let you type in reservations for a trip you plan to take.

Several companies, known as *information utilities,* provide access to many data banks.

You pay a fee to hook up to a utility. When you call the utility, you indicate what information you want. This could be a weather report, today's baseball scores, an encyclopedia article on space missions, or reviews of a new movie.

Information utilities usually provide another service: electronic bulletin boards. These are used for exchanging messages with other computer owners. To use one, you turn on your computer and dial the bulletin board. When the phone answers, your computer automatically connects to the bulletin board computer. You can type in messages for other people or ask to see messages that were left for you.

Shopping and Banking at Home. Companies are beginning to offer consumers computer shopping services. Information about items for sale is shown on the screen. If you want to order an item, you simply press certain keys on the computer. The object is mailed to you, and its cost is billed to your credit card account. In some places, it's even possible to use a home computer to do grocery shopping. You enter your order via the modem, and later in the day the store has someone deliver your groceries.

Several dozen experimental banking programs are now underway. They let you use your computer to do simple banking transactions: check account balances, transfer money from one account to another (within the same bank), get an instant record of recent transactions, and pay bills.

Computerized Files. Specialized software makes it easy for people to store various information in computerized files. There are genealogical programs for people who gather data on their ancestors. There are programs that let you keep an inventory of all your personal belongings.

Perhaps you have a record collection. Which records contain Song A? Which are performed by Singer X? It's relatively easy to set up a computer file on a collection. The file can contain almost any kind of information you wish, it's easy to keep up to date, and it takes up much less space than a paper file.

Let's Play! Entertainment—having fun—is one of the main uses of home computers. There are many types of computer games.

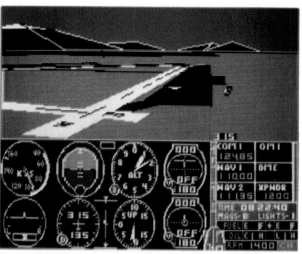

Some computer games are simulations—such as Flight Simulator, which just about puts you in the pilot's seat.

Some are target-shooting games that require co-ordination and split-second timing. Others, such as chess, require an ability to plan ahead. Mystery stories and adventure games involve reasoning—you are given information that you must use to find the solution.

Some software can be used for both entertainment and work. Graphics programs let you create pictures on the screen. You can draw computer pictures for pleasure. Or you can create charts and graphs for school projects or business purposes. You can have your computer save the pictures so that they can be looked at over and over again, or you can have the computer print the pictures on paper.

And Many More . . . Look through a computer magazine or visit a store that sells software. A quick glance will show you that there are many additional uses to which you can put your home computer. You may see a program that allows you to control a home security system. You may see one that will turn electrical appliances on and off. You may see a peripheral that gathers weather information and feeds it into your computer so that the computer can predict how warmly you should dress if you're going outdoors. What other software is available? Go and see!

JENNY TESAR
Designer, Computer Programs

GREAT GADGETS

What do you buy for the person who has everything? It seems that manufacturers will never run out of answers to that question—especially with the rapid changes that are taking place in the field of electronics. Here are just a few of the new gadgets that you could buy in 1984. What will inventors think of next? That's anybody's guess!

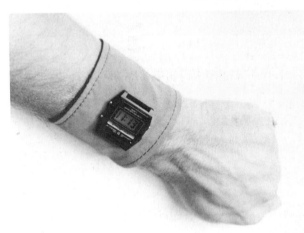

You probably don't like to carry a wallet when you go out to jog or play tennis. It gets in the way, and you might lose it. But what do you do with your money and your keys? Here's one solution—a sports watch with a band that's really a fabric wallet. The band wraps snugly around your wrist and has zippered compartments for keys, money, and an I.D. card. The watch is waterproof and has a fifteen-minute timer, so you can pace yourself as you jog.

"How may I serve you?" Hubot asks each time he's switched on. And Hubot can serve in lots of ways—this robot is a versatile home helper and an entertainment machine, too. He has a television, a radio, a tape deck, a clock, and a video-game system built right in. He has a vocabulary of 1,200 words, and he can be taught to move anywhere in your house. Hubot can wake you up, serve you a cold drink or a snack, chat with your friends, and tell you when it's time for bed. With various attachments, he can vacuum the rug, turn appliances on and off, act as a smoke alarm, and sense when objects are in his path.

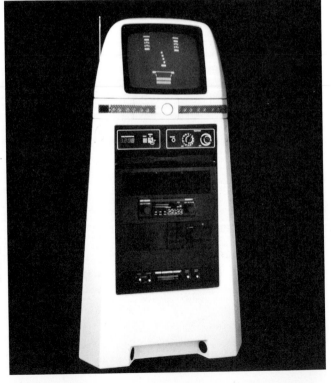

No, this isn't the latest NASA design for space travel. It's a special helmet designed for hay fever sufferers. The helmet is connected by a plastic hose to an air filter, which clips onto a belt. The filter screens out pollen, dust, and other irritants, and a battery-operated fan moves the purified air through the helmet. The wearer can do jobs like gardening and lawn mowing—or maybe just take a walk in the fields—without risking an attack of sniffles and sneezes.

You can watch your favorite programs practically anywhere on the world's first pocket-size color television, which is about the size of most personal cassette players. It uses a color liquid crystal display instead of a picture tube, and it can operate for up to five hours on batteries. The screen measures just 2 inches (5 centimeters) diagonally. But while the television is small, the price is not—the new portable costs more than some full-size sets.

The cars of the future will be sleek, smooth, comfortable, and computerized.

CARS OF THE FUTURE

A pod-like city car with rear wheels that can be steered, to slip into tight parking spots . . . a three-wheeler that seats two people . . . a car with computerized sensors that detect objects in its path . . . an "outrigger" car with wheels that extend from its body at slow speeds and are drawn in close to the body at high speeds.

These are just a few of the cars that you may see driving down the highway in the not too distant future. They're on designers' drawing boards right now. They're smooth and sleek and shiny, and some of them almost look as though they could take off from the highway and head for outer space.

The designs are based on some trends that can be seen now. There are more and more people in the world, but families are getting smaller. This means that in the future there may be more cars, each carrying fewer people. People are also more concerned with safety and comfort in their cars. And our supplies of fuel are running low.

With these trends in mind, some designers think that the cars of the future will fall into several distinct types. There will be little three-wheeled, one- or two-passenger commuter cars, designed to go as far as 75 miles (120 kilometers) on each gallon of gasoline. There will be slightly larger versions that seat three people abreast. And there will be low-slung, sleek vans to replace the station wagons and boxy vans of today. Some designers envision a basic three-seater that can be attached to various rear ends, to become a truck, a van, or a larger passenger car.

All the cars will be rounder and smoother in shape. The sleek shapes will have a purpose: They'll cut wind resistance at high speeds and therefore save fuel. The cars will save fuel in other ways, too. They'll be lighter, with more parts made of tough, space-age plastics and ceramics. Some cars of the future may even burn alcohol or natural gas instead of gasoline.

Lots of comfort and convenience features are already built into cars. But tomorrow's cars will have even more. For example, your car might have a replaceable engine that pops out for easy servicing. You could drop the engine off at the service station and plug in a spare engine while it's being tuned up.

But the greatest advances in convenience and safety will come from computers that will be built right into cars. Some computers will constantly monitor the car's engine, brakes, and electrical systems. If your oil is low or your turn signals aren't working, the computer will tell you—often in a human voice! It will also tell you your speed, how much fuel you have, and how far you have to go to your destination. Other computers will adjust your seat and tune your radio automatically. You may even be able to tell them what to do just by speaking to them. Door and ignition locks may be keyless and respond to computer passwords.

Cars may be equipped with radar that can sense objects in their paths or with special sensors that follow guiding marks built into roadways. The sensors would be connected to the car's steering and brakes, so the car would stay safely on course.

The dashboard of the future car may be equipped with a video screen. The screen

All future cars may have video maps on the dashboards.

could take the place of a rear-view mirror and show what's behind the car. It might also display the owner's manual. Or the car's computer could communicate with a satellite that would radio back your position. The position would be shown on a video map, so you'd know exactly where you were. The satellite could also radio for help if you had trouble on the road.

What will the cars of the future really be like? No one knows for sure. But if the designers' visions come true, they're certain to be exciting.

This 3-wheeled commuter will get 75 miles to the gallon.

TOMORROW'S DESIGNERS

The cars of the future are getting ready to roll—in the studios of a school in Pasadena, California. The school is the Art Center College of Design. It has trained more professional automobile designers than any other school in the world.

The college was founded in 1930 in Los Angeles. Today it's housed in modern buildings set in parklike surroundings. There, students who are majoring in transportation design complete a four-year program that includes academic studies as well as studio courses.

The students design more than cars—in some courses, they put their felt-tipped pens to work on vehicles that range from space capsules to motorcycles. But cars are the focus of the program. At the end of the line is a bachelor's degree and, in all likelihood, a job on the design staff of a major car maker. The chances are strong that at least some of the cars of the future will have their start on drawing boards in Pasadena.

MAKE & DO

Have a smashing time at your next party —with a treat-filled Mexican piñata. In Mexico, piñatas are made at Christmastime from decorated clay jars and papier-mâché. But you can have a piñata anytime. The piñata is stuffed full of candy and gifts and hung from the ceiling. Then children take turns, putting on a blindfold and trying to hit it with a stick. When it breaks, the candy and gifts shower down.

MARK THAT PAGE!

Bookmarks are fun to make, to use, even to give as presents. There are unlimited design possibilities. Here are four types that can be made quickly and easily.

Clownin' Around. The bookmarks shown below are made with posterboard. They are comparatively thick, which makes them particularly useful for marking pages in magazines. To make these bookmarks you need posterboard, white construction paper, crayons or felt-tipped markers, and glue.

1. Cut out a rectangular piece of posterboard. It should be approximately 1½ inches wide by 6 inches long (4 centimeters wide by 15 centimeters long).

2. The design at the top of the bookmark consists of two pieces, a front and a back. First, draw the front design on a piece of construction paper and cut it out.

3. To make the back, place the front design on another piece of construction paper. Trace around it, draw your design on it, and cut it out.

4. Glue the front design onto the top of the posterboard rectangle. Then glue the back design onto the back of the front design.

5. Gift suggestion: If your mother likes to mark recipes in magazines, you can make a series of fruit and vegetable bookmarks for her. If she is more likely to mark articles on interesting travel spots, make a series of bookmarks decorated with cars, ships, and airplanes.

Rainbow Ribbons. The ribbon bookmarks shown above enable a reader to mark several pages at the same time—the ribbons hang free of each other and so can be placed in different parts of the book or magazine. To

2. Give the bookmark a tongue by carefully cutting out a thin sliver of paper in the center. The tongue should be as symmetrical as possible.

3. Using crayons or felt-tipped pens, decorate the bookmark with initials or a design.

Stars & Stripes. To make the colorful bookmarks shown below, you need three ribbons of different widths, stickers or construction paper, and glue.

1. Cut equal lengths of the three ribbons. Glue the pieces together, with the narrowest ribbon on top and the widest ribbon on the bottom.

2. You need two copies of a sticker or of a construction paper design, one for the front and one for the back. Place the designs back to back and glue them onto the top of the ribbons.

3. More ideas: Glue stars or other tiny stickers down the center of the bookmark . . . cut the bottom of the ribbons so they form a point or a slanted line . . . use red and white ribbons topped by a heart for a Valentine's Day gift.

make these bookmarks you need paper, felt, ribbons of equal width, and glue.

1. Begin by drawing an animal or other design on a piece of paper. The design should be at least as wide as the ribbons.

2. Cut out the design. Use it as a pattern to make two felt pieces, front and back. Small details, such as eyes and a mouth, can be drawn on with a felt-tipped pen.

3. Cut three or more lengths of ribbon. They can be of equal length. Or they can be graduated, with the shortest pieces on top.

4. Glue or staple together the tops of the ribbons.

5. Glue one felt design onto the front of the ribbons. Glue the other onto the back.

Paper Clips. The bookmarks shown above are best made from lightweight, flexible paper. Construction paper is ideal. Because these bookmarks are relatively thin, they are excellent for marking pages in paperback books. Use them as you would a paperclip, with the "tongue" on one side of the page and the rest of the bookmark on the other side.

1. Draw the shape of the bookmark on the construction paper, and cut it out.

HIDDEN RIVERS

The Mississippi is one of the most famous rivers in North America. On its banks is an equally famous city—New Orleans. This city was the site of the 1984 World's Fair, whose theme was "The World of Rivers . . . Fresh Water as a Source of Life."

The Mississippi and 24 other well-known rivers of the United States and Canada are listed below (in the left column). Match each to a city that is located on its banks (in the right column). You may wish to use an atlas to help you.

1. Alabama		a.	Billings, Montana
2. Arkansas		b.	Boston, Massachusetts
3. Bow		c.	Calgary, Alberta
4. Brazos		d.	Chattanooga, Tennessee
5. Charles		e.	El Paso, Texas
6. Colorado		f.	Fairbanks, Alaska
7. Connecticut		g.	Harrisburg, Pennsylvania
8. Delaware		h.	Lewiston, Idaho
9. Fraser		i.	Louisville, Kentucky
10. Hudson		j.	Montgomery, Alabama
11. Kansas		k.	New Orleans, Louisiana
12. Mississippi		l.	New York, New York
13. Missouri		m.	Omaha, Nebraska
14. Ohio		n.	Portland, Oregon
15. Potomac		o.	Quebec, Quebec
16. Red		p.	Shreveport, Louisiana
17. Rio Grande		q.	Springfield, Massachusetts
18. Saint Lawrence		r.	Terre Haute, Indiana
19. Snake		s.	Topeka, Kansas
20. Susquehanna		t.	Trenton, New Jersey
21. Tanana		u.	Tulsa, Oklahoma
22. Tennessee		v.	Vancouver, British Columbia
23. Wabash		w.	Waco, Texas
24. Willamette		x.	Washington, D.C.
25. Yellowstone		y.	Yuma, Arizona

ANSWERS: 1.j; 2.u; 3.c; 4.w; 5.b; 6.y; 7.q; 8.t; 9.v; 10.l; 11.s; 12.k; 13.m; 14.i; 15.x; 16.p; 17.e; 18.o; 19.h; 20.g; 21.f; 22.d; 23.r; 24.n; 25.a.

Next, go on a hunt. All 25 rivers are hidden in this search-a-word puzzle. Try to find them. Cover the puzzle with a sheet of tracing paper. Read forward, backward, up, down, and diagonally. Then shade in the letters of each river as you find it. One river has been shaded in for you.

Some letters will be left over after you have found all the rivers. Circle all the unused letters. If you read them from left to right, you will find a hidden title for the puzzle.

Y	B	O	W	F	E	E	S	S	E	N	N	E	T
E	O	A	M	A	L	A	B	A	M	A	O	U	S
L	R	I	P	P	I	S	S	I	S	S	I	M	I
L	E	V	H	E	R	A	S	N	O	S	D	U	H
O	D	S	O	O	S	S	T	D	U	S	F	E
W	N	N	O	N	O	O	D	L	A	S	A	R	T
S	A	F	A	U	Z	E	S	A	R	Q	S	P	T
T	R	K	R	A	L	E	N	W	O	U	N	D	E
O	G	I	R	A	L	T	A	R	L	E	A	T	M
N	O	B	W	R	S	H	K	E	O	H	K	O	A
E	I	A	A	A	E	E	E	N	C	A	R	M	L
M	R	H	E	R	I	D	R	C	C	N	A	A	L
E	C	T	U	C	I	T	C	E	N	N	O	C	I
T	A	N	A	N	A	A	W	A	B	A	S	H	W

MANY FRIENDS COOKING

BROONIE (Irish Gingerbread), from Ireland

The Irish are famous for home-baked potato bread and soda bread. Both are unusual and flavorful. Less well known but just as good is Broonie, an Irish bread that's almost a cake. Broonie is chewy and dark in color. It is full of oats—a grain grown in this cool, wet land. Broonie, which is a little sweet, goes perfectly with hot tea or cold milk.

INGREDIENTS

1 or 2 teaspoons butter
2 cups flour
1½ teaspoons baking soda
1 teaspoon cinnamon
1 teaspoon ground ginger
¾ teaspoon salt
½ cup soft butter
½ cup sugar
1 egg
2 egg yolks
1 cup molasses
½ cup quick-cooking oatmeal
1 cup hot water

EQUIPMENT

8-inch-square baking pan
measuring cups
measuring spoons
sifter
piece of waxed paper
mixing bowl
mixing spoon

HOW TO MAKE

1. Preheat the oven to 350°F.

2. Grease the bottom of the baking pan with 1 or 2 teaspoons of butter.

3. Measure the flour, baking soda, cinnamon, ginger, and salt, and sift them together onto the piece of waxed paper.

4. In the mixing bowl, combine the ½ cup of butter with the sugar by stirring them with the mixing spoon until they are well blended.

5. Add the egg and egg yolks.

6. With the mixing spoon, beat the mixture until it is fluffy.

7. Stir in the molasses.

8. Add the sifted dry ingredients, the oatmeal, and the hot water a little at a time to the egg-and-molasses mixture, stirring after each addition.

9. Pour the mixture into the greased pan.

10. Bake the Broonie 50 to 55 minutes.

11. Cut into squares and serve warm.

This recipe makes 6 pieces.

QUICK QUICHE, from France

It's foolproof! With this simple entrée from France, you can't go wrong for brunch, lunch, or dinner. It's a pie without a crust, filled with vegetables mixed with eggs, and then baked until puffed and brown. Add any combination of vegetables, such as potatoes, zucchini, cauliflower, or carrots. A traditional quiche is cooked in a pastry shell. You can cook yours this way, too. If you do, be sure to use a 9-inch shell.

INGREDIENTS

- 1 medium onion
- 2 tomatoes
- 1 small eggplant or 2 medium zucchini
- 12 mushrooms
- ¼ cup Parmesan cheese
- 12 ounces Swiss cheese
- ⅛ cup vegetable oil
- 4 eggs
  dash garlic salt
- ½ cup milk
- 1 tablespoon flour
  salt and pepper to taste

EQUIPMENT

paring knife	mixing spoon
measuring cups	mixing bowl
grater	fork
large iron skillet	measuring spoons

HOW TO MAKE

1. Peel and chop the onion, tomatoes, and eggplant (or zucchini). Wash and slice the mushrooms. Grate the cheeses.

2. Heat the oil in the skillet over low heat.

3. Add the vegetables and stir for 15 minutes until the vegetables are soft.

4. Preheat the oven to 400°F.

5. Beat the eggs with the fork and add to the mixture. Add the garlic salt, milk, flour, cheeses, salt, and pepper. Combine well.

6. Put the skillet in the oven for 25 minutes. Cut the quiche into wedges to serve.

Note: If you don't have an iron skillet, you can sauté the vegetables in a frying pan and add the other ingredients. Then pour the mixture into a greased 8-inch-square baking pan or a 9-inch pie plate to bake in the oven.

This recipe serves 6 people.

STAMP COLLECTING

The United States issued more than 50 new stamps and items of postal stationery during 1984. But this was just a drop in the bucket—some 7,000 new stamps were issued worldwide. Among those most interesting for collectors were stamps that celebrated the 1984 Olympic Games and that honored famous people and places in many countries.

U.S. STAMPS

October was National Stamp Collecting Month, and a special stamp was issued to mark it. The stamp was the first ever designed by a student—18-year-old Molly LaRue of Shaker Heights, Ohio. Her drawing expressed the theme of family unity by showing three stick figures with hearts for bodies, drawn as a young child might draw them. Later in the year a second student-designed stamp was issued, for the Christmas holidays. Drawn by 8-year-old Danny LaBoccetta of Jamaica, New York, it showed Santa Claus. Both stamps were chosen from more than 500,000 designs submitted by children.

The Postal Service used a new process, called quadrant printing, to produce four commemoratives. The stamps honored several goals of President Franklin Delano Roosevelt's New Deal—soil and water conservation, government insurance for bank deposits, and the establishment of credit unions—as well as the National Archives. The designs were printed together in sheets of 200 (50 of each design) but released at different times.

Plants and animals proved popular subjects for several 1984 issues. Some of the prettiest U.S. stamps showed orchids, which are found all over the world. Four varieties native to different parts of the United States were depicted. Another issue marked the 100th anniversary of the American Kennel Club. The four stamps showed eight dogs— a beagle and a Boston terrier, a Chesapeake Bay retriever and a cocker spaniel, an Alaskan malamute and a collie, and an American foxhound and a black-and-tan coonhound.

Waterfowl were featured on two stamps.

One marked the 1984 Louisiana World Exposition, which took rivers as its theme. The other commemorated the 50-year-old "duck stamp" program. "Duck stamps" are hunting permit stamps, and the income from their sale has helped preserve wetland habitats.

Another animal was also honored on a stamp—Smokey the Bear, who since 1944 has been the symbol of a campaign for the prevention of forest fires. The original Smokey was a bear cub that was rescued from a fire by forest rangers.

Historical events were also marked by stamps. One stamp showed the ships that brought the first settlers to the colony of Maryland, in 1634. Other stamps commemorated the 25th anniversaries of statehood for Alaska and Hawaii. The United States and Canada got together to issue stamps marking the 25th anniversary of the opening of the St. Lawrence Seaway, which they had built jointly. The stamps used similar designs to show different views of the seaway.

As always, there were special stamps honoring special people. These included President Harry S. Truman and Eleanor Roosevelt, both of whom were born in 1884. The newest stamp in the Literary Arts series showed the 19th-century author Herman Melville, best known for his novel *Moby Dick*. Douglas Fairbanks, the silent-film hero of many swashbuckling adventures, was shown on a new issue in the Performing Arts series. Another commemorative honored Horace Moses, who was the founder of the Junior Achievement program. This program helps young people gain business skills and experience.

Two sports figures were honored. One was Jim Thorpe, whose success in many sports in the early 1900's made him one of the most versatile athletes ever. The other was Roberto Clemente, the baseball star who died in a plane crash in 1972 while delivering supplies to earthquake victims in Nicaragua.

STAMPS FROM AROUND THE WORLD

Stamps on several themes were issued by the United Nations during the year. A group of six was devoted to the organization's ef-

**1984 STAMPS
FROM AROUND
THE WORLD**

A TOPICAL COLLECTION OF OLYMPIC STAMPS

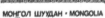

forts to help refugees. The stamps carried expressive designs showing refugees from around the world, drawn by the Swiss artist Hans Erni. Another group of six U.N. stamps, in the World Heritage series, showed natural wonders and famous ancient cities. The natural sites were the Grand Canyon (United States), Los Glaciares National Park (Argentina), and Serengeti National Park (Tanzania). The cities were Valleta (Malta), Polonnaruwa (Sri Lanka), and Shibam (Yemen). The U.N. also continued its flag series with sixteen new stamps, and it issued a special set of stamps on the theme of hunger.

Canada marked two important anniversaries with new stamp issues. One commemorated the 450th anniversary of Jacques Cartier's first voyage to North America. (France, Cartier's homeland, also issued a stamp in his honor in 1984.) The second Canadian stamp honored Yellowknife, the gold-mining community in the Northwest Territories, which celebrated its 50th birthday. A stamp honoring this event showed the entrance of a gold mine rising out of a prospector's pan.

A dozen Canadian commemoratives offered stamp collectors an armchair tour of the country, showing scenes from each of the ten provinces and two territories. And still another attractive Canadian issue showed early lighthouses, in a block of four stamps. The 1984 visit of Pope John Paul II to Canada was also marked with new stamps.

Several of the many stamps issued by countries in South and Central America had themes of interest to young people. Children's games were featured on stamps from Argentina, and world scouting was honored in a Colombian issue. The Caribbean nation of St. Kitts-Nevis honored 4-H clubs on four of its stamps. The stamps showed members planting trees, tending farm animals, and marching behind the organization's flag.

Some of the most colorful stamps of the year were produced by Britain. Four stamps showed coats-of-arms of noble families. The intricate designs were reproduced in as many as eight colors, ranging from blue-green to rose red. Another issue showed British cattle breeds, which have been the cornerstones of many beef and dairy herds throughout the world.

There were several omnibus issues—stamps with a single theme produced by many countries. The 1984 Europa stamps, issued by member countries of the Congress of European Postal and Telecommunication Administrations, took bridges as their theme. And since 1984 was the Year of the Rat in the Chinese Lunar calendar, several Asian countries produced stamps showing rats or mice. Taiwan's had a whimsical, stylized rat. Japan showed a folk toy—a mouse riding a small hammer.

But the most common theme for stamps from countries around the world was the 1984 Olympic Games. In fact, there have been so many Olympic stamps that they would be a good choice for a topical collection—a collection built around a single theme.

A TOPICAL COLLECTION OF OLYMPIC STAMPS

Olympic stamps are a tradition in many countries. The United States issued its first Olympic stamp in 1932, to mark the Winter Games held that year in Lake Placid, New York. Other U.S. stamps commemorated the Games in 1960, 1972, 1976, and 1980. And for the 1984 Olympics, the United States produced its largest Olympic issue ever—24 individual stamps, three postal cards, and one overseas aerogramme.

But almost every country had its own Olympic stamps in 1984. Among the most interesting issues were a group from Liberia, showing black winners in past Games, and a group from the Pacific island of Niue, showing athletes as depicted on ancient Greek pottery. Most other countries showed various sports, especially sports at which their athletes excelled.

Your topical collection could concentrate on stamps from one country or from all over the world. It could cover just the 1984 Games or the Games of the past. However you arrange it, your stamp collection will be a record of the world's most important sporting event.

CHARLESS HAHN
Stamp Editor
Chicago Sun-Times

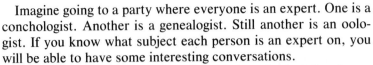

MEET THE EXPERTS

Imagine going to a party where everyone is an expert. One is a conchologist. Another is a genealogist. Still another is an oologist. If you know what subject each person is an expert on, you will be able to have some interesting conversations.

All the people at the party are listed below, in the left column. Match them with their subjects, which are listed in the right column.

THE EXPERTS	THEIR SUBJECTS
1. biologist	a. ancient animal life
2. conchologist	b. animals
3. cosmetologist	c. birds
4. cosmologist	d. birds' eggs
5. dermatologist	e. blood
6. entomologist	f. cosmetics
7. genealogist	g. diseases
8. geologist	h. drugs
9. hematologist	i. ears, nose, and throat
10. herpetologist	j. earth
11. ichthyologist	k. family histories
12. meteorologist	l. fish
13. oologist	m. fossils
14. ornithologist	n. insects
15. otorhinolaryngologist	o. living things
16. paleontologist	p. moon
17. paleozoologist	q. poisons
18. pathologist	r. reptiles and amphibians
19. pharmacologist	s. shells
20. selenologist	t. skin
21. toxicologist	u. universe
22. virologist	v. viruses
23. volcanologist	w. volcanoes
24. zoologist	x. weather

ANSWERS: 1,o; 2,s; 3,f; 4,u; 5,t; 6,n; 7,k; 8,j; 9,e; 10,r; 11,l; 12,x; 13,d; 14,c; 15,i; 16,m; 17,a; 18,g; 19,h; 20,p; 21,q; 22,v; 23,w; 24,b.

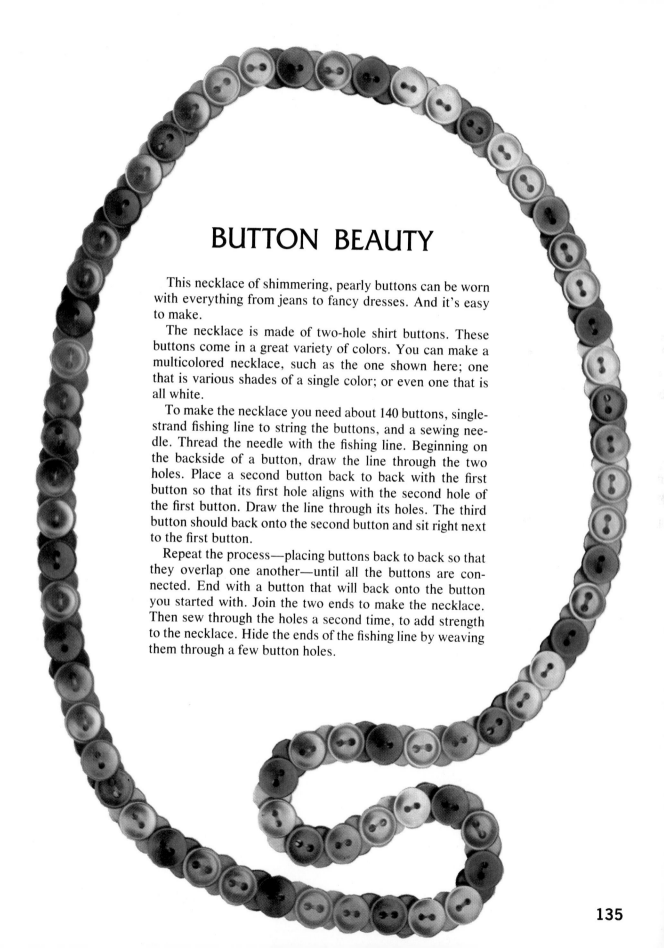

BUTTON BEAUTY

This necklace of shimmering, pearly buttons can be worn with everything from jeans to fancy dresses. And it's easy to make.

The necklace is made of two-hole shirt buttons. These buttons come in a great variety of colors. You can make a multicolored necklace, such as the one shown here; one that is various shades of a single color; or even one that is all white.

To make the necklace you need about 140 buttons, single-strand fishing line to string the buttons, and a sewing needle. Thread the needle with the fishing line. Beginning on the backside of a button, draw the line through the two holes. Place a second button back to back with the first button so that its first hole aligns with the second hole of the first button. Draw the line through its holes. The third button should back onto the second button and sit right next to the first button.

Repeat the process—placing buttons back to back so that they overlap one another—until all the buttons are connected. End with a button that will back onto the button you started with. Join the two ends to make the necklace. Then sew through the holes a second time, to add strength to the necklace. Hide the ends of the fishing line by weaving them through a few button holes.

SHADOW PICTURES

In the 18th century, one of the most popular art forms was the shadow picture. A person who wanted a portrait but who couldn't afford a portrait painter went to an artist who specialized in shadow art. Usually, the artist would seat the person between a candle and a sheet of light-colored paper. The person's head blocked some of the candlelight, so that a shadow of the head appeared on the paper. The artist would trace around the shadow, then cut it out or paint it.

Some artists were very talented. They were able to cut shadow pictures freehand, just by looking at a person. Other artists used various machines in their work. One machine reduced the size of the shadow so that the portrait was very small and could be put in a locket. Another machine, shown in the drawing above, consisted of a chair connected to an easel. Attached to the easel,

between the artist and the sitter, was a piece of glass. And mounted to the glass, on the side facing the artist, was a piece of paper that had been oiled to make it translucent. The artist stood behind the easel to draw the outline of the person's profile.

People who couldn't afford to go to a shadow artist made their own portraits using similar techniques. Shadow art also became a popular hobby. One person who enjoyed cutting portraits out of paper was the French finance minister Étienne de Silhouette. Today, another name for a shadow picture is a silhouette.

With the invention of photography in the mid-1800's, shadow portraits declined in popularity. But the art continues to challenge people who want an unusual and interesting hobby.

To make shadow portraits of family members and friends, you need both light- and dark-colored paper. Smooth, thin paper is better than thick paper. You also need a pencil, paint, scissors, and a flashlight or slide projector. And you need a partner: someone who will draw your silhouette and who will sit while you draw his or her portrait.

Securely set the flashlight or slide projector on a table. The light source should be positioned so that the beam of light travels straight ahead to fall on a blank wall. Tape a piece of light-colored paper on the wall, where the light beam falls. Position a chair sideways between the light and the wall. Sit on the chair so that the shadow of your profile appears on the paper. It may be necessary to adjust the height of the light, paper, or chair to obtain a sharp, accurate silhouette. Sharpness will also improve if the room is as dark as possible.

If you want your silhouette to appear smaller, move the chair closer to the paper. To enlarge the silhouette, move the chair closer to the light.

Your partner should draw around the shadow cast by your head. You must sit very still while your partner is tracing the shadow. If you move your head—even if you talk or laugh—the shadow won't be an accurate replica of your profile.

When the outline drawing is finished, remove the paper from the wall. Then you can do one of two things. You can cut out the silhouette and paste it on a dark sheet of paper. Or you can paint the silhouette with dark paint so that it contrasts with the light-colored background.

If you cut very carefully, you can actually get two shadow pictures from one drawing: Cut out the head and paste it on dark paper. Then take another sheet of dark paper and put it behind the opening left in the original sheet of paper.

Dale B.

IT'S A
FABULOUS
FRAME-UP

"Every picture tells a story," says an old proverb. And the frame that surrounds a picture can add to the story. Imagine, for example, a photograph of you and your best friend at camp, rowing a boat across a lake. Wouldn't it look great framed by cattails and a flock of flying geese? And wouldn't a picture of your grandparents on their wedding day be enhanced by a frame decorated with lacy leaves and flowers?

Making unusual picture frames is a popular craft. Decorative wood, ceramic, and fabric frames are sold in many stores as well as at craft shows. Paper sculpture frames such as those shown on these pages are rarer because they are relatively delicate and must be handled carefully—since they are three-dimensional, they cannot be stacked one atop another. Nor can the pictures these frames contain be covered with glass. But the special handling they require is worth it. Once on the wall, framing favorite prints and photographs, they provide a great deal of pleasure.

The main ingredients of paper sculpture frames are imagination and attention to detail. Begin by considering the picture that you wish to frame. What story does it tell? How can a frame add to the story? Suppose, for example, that you want to frame a photo of your favorite rock singer. You could decorate the frame with gold records and black musical notes. The frame for a photograph of your birthday party could be decorated with paper candles and curling streamers.

Begin with a basic frame. You can cut this yourself from a sheet of posterboard or cardboard. Or you can buy a precut mat. Most photo and art supply stores have mats in many colors. Use construction paper for the decorations. Regular all-purpose white glue can be used to attach the decorations to the frame.

You can create the sculptured, or three-dimensional, effects in a number of ways. The most basic way is to curl the paper decorations. This is easy to do. For example, cut a leaflike shape from a sheet of construction paper. Hold the leaf in your hand, grasping one end with your fingertips. In your other hand, hold a pair of dull scissors—the scissors must be wide open, with your hand carefully gripping them in the center of the

two blades. Place the inner edge of one blade against the leaf, and pull the blade over the leaf from bottom to top. If you apply a fair amount of pressure as you pull the blade over the leaf, the leaf will form a tight curl. Less pressure will make it curl only a little. Practice this procedure with various shapes and sizes of paper leaves to appreciate the different effects you can create.

The curling technique works very well when one piece of paper is placed on top of another piece. For example, you can make five broad petals for a flower, curling each petal slightly. Then cut five thin petals from another color paper, curl them tightly, and place them in the middle of the broad petals. The center of the flower can be a star or a circle or a heart cut from yet another color paper.

To give a leaf a frilly look, cut many slits all around its edges. Then remove a tiny sliver, or wedge, of paper along each slit. Next gently curl the leaf around your finger. This technique can be used on other shapes, too.

Another paper-sculpting technique can be used to make cattails. Cut out long rectangles of brown paper, roll them around a pencil, then glue the edges together to form a tube. In the same way, you can make birthday candles or the body of a spaceship.

Try this technique to create a fanlike effect: Using a compass, cut out a semicircle of paper. Form triangles by folding it from corner to corner two or three times. Scallop or fringe the edge. For an even more decorative effect, take a paper punch and make a hole in the center of the folded semicircle. Then when you fan the paper out, you will have a hole in each triangle.

Once you have practiced these techniques, you are ready to begin designing your frame. First arrange your decorations on a ''dummy'' copy of the frame. (To keep the frame itself clean and undamaged, don't bring it to your working space until you are ready to glue on the decorations.)

This planning stage is the most important step of frame making. As you cut out shapes and sculpt them, you'll find that some things you try just won't look right. But an unusable idea often leads to another, more practical idea. Keep experimenting. If you have difficulty creating complex shapes, such as flying geese or sailboats, trace these from pictures in magazines or newspapers. And keep in mind that it is not necessary or even desirable to sculpt every piece of paper in your design. Some pieces can lie flat on the frame.

Don't glue anything to the frame until all your decorations have been cut, sculpted, and put in place on the dummy frame. Then cover your working area with paper and have a damp cloth handy. Pour a few drops of glue into a dish. Use a small brush or a toothpick to apply the glue to the back of each decoration. Glue only that part of the paper that is to lie flat on the frame. The part

that curves upward should not be glued. For example, if a leaf or flower petal is glued along its center line, it will curve upward on both sides. If a leaf or petal is glued along its bottom edge, the entire structure will curve upward. Both ways are fine—chose the one that looks best on your particular frame.

Neatness is important. Be careful not to put too much glue on the decorations. If excess glue seeps out from under the decorations, wipe it up with the damp cloth. If glue gets on your hands, wipe them clean.

Another type of paper frame is the snowflake frame shown on this page. It's easier to make than the sculptured frames, and it's just as attractive. It is made from paper doilies, which are available in supermarkets and craft stores. Cut out shapes from the doilies and arrange them on the frame so that they form a pleasing pattern. Generally, a symmetrical pattern is best.

Snowflakes can also be combined with paper sculpting. A picture of a snowy landscape could be framed by sculpted evergreen trees and a background sky filled with snowflakes. A photograph of your mother in her wedding dress could be surrounded by snowflakes and pink flowers.

If you want to be especially fanciful, you can make your frame an unusual shape. Nothing requires a frame to be rectangular or oval. Put a graduation picture in a frame that is shaped like an old-fashioned schoolhouse. Put a picture of camp scouts in a tent-shaped frame (complete with sculpted poles). Put a football player's photo in a brown frame shaped like . . . you guessed it . . . a football.

Making these frames takes time. But if you create them with care and thought, they will be a source of great pride and pleasure for many years to come.

COIN COLLECTING

Coins honoring the Olympic Games—among them, the first U.S. gold coin in more than half a century—were some of the highlights for collectors in 1984. Also of interest were commemoratives from many lands and some unusual error coins from the United States.

U.S. $10 gold coin and silver dollar commemorating the 1984 Olympic Games

U.S. COINS

The U.S. gold coin was part of a three-coin tribute to the Summer Olympics held in Los Angeles. It showed male and female runners carrying a torch, and it had a face value of $10—although collectors paid just over $350 for it. A silver dollar coin was also produced in 1984 to honor the Games. It joined a similar dollar coin that had been issued in 1983. Profits from the sale of the coins went to fund athletes' participation in the 1984 and future Games. By the time the Games were over, more than $56,500,000 had been raised through the coins. And sales were to continue through the end of the year.

While the coins were successful in raising money, many collectors were unhappy with the program for two reasons. One reason was that the U.S. Treasury created thirteen versions of the coins, with different combinations of date, mint mark, and finish. (The mint mark shows which of the several U.S. mint facilities produced the coin. The term ''finish'' applies to the coin's surface appearance.) Some collectors felt they had to have an example of every type in order to have a complete collection, and this cost more than $2,000.

Many people were also unhappy with the designs of the coins, especially the 1984 silver coin. It showed the entrance to the Olympic stadium in Los Angeles, with headless statues of two athletes. Some critics said the design looked like a UFO with two weird extraterrestrials aboard.

Collectors welcomed another event—the return of the ''mint set'' after a two-year absence. Sold by the U.S. Mint in a special package, the set contains one example of each denomination (cent through half dollar) and mint mark struck for regular circulation during a given year. This enables collectors to keep their coin sets complete with uncirculated coins, without having to search pocket change for new issues.

Searching pocket change is a favorite pastime for collectors, however. And 1984 saw a nationwide treasure hunt for a pair of valuable error coins, both doubled-die cents. A doubled-die coin has a double image of all or part of the design, one image just a tiny distance from the other. This error occurs when a faulty die is used to strike coins, and it usually results in thousands of error coins entering circulation. When the distance be-

A doubled-die 1983 cent, a valuable error coin

tween the images is great enough to be easily seen, the coins usually take on added collector value.

This was the case with the two types of error coins discovered in 1984. One was a 1983 cent with a double image of the entire reverse design, most noticeable on the words "one cent" at the bottom of the coin. Collectors were paying up to $250 each for these coins. The other coin was a 1984 cent with a double image of Lincoln, most noticeable around his ear. Because this error was much harder to spot, the coin was valued at around $50.

Canada's silver dollar commemorating the 150th birthday of the city of Toronto

COINS AROUND THE WORLD

The United States was not the only country to strike coins in honor of the Los Angeles Olympics. China, Jamaica, San Marino, Western Samoa, Poland, and the Isle of Man

China's 5-yuan coin honoring the 1984 Olympics

also produced gold or silver coins for the event. Plans are already underway for coinage in honor of the 1988 Olympics, which will be held in South Korea and Canada. In fact, South Korea began in 1982 to issue a series of coins for the 1988 Games.

Canada continued its long-running commemorative coin program in 1984 with a trio of coins. A silver dollar honored the 150th anniversary of the city of Toronto. The coin showed an Indian canoeing past the modern skyline of the city. A second commemorative dollar, struck in pure nickel, and a $100 gold coin commemorated the 450th anniversary of French explorer Jacques Cartier's first voyage to North America.

Another explorer, Christopher Columbus, was the subject of a cupronickel coin issued by El Salvador. The coin has a face value of 1 colon (about 40 cents) and was the first

Salvadorean coin of that denomination since 1971. The word "colon" is the Spanish version of the name Columbus.

Still another famous explorer, Marco Polo, was the subject of a series of coins issued by China. The two gold and two silver coins were dated 1983, but they were released in 1984. Polo, a Venetian, crossed Asia by land to visit Cathay (China) between 1271 and 1295.

Reaching further back into history, Egypt issued a 1984 gold coin with a portrait of Cleopatra, queen of Egypt during Roman

Egypt's 100-pound gold coin showing Cleopatra

times. The coin had a face value of 100 Egyptian pounds (about $140) but was sold to collectors for $575.

The worldwide travels of Pope John Paul II have resulted in the striking of a number of coins and medals. In 1984, the South Korean Government issued an official medal for the first visit of a pope to its country. And in Canada, several private mints struck medals to mark the papal visit to their nation.

ROBERT F. LEMKE
Numismatic News

A FIELD OF FELT

It's easy to make a brightly colored felt hanging such as this autumn still life. Felt doesn't ravel or fray, so pieces can be glued rather than sewn. Hangings can be placed anywhere in your home. They can even be used outdoors, as decorations for a party or to announce someone's birthday.

To make this type of hanging you need a large piece of felt for the background and the loops; small pieces of felt in several different colors; two thin dowels; and white fabric glue.

Begin by creating your design. Choose a subject that lends itself to bright colors and that doesn't have lots of fine details. Then "sketch it out," using pieces of construction paper in colors that are similar to those of the felt. Move the pieces around and add or subtract objects until you are satisfied with the design.

Cut the background from the large piece of felt. If you wish, you can glue this onto cardboard cut to the same size.

Use the construction paper pieces as patterns. Pin each piece of paper onto the desired color of felt. Carefully cut out the felt piece.

Arrange the felt pieces on the backing. Then put a little glue around the back edge of each piece of felt, and press the piece firmly in place on the backing.

To make the loops, cut six strips of felt of equal length (eight or more if the hanging is very wide). Fold each strip in half so it forms a loop. Glue the two ends together. Then glue the loops to the back of the hanging.

Sand the ends of the dowels until they are smooth. You might want to paint the dowels, or color them with a felt-tipped marker. When the loops are dry, put the dowels through them. You can then hang the picture by placing the top dowel over two widely spaced nails. Or cut a piece of cord or ribbon twice the length of a dowel. Tie the ends to the ends of the top dowel and place the center of the cord over a nail.

TWIST THAT TONGUE!

Tom Twist twisted his tongue on this hidden tongue twister. And so will you—but first you have to find it.

To discover it, you need a pencil and a sheet of lined paper. Number the lines from 1 through 18, leaving a line of space between numbers. Carefully follow the directions given below. They will lead you to the tongue twister. Hint: It will be easier if you rewrite the complete words at each step.

The solution is on page 381.

1. Print the words TOUGH TONGUE TWISTER, leaving them separated as you continue to work.

2. Remove the first two vowels from the left.

3. Place an S after the second and third T's from the left.

4. Find the fourth consonant from the right. Replace it with an M.

5. Move the third vowel from the left after the third consonant from the left.

6. Remove the seventeenth letter from the right.

7. Replace the second and third T's from the right with K's.

8. Insert an N between every K–S combination.

9. Move the tenth letter from the left so it becomes the eighth letter from the right.

10. Place an I before and after the fifth consonant from the left.

11. Find the second vowel from the right. Replace it with AE.

12. Put a space between the seventh and eighth letters from the right. (You now have 4 words.)

13. Reverse the order of the first four letters of the second word.

14. Reverse the order of the letters of the third word.

15. Remove the fourth vowel from the left.

16. Reverse the order of the last two words.

17. Reverse the order of the first three letters of the third word.

18. Find the seventh and eighth letters from the right. Move them to the beginning of the third word.

Repeat out loud six times. Quickly!

POPULAR CRAFTS

Making something by hand can be an exciting and rewarding experience. Your handmade items reflect your creativity, and they have a special meaning for you that manufactured items seldom have.

During 1984 people everywhere continued to enjoy a wide range of crafts. Some of the most popular were paper and fabric crafts. People used a variety of techniques with paper and fabric to make useful objects, as well as items just for decoration.

A HANDMADE PAPER WALL HANGING

Papermaking is an ancient craft. In recent years, many people have begun to make craft papers at home, using supplies from mail-order firms that specialize in such materials. Handmade papers can be molded into raised designs and dyed in brilliant colors to make a beautiful wall hanging.

The wall hanging begins with plant fibers that are soaked in water to make pulp. Some of the pulp is then formed into sheets with special papermaking molds and allowed to dry. Raised forms—flowers, birds, leaves, or others—are made by pressing pulp against the surfaces of objects that have recessed designs. Look for such designs on vases, glass or crystal ware, and wrought iron objects.

After the paper sheets and the raised forms are dry, they are colored with special high-intensity dyes. The edges of flowers and leaves can be decorated with embroidered designs, using thread in a co-ordinating color. Then the picture is assembled. The backing is a foam-core board covered with fabric. The flat sheets of paper are glued or stitched onto this to make the background. Then the trees, leaves, flowers, and other forms are arranged for the best effect and glued in place.

This whimsical wall hanging was made from handmade craft papers. The papers were molded into raised designs and dyed in brilliant colors.

Above: Make your own old-fashioned valentines using construction paper, colored typing paper, and pictures cut from old magazines. Below: You can turn brightly colored felt into shoulder bags that will be beautiful as well as useful.

PAPER VALENTINES

Handmade greeting cards are a popular paper craft. You can make your own old-fashioned lacy valentines using colored construction paper, colored typing paper, and pictures cut from old magazines.

Each card can be designed to match the interests of the person who will receive it.

To make this charming appliqué wall hanging, pieces of different fabrics were stitched onto a fabric backing.

Search through magazines for pictures around which to build your design. A picture of a puppy might suit a dog-lover, while flowers would be appropriate for a gardener.

Cut hearts and lacy borders from folded sheets of paper. To make hearts, fold a piece of paper in half and cut half the heart shape, beginning and finishing at the folded edge. To make a border, cut a square of typing paper and fold it into quarters. Use scissors and a paper punch to cut your design along the open, unfolded edges.

Use colored construction paper for the folder. Fold the sheet in half and trim it to a size that is larger than your border.

Now you are ready to assemble your valentine. First, paste the border on the front of the folder. Then arrange your pictures and cut-outs and glue them in place. Finally, write a special greeting inside. Your handmade card will be much more meaningful than any card you could buy in a store.

RAINBOW SHOULDER BAGS

Using brightly colored felt, you can make a shoulder bag that will be beautiful as well as useful. Felt is easy to work with because it won't ravel when it is cut, and it holds its shape well.

To make your shoulder bag, choose felt in several colors, contrasting or co-ordinating. The body of the bag is formed by three large pieces of felt—an oval for the back and flap, a half-oval for the front, and a long strip to form the gusset that goes around the sides and bottom. Use a paper pattern to cut these pieces, and cut two of each. One set of pattern pieces will be used for the outside of the bag, and the second set will be used for the lining.

The design on the bag is made with felt cording. To make the cording, cut long, narrow strips of felt. Fold each strip around a piece of bulky yarn the same length as the felt. Stitch so that you enclose the entire length of yarn in the felt. After making the cords, sew them onto the back and flap, and perhaps even the front, of the bag. Make sure that only the rounded, unsewn edges show.

When the design is finished, the lining pieces are added, and the bag is stitched together. The seams are hidden with binding

This Noah's Ark wall hanging was made by gluing pieces of fabric and other objects onto a stiff backing.

strips of contrasting or co-ordinating felt, and shoulder straps are made from other long felt strips. A leather strap and a buckle add the finishing touch.

FABRIC WALL HANGINGS

A colorful fabric wall hanging can brighten any room. Several different techniques can be used to make such hangings. And you can take your design from any source, such as a favorite picture or poster.

One popular technique is appliqué—pieces of fabric stitched onto a fabric backing. Cut a large piece of solid-color cotton or similar fabric for the backing. Select an array of fabrics to make up the pieces of your design. Then make a paper pattern for each piece. Experiment by placing the pattern pieces on the backing and moving them around until you have the effect you want.

The design pieces are cut slightly larger than the pattern pieces. The extra material is folded under and basted in place with large stitches, to make a finished edge. Then each piece is sewn in place with fine stitching, and the basting threads are removed. Details are embroidered with contrasting thread, and the completed hanging is stapled to a picture stretcher.

You can also make a wall hanging by gluing pieces of fabric and other objects in place. This type of hanging is mounted on a stiff backing, such as the art board sold in art-supply stores, covered with fabric. The fabric is glued on with wallpaper paste.

Begin by planning your design, using paper pattern pieces. Then cut your design pieces from scraps of fabric. Use patterned and textured fabrics, such as corduroy, for interesting effects. Glue each piece in place and outline it with colored yarn, to hide the cut edges. Other objects can be glued on, too —braid for borders and trim, buttons for flower centers, and pieces of colored pipe cleaners for flower stems.

WALTER C. LANKENAU
Managing Editor
Creative Crafts & Miniatures magazine

SPORTS

The Olympic Games, a celebration of athletic competition and friendship among nations, is filled with color and tradition. One of the most inspiring rituals is the carrying of the Olympic torch. The flame is lighted by the sun's rays near Olympia, Greece, where the first Games were held many centuries ago. Then the torch is carried by a relay of runners—and by ships or planes when necessary—to the sites of the next Olympics. In 1984, the destinations were Sarajevo, Yugoslavia, and Los Angeles, California. For the Summer Games in Los Angeles, the long journey began in early May. First the torch was flown to New York City. Then a relay of more than 9,000 runners took it zig-zagging across the map. Night and day, through cities and farmlands, the torch was carried in 33 of the 50 states. After 82 days, it arrived at the Los Angeles Coliseum. The final runner circled the stadium track, climbed a long stairway, and used the torch to light a giant flame atop the arena. The 1984 Summer Olympics had begun!

151

THE 1984 OLYMPIC GAMES

The Winter Games—Sarajevo, Yugoslavia

The Olympic Games were first held in ancient Greece, in the city-state of Olympia. Every four years, athletes from all over Greece gathered to compete. Nothing was more important to the Greeks than the Games, and nothing was allowed to interfere. If a war was going on between city-states, a special truce was called. Olympia was sacred ground, and disputes weren't allowed in.

Today the Olympic Games are the most celebrated sporting event in the world. They are also the largest gathering of the nations and peoples of the world. They are full of drama, pageantry, and tradition. But the modern Olympics are different from the ancient Greek Games in one important respect. Political disputes *often* interfere.

In 1984 problems arose again. The Winter Games in Sarajevo, Yugoslavia, went off without a hitch. But the Summer Games in Los Angeles, California, suffered from the absence of fourteen nations due to differences between the United States and the Soviet Union.

THE SOVIET BOYCOTT

On May 7, 1984, the Soviet Union announced that it would not send a team to the 1984 Summer Olympics. It accused the United States of using the Games for "political aims" and expressed concern about the security of Soviet athletes in Los Angeles. Certain groups in the United States were planning to stage anti-Soviet demonstrations and to help Soviet athletes defect—abandon their country to become U.S. citizens. The Soviet Union was upset because the United States wouldn't ban such demonstrations.

Many believed that there was another reason for the withdrawal. In 1980, to protest the Soviet invasion of Afghanistan, the United States had led a 54-nation boycott of the Olympic Games in Moscow. Now, it was thought, the Soviets were trying to retaliate by boycotting the Olympic Games in Los Angeles.

Immediately after the Soviet announcement, the U.S. Government issued its own statement. It called the boycott "a blatant political action for which there is no real justification." The International Olympic Committee, which runs the Games, tried to talk the Soviets out of their decision. But it was too late. The decision was final. The Soviets would not be at the Summer Games.

Over the next few weeks, thirteen other countries decided to go along with the Soviet boycott. Among them were East Germany, Czechoslovakia, Poland, and Cuba—countries with some of the best athletes in the world. Rumania was the one Warsaw Pact country that did attend.

The most disappointed people of all were the athletes themselves. Those from the boycotting countries had trained for years but now couldn't compete. Those from the United States, Canada, and elsewhere—many of whom had missed the 1980 Games—now couldn't test their skills against some of their greatest rivals.

"You work so hard and want to play against the very best," said Cheryl Miller of the U.S. women's basketball team. "And now one of the best is not going to be there." Said gymnast Bart Conner: "I hurt for the Soviet athletes."

THE GAMES GO ON

The boycott raised serious doubts about the future of the Olympics. At the 1972 Games, eleven Israeli athletes had been killed by Palestinian terrorists in Munich, West Germany. In 1976, most African countries had boycotted the Games in Montreal. Then came the U.S.-led boycott in 1980. Now there was another boycott. How long could the Olympics go on?

The 1984 Summer Games opened in Los Angeles on July 28. Despite the boycott, there were more athletes (7,575) from more countries (140) than in any previous Olympics. And during the fifteen days of competition, there were many exciting moments. There was also fine weather, superb organization, and a true spirit of friendship among the athletes. One special bright spot was the first full-fledged participation by a team from China. The boycotting countries were missed, but by the night of the closing ceremonies, few people doubted that the Olympics would live on.

The Summer Games—Los Angeles, California

THE WINTER GAMES

The Games of the XIV Winter Olympiad were everything a Winter Olympics should be. Sarajevo, Yugoslavia, located in the scenic Dinaric Alps, hosted the pageant from February 7 to February 19, The colorful opening parade included more athletes (1,510) from more countries (49) than ever before. There were figure skaters from the United States and hockey players from the Soviet Union. But there were also skiers from Lebanon, Egypt, and Senegal.

The 1984 Games also represented the first time a Winter Olympics had been held in an Eastern European country. Sarajevo gave the Olympics a special character and unique cultural flavor. Athletes and spectators alike would remember the 1984 Winter Games for snow-covered evergreens, traditional Yugoslav costumes, mosques, minarets, narrow twisting streets, and a pointy-nosed wolf named Vucko—the official mascot.

And then, of course, there was the competition itself. On the ski slopes and trails, ice sheets and sled runs, there were all the surprises, disappointments, beauty, excitement, controversy, and plucky performances that one expects in a Winter Olympics. The Soviet Union won the most medals (25), but East Germany took the most golds (9). U.S. athletes earned eight medals overall, four of them gold. Canada won four medals, two of them gold.

Surprises on the Slopes. No sport on the Winter Olympic program attracts more interest than Alpine skiing. The competitions on Mt. Bjelašnica and Mt. Jahorina outside Sarajevo were delayed several days because of heavy snows and high winds. When the skies finally cleared, the sun shone on the American team. Five of the eight medals won by U.S. athletes were earned in Alpine ski races.

The first U.S. triumph came in the women's giant slalom. Debbie Armstrong, a 20-year-old newcomer, unexpectedly swept to victory. Teammate Christin Cooper took second place. It was the first time that U.S. skiers had ever won the gold and silver medals in one Olympic skiing event. Michela Figini of Switzerland won the women's downhill, and Paoletta Magoni of Italy took the women's slalom.

The U.S. men were even more surprising. They were shut out in the giant slalom, won by Max Julen of Switzerland, but then they came on strong. Bill Johnson, a brash 23-

Five of the eight medals won by U.S. athletes at the Winter Games were earned in the Alpine ski races. The first gold came in the women's giant slalom, when 20-year-old Debbie Armstrong unexpectedly swept to victory.

In the ice dancing event, figure skaters Jayne Torvill and Christopher Dean of Britain gave one of the most stunning performances of the entire Olympics.

year-old, charged down Bjelašnica to capture the downhill. It was the first time that an American had won a gold in that event. In fact, Johnson became the first American man ever to win an Olympic gold medal in Alpine skiing.

In the men's slalom, veteran ski twins Phil and Steve Mahre turned in remarkable performances. Phil won the gold medal, and Steve came in second.

Fabulous Figure Skaters. The other three medals won by U.S. athletes at Sarajevo came in figure skating. Scott Hamilton, the reigning world champion, was heavily favored to win the men's singles, and he did. In the women's singles, 19-year-old Rosalynn Sumners finished a close second to the graceful Katarina Witt of East Germany. And in pairs skating, the Soviet duo of Elena Valova and Oleg Vasiliev outpointed the U.S. brother-and-sister team of Kitty and Peter Carruthers.

Perhaps the most memorable performance of the 1984 Winter Games—and certainly the most beautiful—was by Jayne Torvill and Christopher Dean in ice dancing. In their final free-dance program, the British couple performed an imaginative interpretation of Ravel's *Bolero*. The judges gave them twelve perfect scores of 6.

Other Winter Winners. After the grand success of the U.S. Olympic hockey team in 1980, the American squad of 1984 was the focus of much attention and expectation. Although they skated hard, the young U.S. team ended up with a disappointing record of two wins, two losses, and two ties—not good enough to reach the final round. The real power in the tournament was the Soviet Union. The squad from the U.S.S.R. won every game impressively. It defeated a strong team from Czechoslovakia, 2–0, for the gold medal. Sweden defeated Canada, 2–0, for the bronze.

The speed skating competition produced some outstanding individual performances. On the women's side, Karin Enke of East Germany won two gold medals (1,000- and 1,500-meters) and two silvers (500- and 3,000-meters). On the men's side, Canada's Gaétan Boucher won two gold medals (1,000- and 1,500-meters) and one bronze (500-meters). Tomas Gustafson of Sweden won a gold in the 5,000-meter and a silver in the 10,000-meter. Igor Malkov of the Soviet Union won a gold in the 10,000-meter and a silver in the 5,000-meter.

The most individual gold medals by any athlete in Sarajevo went to a 28-year-old woman from Finland named Marja-Liisa

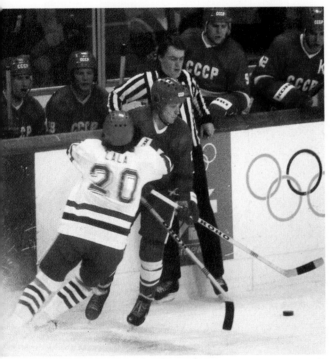

The squad from the Soviet Union (in red) took the gold medal in ice hockey, winning every game impressively.

Canadian speed skater Gaétan Boucher was an outstanding performer, winning two gold medals and one bronze.

Hamalainen. The tall cross-country skier pushed and slid her way to three victories—in the 5-, 10-, and 20-kilometer races. She also earned a bronze in the 20-kilometer relay, won by Norway.

The outstanding performers in ski jumping were Finland's Matti Nykaenen and East Germany's Jens Weissflog. Nykaenen won a gold in the 90-meter jump and a silver in the 70-meter jump. Weissflog, conversely, took the gold in the 70-meter and the silver in the 90-meter.

The bobsled competition featured some exciting runs at Trebević, as well as a controversial new sled introduced by the Soviets. Called the "shark" or "cigar" because of its streamlined shape, the new sled was expected to give the Soviets a slight advantage. It didn't work. East Germany won the gold and silver medals in both the two-man and four-man competitions. The Soviets managed only a bronze in the two-man. East Germany was also strong in the women's luge (small sled) event. Its team took all three medals, with Steffi Martin claiming the gold.

As the Olympic flame was extinguished and the athletes said *dovidjenja* (so long) to Sarajevo, viewers of the 1984 Winter Games could look back on an exciting and colorful two weeks. They could also look ahead to the 1988 Winter Games in Calgary, Canada.

FINAL MEDAL STANDINGS

Winter Games—Sarajevo, Yugoslavia

Country	Gold	Silver	Bronze	Total
Soviet Union	6	10	9	25
East Germany	9	9	6	24
Finland	4	3	6	13
Norway	3	2	4	9
United States	4	4	0	8
Sweden	4	2	2	8
Czechoslovakia	0	2	4	6
Switzerland	2	2	1	5
Canada	2	1	1	4
West Germany	2	1	1	4
France	0	1	2	3
Italy	2	0	0	2
Liechtenstein	0	0	2	2
Britain	1	0	0	1
Japan	0	1	0	1
Yugoslavia	0	1	0	1
Austria	0	0	1	1

THE SUMMER GAMES

The Summer Games of the XXIII Olympiad were held in Los Angeles, California, from July 28 to August 12, 1984. Medals were awarded in 221 events in 24 different sports. New to the Olympic program were synchronized swimming and rhythmic gymnastics, as well as several individual events in established sports. Also on display were two "exhibition" sports—baseball and tennis—in which no medals were awarded.

The various competitions were held at sites throughout southern California. The hub of all the activity was the L.A. Memorial Coliseum. This vast stadium had been built for the 1932 Olympics, also held in Los Angeles. Beautifully renovated, the Coliseum was the site of the lavish opening and closing ceremonies, as well as the track and field competition. For the first time ever, the entire Games were paid for by commercial sponsorships, television revenues, ticket sales, and other nonpublic sources. Los Angeles taxpayers did not have to add a cent.

Partly because of the absence of the Soviet Union, East Germany, and other boycotting countries, the United States won a record 83 gold medals and 174 medals overall. West Germany had a total of 59 medals, including 17 gold. Rumania had 53 medals, 20 of them gold. And Canada took 44 overall, 10 gold.

Track and Field. Track and field competition, the backbone of the Summer Games, featured 41 different events. In front of cheering crowds of nearly 100,000, the host U.S. team took first place in 16 of the events.

Perhaps the most outstanding performer of the entire Summer Games was 23-year-old Carl Lewis of the United States. Lewis equaled the historic feat of Jesse Owens in 1936 by winning gold medals in four events —the 100-meter dash, the 200-meter dash, the long jump, and the 400-meter relay. Another star of the U.S. men's track team was hurdler Edwin Moses. The most difficult Olympic moment for Moses probably came in the Games' opening ceremonies. Taking the official oath on behalf of all the athletes, Moses momentarily forgot the words. When it came to running, however, Moses didn't forget his winning ways. His victory in the 400-meter hurdles was his 105th in a row!

American runner Carl Lewis equaled the historic feat of Jesse Owens in 1936 by winning golds in four events.

157

Maricica Puica of Rumania won the gold in the 3,000-meter, after the two favorites in the race collided.

Britain had two outstanding performers in men's track and field. Daley Thompson scored 8,797 points in the decathlon—a new Olympic record and one point less than the world record—to take his second consecutive gold medal in that event. Countryman Sebastian Coe also repeated his gold-medal performance of 1980 by winning the 1,500-meter. In addition, Coe took a silver medal in the 800-meter, finishing behind surprise winner Joaquim Cruz of Brazil. Another surprise winner was 37-year-old Carlos Lopes of Portugal, who outlasted the field to win the men's marathon.

In women's track and field, the marathon and the 3,000-meter run were held for the first time in an Olympics. In the marathon, U.S. runner Joan Benoit ran strongly for all 26 miles, 385 yards and won easily. In the 3,000-meter, Maricica Puica of Rumania won the gold. The two favorites in the race, Mary Decker of the United States and Zola Budd of Britain, collided halfway through.

The big medal winner in women's track was American Valerie Brisco-Hooks. She took three golds—in the 200-meter dash, the 400-meter run, and the 1,600-meter relay. Another American, Evelyn Ashford, earned the title "fastest woman in the world" by winning the 100-meter dash. Ashford also earned a gold in the 400-meter relay.

Swimming and Diving. The U.S. team found even more gold in the newly built pool at the University of Southern California. American swimmers touched first in 20 of 29 swim races.

The U.S. women lost only three of fourteen races. Nancy Hogshead won a total of four medals, three of them gold—in the 100-meter freestyle (tied with Carrie Steinseifer), the 400-meter freestyle relay, and the 400-meter medley relay—and one silver, in the 200-meter individual medley. Mary T. Meagher, nicknamed "Madame Butterfly," won golds in the 100- and 200-meter butterflys, as well as the medley relay. And Tracy Caulkins earned golds in the 200- and 400-meter individual medleys, as well as the medley relay.

The American men were also dominant. Outstanding among them were triple gold medalists Rick Carey (100- and 200-meter backstrokes, 400-meter medley relay) and

Alex Baumann of Canada set two world records in winning the men's 200- and 400-meter individual medleys.

American Greg Louganis, winner of the springboard and platform events, was said to be the greatest diver ever.

Rowdy Gaines (100-meter freestyle, 400-meter medley relay, and 400-meter freestyle relay).

Perhaps the top male swimmer of all was 20-year-old Michael Gross of West Germany. Nicknamed "The Albatross" because of his wide armspan, Gross won two gold medals in world-record time (100-meter butterfly and 200-meter freestyle) and two silvers (200-meter butterfly and 800-meter freestyle relay).

The swimming competition was also a rich medal haul for the Canadian team. Canada hadn't won an Olympic gold medal in swimming since 1912. In 1984 it collected four golds, three silvers, and three bronzes. Alex Bauman set two world records in winning the men's 200- and 400-meter individual medleys. Victor Davis took the 200-meter breaststroke. And Anne Ottenbrite won the women's 200-meter breaststroke.

Synchronized swimming, new to the Olympic program, was yet another sport in which U.S. athletes excelled. The team of Candy Costie and Tracie Ruiz won the dual competition. And Ruiz also won the solo event.

Finally, the diving competition highlighted the talents of the 24-year-old American Greg

In the gymnastics competition, high-flying Li Ning of China was a great crowd pleaser. He won a total of five medals (three golds, one silver, and one bronze), including a tie for top honors in the rings.

Louganis. Said to be the greatest diver ever, Louganis far outpointed his nearest rivals in both the men's springboard and platform events. Sylvie Bernier of Canada won the women's springboard. And China's Zhou Jihong took the gold in platform. The acrobatic Chinese divers took a total of one gold, one silver, and one bronze medal.

Gymnastics. The gymnastics competition at Pauley Pavilion on the campus of UCLA treated spectators to exciting displays of beauty, grace, strength, balance, and daredevil stunts. And the competition was close.

For the first time in Olympic history, the U.S. men's team surprised everybody by winning the team competition. China won the silver medal, and Japan took the bronze. In the men's all-around competition, veteran Japanese gymnast Koji Gushiken edged out America's Peter Vidmar for the gold. China's Li Ning was third. When it came to individual apparatuses, however, it was the high-flying Li Ning who was most impressive. He won three gold medals and one silver.

In women's gymnastics, the show was stolen by a sprightly 16-year-old American named Mary Lou Retton. In a duel for the all-around gold with Ecaterina Szabo of Rumania, the powerful Retton scored a perfect 10 in the vault and emerged the winner. But Szabo, called the next Nadia Comaneci (the Rumanian star of the 1976 Olympics), led her country to victory in the team competition. Szabo also went on to win three gold medals in individual apparatuses.

In rhythmic gymnastics, a new Olympic event, Lori Fung of Canada came out on top.

Team Sports. The U.S. men's and women's basketball teams were both expected to win gold medals, and they did so in impressive fashion. The men, coached by Bobby

Knight, won their games by an average of 32 points and defeated Spain, 96–65, in the final. The women, coached by Pat Head Summitt, won their games by an average of 33 points and beat South Korea, 85–55, for the gold.

The success of the U.S. volleyball teams was more of a surprise. No American squad had ever won any medal in Olympic volleyball. In 1984, however, the U.S. men took the gold by defeating Brazil in the finals. The women also reached the championship match but were beaten by China for the gold.

The sixteen-team soccer tournament came down to a final matchup between France and Brazil. France won, 2–0, for the gold medal. Yugoslavia took the bronze.

Yugoslavia did even better in other team sports. Its men's squads won gold medals in both water polo (beating out a strong U.S. squad) and team handball. The Yugoslav women also earned the gold in team handball. Finally, in field hockey, the tradition-ally powerful team from Pakistan won the men's tournament, with the Netherlands coming out on top in women's play.

Other Sports. With speed, power, and precise punching, U.S. boxers won a total of nine gold medals in the twelve weight divisions. In freestyle wrestling, Americans won in seven of ten weight classes. Greco-Roman wrestling was more of an international affair, with wrestlers from eight different countries earning golds. China excelled in weight lifting, taking four golds. And in rowing, Rumanian women won five gold medals and one silver in six events; the eight men's races were won by eight different countries.

The 1984 Summer Olympic Games of Los Angeles were a celebration of athletic excellence, friendly competition, and international co-operation. They gave promise for the future of the Olympic movement, and everyone could look forward with confidence to the 1988 Summer Games in Seoul, South Korea.

In women's gymnastics, the show was stolen by 16-year-old Mary Lou Retton of the United States. She became the first American gymnast ever to win the individual all-around gold medal.

161

In women's volleyball, the team from China captured the gold. (Here, they are shown playing Brazil.)

FINAL MEDAL STANDINGS

Summer Games—Los Angeles, California

Country	Gold	Silver	Bronze	Total	Country	Gold	Silver	Bronze	Total
United States	83	61	30	174	Portugal	1	0	2	3
West Germany	17	19	23	59	Jamaica	0	1	2	3
Rumania	20	16	17	53	Norway	0	1	2	3
Canada	10	18	16	44	Turkey	0	0	3	3
Britain	5	10	22	37	Venezuela	0	0	3	3
China	15	8	9	32	Morocco	2	0	0	2
Italy	14	6	12	32	Kenya	1	0	1	2
Japan	10	8	14	32	Greece	0	1	1	2
France	5	7	15	27	Nigeria	0	1	1	2
Australia	4	8	12	24	Puerto Rico	0	1	1	2
South Korea	6	6	7	19	Algeria	0	0	2	2
Sweden	2	11	6	19	Pakistan	1	0	0	1
Yugoslavia	7	4	7	18	Colombia	0	1	0	1
Netherlands	5	2	6	13	Egypt	0	1	0	1
Finland	4	3	6	13	Ireland	0	1	0	1
New Zealand	8	1	2	11	Ivory Coast	0	1	0	1
Brazil	1	5	2	8	Peru	0	1	0	1
Switzerland	0	4	4	8	Syria	0	1	0	1
Mexico	2	3	1	6	Thailand	0	1	0	1
Denmark	0	3	3	6	Cameroon	0	0	1	1
Spain	1	2	2	5	Dom. Republic	0	0	1	1
Belgium	1	1	2	4	Iceland	0	0	1	1
Austria	1	1	1	3	Taiwan	0	0	1	1
					Zambia	0	0	1	1

1984 OLYMPIC GOLD MEDAL WINNERS

WINTER GAMES—SARAJEVO, YUGOSLAVIA

Biathlon
10-km: Eirik Kvalfoss, Norway
20-km: Peter Angerer, W. Germany
30-km Relay: U.S.S.R.

Bobsledding
Two-Man: East Germany
Four-Man: East Germany

Hockey
Team: U.S.S.R.

Luge
Men's Singles: Paul Hildgartner, Italy
Women's Singles: Steffi Martin, E. Germany
Men's Doubles: West Germany

Figure Skating
Men's Singles: Scott Hamilton, U.S.
Women's Singles: Katarina Witt, E. Germany
Pairs: Elena Valova/Oleg Vasiliev, U.S.S.R.
Dance: Jayne Torvill/Christopher Dean, Britain

Speed Skating, Men
500-m: Sergei Fokichev, U.S.S.R.
1,000-m: Gaétan Boucher, Canada
1,500-m: Gaétan Boucher, Canada
5,000-m: Tomas Gustafson, Sweden
10,000-m: Igor Malkov, U.S.S.R.

Speed Skating, Women
500-m: Christa Rothenburger, E. Germany
1,000-m: Karin Enke, E. Germany
1,500-m: Karin Enke, E. Germany
3,000-m: Andrea Schöne, E. Germany

Alpine Skiing, Men
Downhill: Bill Johnson, U.S.
Giant Slalom: Max Julen, Switzerland
Slalom: Phil Mahre, U.S.

Alpine Skiing, Women
Downhill: Michela Figini, Switzerland
Giant Slalom: Debbie Armstrong, U.S.
Slalom: Paoletta Magoni, Italy

Nordic Skiing, Men
15-km Cross-Country: Gunde Svan, Sweden
30-km Cross-Country: Nikolai Zimyatov, U.S.S.R.
50-km Cross-Country: Thomas Wassberg, Sweden
40-km Cross-Country Relay: Sweden
70-m Jump: Jens Weissflog, E. Germany
90-m Jump: Matti Nykaenen, Finland
Combined: Tom Sandberg, Norway

Nordic Skiing, Women
5-km Cross-Country: Marja-Liisa Hamalainen, Finland
10-km Cross-Country: Marja-Liisa Hamalainen, Finland
20-km Cross-Country: Marja-Liisa Hamalainen, Finland
20-km Cross-Country Relay: Norway

SUMMER GAMES—LOS ANGELES, CALIFORNIA

Archery
Men: Darrell Pace, U.S.
Women: Hyang-Soon Seo, S. Korea

Basketball
Men: United States
Women: United States

Boxing
Light Flyweight: Paul Gonzales, U.S.
Flyweight: Steve McCrory, U.S.
Bantamweight: Maurizio Stecca, Italy
Featherweight: Meldrick Taylor, U.S.
Lightweight: Pernell Whitaker, U.S.
Light Welterweight: Jerry Page, U.S.
Welterweight: Mark Breland, U.S.
Light Middleweight: Frank Tate, U.S.
Middleweight: Joon-Sup Shin, S. Korea
Light Heavyweight: Anton Josipovic, Yugoslavia
Heavyweight: Henry Tillman, U.S.
Super Heavyweight: Tyrell Biggs, U.S.

Canoeing, Men
500-m Kayak Singles: Ian Ferguson, New Zealand
500-m Kayak Doubles: New Zealand
1,000-m Kayak Singles: Alan Thompson, New Zealand
1,000-m Kayak Doubles: Canada
1,000-m Kayak Fours: New Zealand
500-m Canoe Singles: Larry Cain, Canada
500-m Canoe Doubles: Yugoslavia
1,000-m Canoe Singles: Ulrich Eicke, W. Germany
1,000-m Canoe Doubles: Rumania

Canoeing, Women
500-m Kayak Singles: Agneta Andersson, Sweden
500-m Kayak Doubles: Sweden
500-m Kayak Fours: Rumania

Cycling
Pursuit: Steve Hegg, U.S.
Team Pursuit: Australia
Sprint: Mark Gorski, U.S.
Points Race: Roger Ilegems, Belgium

Time Trial: Fredy Schmidtke, W. Germany
Road Team Trial: Italy
Road Race, men: Alexi Grewal, U.S.
Road Race, women: Connie Carpenter, U.S.

Equestrian
3-Day Event: Mark Todd, New Zealand
Team 3-Day Event: United States
Dressage: Reiner Klimke, W. Germany
Team Dressage: West Germany
Jumping: Joe Fargis, U.S.
Team Jumping: United States

Fencing, Men
Epee: Philippe Boisse, France
Team Epee: West Germany
Foil: Mauro Numa, Italy
Team Foil: Italy
Saber: Jean-François Lamour, France
Team Saber: Italy

Fencing, Women
Foil: Luan Jujie, China
Team Foil: West Germany

Field Hockey
Men: Pakistan
Women: Netherlands

Gymnastics, Men
All-Around: Koji Gushiken, Japan
Team: United States
Floor Exercises: Li Ning, China
Horizontal Bar: Shinji Morisue, Japan
Parallel Bars: Bart Conner, U.S.
Rings: Koji Gushiken, Japan, and Li Ning, China (tie)
Side Horse: Li Ning, China, and Peter Vidmar, U.S. (tie)
Vault: Lou Yun, China

Gymnastics, Women
All-Around: Mary Lou Retton, U.S.
Team: Rumania
Balance Beam: Simona Pauca, Rumania, and Ecaterina Szabo, Rumania (tie)
Floor Exercises: Ecaterina Szabo, Rumania
Uneven Parallel Bars: Ma Yanhong, China, and Julie McNamara, U.S. (tie)
Vault: Ecaterina Szabo, Rumania
Rhythmic: Lori Fung, Canada

Handball
Men: Yugoslavia
Women: Yugoslavia

Judo
Extra Lightweight: Shinji Hosokawa, Japan
Half Lightweight: Yoshiyuki Matsuoka, Japan
Lightweight: Byeong-Keun Ahn, S. Korea
Half Middleweight: Frank Wieneke, W. Germany
Middleweight: Peter Seisenbacher, Austria
Half Heavyweight: Hyoung-Zoo Ha, S. Korea

Heavyweight: Hitoshi Saito, Japan
Open: Yasuhiro Yamashita, Japan

Modern Pentathlon
Individual: Daniele Masala, Italy
Team: Italy

Rowing, Men
Single Sculls: Pertti Karppinen, Finland
Double Sculls: United States
Quadruple Sculls: West Germany
Coxed Pairs: Italy
Coxless Pairs: Rumania
Coxed Fours: Britain
Coxless Fours: New Zealand
Eights: Canada

Rowing, Women
Single Sculls: Valeria Racila, Rumania
Double Sculls: Rumania
Quadruple Sculls: Rumania
Coxless Pairs: Rumania
Coxed Fours: Rumania
Eights: United States

Shooting, Men
Free Pistol: Xu Haifeng, China
Rapid-Fire Pistol: Takeo Kamachi, Japan
Air Rifle: Philippe Heberle, France
English Small-Bore Rifle: Ed Etzel, U.S.
Small-Bore Rifle, 3 Positions: Malcolm Cooper, Britain
Rifle, Running Game Target: Li Yuwei, China
Shotgun, Clay Target Trap: Luciano Giovannetti, Italy
Shotgun, Skeetshooting: Matthew Dryke, U.S.

Shooting, Women
Sport Pistol: Linda Thom, Canada
Air Rifle: Pat Spurgin, U.S.
Small-Bore Rifle, 3 Positions: Wu Xiaoxuan, China

Soccer
France

Swimming and Diving, Men
100-m Backstroke: Rick Carey, U.S.
200-m Backstroke: Rick Carey, U.S.
100-m Breaststroke: Steve Lundquist, U.S.
200-m Breaststroke: Victor Davis, Canada
100-m Butterfly: Michael Gross, W. Germany
200-m Butterfly: Jon Sieben, Australia
100-m Freestyle: Rowdy Gaines, U.S.
200-m Freestyle: Michael Gross, W. Germany
400-m Freestyle: George DiCarlo, U.S.
400-m Freestyle Relay: United States
800-m Freestyle Relay: United States
1,500-m Freestyle: Michael O'Brien, U.S.
200-m Individual Medley: Alex Baumann, Canada
400-m Individual Medley: Alex Baumann, Canada
400-m Medley Relay: United States
Platform Diving: Greg Louganis, U.S.
Springboard Diving: Greg Louganis, U.S.

Swimming and Diving, Women

100-m Backstroke: Theresa Andrews, U.S.
200-m Backstroke: Jolanda De Rover, Netherlands
100-m Breaststroke: Petra Van Staveren, Netherlands
200-m Breaststroke: Anne Ottenbrite, Canada
100-m Butterfly: Mary T. Meagher, U.S.
200-m Butterfly: Mary T. Meagher, U.S.
100-m Freestyle: Nancy Hogshead and
Carrie Steinseifer, U.S. (tie)
200-m Freestyle: Mary Wayte, U.S.
400-m Freestyle: Tiffany Cohen, U.S.
400-m Freestyle Relay: United States
800-m Freestyle: Tiffany Cohen, U.S.
200-m Individual Medley: Tracy Caulkins, U.S.
400-m Individual Medley: Tracy Caulkins, U.S.
400-m Medley Relay: United States
Synchronized, solo: Tracie Ruiz, U.S.
Synchronized, duet: United States
Platform Diving: Zhou Jihong, China
Springboard Diving: Sylvie Bernier, Canada

Track and Field, Men

100-m Dash: Carl Lewis, U.S.
200-m Dash: Carl Lewis, U.S.
400-m Run: Alonzo Babers, U.S.
400-m Relay: United States
800-m Run: Joaquim Cruz, Brazil
1,500-m Run: Sebastian Coe, Britain
1,600-m Relay: United States
5,000-m Run: Said Aouita, Morocco
10,000-m Run: Alberto Cova, Italy
20-km Walk: Ernesto Canto, Mexico
50-km Walk: Raul Gonzalez, Mexico
100-m Hurdles: Roger Kingdom, U.S.
400-m Hurdles: Edwin Moses, U.S.
3,000-m Steeplechase: Julius Korir, Kenya
Marathon: Carlos Lopes, Portugal
Discus: Rolf Danneberg, W. Germany
Hammer Throw: Juha Tiainen, Finland
High Jump: Dietmar Mogenburg, W. Germany
Javelin: Arto Haerkoenen, Finland
Long Jump: Carl Lewis, U.S.
Pole Vault: Pierre Quinon, France
Shot Put: Alessandro Andrei, Italy
Triple Jump: Al Joyner, U.S.
Decathlon: Daley Thompson, Britain

Track and Field, Women

100-m Dash: Evelyn Ashford, U.S.
200-m Dash: Valerie Brisco-Hooks, U.S.
400-m Run: Valerie Brisco-Hooks, U.S.
400-m Relay: United States
800-m Run: Doina Melinte, Rumania
1,500-m Run: Gabriella Dorio, Italy
1,600-m Relay: United States
3,000-m Run: Maricica Puica, Rumania
100-m Hurdles: Benita Brown-Fitzgerald, U.S.
400-m Hurdles: Nawal El Moutawakel, Morocco

Marathon: Joan Benoit, U.S.
Discus: Ria Stalman, Netherlands
Heptathlon: Glynis Nunn, Australia
High Jump: Ulrike Meyfarth, W. Germany
Javelin: Tessa Sanderson, Britain
Long Jump: Anisoara Stanciu, Rumania
Shot Put: Claudia Losch, W. Germany

Volleyball

Men: United States
Women: China

Water Polo

Team: Yugoslavia

Weight Lifting

Flyweight: Zeng Guoqiang, China
Bantamweight: Wu Shude, China
Featherweight: Chen Weiqiang, China
Lightweight: Yao Jingyuan, China
Middleweight: Karl-Heinz Radschinsky, W. Germany
Light Heavyweight: Petre Becheru, Rumania
Middle Heavyweight: Nicu Vlad, Rumania
Heavyweight: Rolf Milser, W. Germany
Second Heavyweight: Norberto Oberburger, Italy
Super Heavyweight: Dinko Lukim, Australia

Wrestling, Freestyle

Paperweight: Robert Weaver, U.S.
Flyweight: Saban Trstena, Yugoslavia
Bantamweight: Hideaki Tomiyama, Japan
Featherweight: Randy Lewis, U.S.
Lightweight: In-Tak You, S. Korea
Welterweight: Dave Schultz, U.S.
Middleweight: Mark Schultz, U.S.
Light Heavyweight: Ed Banach, U.S.
Heavyweight: Lou Banach, U.S.
Super Heavyweight: Bruce Baumgartner, U.S.

Wrestling, Greco-Roman

Paperweight: Vicenzo Maenza, Italy
Flyweight: Atsuji Miyahara, Japan
Bantamweight: Pasquale Passarelli, W. Germany
Featherweight: Weon-Kee Kim, S. Korea
Lightweight: Vlado Lisjak, Yugoslavia
Welterweight: Jouko Salomaki, Finland
Middleweight: Ion Draica, Rumania
Light Heavyweight: Steven Fraser, U.S.
Heavyweight: Vasile Andrei, Rumania
Super Heavyweight: Jeff Blatnick, U.S.

Yachting

Finn: Russell Coutts, New Zealand
Flying Dutchman: United States
470: Spain
Soling: United States
Star: United States
Tornado: New Zealand
Windglider: Stephan Van Den Berg, Netherlands

OLYMPIC MOMENTS

For the young men and women who take part in the Olympics, the Games provide memorable experiences. Some athletes find triumph, others disappointment. Some muster courage they never knew they had, others have plain bad luck. In 1984, the Winter and Summer Games showcased some special moments in the lives of special people.

MILES OF COURAGE

Joan Benoit of the United States won the women's marathon in Los Angeles, but 43 other runners completed the 26-mile, 385-yard course. One of them gave a moving display of courage.

About 20 minutes after Benoit had crossed the finish line, 29-year-old Gabriela Andersen-Schiess of Switzerland entered the Los Angeles Coliseum for the final yards of the race. She had only one lap to go, but she was near physical breakdown. Suffering from heat exhaustion, she wobbled down the track like a newborn colt learning to walk. Doctors, aides, and officials trailed behind, wondering whether to stop her. But with the crowd yelling encouragement, Andersen-Schiess continued around the track, dazed. Finally, she collapsed across the finish line into the arms of a team of doctors. She finished in 37th place, but she had accomplished her goal. (Within hours after the race, Andersen-Schiess was well and back on her feet.)

THE DECKER-BUDD AFFAIR

The showdown had been building for months: Mary Decker versus Zola Budd in the women's 3,000-meter run.

At age 26, Mary Decker of the United States was a veteran distance runner. She held many championships and records, but injuries and other problems had kept her from participating in previous Olympics. Now in 1984 she felt ready to win a gold medal.

Zola Budd was 18. Weighing only 82 pounds and running in bare feet, she looked like a little girl searching the neighborhood for her dog. But Zola Budd was a record-holding distance runner. She grew up in South Africa, a country that isn't allowed at the Olympics because of its racial policies. As a young girl, she had a poster of her idol, Mary Decker, over her bed. In early 1984, Budd became a British citizen and made plans to run in her first Olympics.

In pain and frustration, Mary Decker watches the other runners continue after her collision in the 3,000-meter run.

The day of the 3,000-meter finals, everybody was talking about Decker versus Budd. Halfway through the race, Decker was in the lead. Then the barefoot Budd moved in front. It all happened in a second. Decker's spikes caught Budd's heel, and their legs got tangled. Decker fell and couldn't get up. Budd ran on, but she was too upset to concentrate. She finished seventh.

After the race, Decker said the accident had been Budd's fault. Budd said she was sorry but didn't think she had been responsible. No matter who was at fault, it was a sad moment in the careers of two fine runners.

BROTHERS

Several events in the 1984 Summer and Winter Games could have been called "family affairs." In freestyle wrestling, for example, two pairs of American brothers grappled their way to victory. In the welterweight class, 25-year-old Dave Schultz defeated a West German wrestler for the gold medal. The next day, his 24-year-old brother, Mark, equaled the accomplishment by defeating a Japanese middleweight in the finals. Meanwhile, a burly set of twins was working on its own family affair. Ed Banach outpointed a Japanese foe in the light heavyweight finals. Then brother Lou pinned a Syrian opponent for the heavyweight title.

In the Winter Games, men's slalom skiing featured 26-year-old twins Phil and Steve Mahre. Phil, a three-time World Cup champion and in his last season, twisted and slashed his way to a surprise gold medal. Not far behind was brother Steve, who took the silver. All in all, it was a great day for the Mahre family. As he left for the medal ceremony, Phil learned that his wife had just given birth to a baby boy.

STICK-TO-ITIVENESS

What do a super-heavyweight wrestler and a skier from Egypt have in common? The answer is stick-to-itiveness, an unwillingness to give up.

The headline in one newspaper called him "Battlin' Blatnick." It was referring to 6'4", 248-pound Greco-Roman wrestler Jeff Blatnick. The 27-year-old giant had beaten the best super heavyweights in the world to win the gold medal. But his real battle had been fought long before the Olympics even

The Mahre twins—Phil and Steve—capped brilliant careers by finishing one-two in the Olympic slalom.

started. In 1981, Blatnick learned that he had Hodgkin's disease, a form of cancer. He underwent surgery and radiation therapy. Then he began his difficult comeback. He trained long and hard, slowly building himself up. After many months he was ready for the Olympics. When his final match was over, the massive wrestler was so overcome with emotion that he broke down and cried in a TV interview. Everyone shared his joy. Blatnick was chosen to carry the U.S. flag in the Games' closing ceremony.

The Egyptian "team" at the Sarajevo Winter Games had only one member. He was 18-year-old skier Jamil el-Reedy. El-Reedy knew he wouldn't win any medals, but he was determined to do his best. To toughen himself up for the competition, he lived in a desert cave for 40 days. On the snow-covered mountains of Yugoslavia, however, el-Reedy had problems. He fell in the giant slalom, and then again in the downhill. In the downhill, he climbed back on his skis and finished the race. His time was a full two minutes slower than that of the winner. But el-Reedy was still not ready to give up. "I'll try again in 1988," he vowed.

BASEBALL

"Wire to wire" is a term used in horse racing when one horse leads a race from the very start all the way to the finish line. In 1984 the term was also used to describe the run by the Detroit Tigers for the championship of major league baseball.

The Tigers opened the season by winning their first 9 games and 35 of their first 40—a record. That gave them a huge lead in the American League Eastern Division, and they never looked back. They completed the 162-game season with 104 victories, good enough for a fifteen-game margin in their division. Then, in the league Championship Series, they won three straight from the Kansas City Royals to claim the pennant. And, finally, in the World Series, they defeated the San Diego Padres, 4 games to 1, to become the champions.

In leading all the way, the Tigers matched the achievement of the legendary 1927 New York Yankees (Babe Ruth, Lou Gehrig, &

Co.). In doing so, the Tigers' George ("Sparky") Anderson became the first manager to win the World Series with a team in each league. (He had won with Cincinnati in 1975 and 1976.)

All year long Anderson made the most of a well-balanced roster. Alan Trammell played a superior shortstop and posted the club's highest batting average, .314. Catcher Lance Parrish had 33 home runs and 98 runs batted in (RBI's), and outfielder Kirk Gibson had 27 homers and 91 RBI's. Three starting pitchers were models of consistency: Jack Morris (19–11), Dan Petry (18–8), and Milt Wilcox (17–8). And perhaps the best of all were bull-pen hurlers Aurelio Lopez and Willie Hernandez. The right-handed Lopez (10–1) had 14 saves and a 2.94 ERA. The left-handed Hernandez (9–3) appeared in 80 games, had 32 saves in 33 opportunities, and posted a 1.92 ERA. After the season, Hernandez was named Most Valuable Player

Alan Trammell of the Detroit Tigers was honored as Most Valuable Player in the World Series. The hard-hitting shortstop cracked two home runs in Game 4 and batted .450 overall, with 6 RBI's.

(MVP) in the American League, as well as the winner of the Cy Young Award as the league's top pitcher.

The Tigers' pitching staff was awesome in the American League playoffs. Morris, Petry, and Wilcox turned back the Royals by scores of 8–1, 5–3 (11 innings), and 1–0 respectively; Hernandez relieved in all three contests, and Lopez in one.

In the National League, San Diego played the Chicago Cubs for the pennant. The Padres had finished on top of the Western Division for the first time in the team's sixteen-year existence. The Cubs, who hadn't reached the World Series since 1945, delighted their long-suffering fans by winning the Eastern Division. Chicago continued its heroics in the first two games of the National League Championship Series, winning 13–0 and 4–2. But the Padres just wouldn't give up. They won the next three games—7–1, 7–5, and 6–3—to become the first National League team ever to recover from a 0–2 deficit in the playoffs.

The first two games of the World Series were played in San Diego. In the first game, Detroit's Morris was the winning pitcher in a close 3–2 decision—a two-run homer by outfielder Larry Herndon in the fifth inning provided the margin of victory. The Padres responded with a 5–3 triumph in the second game, overcoming an early three-run Tiger lead—a three-run homer by Padre designated hitter Kurt Bevacqua gave the winning edge.

But that was the last hurrah for San Diego. The series moved to Tiger Stadium, where the home team won three straight. In the third game, Padre hurlers walked eleven batters, as Detroit won 5–2. In the next game, Morris pitched his second complete game of the Series, and Trammell hit two, two-run homers for a 4–2 triumph. And in the finale, Gibson cracked a two-run homer and a three-run homer, as the Tigers roared to an 8–4 victory—and the world championship. Trammell, who had nine hits for a .450 average in the five games, was voted MVP of the Series.

After the season, disappointed Chicago Cub fans took some consolation in the voting for two important awards. Cub second baseman Ryne Sandberg was named MVP of the

Rick Sutcliffe (16–1) led the Chicago Cubs to a division title and won the National League Cy Young Award.

National League. And Cub right-hander Rick Sutcliffe won the Cy Young Award as the league's top pitcher.

In other highlights of the 1984 season, Pete Rose became only the second player to reach 4,000 career hits (Ty Cobb was the other); Reggie Jackson became only the thirteenth player to hit 500 career home runs; and Peter V. Ueberroth took over from Bowie Kuhn as baseball commissioner on October 1.

1984 WORLD SERIES RESULTS

		R	H	E	Winning/Losing Pitcher
1	San Diego	2	8	1	Mark Thurmond
	Detroit	3	8	0	Jack Morris
2	San Diego	5	11	0	Andy Hawkins
	Detroit	3	7	2	Dan Petry
3	Detroit	5	7	0	Milt Wilcox
	San Diego	2	10	0	Tim Lollar
4	Detroit	4	7	0	Jack Morris
	San Diego	2	5	2	Eric Show
5	Detroit	8	11	1	Aurelio Lopez
	San Diego	4	10	1	Andy Hawkins

Home team listed first, visiting team second

MAJOR LEAGUE BASEBALL FINAL STANDINGS

AMERICAN LEAGUE

Eastern Division

	W	L	Pct.	GB
*Detroit	104	58	.642	—
Toronto	89	73	.549	15
New York	87	75	.537	17
Boston	86	76	.531	18
Baltimore	85	77	.525	19
Cleveland	75	87	.463	29
Milwaukee	67	94	.416	36½

Western Division

	W	L	Pct.	GB
Kansas City	84	78	.519	—
California	81	81	.500	3
Minnesota	81	81	.500	3
Oakland	77	85	.475	7
Chicago	74	88	.457	10
Seattle	74	88	.457	10
Texas	69	92	.429	14½

NATIONAL LEAGUE

Eastern Division

	W	L	Pct.	GB
Chicago	96	65	.596	—
New York	90	72	.556	6½
St. Louis	84	78	.519	12½
Philadelphia	81	81	.500	15½
Montreal	78	83	.484	18
Pittsburgh	75	87	.463	21½

Western Division

	W	L	Pct.	GB
*San Diego	92	70	.568	—
Atlanta	80	82	.494	12
Houston	80	82	.494	12
Los Angeles	79	83	.488	13
Cincinnati	70	92	.432	22
San Francisco	66	96	.407	26

* pennant winners

MAJOR LEAGUE LEADERS

AMERICAN LEAGUE

Batting
(top 10 qualifiers)

	AB	H	Pct.
Mattingly, New York	603	207	.343
Winfield, New York	567	193	.340
Boggs, Boston	625	203	.325
Bell, Texas	552	174	.315
Trammell, Detroit	555	174	.314
Easler, Boston	601	188	.313
Hrbek, Minnesota	559	174	.311
Collins, Toronto	441	136	.308
Murray, Baltimore	588	180	.306
Ripken, Baltimore	641	195	.304

NATIONAL LEAGUE

Batting
(top 10 qualifiers)

	AB	H	Pct.
Gwynn, San Diego	606	213	.351
Lacy, Pittsburgh	474	152	.321
C. Davis, San Francisco	499	157	.315
Sandberg, Chicago	636	200	.314
Cruz, Houston	600	187	.312
Ray, Pittsburgh	555	173	.312
Hernandez, New York	550	171	.311
Cabell, Houston	436	135	.310
Raines, Montreal	622	192	.309
Guerrero, Los Angeles	535	162	.303

Pitching
(top qualifiers, based on percentage)

	W	L	Pct.
Alexander, Toronto	17	6	.739
Blyleven, Cleveland	19	7	.731
Petry, Detroit	18	8	.692
Wilcox, Detroit	17	8	.680
Niekro, New York	16	8	.667
Stieb, Toronto	16	8	.667

Pitching
(top qualifiers, based on percentage)

	W	L	Pct.
Sutcliffe, Chicago	16	1	.941
Dawley, Houston	11	4	.733
Soto, Cincinnati	18	7	.720
Pena, Los Angeles	12	6	.667
Gooden, New York	17	9	.654

Home Runs

	HR
Armas, Boston	43
Kingman, Oakland	35
Murphy, Oakland	33
Parrish, Detroit	33
Thornton, Cleveland	33

Home Runs

	HR
Murphy, Atlanta	36
Schmidt, Philadelphia	36
Carter, Montreal	27
Strawberry, New York	26
Cey, Chicago	25

LITTLE LEAGUE BASEBALL

Participating in its first Little League World Series, South Korea won the 1984 championship in convincing fashion. In the final game of the 38th annual tournament, the team from Seoul, South Korea, defeated Altamonte Springs, Florida, by a score of 6–2. The two runs scored by Altamonte Springs were the first ones given up by Seoul in their three games at the Williamsport, Pennsylvania, tournament.

Seoul's success ended a two-year winning streak by U.S. teams. Kirkland, Washington, won the tournament in 1982, and Marietta, Georgia, took the title in 1983. Prior to that, entries from Taiwan had won the series five years in a row. In 1984, the South Koreans earned their first trip to Williamsport by defeating Taiwan in the Far East regional playoff. Then in Williamsport, Seoul shut out Panama City, Panama (4–0), and Coquitlam, British Columbia, Canada (10–0). Altamonte Springs, meanwhile, advanced to the final by defeating Los Gatos, California (2–1), and Southport, Indiana (4–2).

A crowd of 35,000 spectators—as well as a national TV audience—watched the championship game at Williamsport. As it turned out, the youngsters from South Korea wrapped up the title in the first inning by scoring four runs. The U.S. team managed one run in the fourth inning on a double, a walk, and a single. Then Seoul added two more tallies in the fifth inning. And, finally, Altamonte Springs scored its second run in the sixth inning on a home run by Chris Radcliff. South Korea's pitchers, Dae Ik Cho and Myong Kwan Lee, gave up only four hits in the 6–2 victory.

The 1984 tournament also marked an important "first." Victoria Roche, a 12-year-old reserve outfielder for Brussels, Belgium, became the first girl ever to appear in a Little League World Series. Girls have played Little League baseball since 1974, but none had ever reached the Williamsport competition. In the fifth inning of Brussels' game against British Columbia, Victoria stepped to the plate as a pinch hitter. She walked.

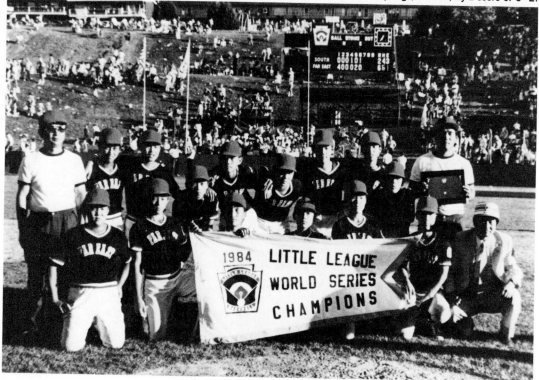

Little Leaguers from Seoul, South Korea, captured the 1984 World Series. They defeated the team from Altamonte Springs, Florida, by a score of 6–2.

BASKETBALL

The Boston Celtics have been one of the most successful teams in all professional sports. In 1984 they won their fifteenth National Basketball Association (NBA) championship. Led by star forward Larry Bird, the Celts defeated the Los Angeles Lakers 4 games to 3 in the playoff finals.

The championship series matchup came as no surprise. The Celtics (62–20) and the Lakers (54–28) had the NBA's best won-lost records during the regular season, and both were favored to survive the playoffs. Boston won the Eastern Conference by defeating Washington (3 games to 1), New York (4 games to 3), and Milwaukee (4 games to 1). Los Angeles breezed through the Western Conference by ousting Kansas City (3 games to 0), Dallas (4 games to 1), and Phoenix (4 games to 2).

What was unexpected was the bruising, roller coaster battle that developed in the coast-to-coast finals. Several times the talented Lakers were on the verge of taking complete control. They ran to a 115–109 victory in the opening game at the Boston Garden, and they were within 18 seconds of making it two straight on the Celtics' home court. But the Bostonians escaped that embarrassment when guard Gerald Henderson intercepted a Laker pass and made a layup for a 113–113 tie. The Celtics went on to win in overtime, 124–121, to even the series.

The fast-breaking Lakers were a blur in the third game, rolling to an impressive 137–104 triumph at the Los Angeles Forum. Earvin ("Magic") Johnson contributed 21 assists, 11 rebounds, and 14 points; 37-year-old center Kareem Abdul-Jabbar scored 24 points.

Few teams could have recovered from a 33-point trouncing, but the Celtics made another hairbreadth escape in the fourth game.

Star forward Larry Bird led the Boston Celtics to their 15th NBA championship. The Celts defeated the Los Angeles Lakers in the decisive seventh game of the playoff finals. Bird was named most valuable player of both the playoffs and the regular season.

NBA FINAL STANDINGS

EASTERN CONFERENCE
Atlantic Division

	W	L	Pct.
Boston	62	20	.756
Philadelphia	52	30	.634
New York	47	35	.573
New Jersey	45	37	.549
Washington	35	47	.427

Central Division

	W	L	Pct.
Milwaukee	50	32	.610
Detroit	49	33	.598
Atlanta	40	42	.488
Cleveland	28	54	.341
Chicago	27	55	.329
Indiana	26	56	.317

WESTERN CONFERENCE
Midwest Division

	W	L	Pct.
Utah	45	37	.549
Dallas	43	39	.524
Denver	38	44	.463
Kansas City	38	44	.463
San Antonio	37	45	.451
Houston	29	53	.354

Pacific Division

	W	L	Pct.
Los Angeles	54	28	.659
Portland	48	34	.585
Seattle	42	40	.512
Phoenix	41	41	.500
Golden State	37	45	.451
San Diego	30	52	.366

NBA Championship: Boston Celtics

COLLEGE BASKETBALL

Conference	Winner
Atlantic Coast	North Carolina (regular season) Maryland (tournament)
Big East	Georgetown
Big Eight	Oklahoma (regular season) Kansas (tournament)
Big Ten	Purdue, Illinois (tied)
Ivy League	Princeton
Metro	Louisville, Memphis State (tied, regular season) Memphis State (tournament)
Missouri Valley	Illinois State, Tulsa (tied, regular season) Tulsa (tournament)
Pacific Ten	Washington, Oregon State (tied)
Southeastern	Kentucky
Southwest	Houston
Western Athletic	Texas-El Paso

NCAA: Georgetown

NIT: Michigan

This time the Lakers were only 56 seconds away from victory. Again the Celtics stole a key pass, forced the game into overtime, and went on to victory, 129–125. The fabulous Bird—who won most valuable player (MVP) honors for both the playoffs and the regular season—scored 29 points and collected 21 rebounds. Another Celt star was Dennis Johnson, who had 22 points and did an extraordinary job guarding the Lakers' Magic Johnson.

In the fifth game, at the Boston Garden, where the temperature was nearly 100°F, the Lakers wilted and the Celtics took the series lead. They outscored Los Angeles by 16 points in the second half and won 121–103.

The roller coaster returned to Los Angeles for the sixth game, and the Lakers rallied. Facing a 84–73 deficit in the second half, they surged to a 119–108 victory and a 3–3 tie in the series.

In the seventh-game showdown in Boston, the strong Celtics prevailed over the swift Lakers. The visitors pulled within 3 points late in the game, but the Celtics' aggressive rebounding and defense carried them to a 111–102 triumph. It was the eighth time that the Celtics had faced the Lakers in the finals and the eighth time they had won.

A highlight of the season came on April 5, when Jabbar of the Lakers surpassed Wilt Chamberlain's career scoring record of 31,419 points.

College Play. The winner of the pressure-packed National Collegiate Athletic Association (NCAA) tournament is never easy to predict. In 1984 it was the Georgetown University Hoyas. Coached by John Thompson, led by 7-foot center Pat Ewing, and with enough talented players for two good teams, the Hoyas finished with a 34–3 record and won their first national title. In the championship game, Georgetown defeated the University of Houston Cougars, 84–75. The Cougars, led by their own awesome center, Akeem Olajuwon, had reached the title match for the second year in a row.

In the National Invitation Tournament (NIT), Michigan beat Notre Dame, 83–63, for the championship. And the University of Southern California captured its second straight NCAA women's crown with a 72–61 victory over Tennessee.

FOOTBALL

The Los Angeles Raiders and the Washington Redskins went at each other in Super Bowl XVIII on January 22, 1984, and what was expected to be a slugfest turned into a rout. Before some 73,000 fans at Tampa Stadium in Tampa, Florida, the Raiders racked up a 38–9 victory. The Raiders' 38 points were the most ever scored in a Super Bowl, and their 29-point winning margin was also a Super Bowl record.

Leading the way for the Raiders was crack running back Marcus Allen. He rushed for 191 yards, breaking the year-old Super Bowl record of 166 yards set by Redskin John Riggins. In 1984, the Raider defense held Riggins to 64 yards. Allen, who was named the game's most valuable player, scored two touchdowns, one of which came on the longest run from scrimmage in Super Bowl history—74 yards.

Other Raider stars included Derrick Jensen, who blocked a Redskin punt and then fell on the ball in the end zone for a touchdown; and Jack Squirek, who intercepted one of Redskin quarterback Joe Theismann's passes and returned it for a touchdown. The fifth Raider touchdown came on a 13-yard pass from quarterback Jim Plunkett to wide receiver Cliff Branch.

THE UNITED STATES FOOTBALL LEAGUE

Pro football's newest league—the United States Football League—had its second season in 1984. Fans continued to show interest in the league's February-through-July schedule. But the championship game, though played in the same stadium as was the National Football League's Super Bowl, drew some 20,000 fewer fans than the Raider-Redskin contest.

The championship game, played on July 15, matched the Philadelphia Stars and the Arizona Wranglers. The Stars, who had lost the 1983 championship game to the Michigan Panthers, thoroughly outclassed their opponents, winning 23–3. A strong rushing game was one of the Stars' weapons. The attack was led by Kelvin Bryant's 115 yards on 29 carries, including a 4-yard touchdown run. Quarterback Chuck Fusina's arm was another potent weapon, as he completed his first 10 passes and 12 of 17 overall for 158 yards. Fusina was named the game's most valuable player. The Stars also shone on defense, frustrating the Wranglers' drives and limiting them to one field goal.

THE NFL REGULAR SEASON

During the 1984 regular season in the Na-

Miami quarterback Dan Marino (*left*) and Chicago running back Walter Payton (*right*) set new records in 1984.

tional Football League (NFL), two teams dominated the standings. The San Francisco 49ers easily led the National Conference Western Division, entering the playoffs with a superb 15–1 record. Nearly as superb were the Miami Dolphins, who topped the American Conference Eastern Division with a 14–2 mark.

The other division titlists were Pittsburgh (9–7) and Denver (13–3) in the American Conference; and Washington (11–5) and Chicago (10–6) in the National Conference. The American Conference wild-card playoff teams were Seattle (12–4) and the Los Angeles Raiders (11–5). In the National Conference, the wild-card teams were the Los Angeles Rams (10–6) and the New York Giants (9–7).

Two of the NFL's premier running backs set important records during the season. Chicago's Walter Payton broke Jim Brown's career rushing mark of 12,312 yards. Payton finished the season with 13,309. And Eric Dickerson of the Los Angeles Rams rushed for 2,105 yards, exceeding O. J. Simpson's one-season mark of 2,003. No less outstanding was Dan Marino of Miami, who became the first quarterback to pass for more than 5,000 yards in a single season, finishing with 5,084. He also set a season record of 48 touchdown passes, breaking the record of 36 shared by George Blanda and Y. A. Tittle. Finally, Art Monk of Washington caught 106 passes, breaking Charlie Hennigan's one-season mark of 101.

THE CANADIAN FOOTBALL LEAGUE

It had been 22 years since the Winnipeg Blue Bombers had last won the Grey Cup, the symbol of the championship of the Canadian Football League. In the 1984 Grey Cup game, played in Edmonton, Alberta, the Blue Bombers decided that a 22-year wait was long enough. They trounced the Hamilton Tiger-Cats, 47–17. The score was even more remarkable in light of the fact that the Blue Bombers were behind early in the game by a score of 17–3. Tom Clements, the Winnipeg quarterback, was tabbed as the game's most valuable player.

COLLEGE PLAY

Only one major college team went undefeated through the entire regular schedule:

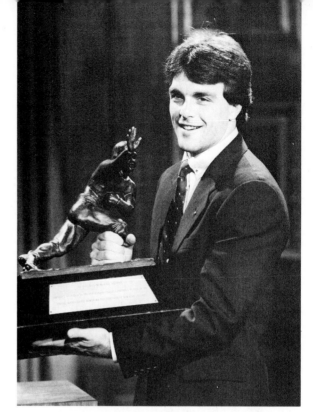

Boston College quarterback Doug Flutie won the 1984 Heisman Trophy, as the best collegiate player.

Brigham Young University (BYU) finished 12–0–0. Fittingly, BYU was ranked number one. Prior to the season-ending bowl games, the University of Oklahoma (9–1–1) was ranked second. Ranked third in one poll was the University of Florida (9–1–1), and in another poll, the University of Washington (10–1–0).

Quarterback Doug Flutie of Boston College won the Heisman Trophy. In doing so, he broke a twelve-year string during which only running backs had won college football's highest individual honor. Flutie became the first quarterback to pass for more than 10,000 yards in a college career—his four-year total was 10,579. In 1984 alone, he completed 233 of 386 passes for 3,454 yards and 27 touchdowns.

Oklahoma met Washington in the Orange Bowl; Louisiana State (8–2–1) faced Nebraska (9–2–0) in the Sugar Bowl; Ohio State (9–2–0) took on Southern California (8–3–0) in the Rose Bowl; Houston (7–4–0) vied with Boston College (9–2–0) in the Cotton Bowl; and South Carolina (10–1–0) played Oklahoma State (9–2–0) in the Gator Bowl.

USFL FINAL STANDINGS

EASTERN CONFERENCE

Atlantic Division

	W	L	T	Pct.	PF	PA
Philadelphia	16	2	0	.889	479	225
New Jersey	14	4	0	.778	430	412
Pittsburgh	3	15	0	.167	259	379
Washington	3	15	0	.167	270	492

Southern Division

	W	L	T	Pct.	PF	PA
Birmingham	14	4	0	.778	539	316
Tampa Bay	14	4	0	.778	498	347
New Orleans	8	10	0	.444	348	395
Memphis	7	11	0	.389	320	455
Jacksonville	6	12	0	.333	327	455

WESTERN CONFERENCE

Central Division

	W	L	T	Pct.	PF	PA
Houston	13	5	0	.722	618	400
Michigan	10	8	0	.556	400	382
San Antonio	7	11	0	.389	309	325
Oklahoma	6	12	0	.333	251	459
Chicago	5	13	0	.278	340	456

Pacific Division

	W	L	T	Pct.	PF	PA
Los Angeles	10	8	0	.556	338	373
Arizona	10	8	0	.556	502	284
Denver	9	9	0	.500	356	413
Oakland	7	11	0	.389	242	348

USFL Championship: Philadelphia Stars

COLLEGE FOOTBALL

Conference	Winner
Atlantic Coast	Maryland
Big Eight	Oklahoma
Big Ten	Ohio State
Pacific Coast	Nevada—Las Vegas
Pacific Ten	Southern California
Southeastern	Florida
Southwest	Southern Methodist
Western Athletic	Brigham Young

Cotton Bowl: Boston College 45, Houston 28
Gator Bowl: Oklahoma State 21, South Carolina 14
Orange Bowl: Washington 28, Oklahoma 17
Rose Bowl: Southern California 20, Ohio State 17
Sugar Bowl: Nebraska 28, Louisiana State 10

Heisman Trophy: Doug Flutie, Boston College

NFL FINAL STANDINGS

AMERICAN CONFERENCE

Eastern Division

	W	L	T	Pct.	PF	PA
* Miami	14	2	0	.875	513	298
New England	9	7	0	.563	362	352
N.Y. Jets	7	9	0	.438	332	364
Indianapolis	4	12	0	.250	239	414
Buffalo	2	14	0	.125	250	454

Central Division

	W	L	T	Pct.	PF	PA
Pittsburgh	9	7	0	.563	387	310
Cincinnati	8	8	0	.500	339	339
Cleveland	5	11	0	.313	250	297
Houston	3	13	0	.188	240	437

Western Division

	W	L	T	Pct.	PF	PA
Denver	13	3	0	.813	353	241
Seattle	12	4	0	750	418	282
L.A. Raiders	11	5	0	.688	368	278
Kansas City	8	8	0	.500	314	324
San Diego	7	9	0	.438	395	413

NATIONAL CONFERENCE

Eastern Division

	W	L	T	Pct.	PF	PA
Washington	11	5	0	.688	426	310
N.Y. Giants	9	7	0	.563	299	301
Dallas	9	7	0	.563	308	308
St. Louis	9	7	0	.563	423	345
Philadelphia	6	9	1	.406	278	320

Central Division

	W	L	T	Pct.	PF	PA
Chicago	10	6	0	.625	325	248
Green Bay	8	8	0	.500	380	309
Tampa Bay	6	10	0	.375	335	380
Detroit	4	11	1	.281	283	408
Minnesota	3	13	0	.188	276	484

Western Division

	W	L	T	Pct.	PF	PA
* San Francisco	15	1	0	.938	475	227
L.A. Rams	10	6	0	.625	346	316
New Orleans	7	9	0	.438	298	361
Atlanta	4	12	0	.250	281	382

* **Conference Champions and Super Bowl Contenders**

In 1984, Hollis Stacy (*left*) won the U.S. Women's Open, and Ben Crenshaw (*right*) won the Masters.

GOLF

PROFESSIONAL		AMATEUR	
	Individual		**Individual**
Masters	Ben Crenshaw	**U.S. Amateur**	Scott Verplank
U.S. Open	Fuzzy Zoeller	**U.S. Women's Amateur**	Deb Richards
Canadian Open	Greg Norman	**British Amateur**	Jose-Maria Olazabal
British Open	Seve Ballesteros	**British Ladies Amateur**	Jody Rosenthal
PGA	Lee Trevino	**Canadian Amateur**	Bill Swartz
World Series of Golf	Denis Watson	**Canadian Ladies Amateur**	Kim Williams
U.S. Women's Open	Hollis Stacy		
Ladies PGA	Patty Sheehan		**Team**
		Curtis Cup	United States
	Team		
World Cup	Spain		

HOCKEY

The Edmonton Oilers, who entered the National Hockey League only five years before, won the Stanley Cup in 1984. By defeating the defending champion New York Islanders 4 games to 1 in the final playoff series, the Oilers became the first NHL team west of Chicago to win the championship. They also foiled the Islanders' bid to capture a record-tying fifth straight Stanley Cup. (The Montreal Canadiens took five straight from 1956 through 1960.)

Edmonton rose to the top of the heap faster than any expansion team in league history. The Oilers were admitted to the NHL in the 1979 merger with the old World Hockey Association (WHA). After two difficult years, they came into their own. Led by young superstar Wayne Gretzky, the Oilers broke team scoring records the next three years in a row. Their single-season total reached a high of 446 goals in the 1983–84 season. "The Great Gretzky" won his fourth consecutive scoring title (205 points) and was voted the league's most valuable player for a record fifth straight year.

Until 1984, however, the Oilers had been frustrated in post-season play. Their most humiliating defeat was a four-game sweep by the Islanders in the 1983 cup finals. Including regular-season and playoff competition, the New Yorkers had defeated Edmonton in ten consecutive games, going back to December, 1981.

That string was snapped in the opening match of the 1984 playoff finals at Nassau Coliseum on Long Island, New York. Edmonton goalie Grant Fuhr fended off 34 shots, and hard-checking center Kevin McClelland scored early in the third period to give the Oilers a 1–0 victory.

In the second game, also in New York, it appeared that the Islanders were back on the beam. The defending champs tied the series with a one-sided 6–1 triumph. Clark Gillies had the "hat trick" (three goals), Bryan Trottier scored twice, and Greg Gilbert once. As it turned out, however, the Isle victory was just a brief interruption in the surge of the young Oilers.

The next three games were played in Edmonton—and the series ended there. The Oiler scoring machine—led by Gretzky, Paul Coffey, Jari Kurri, Mark Messier, and Glenn Anderson—finally got untracked, tal-

The Edmonton Oilers, led by center Wayne Gretzky (*left*), dethroned the New York Islanders as NHL champions.

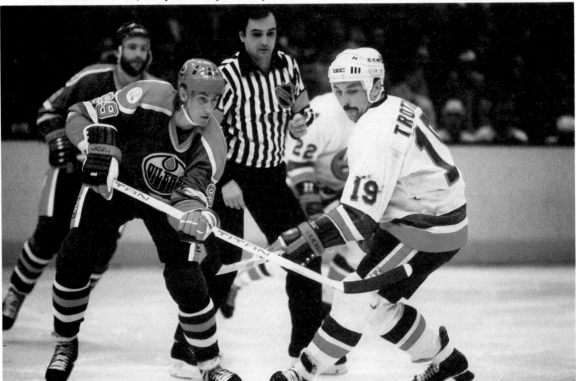

lying goals in bunches. Another star was goalie Andy Moog, who replaced the injured Fuhr in the last three games.

The third game was tied 2–2 until the last minute of the second period, when Anderson and Coffey scored rebound goals 17 seconds apart. That triggered an avalanche, and the Oilers went on to win 7–2.

In game four, Gretzky—whom the Islanders had held without a goal in seven straight final playoff games—finally broke the ice. He scored the first and last goals of the game on breakaways, leading the Oilers to another 7–2 win.

Gretzky rose to the occasion again in the fifth game, delivering two early scores. Edmonton won 5–2, and the Stanley Cup was theirs. Left-winger Mark Messier was awarded the Conn Smythe Trophy as the most valuable player in the playoffs.

For the Oilers, the championship capped a superb season. In addition to setting the team scoring mark, they had the league's best record during the regular season (57 victories, 18 defeats, 5 ties). Amazingly, five different Oilers ended the regular season with 99 or more points. As for Gretzky, the personal records and achievements included scoring at least one point (a goal or assist) in the season's first 51 games.

Canada Cup. The third international Canada Cup hockey tournament was played in September, 1984. Six countries took part in the event: Canada, Czechoslovakia, the Soviet Union, Sweden, the United States, and West Germany. The competition highlighted the best players in the world, including many stars of the NHL.

The Soviet team was favored to win the championship. But to the joy of the host-country fans, Team Canada emerged victorious. In an exciting semifinal contest, Canada upset the Soviet Union, 3–2. In the other semifinal matchup, Sweden overwhelmed the United States, 9–2. Then, in the best-of-three championship series, Canada defeated Sweden 2 games to 0. In the first contest, Michel Goulet (who also plays for the Quebec Nordiques of the NHL) scored two goals and set up a third in a 5–2 triumph. In the second game, Team Canada unleashed a five-goal assault in the first period, then held off a spirited rally by Sweden, to win 6–5. The Canada Cup belonged to Canada.

NHL FINAL STANDINGS

WALES CONFERENCE

Patrick Division

	W	L	T	Pts.
N.Y. Islanders	50	26	4	104
Washington	48	27	5	101
Philadelphia	44	26	10	98
N.Y. Rangers	42	29	9	93
New Jersey	17	56	7	41
Pittsburgh	16	58	6	38

Adams Division

	W	L	T	Pts.
Boston	49	25	6	104
Buffalo	48	25	7	103
Quebec	42	28	10	94
Montreal	35	40	5	75
Hartford	28	42	10	66

CAMPBELL CONFERENCE

Norris Division

	W	L	T	Pts.
Minnesota	39	31	10	88
St. Louis	32	41	7	71
Detroit	31	42	7	69
Chicago	30	42	8	68
Toronto	26	45	9	61

Smythe Division

	W	L	T	Pts.
Edmonton	57	18	5	119
Calgary	34	32	14	82
Vancouver	32	39	9	73
Winnipeg	31	38	11	73
Los Angeles	23	44	13	59

Stanley Cup: Edmonton Oilers

OUTSTANDING PLAYERS

Hart Trophy (most valuable player)	Wayne Gretzky, Edmonton
Ross Trophy (scorer)	Wayne Gretzky, Edmonton
Vezina Trophy (goalie)	Tom Barrasso, Buffalo
Norris Trophy (defenseman)	Rod Langway, Washington
Selke Trophy (defensive forward)	Doug Jarvis, Washington
Calder Trophy (rookie)	Tom Barrasso, Buffalo
Lady Byng Trophy (sportsmanship)	Mike Bossy, N.Y. Islanders
Conn Smythe Trophy (Stanley Cup play)	Mark Messier, Edmonton

ICE SKATING

SKIING

FIGURE SKATING

World Championships

Men	Scott Hamilton, U.S.
Women	Katarina Witt, E. Germany
Pairs	Barbara Underhill/Paul Martini, Canada
Dance	Jayne Torvill/Christopher Dean, Britain

United States Championships

Men	Scott Hamilton
Women	Rosalynn Sumners
Pairs	Caitlin Carruthers/Peter Carruthers
Dance	Judy Blumberg/Michael Seibert

SPEED SKATING

World Championships

Men	Oleg Boziev, U.S.S.R.
Women	Karin Enke, E. Germany

WORLD CUP CHAMPIONSHIPS

Men	Pirmin Zurbriggen, Switzerland
Women	Erika Hess, Switzerland

U.S. ALPINE CHAMPIONSHIPS

Men

Downhill	Bill Johnson
Slalom	Steve Mahre
Giant Slalom	Steve Mahre
Combined	Andy Chambers

Women

Downhill	Lisa Wilcox
Slalom	Tamara McKinney
Giant Slalom	Christin Cooper
Combined	Eva Twardokens

Left: Steve Mahre finished first in the slalom and giant slalom at the 1984 U.S. alpine championships.
Right: Paul Martini and Barbara Underhill of Canada won the 1984 world pairs figure-skating title.

GOLD ON ICE

After 4½ minutes of breathtaking jumps, whirling loops, and rapid-fire dance steps, the young figure skater ends his routine with a move called the "toe spin." He stretches to his full height of 5 feet, 3 inches (160 centimeters), lifts one foot from the ice, draws in his arms, and starts to spin. Turning faster and faster with each revolution, he becomes a blur. He looks like a human power drill about to bore through the ice.

The whirling dervish begins to slow. He comes to a stop, drops to one knee, and bows his head. The routine is over. The crowd is on its feet, wildly applauding his performance—for nobody does it better or with more enthusiasm than Scott Hamilton.

Despite his small size, Scott Hamilton is a giant in his field. He is probably the most dynamic, most talented, and most popular champion ever to lace up a pair of ice skates. In 1981 he became the U.S. and world men's figure skating champion—and he just went right on winning competition after competition. At the 1984 Winter Games in Sarajevo, Yugoslavia, the 25-year-old skater from Denver, Colorado, achieved his biggest goal —winning an Olympic gold medal.

Scott's story is one of adversity. He was born on August 28, 1958, and was adopted at the age of six weeks. His adoptive parents were professors in Bowling Green, Ohio. At the age of 2, Scott suddenly stopped growing. For the next six years, the doctors couldn't figure out the problem. Then it was diagnosed that he had a rare disease called Shwachman's syndrome: His food wasn't being properly digested.

When Scott was about 8, he went to watch his sister ice skate. He had a feeding tube leading to his stomach, but he wanted to try skating anyway. He loved it. The next year, Scott's disease disappeared just as mysteriously as it had come. Although he would never reach normal size, he did begin to grow. And so did his love of ice skating.

With daily practice, expert coaching, and frequent competition, Scott became a world-class competitor. He carried the American flag during the opening ceremonies of the 1980 Olympics in Lake Placid. He was chosen to lead the U.S. team because of his

Scott Hamilton is one of the most popular figure-skating champions ever. His coach has said of him: "To know Scott Hamilton is to know that nice guys finish first."

courage in overcoming his childhood disease. But he didn't win a medal in those Games.

By the 1984 Games, everyone expected Scott to win the gold. He not only wanted to win, he also wanted to give the "performance of his life." Although he wasn't quite up to his usual standard, Hamilton was still better than all the rest. "It wasn't my best," he said, "but I did it!"

The Chicago Sting (dark jersies) defeated the Toronto Blizzard, 2 games to 0, for the 1984 NASL championship.

SOCCER

NORTH AMERICAN SOCCER LEAGUE
FINAL STANDINGS

Eastern Division

	W	L	GF	GA	Pts.
Chicago	13	11	50	49	120
Toronto	14	10	46	33	117
New York	13	11	43	42	115
Tampa Bay	9	15	43	61	87

Western Division

	W	L	GF	GA	Pts.
San Diego	14	10	51	42	118
Vancouver	13	11	51	48	117
Minnesota	14	10	40	44	115
Tulsa	10	14	42	46	98
Golden Bay	8	16	61	62	95

Championship Series: Chicago Sting

NORTH AMERICAN SOCCER LEAGUE
INDOOR
FINAL STANDINGS

	W	L	Pct.	GF	GA
San Diego	21	11	.656	196	148
New York	20	12	.625	219	198
Chicago	20	12	.625	183	148
Golden Bay	19	13	.594	206	190
Vancouver	12	20	.375	187	209
Tulsa	11	21	.344	166	216
Tampa Bay	9	23	.284	177	225

Championship Series: San Diego Sockers

SWIMMING

WORLD SWIMMING RECORDS SET IN 1984

EVENT	HOLDER	TIME
	Men	
200-meter freestyle	Michael Gross, W. Germany	1:47.44
200-meter backstroke	Sergei Zabolotnov, U.S.S.R.	1:58.41
100-meter breaststroke	Steve Lundquist, U.S.	1:01.65
200-meter breaststroke	Victor Davis, Canada	2:13.34
100-meter butterfly	Michael Gross, W. Germany	53.08
200-meter butterfly	Jon Sieben, Australia	1:57.04
200-meter individual medley	Alex Baumann, Canada	2:01.42
400-meter individual medley	Alex Baumann, Canada	4:17.41
400-meter freestyle relay	United States	3:19.03
800-meter freestyle relay	United States	7:15.69
400-meter medley relay	United States	3:39.30
	Women	
50-meter freestyle	Dara Torres, U.S.	0:25.61
200-meter freestyle	Kristin Otto, E. Germany	1:57.75
100-meter backstroke	Ina Kleber, E. Germany	1:00.59
100-meter breaststroke	Sylvia Gerasch, E. Germany	1:08.29
400-meter freestyle relay	East Germany	3:42.41
400-meter medley relay	East Germany	4:03.69

West German swimmer Michael Gross sets a world record in the 100-meter butterfly.

John McEnroe reigned supreme in men's tennis in 1984.

TENNIS

Professional tennis in 1984 was dominated by two players. John McEnroe reigned supreme among the men, winning both the Wimbledon tournament and the U.S. Open. And Martina Navratilova was virtually unbeatable in women's play. By September she had won her 56th straight match, breaking the record of Chris Evert Lloyd.

McEnroe's chief rivals in the top tournaments were fellow American Jimmy Connors and Ivan Lendl of Czechoslovakia. At the century-old Wimbledon tournament in England, McEnroe met Connors in the final. McEnroe won the match with astonishing ease, 6–1, 6–1, 6–2. That gave the 25-year-old New Yorker his second straight—and third overall—Wimbledon singles crown.

In the U.S. Open, McEnroe and Connors collided again in the semifinals. This time the 32-year-old Connors put up a good fight, but McEnroe once more emerged the winner, 6–4, 4–6, 7–5, 4–6, 6–3. In the finals, McEnroe breezed to his fourth U.S. Open title with an easy triumph over Ivan Lendl, 6–3, 6–4, 6–1. For "Mac," the defeat of Lendl was sweet revenge. Earlier in the year, the 24-year-old Czech had beaten McEnroe in the finals of the French Open.

In women's tennis, Martina Navratilova was regarded by some long-time observers as the greatest player ever. The powerful 28-year-old from Czechoslovakia, now a U.S. citizen, became only the third woman in history to win the Grand Slam—consecutively sweeping the Wimbledon championship, U.S. Open, Australian Open (all 1983), and French Open (1984).

Through it all, Chris Evert Lloyd was the only player to mount any challenge at all. She reached the finals against Navratilova in the French Open, at Wimbledon, and in the U.S. Open. Navratilova won the first two matches easily (6–3, 6–1 and 7–6, 6–2). Then at the U.S. Open, Evert Lloyd played some of her best tennis in years and even won the first set. But Navratilova returned to her unstoppable form and took the next two sets, for a close 4–6, 6–4, 6–4 victory. It was her second straight U.S. Open championship and her sixth straight triumph in a Grand Slam event.

TOURNAMENT TENNIS

	French Open	Wimbledon	U.S. Open	Australian Open
Men's Singles	Ivan Lendl, Czechoslovakia	John McEnroe, U.S.	John McEnroe, U.S.	Mats Wilander, Sweden
Women's Singles	Martina Navratilova, U.S.	Martina Navratilova, U.S.	Martina Navratilova, U.S.	Chris Evert Lloyd, U.S.
Men's Doubles	Yannick Noah, France/ Henri Leconte, France	John McEnroe, U.S./ Peter Fleming, U.S.	John Fitzgerald, Australia/ Tomas Smid, Czechoslovakia	Mark Edmondson, Australia/ Sherwood Stewart, U.S.
Women's Doubles	Martina Navratilova, U.S./ Pam Shriver, U.S.	Martina Navratilova, U.S./ Pam Shriver, U.S.	Martina Navratilova, U.S./ Pam Shriver, U.S.	Martina Navratilova, U.S./ Pam Shriver, U.S.

Davis Cup Winner: Sweden

TRACK AND FIELD

WORLD TRACK AND FIELD RECORDS SET IN 1984

EVENT	HOLDER	TIME, DISTANCE, OR POINTS
	Men	
300-meter run	Kirk Baptiste, U.S.	31.70
10,000-meter run	Fernando Mamede, Portugal	27:13.81
20,000-meter walk	Ernesto Canto, Mexico	1:18:39.90
400-meter relay	United States	37.83
High jump	Zhu Jianhua, China	7′10″
Pole vault	Sergei Bubka, U.S.S.R.	19′ 5¾″
Hammer throw	Yuri Sedykh, U.S.S.R.	283′ 3″
Javelin	Uwe Hohn, E. Germany	343′ 10″
Decathlon	Jurgen Hingsen, W. Germany	8,798 pts.
	Women	
100-meter run	Evelyn Ashford, U.S.	10.76
1-mile run	Natalya Artyemova, U.S.S.R.	4:15.80
2,000-meter run	Tatyana Kazankina, U.S.S.R.	5:28.72
3,000-meter run	Tatyana Kazankina, U.S.S.R.	8:22.62
5,000-meter run	Ingrid Kristiansen, Norway	14:58.89
10,000-meter run	Olga Bondarenko, U.S.S.R.	31:13.78
1-mile walk	Giuliana Salce, Italy	6:43.59
3,000-meter walk	Giuliana Salce, Italy	13:09.09
400-meter hurdles	Margarita Ponomaryova, U.S.S.R.	53.58
1,600-meter relay	East Germany	3:15.92
High jump	Ludmila Andonova, Bulgaria	6′ 9½″
Shot put	Natalya Lisovskaya, U.S.S.R.	73′ 11″
Discus	Zdena Silhava, Czechoslovakia	224′ 7″
Heptathlon	Sabine Paetz, E. Germany	6,867 pts.

Ludmila Andonova of Bulgaria leaps to a world record in the high jump.

LIVING HISTORY

This old print shows the waterfront of Toronto as it appeared in 1840, when the city was young. Today, Toronto is the capital of the Canadian province of Ontario and a bustling center of commerce. In 1984, Toronto and Ontario celebrated a double birthday—the 150th birthday of the city, and the 200th birthday of the province.

A DOUBLE BIRTHDAY CELEBRATION

Once upon a time this Canadian city on Lake Ontario was an important livestock market, and it was called Hogtown. Today it is known as People City because of its rich ethnic diversity. Through the years it has had a variety of names. But its true name has always been Toronto, which was derived from an Indian word meaning "place of meeting." And in 1984, Toronto was definitely the place to meet—as it celebrated its 150th birthday with parades, fireworks, science fairs, sports tournaments, and an international performing arts festival.

Toronto is the capital of the province of Ontario. It is also one of the most spectacular cities in North America. And its celebrations were really just the icing on an even bigger birthday cake—for 1984 was also Ontario's 200th birthday. All across the province, in communities large and small, there were special celebrations. Tall ships sailed up the St. Lawrence Seaway, from the Atlantic to Lake Ontario. Balloonists gathered in Barrie for the Canadian Hot Air Balloon Championships. In Orono, people wore ethnic costumes to a giant barn dance. In Sault Sainte Marie, a fashion show displayed two centuries of frocks, smocks, and gala gowns —and bonnets, buttons, and bows.

In Toronto, people re-enacted one of Ontario's most important battles, which occurred during the War of 1812. At that time Toronto was a settlement named York, after Britain's Duke of York. York, and indeed all of Ontario, was ruled by Britain, which was at war with the United States. British soldiers were stationed at Fort York. When U.S. troops invaded the fort in 1813, the British were forced to retreat. But before they left, they mined the fort's magazine,

Toronto, the capital of Ontario, is one of the most spectacular cities in North America. In 1984 it celebrated its 150th birthday. Shown here is Toronto's new city hall, in the downtown area. It is a landmark in modern architectural design.

If you visit Toronto, you may want to explore Casa Loma, a 98-room castle. An excellent example of French chateau architecture, Casa Loma is now a museum.

which blew up as the Americans arrived. The Americans proceeded to burn and loot houses and other buildings in York. (In retaliation, the British burned part of Washington, D.C., in 1814.) Fort York has now been restored, and it includes eight original log, stone, and brick buildings. During the 1984 celebrations, visitors got a good idea of what it was like to be a British soldier in the early 1800's. They watched scarlet-clad members of the Fort York Guard march, fire musket volleys, and salute to the strains of the fife and drum.

York had fewer than 1,000 inhabitants when the War of 1812 ended. But by the time it was incorporated as the city of Toronto in 1834, its population had grown to 9,000. Today its population is about 3,000,000. Only about ten percent of its citizens were born in Toronto. One third were born outside Canada—since World War II the city has been a haven for people from other countries. (The same is true for the province as a whole. Ontario is home to more Italians than is Florence, Italy. More Germans live in Ontario than in Nuremberg, West Germany. Of course, Ontario is much larger than these other places. It is as big as France, Germany, and Italy combined.)

The racial and ethnic mix has helped give Toronto the cosmopolitan atmosphere that both residents and visitors find so appealing. On Spadina Avenue, Filipino, Korean, and Hungarian shops sit side by side. At Kensington Market there are kosher butchers, Portuguese fishmongers, and West Indian greengrocers. And food critics consider Toronto one of the best places to dine in all of North America. Its restaurants offer foods from all over the world: hot Indian curries, spicy Chinese soups, Middle Eastern shish kebabs, Italian pastas, U.S. southern-fried chicken and chitlins.

If you visit Toronto, you can tour the exciting Ontario Science Centre. At the University of Toronto, you can see where penicillin and the electron microscope were developed. You can explore Casa Loma, a 98-room castle with huge stables where horses drank from porcelain troughs. At the Royal Canadian Military Institute, you can view the cockpit of the plane flown by Baron von Richthofen. The Red Baron, as this German pilot was called, was shot down by a Canadian flying ace in 1918.

Toronto is a city that offers visitors many delights, even when it isn't having a giant birthday party!

As long ago as 3000 B.C., people were playing board games. Here, ancient Egyptians are playing *senet*.

FUN & GAMES

The year is 1984—B.C. The sun is setting slowly in the western desert, and a cool breeze has sprung up. The waters of the Nile lap gently against the riverbank. Inside their house, the members of an Egyptian family light their oil lamps and talk quietly among themselves. How will they spend this cool and peaceful evening?

They'll play a board game, just as you might on a similar night at home. People were playing board games as long ago as 3000 B.C., and some of their games remained popular for thousands of years. In fact, some games that *you* play may be thousands of years old.

At different times and in different places, different games became something of a passion with people. They spent hours playing them—and sometimes small fortunes on elaborate pieces and boards. The games they made were not just ways to spend free time. They were works of art. And even when an ancient game is no longer played, the boards and pieces may still exist.

GAMES OF THE ANCIENT MIDEAST

The most popular game of ancient Egypt seems to have been senet, which means "passing." Archeologists have found stone boards that were used to play this game about 4,000 years ago. And they've found evidence that the game was popular for more than 2,000 years, not just in Egypt but throughout the Middle East.

What the archeologists haven't found is how to play the game. Senet boards can be bought today. But the rules of the modern game were thought up by people who studied the ancient Egyptians and guessed about how they might have played it.

Senet was played on a board with three rows of ten spaces each. Some people think the game may have had some religious or philosophical meaning. One theory has it that as players moved their pieces from space to space, they duplicated the journey of a soul through the underworld.

Senet seems to have found favor with people in all walks of life. Some senet boards have been found scratched onto tombs and temples, showing that workers in these buildings probably played it. Peasants probably drew senet boards in the sand and used pebbles for pieces. But royalty played on boards of rare woods and ivory. The tomb of the pharoah Tutankhamen contained four such boards, each perfectly preserved.

GAMES OF STRATEGY

The Asian game Go, or Wei-Chi, may hold the title as the world's longest-lived game. Go originated in China about 2300 B.C., and it is still played by millions of people in China, Japan, and elsewhere in Asia.

Go can be described as a game of warfare. It is played on a grid, which is empty at the start of the game. The two players place small black or white pieces on the grid, each trying to encircle and capture the other's pieces. The game sounds simple—but Go is actually one of the most complicated games ever invented. Masters of the game were honored as wise men in ancient China. And until 1600, students at Japan's military academy were taught the game as a way of learning military strategy.

Go is also played in Western countries. But a game of strategy that you may be more familiar with is chess. Chess originated in India in the 500's and then spread to Persia.

Senet was the most popular game of ancient Egypt, and it was played by people from all walks of life. Royalty played on boards of rare woods and ivory. The senet games above were found in the tomb of the pharoah Tutankhamen. Below, Japanese men play Go, which may hold the title as the world's longest-lived game. It originated in China about 2300 B.C. and is still played by millions of people.

Pachisi, India's national game, has been played there for centuries. It became popular in Europe in the 1800's, and several versions were developed. One version popular in Germany was called *chinesenspiel* (left)—a game for children in which small Chinese figures were used as the playing pieces.

It was brought to Europe by the Arabs, and there the game won lasting popularity. One story recounts that when King John of England was besieged in the city of Rouen in 1204, he refused to see to the city's defense until he had finished a long-running game of chess.

As the game developed in Europe, chess mirrored not only battle but society. The playing pieces—kings, queens, knights, castles, bishops, and pawns—were often carved and painted in great detail to show people from society's different levels. And the boards themselves were often inlaid with ivory and other precious materials.

Checkers, a much simpler game, was played with pieces that were no less beautiful. The checkers themselves were often carved with various designs, and Queen Elizabeth I of England played on an emerald-studded board. The origins of checkers are unclear. But one school of thought believes that it was developed in medieval Europe, using the board of chess and the pieces from another game, backgammon.

GAMES OF SKILL—AND LUCK

In backgammon, players need luck as well as skill—they move their pieces around the board according to the roll of dice. Back-gammon is one of the world's most ancient games. It was probably brought to Europe from the Middle East by the Crusaders in the early 1100's. And it has been played in many countries under many names—*tric-trac* in France, *puff* in Germany, *tarola reale* in Italy. The English name is said to come either from the Welsh words *back* and *gammon* ("little battle") or the Saxon words *bac* and *gamen* ("back game").

Backgammon has been popular for centuries in India, and it is thought to have been the forerunner of India's national game—pachisi. In this game, the pieces move around a cross-shaped board as dictated by throws of cowrie-shells. The pachisi board built by the Moghul emperor Akbar in the 1500's may have been the most elaborate game board ever made. It was built to human scale and inlaid with marble—and the playing pieces were slaves from Akbar's harem.

Pachisi became popular in Europe in the 1800's, and several versions were developed. One version popular in Germany was *chinesenspiel*—a simplified game for children in which small Chinese figures were the playing pieces. A popular version today played in Western countries is Parcheesi, which uses a somewhat different board and regular dice.

Another game that requires a bit of luck is dominoes, which is played with flat, oblong blocks. Players try to match the number of dots on the blocks they hold with the dots on blocks that have already been played. This game was known in the 1700's in Italy, but its actual origins have never been definitely established.

Mah-jongg is a very old Chinese game that may have developed from dominoes. It is played with ivory tiles that bear colorful pictures and symbols. This game was all the rage in the United States in the 1920's, and even today it has a number of enthusiasts. The game is very popular in Japan, where many towns have mah-jongg parlors.

GAMES FOR GAMBLERS AND TEACHERS

Like many games of chance, mah-jongg and dominoes have often attracted gamblers. So has cribbage, a card game in which a decorative pegboard is used to keep score. Pegboards thousands of years old have been found, but cribbage itself is said to have been invented in England in the 1600's by Sir John Suckling. According to a writer of the time, Suckling "played at Cards rarely well, and did use to practise by himselfe a-bed." But, the account states, he was a bit of a cheat—he made his own cards and marked them, so he could read his opponents' hands.

Suckling's honesty notwithstanding, the game gained in popularity through the 1800's. Elaborate inlaid cribbage boards and tables were ordered by the upper classes. And sailors to the New World whiled away shipboard hours with the game, keeping score on cribbage boards carved by Eskimos from walrus tusks.

Lotto is another game of chance that became popular at about the same time as cribbage. It was developed from the Italian national lottery, which has been run almost without interruption since 1530. Lotto was a forerunner of bingo, and it is played in much the same way. Players receive a game card bearing numbers. Then the game organizer draws numbers at random. If the number drawn is on a player's card, it's blocked off. The player who blocks off the entire board first wins.

But not all versions of the game have been based on luck. The Japanese developed a version of lotto called *karuta,* or "one hundred poems." In this game, the organizer reads the first line of a Japanese poem, and the players must select the correct last line from their cards. And in Western countries, various educational versions were developed in the 1800's—spelling lotto, botanical lotto, historical lotto. In these games, pictures and letters were added, and they tested the players' knowledge of various subjects.

Other educational games were also popular in the past. One elaborate game, made of rare woods and ivory and dedicated to a British princess, taught the fundamentals of music. Another, the game of goose, was a spiral board game. Depending on the pictures used in the spaces, it was used to teach history, literature, or the rewards of virtuous conduct.

But whether they were used to teach, to gamble, or simply for fun, the board games of the past make one thing clear: At all times and in all places, people love to play games.

Goose, a spiral board game of the past, was educational as well as fun. It was used to teach various subjects, depending on the kinds of pictures shown in the spaces.

LARGER THAN LIFE

What can travel a mile in a hop, a step, and a jump? Carry a coach-and-four slung over one shoulder? Uproot a tree as if it were a blade of grass?

A giant, of course. From ancient times to the present, stories and legends have told of these marvelous mythical creatures—like humans but vastly larger and stronger. Some have been portrayed as evil monsters, plundering the countryside and devouring human flesh. Others have been described as helpful and kindly, although perhaps a bit clumsy. And all kinds of wonderful feats are said to have been accomplished by giants. According to some stories, giants even shaped the landscape of the earth.

GIANTS IN ANCIENT MYTH

Legends from many parts of the world tell of giants who roamed the earth before people appeared. Some Indian tribes, for example, believed that giant Indians once lived in North America. They were tall enough to carry buffalo over their shoulders. Some Norse myths tell that the world was created from the body of a terrible giant, Ymir, who was killed by the gods. From his flesh they made the soil; from his blood, the seas; from his bones, the mountains; from his hair, the trees; from his skull, the sky. The gods then walled off the world of humans with Ymir's eyelashes, to protect it from other giants.

The ancient Greeks also believed that gigantic creatures lived long before the first people were born. These giants were the children of the Earth (Gaea) and the Sky (Uranus). Three of them were enormously huge and strong, with a hundred arms and fifty heads each. Three others were cyclops—they had just one eye each, right in the middle of the forehead. The rest were the Titans, just as huge and strong but not quite as evil as the others. According to legend, a Titan named Cronus rebelled against Uranus and wounded him.

Cronus ruled the universe for ages, until his son, the god Zeus, revolted. In the war between the Titans and the gods, the Titans were defeated. The Titans were eventually banished beneath the surface of the earth. But according to other legends, there were still some cyclops roaming about.

The most famous of these was Polyphemus. On his way home from the Trojan War, the Greek hero Odysseus led his men unawares into Polyphemus' cave. Before long, the giant came home, herding his sheep into the cave and rolling a huge stone across the entrance to block it. The men were trapped. And when Polyphemus saw them, he started to make them his dinner. But Odysseus tricked the giant. First, he gave him strong wine to drink. When the giant fell asleep, Odysseus and his men put out his single eye. Enraged, the blinded giant opened the cave and waited with his hands outstretched to catch the men as they ran out. But Odysseus had tied each of his men to the belly of a sheep, so the giant felt only sheep go by.

Michele

195

THE GIANTS OF BRITAIN

A race of giants was said to have lived in England in early times, too. People believed that these giants built Stonehenge, a prehistoric ring of towering rocks in southern England, and set up similar stones elsewhere. The giants were supposed to be the children of 33 evil daughters of the Roman emperor Diocletian, each of whom had murdered her husband. The daughters were set adrift in a boat and arrived in England, where they married demons and gave birth to the giants.

The giants were the only inhabitants of England for many years. Then, the stories tell, the hero Brut—who was also returning from the Trojan war—arrived to fight them. He dug a huge trench and hid it with branches, so that when the giants charged in battle they fell in. Those who weren't killed were driven to Cornwall, in the far southwest. But the two most powerful giants, Gog and Magog, were taken prisoner. They were chained to the gates of Brut's palace in London and made to serve as porters. Today statues of Gog and Magog guard the doors of the London Guildhall, which is said to stand on the site of Brut's palace.

If folk tales can be believed, though, there were still plenty of giants around—especially in Cornwall. One of the best known of

these tales concerns a Cornish boy named Jack, who lived at the time of King Arthur. He set out to rid his neighborhood of a dreadful pest—the giant Cormoran.

Cormoran was 18 feet tall and 9 feet around. He was a fearsome monster who raided the countryside, carrying off half a dozen oxen and three times that many sheep and hogs at a time. But Jack killed him with the same trick Brut had used: a concealed pit. From there Jack went on to kill five more giants—or perhaps many more, depending on the version of the story you read. He became known far and wide as Jack the Giant-Killer.

Not all the British giants were pests like Cormoran. The giant of Grabbist, in Somerset, was a helpful soul. He even waded into the sea to save small boats that were foundering in storms.

A LAND OF GIANTS

Can you picture a country in which everything—from flies to fields of wheat—is scaled to giant size? Such a land was described by the British writer Jonathan Swift in *Gulliver's Travels,* which was published in 1726.

In the story, Gulliver's ship is blown off course and stops to pick up water along a strange coast. By accident, Gulliver is left

behind. He soon finds himself walking through a field of grain—grain that is 40 feet high! Before long he is captured by a farmer, who "appeared as tall as an ordinary spire-steeple and took about ten yards at every stride." Gulliver is a great curiosity to the farmer and his family, and the farmer begins to carry him from town to town to show him off. Eventually he is bought by the queen of the country. He is kept in a little carrying box that to him is the size of a room, and he becomes the pet of the royal family.

In this strange country, which is called Brobdingnag, flies are the size of songbirds. Songbirds are the size of swans. Horses are 60 feet tall. The giants' voices sound like thunder. And Gulliver nearly loses his life when he is picked up and cuddled by a giant-size monkey.

Gulliver finally escapes from Brobdingnag when his "room" is carried off by an enormous eagle and dropped in the ocean. In another part of the book, he visits Lilliput. There the people are just 6 inches high. To them, Gulliver is a giant!

GIANTS IN AMERICA

Britain isn't the only country that has tales of giants, of course. There are stories from all over the world. A German tale tells of a young man who must fetch three golden hairs from the head of a giant in order to win the hand of a princess. There are Danish stories about a ghostly giant who haunts a forest called the Grunewald. And nearly every country has its own version of Jack and the Beanstalk, in which a boy climbs up a magic stalk to steal the treasures of a giant.

American folklore has its own giants. One of the most famous is Paul Bunyan, the legendary lumberjack.

Stories about Bunyan began in Canada—in Quebec or northern Ontario. Scholars say the first stories were based on the exploits of a real, human-size logger who lived in the mid-1800's. These stories spread throughout the logging camps of the American northwest. But when the Paul Bunyan stories were first written down, in the early 1900's, they had changed. The Bunyan of these stories was a giant. And the stories themselves were tall tales, each more outlandish than the last.

One story has it that Bunyan carved the Grand Canyon by accident, by dragging his pick across the ground. Another tells how he built a hotel, with the top seven stories hinged to let the moon pass by. He used a charred pine tree as a pencil. And he invented logging. He transported the logs in bundles that were tied around the neck of his pet—an enormous bright blue ox named Babe. Babe's footprints were so large that when they filled with water, ponds formed. People who fell in could drown. The Mississippi River formed by accident from a leak in Babe's water tank.

Thus—according to legend, at least—the New World, like the old, was shaped by giants.

"1984"

On one wall of Winston Smith's apartment is a large tele-screen. The telescreen is always on—it can't be turned off. It wakes Winston up in the morning, tells him to do stretching exercises, and drones on all day telling him what the government wants him to know. Winston always does what the screen says because it does more than send messages. It's a camera, too, and it records his every move.

Winston lives in London, a city in Oceania, one of the three superstates of the world. Everyone in Oceania has a telescreen like his, and everyone is watched. Just to remind people of this, the government has put up posters everywhere. They show a stern man's face peering out, and they carry the words "Big Brother Is Watching You." Big Brother is the ruler of Oceania. But no one has ever seen him.

Winston works for the government, at the Ministry of Truth. His job is to rewrite back issues of newspapers to agree with the government's current positions. For example, if the government made forecasts of industrial output that weren't met, the back issues would be rewritten to show correct forecasts. The ministry has three slogans: War Is Peace, Freedom Is Slavery, and Ignorance Is Strength.

There are two other major government ministries. The Ministry of Peace is in charge of war—Oceania is always at war with the other two superstates. The other ministry is the Ministry of Love. Winston has never been there, nor has anyone he knows. But when people don't follow the government line, the Thought Police take them to the Ministry of Love, and they disappear.

This is the chilling world of George Orwell's *1984,* a novel that tells of life in a totalitarian state. Orwell wrote the book in 1949, as a picture of a world that might someday come to be—a world without freedom, privacy, or free thinking.

1984 became an immediate best-seller. Over the years it was translated into more than 60 languages, and some 10,000,000 copies were sold. In the year 1984, sales of the book soared again. People everywhere wondered how accurate Orwell's picture of the future had been.

A WRITER WHO FOUGHT INJUSTICE

George Orwell was the pen name of Eric Arthur Blair, who was born to British parents in India on June 25, 1903. When he was about 5 years old, his mother brought him back to England. There he attended the best schools and won a scholarship to Eton. But school wasn't a good experience for him. "I had no money, I was weak, I was unpopular," he later recalled.

Blair left Eton in 1921 to join the Indian Imperial Police. He was sent to Burma, where he served for five years. This service left him with a lasting distaste for British imperialism. When he returned to England, he resolved to be a writer and to work on the side of people who were oppressed.

He had no steady work for five years, and his experiences during that time led to his first book, *Down and Out in Paris and London* (1933). He chose the pen name George Orwell for the book so that he wouldn't embarrass his family with his tales of hard times. After that book's success, he wrote about the hardships of English coal miners in *The Road to Wigan Pier* (1937).

Orwell's political views favored democratic socialism. In 1936, he went to Spain to fight against the dictator Franco in the Spanish Civil War. *Homage to Catalonia* (1938) describes the hopes and dreams of that fight. But he became bitterly disillusioned with the Spanish Communists, who opposed Franco but were in league with the Soviet Union.

His distaste for Soviet Communism led him to write *Animal Farm* (1945), a parody of the Russian revolution. In this book, barnyard animals revolt and take control of a farm. But the animals themselves then fall under the control of the pigs, who are the cleverest.

Animal Farm was a great success. Then personal tragedy struck. Eileen, Orwell's wife since 1936, died suddenly, leaving him with an adopted son. And Orwell himself developed tuberculosis. Over the next few years, as he worked on the manuscript that was to become *1984,* his health gradually declined. The book was finally published in 1949. Later that year, he married Sonia Brownell, an editor. Orwell died four months later on January 21, 1950, in London.

PREDICTION OR POSSIBILITY?

The book *1984* describes the effort of Winston Smith to express some individuality in the government-controlled society of Oceania, where even the act of keeping a diary is a crime. Winston is unsuccessful, and the book ends on a grim and hopeless note.

The world in the real year 1984 was certainly nothing like the 1984 of Orwell's book. But Orwell didn't intend his book to be a prediction of what would happen in 35 years. His intent was to show the possible consequences of the totalitarian ideas that were taking hold in the 1930's and 1940's. "I do not believe the kind of world I described will arrive," he wrote shortly after the book was published, "but I believe . . . that something resembling it could arrive." And many people have found parallels between modern societies and the society of *1984.*

When the book first came out, many saw it as a criticism of Communism, especially the kind of Communism that developed in the Soviet Union. A number of the details in

The oppressive world of George Orwell's novel *1984* is portrayed in this scene from a 1955 motion picture.

1984 were taken straight from the Soviet system. And the Soviets themselves banned the book.

Later, some people saw signs of *1984* in Western societies. Today, for example, computers hold quantities of information on people. There are other similarities, too. "Newspeak," the official language of Oceania, obscured the truth and twisted facts. But so does some modern government jargon—"peacekeeper," for example, for a deadly missile. And like Oceania, the West is continually preparing for war by stockpiling nuclear weapons.

Orwell's book was a warning of things that might come to be. Even though our world is not the world described in *1984,* many people think the warning should still be heeded.

THE GOLDEN WEST.

HEROES OF THE WILD WEST

The early settlers of the Wild West believed it to be a Garden of Eden, and they braved great dangers in trying to reach it. These trailblazers included such folk heroes as Daniel Boone and Kit Carson—both of whom celebrated anniversaries in 1984.

In this age of jet aircraft and space shuttles, it's hard to believe that people once traveled great distances across North America on foot, on horseback, and by covered wagon drawn by oxen. But that's the way it was 200—and even 100—years ago, when our pioneer ancestors marched westward toward the Pacific.

Back then, there was a saying that if you could see the smoke from your neighbor's chimney, it was time to move on. The great heroes of the American frontier were often restless adventurers. But it was they who braved the dangers of the wilderness to hack out slender pathways that armies of settlers would follow. They included early trailblazers like Daniel Boone and Davy Crockett

and the later generation of frontier scouts like Kit Carson and ''Buffalo Bill'' Cody.

For two of these folk heroes, 1984 was an anniversary year. The legendary backwoodsman Daniel Boone was born 250 years earlier, and Kit Carson, equally famous as a scout and hunter, was born 175 years earlier.

DANIEL BOONE—A GREAT TRAILBLAZER

Daniel Boone was born into a family of Quaker farmers, on November 2, 1734—just two years after the birth of George Washington. But while the future first president was growing up in a fine manor house in Virginia, Daniel Boone spent his boyhood in a log cabin near the present-day city of Reading, Pennsylvania. And while George was learning how to be a proper gentleman, Daniel was learning how to shoot, hunt, and survive in the wilderness.

When Daniel was 16, the Boones moved south, finally settling in North Carolina. Shortly after, in 1754, the French and Indian War broke out. Boone served as a wagon driver in General Edward Braddock's expedition of British regulars and American colonial militia. When the French and their Indian allies ambushed the troops and killed Braddock, Boone and the other wagoners had to run for their lives.

During that military stint, Boone had heard stories from fellow teamster John Finley about a fertile land west of the Appalachian Mountains that the Indians called Kentucky. According to Finley, it was a lush, game-filled region where herds of buffalo blanketed the meadows. Only a few hunters had ever been there. Boone's adventurous appetite was whetted, but there was no known trail to this fabled territory. So Boone returned home, married, raised a family, and farmed and hunted.

Years later, by coincidence, John Finley showed up at the Boones' cabin. Finley now knew of an old Indian trail to Kentucky. Spurred by this information, Boone and a small group of frontiersmen headed west, picked up the Indian trail, and made their way through the Cumberland Gap into Kentucky. There, Boone found what he called "a second paradise."

Boone explored the region from 1769 to 1771. When he returned to North Carolina he convinced several families to settle in Kentucky, and they set out in the autumn of 1773. On the way, they were attacked by Indians. Boone's son James and several others were killed, and the party turned back.

Boone, however, was still determined to settle Kentucky. Hired by a land-settlement company, he and a group of woodsmen cleared a pathway into the territory. This pathway was the famous Wilderness Road, which was later used by generations of pioneers as they journeyed westward. Boone and his comrades also built a small fort on the Kentucky River. And in 1775 he brought his family to the territory.

The fort was named Boonesborough, and by the time the Declaration of Independence was signed in 1776, it was a small but thriving settlement. During these years, Boone had many close brushes with death. On several occasions he was captured by Indians. In February, 1778, a war party of Shawnees surprised Boone and other settlers while they were making salt at a distant spring. The Indians formed two lines and forced Boone to run between them, as they stood ready to attack him with war clubs and tomahawks. With speed and agility, the frontiersman sidestepped the blows and emerged unharmed. Impressed by this, the Shawnees adopted him into their tribe. Boone became the "son" of Chief Blackfish and received the name Sheltowee, or "Big Turtle."

Boone lived with the Indians for several months, pretending to be happy while secretly looking for a way to escape. When he learned of Indian plans to attack Boonesborough, he slipped away from the Indian camp to warn his friends. The hardy frontiersman traveled 160 miles (258 kilometers)—on foot —in only four days. Boone and his handful of settlers fought off repeated attacks by 400 Shawnees, saving the settlement.

Daniel Boone, the legendary backwoodsman, was an expert at shooting, hunting, and surviving in the wilderness.

When Boone finally reached the fabled territory of Kentucky, he described it as "a second paradise."

Despite his celebrated status as a frontier hero, Boone fell on hard times after the Revolutionary War. He lost his Kentucky lands because he had failed to get legal title to them. For a while, Boone lived in what is now West Virginia (then Virginia). He was made a colonel of the militia and was a representative to the Virginia state legislature.

But his spirit remained restless. In 1799, Boone headed west again with his family, this time to the Spanish-held Missouri territory. There, the Spanish authorities gave him a tract of land and made him magistrate, which meant he had to judge law cases and keep order in the district.

When the United States gained control of Missouri in 1803 (as a result of the Louisiana Purchase), Boone again lost his land. But in 1814 the U.S. Government gave him 850 acres, citing his efforts as a pathfinder who had "opened the way for millions of his fellow men."

Daniel Boone remained active well into his 80's, going out on hunting expeditions whenever he could. He died on September 26, 1820, at the age of 86, leaving behind a legacy of courage and resourcefulness. For decades after his death, people referred to a smart frontiersman by saying, "He's a regular Dan'l Boone."

KIT CARSON—A SKILLED GUIDE

Just eleven years before Boone's death, on December 24, 1809, Christopher Carson —better known as Kit—was born in Madison County, Kentucky. Interestingly, the Carson family practically followed in the footsteps of Daniel Boone. Originally from North Carolina, they took the trail Boone had blazed to Kentucky and then—still looking for open space—they headed for Missouri in 1810.

Kit spent his early years in a stockaded frontier settlement, where schooling was mainly learning to use a gun and till the land. When he was 15, he was made an apprentice to a saddle maker. But the job was too tame for an adventurous youth like Kit, and a year later he ran away to join a group of traders heading for the New Mexico territory.

In New Mexico, Carson became friendly with an experienced fur trapper named Ewing Young. The two men journeyed to the Rocky Mountains where Carson learned how to trap and skin beavers. From the late 1820's to the early 1840's, Carson wandered over the far western frontier, hunting and trapping from the Rockies to California and as far north as Wyoming. These were rough-and-tumble times, and Carson had to match wits with fur thieves, hostile Indians, and

204

rival trappers. Before he left the Rocky Mountain beaver country, he married an Indian girl who bore him a daughter.

Carson's big break, which led to national fame, occurred in 1842, during a trip to Missouri to visit his relatives. While on a steamboat headed up the Missouri River, he met a young army officer, John C. Frémont. Frémont had been ordered to survey and map a portion of the Rocky Mountains, and he was looking for a guide.

According to Carson's own account, he brazenly approached the army officer and firmly said, "Sir, I have been some time in the mountains and I think I can guide you to any point there you wish to reach."

Frémont was favorably impressed by Carson, and after looking into his background he hired him to guide him over the rugged Rockies. The expedition set out on June 10, 1842, and after many adventures the most favored route to Oregon was charted.

Frémont's lively report of the expedition was widely read. Filled with glowing references to Carson's scouting abilities, it made the guide one of the best-known frontiersmen of his day. Between 1843 and 1845, Carson guided Frémont on two more exploring trips—the first to the Oregon territory and the second across the Rockies to California.

When the Mexican War broke out in 1846, Carson and Frémont returned to California. There they joined American settlers in a revolt against the Mexicans who controlled the area. Carson performed heroic services as a guide for General Stephen W. Kearny. Kearny's troops were attacked and surrounded by Mexicans not far from present-day San Diego. When all seemed hopeless, Carson volunteered to sneak through the enemy lines to get help. Accompanied by two other scouts, he walked, ran, and crawled the 30 miles (48 kilometers) to San Diego, where there were additional American troops. Thanks to his efforts, a relief column arrived in time to save Kearny's force from being overwhelmed.

In the years between the Mexican and Civil wars, Carson was U.S. Indian agent at Taos, New Mexico. He treated the Indians fairly and won their respect. When the Civil War broke out in 1861, he offered his ser-

Kit Carson was a skilled scout and hunter, and he guided an expedition over the rugged, unmapped Rockies.

vices to the Union government. He organized the New Mexico Volunteer Regiment and was made its colonel.

Carson's regiment fought battles in Texas and New Mexico against both Confederate troops and Indians. By the end of the war, he had risen to the rank of brigadier general. Ill health forced him to leave the army in 1867, and a year later, on May 23, 1868, he died.

Kit Carson and Daniel Boone are no more. But the spirit of adventure and exploration lives on in those daring astronauts who blaze trails into space. Perhaps one day people will follow planet-hopping pathfinders to new settlements in the far corners of the universe —just as they once followed Daniel Boone and Kit Carson to the uncharted lands of the American West.

HENRY I. KURTZ
Author, *John and Sebastian Cabot*

ABRAHAM LINCOLN AND HARRY S. TRUMAN

An Anniversary Album

The United States celebrated two important birthdays in 1984. The year marked the 175th anniversary of the birth of Abraham Lincoln, who was president of the United States from 1861 to 1865. Lincoln is known as the Great Emancipator—the person who freed black slaves from bondage. He led the country through the turmoil of the Civil War and died tragically from an assassin's bullet.

The year 1984 was also the 100th anniversary of the birth of Harry S. Truman, who served as president from 1945 to 1953. Truman led the country during the closing months of World War II, and he helped establish the United States as a major world power after the war. He also made progress toward achieving equal opportunity and financial security for all U.S. citizens. Lincoln has long been one of the country's most famous presidents. But historians are only today beginning to realize Truman's importance as president.

Abraham Lincoln was born in a one-room log cabin near Hodgenville, Kentucky, on February 12, 1809. His father, a carpenter and farmer, later moved the family to similar homes in Indiana and Illinois. School was an on-and-off thing for the boy—in his entire life, his schooling added up to less than a year. But he became an avid reader and studied on his own. As he grew older he earned money as a hired hand and store clerk. When Lincoln was in his 20's, he decided to run for the Illinois state legislature. He lost in his first try but won in 1834 and was re-elected three times. Meanwhile, he studied law and received his law license. (Right: Lincoln as a boy, reading by firelight in his log-cabin home.)

After leaving the state legislature, Lincoln practiced law in Springfield, Illinois. He served one term in Congress as a representative from that state, from 1847 to 1849, but then decided to leave politics. The issue that brought him back was the Kansas-Nebraska Act of 1854, which threatened to extend slavery to new territories. He helped form the Illinois branch of the newly founded Republican Party, and in 1858 he ran for the U.S. Senate. His opponent was Stephen A. Douglas, a Democrat. Lincoln lost the election, but a celebrated series of debates between the candidates brought him national attention. (Below: Lincoln debating Douglas during the campaign.)

In 1860, Lincoln won the Republican presidential nomination. His opposition to the spread of slavery made him popular with many people in the North. So did his reputation as a hard-working, honest person. The Democrats split over the issue of slavery and fielded two candidates, Douglas and John C. Breckinridge. Lincoln didn't get a majority of the popular vote, but he outpolled the other candidates in enough states to win the election. (Above: Lincoln was nicknamed the Railsplitter, a reference to his humble background.)

The Southern leaders who had opposed Lincoln most strongly had threatened to withdraw from the Union if he were elected president. And on December 20, 1860, South Carolina seceded. Ten other Southern states eventually followed suit. Lincoln entered Washington, D.C., secretly because of an assassination threat, and he was inaugurated under heavy guard. On April 12, 1861, Confederate guns fired on Fort Sumter in South Carolina, beginning the Civil War. At Bull Run and other early battles of the war, Northern forces met defeat. People quickly realized that the war would be a long one. (Left: Fort Sumter under attack.)

In 1842, Lincoln had married Mary Todd, a high-spirited woman from Kentucky. She had also been courted by Stephen A. Douglas, Lincoln's political opponent. The Lincolns had four sons—Robert Todd, Edward, William, and Thomas (Tad). But to their sorrow, two of their children died young—Edward at the age of 4, and William at 11, after his father had taken office. By this time Robert Todd was in college; Tad, who lived at the White House, was his father's favorite. (Above: The Lincolns at the White House in 1862, after William's death.)

In 1862, Lincoln issued the Emancipation Proclamation, which freed slaves throughout the Confederacy and set the stage for the end of slavery in the United States. Meanwhile, the war continued, with major Union victories at Gettysburg, Pennsylvania, and Vicksburg, Mississippi, in 1863. Lincoln's famous Gettysburg Address gave new heart to the Union effort. In 1864 armies led by Ulysses S. Grant and William T. Sherman began to sweep through Confederate territory. The war had made Lincoln increasingly unpopular. But a string of Union victories in 1864 helped him win re-election. And on April 9, 1865, Confederate forces under Robert E. Lee surrendered, ending the war. (Right: A poster from Lincoln's 1864 election campaign calls for the preservation of the Union.)

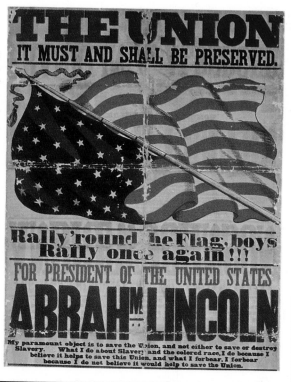

Lincoln had already begun to make plans for rebuilding the South. But he didn't live to see his plans take effect. On April 14, 1865, he was shot while attending a play at Ford's Theatre in Washington. He died the next morning. The assassin was John Wilkes Booth, a well-known actor. He was killed a few days later, while trying to escape arrest. Several people who were thought to have helped him were arrested, tried, and convicted for conspiracy in the crime. (Above: Booth takes aim at Lincoln in Ford's Theatre.)

Lincoln was buried in Springfield, Illinois. His coffin was sent there by train, and thousands of mourners lined the tracks to watch it pass. His loss was felt by everyone. But he had succeeded in preserving the Union and in ending slavery, and today he remains one of the most honored U.S. presidents. (Left: The Lincoln Memorial in Washington, D.C., houses a statue by the sculptor Daniel Chester French. It shows the President in a typically thoughtful pose.)

Harry S. Truman was born on May 8, 1884, in Lamar, Missouri. He spent most of his childhood in the Missouri town of Independence. Poor eyesight, which required him to wear glasses, kept him from playing many sports and from attending the U.S. Military Academy at West Point after high school graduation. Instead, he worked at several jobs and then served in the armed forces during World War I. After the war, he and a friend opened a men's clothing store in Kansas City. The store failed, and Truman entered politics. He became a county judge in 1922 and a U.S. senator in 1934. In 1944, he was chosen as President Franklin D. Roosevelt's running-mate, and he became vice president. (Right: Truman in his World War I uniform.)

Roosevelt died suddenly on April 12, 1945, and Truman was sworn in as president. He told reporters: "If you ever pray, pray for me now." World War II was drawing to a close in Europe—Germany surrendered on May 7. But the war still raged in the Pacific. Truman made the decision to drop two atomic bombs on Japanese cities, and Japan surrendered on September 2. (Right: Truman is sworn in. Next to him are his wife, Bess, whom he married in 1919, and their daughter, Margaret.)

Relations with the Soviet Union worsened after the war, and the Cold War developed. Truman's answer was a policy of open resistance to the spread of Communism. This policy, called the Truman Doctrine, was extended in 1947 by the Marshall Plan, which provided economic aid to the war-torn countries of Europe. In the United States, Truman pressed for better protection of minority rights and a broader social security program. (Left: A French poster promoting the Marshall Plan.)

Truman's popularity was low, and in the election of 1948 many Democrats supported small-party candidates. Victory seemed certain for Thomas E. Dewey, the Republican candidate—so certain that on election night some newspapers printed their headlines before the votes were counted. But Truman had crossed the country by train in a "whistle-stop" campaign and managed to pick up support. He defeated Dewey in what was one of the biggest political upsets in U.S. history. (Right: A victorious Truman displays a newspaper that jumped the gun and announced his defeat.)

In Truman's second term, the United States helped form NATO and expanded aid to Asian countries threatened by Communism. In 1950 the Korean War broke out, and Truman sent U.S. troops to help South Korea. Meanwhile, people began to wonder if Truman would seek another term. (The constitutional amendment limiting presidents to two terms had not yet taken effect.) Truman ended the suspense in March of 1952 by announcing that he wouldn't run. (Left: This political cartoon reflects the speculation over whether Truman would run for another term.)

Truman retired to Independence, Missouri, in 1953. He lived there quietly and wrote two autobiographical books, *Year of Decisions* and *Years of Trial and Hope.* He died on December 26, 1972, and was buried in Independence. Truman left office as an unpopular president. But over the years people began to realize the importance of the things he had accomplished. Today many historians rank him among the best of the past presidents of the United States. (Right: On vacation in Key West, Florida, the retired Truman catches up on his reading—which includes a book on Abraham Lincoln.)

Crown of St. Edward—Britain's coronation crown.

Orb of Sweden's Eric XIV, who became king in 1560.

CROWN JEWELS

In 1671, a bold thief by the name of Colonel Blood crept into the Tower of London and stole the greatest treasure in all of England—the royal crown. The loss of the crown was not only a financial blow to the royal family, it was also a blow to its prestige. Encrusted with legends as thickly as with gems, the British crown—as well as the other crown jewels of Europe—was a symbol of wealth and power.

The "mother" of all the crowns of Europe can be traced back to the Middle Ages. This was the crown worn by Charlemagne at his coronation in 800. Charlemagne was the first ruler of the Holy Roman Empire, and his crown became its symbol. No one knows what happened to that coronation crown. But over the years, three other crowns were fashioned that became known as the Crown of Charlemagne—although none was ever worn by him. The first of the crowns that bore his name was made around 960. It was set with emeralds, amethysts, rubies, pearls, and sapphires. The Crown of Charlemagne was sought after by emperors and kings from the 900's to about 1800.

In theory, all the kings of Europe were vassals of the Holy Roman Emperor. But the empire's power gradually weakened. Kings declared themselves emperors in their realms, and they took on all the trappings of

Coronation sword of Charles X, the last king of France.

rule. In addition to crowns, they possessed other symbols of royalty. The orb was a globelike sphere carried by the ruler, to symbolize domination of the world. The scepter was a staff, symbolizing the ruler's power as a judge. And the coronation sword symbolized the ruler's military power.

Some crowns became symbols of nationalism. Hungary's Crown of St. Stephen, made about the year 1000, was one. It was honored so highly that it had its own troop of guards. At the end of World War II, it was taken to the United States. Years of negotiations brought it back to Hungary in 1978.

As their wealth and power increased, rulers amassed great collections of precious objects. In addition to crowns, orbs, scepters, and swords, these royal objects included necklaces, rings, bracelets, religious crosses, inkwells, snuff boxes—anything that could be considered "treasures of the crown." They were handed down from ruler to ruler, from generation to generation. But often rulers were forced to pawn their treasures to meet expenses. And a number of these fabulous objects were stolen. The coronation sword of Charles X of France, encrusted with over 1,500 diamonds, was stolen in modern times and has never been found.

And whatever happened to Colonel Blood? He was caught—but he wasn't executed for his bold crime. The king, Charles II, offered the daring burglar a post in his guard instead!

Crown of 16th-century Holy Roman Emperor Rudolf II.

Crown of Charlemagne, made about A.D. 960.

Snuffbox of Frederick the Great, Prussia's most famous king.

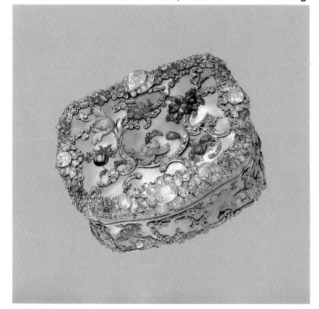

ARE YOU SUPERSTITIOUS?

Did you see the new moon over your left shoulder last night? Well, keep your fingers crossed—it looks like you might be in for some good luck. Things don't look so bright, though, if you spilled the salt at dinner or if you broke a mirror recently. Then, some people say, your luck will be bad.

These are superstitions—beliefs based on faith in magic or chance. People who are superstitious believe that certain actions will influence events, even when those actions have no logical connection to the events. Many superstitions date back to ancient times, when people didn't understand why or how things happened. But even though we may know better today, many people are still superstitious.

Dale Barsamian

KNOCK ON WOOD

Touching or knocking on wood is another custom that's thought to help good things happen. This belief has its roots in ancient folklore. In early times, trees were often thought to be the homes of friendly spirits. People touched or knocked on a tree to ask a favor of the spirit that lived there. Some people also thought that knocking loudly on wood would keep evil spirits from hearing them talk about good news—so that the spirits wouldn't step in to spoil things for them.

DON'T BREAK A MIRROR

The belief that mirrors have special magical powers is an ancient one. Early peoples thought that they were seeing their souls when they saw their reflections in lakes and ponds—how else, they wondered, could there be "other beings" exactly like themselves? When people began to make mirrors, they thought that the mirror actually held the other self, or soul, of whoever looked into it. If the mirror broke, then, something bad would surely happen to that person.

The ancient Romans added the notion that breaking a mirror would bring seven years of poor health. They believed that life renewed itself every seven years, so after that time a person's health would be renewed. Thus if a person's other self were shattered in a mirror, his or her health would also be "broken," and it would take seven years to get well. Gradually the superstition changed from poor health to poor luck. But superstitions aside, a person in ancient times had good reason not to break mirrors— they were expensive and rare.

KEEP YOUR FINGERS CROSSED

When you hope something good will happen, do you ever cross your fingers? Ancient peoples believed that the cross was a powerful symbol, with the power to prevent evil and bring good. By crossing their fingers when they made a wish, they thought they could trap the wish at the place where the two fingers met, so it couldn't slip away before it came true. At first, two people made the sign—the wisher would hold out one finger, and a friend would place a finger on top to form the cross. Later the custom changed, and people made the sign themselves with their index and middle fingers.

REACHING FOR BREAD AT THE SAME TIME

In early times, bread was considered sacred. It stood for the essentials of life—water and grain (used in making the bread) and the earth and sun (needed to grow the grain). As a result, many superstitious beliefs grew up about bread. One was that it was bad luck to cut a loaf at both ends. Another was that it was good luck to accidentally drop bread—and if you made a wish as you picked it up, your wish would come true. This superstition didn't apply if you dropped your bread butter side down, though—that was bad luck. People also thought that if two people reached for bread at the same time, someone would visit the house soon. And dreaming about bread was considered a sign of a happy event to come.

DON'T SPILL SALT

Salt was hard to get and very expensive in ancient times. If people spilled it, they thought that evil spirits must have been around to cause the unhappy accident. And these evil spirits would surely cause more trouble before they were done. Some people thought that their bad luck would last until they had cried a tear for every grain of salt that had spilled. But there was a way to ward off the bad luck. Evil spirits were thought to always stand behind a person to the left. So if you took a pinch of salt and threw it over your left shoulder, you could bribe the spirits into leaving you alone.

MAKE A WISH . . .

. . . on a star, on the new moon, on the breastbone of a chicken, on the candles of your birthday cake. Each of these superstitions has a long history.

The belief that the stars govern luck goes back to the ancient Middle East, where people thought that each person's destiny was ruled by the stars. If a person was born under an evil star, bad things would happen. But if a good star ruled, it would bring good luck.

The new moon was thought to be a symbol of good luck by people in many places. If you first saw it over your left shoulder, you were sure to be lucky. And any wish made at first sight of the new moon was certain to come true.

The custom of wishing on a chicken's breastbone dates to early Roman times. The Romans sacrificed chickens to their gods and hung the breastbones up to dry for luck. This grew into another custom—two people would grasp the ends of the bone and snap it as they each made a wish. Whoever got the longer piece would also get his or her wish.

And when you blow out the candles on your birthday cake, you're following still another ancient superstition. Long ago, people lit fires as protection from cold and from wild animals. Gradually any fire—even a candle—came to be a symbol of magical protection. For example, the ancient Greeks and Romans lit candles when they prayed, so that the flames would carry their prayers to the gods. Later, candles were placed on birthday cakes to ward off evil spirits. And today many people try to blow out all their birthday candles with one puff—to make their wishes come true.

Dale Barsamian

YOUTH

These two boys aren't dressed for Halloween. They're on stage with one of the world's leading opera companies in New York City, for a production of Benjamin Britten's A Midsummer Night's Dream. In recent years children have broken new ground in opera, taking over roles that were formerly sung by adult sopranos.

CAPITAL CHILDREN'S MUSEUM

"I hear and forget, I see and remember, I do and understand," goes an old Chinese proverb. This proverb is the fitting motto of the Capital Children's Museum, in Washington, D.C.—a museum where almost everything is designed to be touched, used, and played with.

In the museum's various exhibits, you can "talk" with a computer, pretend to drive a car or a bus, telephone your friends in another part of the museum, weigh yourself on a metric scale, and grind corn to make your own tamales and tortillas. Everything in the museum is scaled to children's size—all the exhibits are easy to reach and see. As the museum's director explains it, "We've taken the concept of learning through doing, of having kids play with things, handle them, test them, as far as we possibly can."

When the museum began in the mid-1970's, it was housed in four rooms of a Washington elementary school. It grew so quickly that by 1978 it had to look for a larger home. A year later the museum opened its doors at a former convent on Capitol Hill.

Since then it has continued to grow, and today there are three main exhibit areas: Communication, Changing Environments, and International Hall. There is also a fourth area, the Future Center. This is a classroom equipped with 20 microcomputers, where the museum teaches computer programming.

MESSAGES PAST AND PRESENT

The Communication area is the newest and one of the most exciting areas in the museum. The basic idea of this area is to show how people have communicated with each other from ancient times to the present —and also to take a look at some of the communications technology of the future.

You start by walking past a colorful mural —drawn by a computer—to a replica of an ice-age cave. Water drips down the walls of the cave, and you can hear the sound of wolves howling. A sound-and-light show begins, and you see that the cave walls are covered with paintings like those made by Stone Age people. Long before writing was invented, people used drawings like these to record information about hunting, tools, and perhaps even their religion.

The Communication area at the Capital Children's Museum shows how people have communicated with each other through the ages. First you will come upon ice-age cave paintings—possibly the first form of communication.

You will end up at the computer exhibit—the modern version of cave paintings and the newest form of communication.

Beyond the cave is a section called "How We Communicate," which shows how to use codes to send messages. Typewriters, telephones, television screens, and computers explain codes that range from pig Latin to sign language. You can learn how ships communicate at sea by using naval signal lamps to flash Morse code. You can also find out how people used codes in ancient times—by signaling with torches, as the ancient Greeks did, or with African drums.

In the Scriptorium next door, you can write with a quill pen. Then you can contrast this method of communication with printing. There is a working model of an 18th-century printing press, and the museum holds workshops on printing and papermaking.

The photography section of the Communication area gives you a chance to make your own slides and filmstrips. You can also see a hologram, a three-dimensional picture made by laser beams. And if you've ever wondered what the inside of a camera looks like, you can find out—by walking right through a giant replica of one. This section of the museum also contains the facade, or front, of an old-time nickelodeon—an early movie theater. If you walk inside, you can see your silhouette projected and captured for a few seconds on a chemically treated wall.

Then climb upstairs through the Tower of Babel—a staircase with speakers that let you hear languages from all over the world. A working model of a communications satellite hangs from the ceiling at the top of the stairs. You can operate a miniature Earth station to bounce messages off the satellite to the other side of the room. The museum also has a real satellite dish outside. It picks up television signals from more than 40 cable stations that you can tune in on TV sets inside.

All the exhibits on this upper floor deal with telecommunications. In one section, you can learn all about telephones. All the telephones on display work—some play recorded messages on the history of telephones, and others are connected to each other by space-age fiberoptic cables. You can use these phones to talk to your friends in the museum. You can also hook up calls on a working model of a 1910 switchboard.

There is also a working radio station, where the museum holds workshops. But the most popular part of the Communication section is the computer exhibit.

You enter this exhibit by walking past a replica of a giant 1950's computer. A videotape shows a scientist of that time performing a calculation with the computer. Then you see a tiny microcomputer of today—the kind many people have at home—do the same problem in a fraction of the time.

Inside the exhibit room, microcomputers are set up for you to use. One computer is called Wisecracker. It calls out to you with a voice synthesizer, inviting you to come over and "talk." This computer will "speak" words typed into it, but only if you type the words phonetically.

Other computers let you draw pictures, tap into a database, compose music, and play games. One takes you through the steps in launching a communications satellite. You can also find out something about the inner workings of these marvelous machines, through an exhibit that gives you a close-up look at a computer's tiny memory chip.

The computers are the final exhibit in the Communication area. They're the modern version of the cave paintings that began your tour—the newest of the many ways that people through the ages have found to record information.

The Simple Machines room is filled with working models of basic machines that you can operate yourself—such as these pulleys.

THE OTHER EXHIBIT AREAS

Changing Environments is especially popular with younger children. This section of the museum explains many things that people meet in everyday life. In the City Room, for example, you can pop through a manhole in a city street to see the pipes and cables that supply buildings with water, gas, and electricity. On the street itself are a bus and a car that you can pretend to drive and life-size phone booths with working phones. You can work in a real kitchen, visit an eye doctor's office, and dress up as a fireman, a postal carrier, or a traffic cop.

In Metricville, you can measure and weigh yourself and other objects in meters and kilograms instead of feet and pounds. The exhibit includes a metric store where vegetables can be bought—by the kilogram, of course. There is also a computer game called Centimeter Eater, in which you try to guess the length of a line in centimeters before an inch worm munches it up.

In the Simple Machines room, you will see how basic machines work and how they can be combined to make more complicated machines. It's filled with working models that you can operate yourself. There are hoists and pulleys that lift concrete blocks, and a model Archimedian screw that bails water from a tank. You can tinker with a typewriter or play on a set of swings that balance like scales.

There are other exhibits in Changing Environments, too. Pattern and Shape uses puzzles, building blocks, and geometric objects to explain math concepts. The Living Room is an exhibit you make yourself. It's filled with objects—foam rubber, fishnets, plastic pipes, and more—that you can rearrange to suit your own ideas. The Factory is an automated garment factory, where you can see how clothes are made.

International Hall focuses on Mexico, and visiting this exhibit is like taking a trip to a Mexican village. There is a chapel with tall arches and columns, a public square with trees and a tile fountain, and a straw market where you can dress up in Mexican clothes. Mexican music fills the air. You can visit a Mexican post office and a turquoise-colored grocery store that sells Mexican food. You can feed a goat or draw water from a well.

A visit to International Hall is like strolling through a Mexican village. You can do such things as grind chocolate with a mortar and pestle and play with Rosie the goat.

There is also a replica of a log house with a sod floor, where you can grind corn into meal and cook it on a little stove.

In a city filled with museums, the Capital Children's Museum is unique. You don't just see and hear the exhibits—you touch them, taste them, try them on, and use them. Visitors to this museum truly learn by doing—and by having fun.

YOUNG PLAYWRIGHTS

"Sometimes I'm so isolated I feel like I'm abnormal," says a teenager named Mark in the play *Meeting the Winter Bike Rider*. This play was one of five presented at the 1984 Young Playwrights Festival in New York City. All the plays were written by young people, aged 12 to 18. And all dealt with the trouble people have in reaching out to make emotional contact with others.

For this year's festival, the third to be held, young people in all 50 states submitted more than 1,100 plays. A selection committee of theater professionals chose the five that would be given full productions—with professional actors and professionally designed sets—at New York's Public Theater. Five other plays were presented in readings.

Meeting the Winter Bike Rider, by 17-year-old Juan Nunez, is about two teenagers who meet by chance on a cold night. One is a gas station attendant; the other is running away from home. The two try to find out what they have in common, and they form a momentary friendship before they part.

Tender Places was written by the youngest finalist in this year's festival, 12-year-old Jason Brown. It's about a boy whose parents divorce. At first, both parents try to win his affection with bribes, and he takes advantage of them. But in the end, he comes to understand the situation.

In the Garden, by Anne Harris, 17, tells of two middle-aged sisters who decide to live together after their mother's death. Despite some initial attempts to understand each other, they end up barely speaking. *Romance*, by 18-year-old Catherine Castellani, shows the efforts of two young lovers to ignore the drab poverty and bleak surroundings that they live in.

Fixed Up, by 16-year-old Patricia Durkin, takes a humorous look at a blind date. In between the awkward moments, the girl slowly reveals her lack of self-confidence. But by the end of the play, the two teenagers have made contact, and the boy has managed to convince her that she's really a nice person.

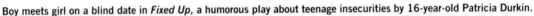

Boy meets girl on a blind date in *Fixed Up*, a humorous play about teenage insecurities by 16-year-old Patricia Durkin.

Meeting the Winter Bike Rider, by 17-year-old Juan Nunez, is about two teenage boys who meet by chance and establish a fleeting friendship.

Tender Places, by 12-year-old Jason Brown, is a clever and insightful play about a boy caught in the middle of his parents' divorce.

YOUNG HEADLINERS

Got a problem? Ask **Mark Godes** of Chelsea, Massachusetts—the teenage version of Ann Landers. Mark, 14, writes a weekly advice column for young people under the pen name Bobby Simpson. Each week, he receives more than two dozen letters asking questions that range from how much allowance kids should get to whether girls or boys are smarter. He answers three or four in his column, which appears in the *Boston Herald*.

The newest face on the Yellow Brick Road is that of **Fairuza Balk,** who is starring as Dorothy in the film *OZ*. The movie brings the familiar characters of *The Wizard of Oz* together again for some new adventures. Fairuza, a 10-year-old from Vancouver, British Columbia, who had no previous film experience, was chosen over 800 other girls.

Alfonso Ribeiro danced his way to stardom in 1984. The 12-year-old from New York City won the lead role in the Broadway show *The Tap Dance Kid,* and his fancy footwork brought cheers from audiences and critics. Alfonso had no formal dance training. But now he has appeared in several TV roles and in a commercial with Michael Jackson.

In 1984, 15-year-old **Scott Berkowitz** of Glen Rock, New Jersey, volunteered as a political fund raiser for Senator Gary Hart of Colorado. He put in 14-hour days, came up with some major money-making projects, and raised over $125,000 for Hart, who sought the Democratic presidential nomination. Scott plans to enter politics himself someday—after he's old enough to vote.

David Stuart, 18, won a $128,000 award in 1984 for work on ancient Mayan Indian hieroglyphics. The money was given by the MacArthur Foundation. David, from Silver Spring, Maryland, became interested in the hieroglyphics in 1974 when he traveled to Mexico with his father, an archeologist. He has since become known as an expert on them.

Another young scientist, **India Wood,** 17, of Colorado Springs, Colorado, made headlines in 1984 with an important find—the nearly complete skeleton of a dinosaur. Wood found the first bone when she was 13. Over the years she collected more. Then she asked scientists at the Denver Museum of Natural History to identify the creature. It turned out to be an allosaurus, a 35-foot-long predator. The scientists helped India unearth the rest of the bones, which will eventually be displayed at the museum.

Richard Pavlicek, Jr., of Fort Lauderdale, Florida, has been attending bridge tournaments since the age of three weeks. Both his parents play professionally. Richard took up the game himself in 1980. And three years later, at age 13, he became the youngest Life Master of the game. Unlike his parents, however, he doesn't plan to make bridge his career. He hopes to become a computer engineer.

Nguyen Vu Tran Nguyen, a fifth-grader from Atlanta, Georgia, was one of 17 children from around the world who received 1984 International Children's Peace prizes. The awards are given by the Round Table Foundation, a California-based group. Entrants in the contest submitted essays and pictures on the theme of peace, which were then judged by a panel of children. Nguyen's entry was judged the best one from the United States.

CHILDREN OF THE OPERA

The curtain is about to go up on another lavish production at the Metropolitan Opera in New York City. The audience has begun to arrive, and the orchestra is warming up. Stagehands rush to put the last props in place. The performers wait anxiously in their dressing rooms, nervously reviewing their parts and making last-minute adjustments to their costumes. But one group of performers doesn't seem worried. They're busy—talking, laughing, watching television, playing games, eating candy bars.

These are the members of the Met Children's Chorus, one of the few groups of its kind in the world. There are about 95 members, aged 7 through 15, all talented singers. And they're some of the coolest professionals to appear on stage. Looking at them, you'd never guess that they're making opera history.

Not long ago, few children were seen in opera productions. There were roles for young people, but these roles were usually sung by adult female sopranos. The children at the Met, however, have changed all that —they've proved that kids can hold their own on stage. Now nearly every Met season includes a solo part for a child, as well as parts for the chorus as a whole. And in the opera *Hansel and Gretel,* children make up most of the cast.

Some of the children joined because their parents are associated with the opera. Others tried out in auditions at public schools in New York. Between 10 and 30 chorus members are used in a typical performance. Each earns about $10. And the Met kids are in demand. They also appear in traveling productions and in operas staged by the City Opera and smaller companies.

On stage, the roles vary. The children may just stand quietly in the background, or they may have more complicated singing parts. Some may be understudies who stand by in case one of the other children can't perform. But it's rare for these professionals to miss a performance. Some are opera fans and hope their careers will continue. Others confess that they'd just as soon listen to rock. But every one of them loves to appear on stage.

These are some of the members of the Metropolitan Opera's Children's Chorus. They are appearing in Puccini's *La Bohème* (above left); Ravel's *L'Enfant et les Sortilèges* (above right and below right); and Strauss' *Der Rosenkavalier* (below left).

TYPICAL TEENAGERS

Their most important goals are career success and happiness. They spend a third of their time talking to others, often on the telephone, and six hours a day watching television or listening to the radio. They like school, chiefly because their friends are there. Their moods change often, swinging from bubbly happiness to deep sadness but rarely lasting long.

Do these sound like people you know? They could well be. The people described above are typical American teenagers, as pictured in two research studies that were released in 1984. One study was nationwide and polled young people in seventh through twelfth grades about their attitudes and goals in life. The other study took a closer look at 75 students in a Chicago-area high school. These students wore electronic paging devices that beeped several times a day. Each time their pagers beeped, they would write down what they were doing and what their thoughts and feelings were at the time.

Here are some of the interesting—and even surprising—things that the researchers learned about today's teenagers.

IN SCHOOL

U.S. teenagers spend about 38 hours a week in school or studying. This is about one fourth of their waking hours. But it is much less time than teenagers in some other countries spend at their studies. In the Soviet Union, for example, students spend more than 50 hours a week. Japanese teenagers spend 59 hours a week at school or studying.

Most U.S. teenagers consider math and English to be the most important subjects in school. Computer science and foreign languages rank high as subjects they think should be added to their schools' course listings. And they like their schools and their teachers. They have far more confidence in school administration than the teenagers of ten years ago—nearly 80 percent feel that their principals understand student problems, compared to 50 percent in 1974.

Another change since the 1970's is that more teenagers plan to get four-year college educations—more than half in 1984, compared to about a third in 1974. But only 17 percent of the students said they liked school for the education it provided. An overwhelming majority—almost 72 percent—listed friends as an important reason for liking school. Another 31 percent listed sports.

OUT OF SCHOOL

U.S. teenagers spend more hours a week in leisure activities than in school—about 42 hours on the average. They watch television, listen to music, play sports and games, and read about two books a month. Four out of five enjoy watching football games. But a large part of their leisure time is spent socializing with others, especially their friends.

The average teenager spends about 30 percent of his or her time with friends. Another

23 percent is spent with classmates, and a similar amount with parents or other family members. One of the studies found that teenagers who spent more time with their families and less with their friends generally did better in school.

What do teenagers do with the rest of their time? They spend a fourth of their waking hours alone, often reading or listening to music in the privacy of a bedroom. The researchers found that this solitude is very important to teenagers. It allows them to concentrate on projects and homework, and they seem to enjoy being with their friends more after they spend some time alone.

The teenagers in the Chicago study often reported feeling very low, especially when they were alone. But these moods didn't seem to last as long as adult moods. And the teenagers whose moods changed most often seemed on the whole to be just as happy as the rest.

THOUGHTS AND BELIEFS

The teenagers of 1984 are more cautious and traditional in their thoughts and beliefs than their counterparts of 1974. Almost half of them think that drugs are the worst influence on young people, followed by alcohol and peer pressure. They oppose the legalization of marijuana.

Unemployment, inflation, and crime are seen by the teens as the worst problems in the United States. Many have strong feelings about law and order, supporting capital punishment and handgun control. Less than 3 percent list ecology and racial tension as major problems. Internationally, the teens say the greatest problem is the threat of nuclear war. A majority—65 percent—say they go to church regularly. In 1974, by contrast, only 25 percent listed themselves as churchgoers.

In many areas, the teenagers of 1984 hold views very similar to those of their parents. The "generation gap" between adults and teens of the 1970's seems to have almost disappeared—three fourths of the teens say they have no difficulties with their parents, compared to half in 1974. There are a few areas where parents and teenagers disagree, though. One is the need for discipline at school (the parents want more). Another is after-school jobs (the teens say yes, the parents say no).

Career success and happiness are the teens' goals for the future. In the surveys, boys tended to list career success as their most important goal more often than girls did, while the girls tended to put happiness first.

For about 20 percent of U.S. teenagers, marriage and family are the most important goals. About 13 percent plan to marry right after high school, up from 6 percent in 1974. Nearly all the teens plan to marry eventually and hope to raise two or three children of their own. Only 5 percent say they don't want to have children.

On the whole, the surveys show that the old picture of teenagers as rebels seeking to break with tradition is no longer correct. Most teens today like best to relax and have fun with their friends. But they're cautious and conservative, and they want traditional things from life. How about you?

YOUNG PHOTOGRAPHERS

Is photography a form of magic? So it would seem from the pictures shown here. In some, the magic is obvious—double exposures have put a human being in a tiny jar and brought a computer to life. In other pictures, the magic is more subtle. The photographers—all young people—have found new beauty and texture in simple objects and everyday scenes.

These pictures were among the winners in the 1984 Scholastic/Kodak Photo Awards Program. The contest is open to junior and senior high school students in the United States and Canada, and it offers scholarships and other awards. Even without the contest, though, photography provides young people with something special—the chance to practice a bit of magic.

Jarred Up, **by Lance Moritz, 17, Havelock, North Carolina**

Togetherness, **by Jeff Kozlowski, 17, Wausau, Wisconsin**

Untitled, by Kerry Green, 17, Lakewood, Colorado

Grandma's Corner, by Terri Piekut, 17, Cicero, New York

Untitled,
by Andrew Ward, 16,
Oakland, California

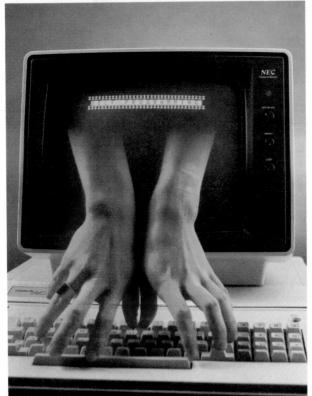

Self Programming Computer,
by William Evans, 18,
Anaheim, California

Blinded,
by Tyler Smith, 17,
Naples, Florida

Untitled,
by Sean Oertle, 17,
Provo, Utah

CREATIVITY

Edgar Degas' The Millinery Shop *is typical of this famous French painter's work. It displays his use of brilliant colors and unusual perspectives. Degas was a leader of the impressionist art movement in the late 1800's. In 1984, the world celebrated the 150th anniversary of his birth and that of another, equally famous impressionist painter, James Whistler.*

241

BONSAI—A LIVING ART

Japan is a land of great natural beauty—rugged mountains, rocky coasts, green hillsides, and sparkling inland seas. And the Japanese have a special art form that brings that natural beauty right into their gardens: the art of bonsai.

Bonsai (pronounced bone-sigh) are miniature plants, usually trees, that are grown in shallow containers. They have been carefully dwarfed and shaped by special techniques. The magic of bonsai is that they duplicate the appearance of full-size trees in their natural settings—perhaps a hardy pine sprouting from a mountain crevice or a stately elm towering over a plain. And they please the eye, projecting an air of tranquility and simplicity.

AN ANCIENT ART

The origins of this unique art form are shrouded in time. The Japanese name "bonsai" comes from the Chinese words *p'en tsai,* meaning "tray planted." It's thought that bonsai were first created in China 700 or 800 years ago. Many scholars think that bonsai traveled from China to Japan in the 1300's, although some say the Japanese may have taken up the art earlier.

One thing, however, is certain: The Japanese have so refined the art of growing bonsai that today this art is considered their own. Japanese gardeners may spend lifetimes working on bonsai, and they pass on their art to their children. Some Japanese bonsai are hundreds of years old. These an-

Bonsai are miniature trees that are grown in shallow containers. They began as normal trees—but then were carefully dwarfed and shaped by special techniques. Flowering trees, such as this Taiwan cherry, make especially beautiful bonsai.

The first step in creating a bonsai is to prune the plant and its roots. This reveals the structure of the trunk and branches and encourages compact growth. New growth is then pinched back regularly. One way to develop the form of the bonsai is to wrap soft copper wire around the trunk and branches and then bend the parts into the desired shape. The wire is removed as the trunk or branch thickens.

cient trees, twisted and gnarled, are the work of many hands. Each gardener subtly shaped the tree and influenced its growth according to his or her own designs.

Small wonder that the graceful bonsai, which are said to symbolize mortality and the seasons, are prized in Japan—and in other countries, too. Many people in the United States and Canada enjoy creating bonsai. And the U.S. National Arboretum in Washington, D.C., includes a collection of 53 bonsai, a gift from Japan to mark the U.S. Bicentennial in 1976. The plants range from 30 to 350 years in age. One is a 180-year-old red pine that once belonged to Japan's imperial household.

HOW BONSAI ARE CREATED

Typical bonsai are 2 to 3 feet (60 to 90 centimeters) tall. They are usually developed from young plants found in nature or pur-chased in nurseries. As the plants grow, they are pruned, pinched, and trained to dwarf and shape them.

Occasionally a bonsai is developed from a tree found in the wild that has been dwarfed by nature—especially one that has been beaten and buffeted by wind and weather so that it has already taken on an interesting shape. All that remains to be done is to refine and complete what nature has begun. Most of the very old bonsai began in this way.

The plants usually used for bonsai are hardy trees and shrubs. Evergreens such as pine and juniper are especially popular, and varieties of holly, maple, and flowering trees are often used. The best plants are those that naturally have small leaves, flowers, and fruits. Even when a tree is being grown as a miniature, it will bear full-size fruits and flowers. If they are large, the effect of the miniature will be spoiled.

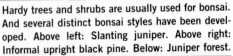

Hardy trees and shrubs are usually used for bonsai. And several distinct bonsai styles have been developed. Above left: Slanting juniper. Above right: Informal upright black pine. Below: Juniper forest.

The first step in creating a bonsai is to prune the plant, to reveal the structure of the trunk and branches. At the same time, the roots are pruned sharply. From then on, new growth is pinched back regularly, as often as the growing pattern of the plant requires, to encourage compact growth. And the plant is repotted every so often, to prune the roots again and to add fresh soil.

To bend trees into interesting shapes that mimic nature, bonsai gardeners use several techniques. One is to wrap soft copper wire around the trunk and branches and then bend the parts into the desired shape. The wire is removed as the trunk or branch grows thicker. To bend a tree over, wires are attached from the tree to the rim of the pot. And weighted strings are sometimes attached to branches, to make them sweep gracefully down.

The techniques that are applied to the plant are aimed at developing the characteristics of a large, mature tree. The actual age of the bonsai is not important. What is important is that the bonsai must *look* old. For example, a good bonsai should have a trunk that is wide at the base and tapers naturally toward the top. Exposed roots help the effect, especially if they are gnarled.

Even mature bonsai require a lot of care. In Japan, most are kept outdoors, sometimes under a lathe shelter. The shelter—made of evenly spaced strips of wood—allows light to enter but protects the plants from hot sun, driving rain, and strong winds. Hardy trees such as pines and maples grow best outdoors. They need the period of dormancy that cold winter weather brings.

Fig trees and other subtropical species are sometimes grown as indoor bonsai. Indoor bonsai are especially popular in the United States. These plants grow faster than outdoor bonsai because they aren't dormant during the winter. And their naturally shallow root systems adapt well to pots.

Whatever their location, the trees are watered daily, misted often, and fed at different times depending on the species of tree. Major pruning is done in spring.

BONSAI STYLES AND SETTINGS

Over the centuries, several distinct styles of bonsai have developed. What style a gardener chooses to create depends as much on the natural growth pattern of the tree as on personal preference.

Perhaps the easiest and simplest is the informal upright style. The tree is trained to grow with a gently curving trunk and three or more branches—usually one to the left, one to the right, and one to the rear for a sense of depth.

Also popular is the slanting style, with a leaning trunk and just one or two graceful, sweeping branches. The slanting, windswept style mimics the look of weatherbeaten trees: All the branches are trained to grow on one side.

The cascade style is an extreme version of the slant—the top of the tree extends below the bottom of the container. To create a slanting or cascade effect, gardeners sometimes set the tree into the pot at an angle.

There are also multiple-trunk and ''forest'' bonsai. A multiple-trunk bonsai is a single tree with a trunk that divides at soil level. A forest bonsai is made up of several trees.

Trees of the same species are generally used, but two different species may also be effective. Sometimes a bonsai forest is created from a single tree. The tree is placed in a pot on its side and covered with soil, and its side branches grow up to become the miniature trees of the arrangement.

A special style is *mame* (pronounced mahmay), which means ''little bean.'' *Mame* are miniature miniatures—bonsai less than 6 inches (15 centimeters) tall. The same techniques are used as for larger bonsai, and the same styles are created. But because of the size of the plants, there are rarely more than three branches on a *mame*.

Just as important as the shape of the tree are the container and the setting of the bonsai. Containers should be simple, in muted colors. The idea is to complement the tree, not draw attention away from it, so wood and earthenware are commonly used.

Most containers are shallow, not more than a third as tall as the tree itself. As a rule, the tree's branches should extend beyond the sides of the container. Upright, slanted, and windswept trees often look best in shallow oval or rectangular pots, especially when they are placed slightly off center. Cascade bonsai are often planted in somewhat deeper pots. The pot is then placed on a stand of some sort, so that the tree's branches can sweep down below it.

The bonsai's planting should reflect the setting that a full-size tree would have in nature. Upright and gently slanting styles are usually surrounded by level or slightly sloping soil, and the soil may be covered with a layer of soft green moss, suggesting a meadow. Small figurines can be added—perhaps a house or a tiny bridge. In Japan, these miniatures are called *bonkai*.

To suggest a rugged cliff, the roots of the plant can be exposed and trained over a rock. Such ''stone-clasping'' bonsai are among the most attractive. Sometimes several bonsai are grouped in the crevices of a large rock, suggesting a windswept islet.

Whatever setting is selected for a bonsai, the tree should remain the central feature. And the arrangement should have what the Japanese call *gei*, a quality of pleasing harmony. A bonsai is truly a living work of art —a bit of nature scaled down and perfected.

Shirley MacLaine (best actress), Debra Winger, and Jack Nicholson (best supporting actor) in *Terms of Endearment* (best motion picture).

1984 ACADEMY AWARDS

CATEGORY	WINNER
Motion Picture	*Terms of Endearment*
Actor	Robert Duvall (*Tender Mercies*)
Actress	Shirley MacLaine (*Terms of Endearment*)
Supporting Actor	Jack Nicholson (*Terms of Endearment*)
Supporting Actress	Linda Hunt (*The Year of Living Dangerously*)
Director	James L. Brooks (*Terms of Endearment*)
Cinematography	Sven Nykvist (*Fanny and Alexander*)
Song	"What a Feeling" (*Flashdance*)
Foreign Language Film	*Fanny and Alexander* (Sweden)
Documentary Feature	*He Makes Me Feel Like Dancin'*
Documentary Short	*Flamenco at 5:15*

Robert Duvall (best actor) and
Allan Hubbard in *Tender Mercies*.

Bertil Guve and Pernilla Allwin
in *Fanny and Alexander* (best
foreign language film).

TWO GREAT ARTISTS

In the 1860's, a group of artists met regularly at the Café Guerbois in Paris. They were rebels against the formal art style that was popular in their day: Rather than painting detailed scenes from history and mythology, these artists wanted to capture fleeting impressions of the present on their canvases. This desire ultimately led them to develop an entirely new style of painting—called impressionism.

Among the people at the café, one man stood out. This was Edgar Degas—aristocratic and aloof, feared for his biting wit and admired for his enormous talent. Degas had a reputation as an intellectual, a painter who was fascinated by the ideas behind the changes that were taking place in art.

Occasionally, another visitor would steal the limelight—James Whistler, an American-born painter who spent most of his time in Britain. Flashily dressed and sporting a monocle, Whistler was known as an eccentric. But his wit was no less sharp than Degas', and his talent was equally respected.

These two great artists had something else in common. They were born in the same year, 1834, just nine days apart. During 1984, which was the 150th anniversary of their births, there were special exhibits marking both their careers.

A STUDENT OF LINE

Hilaire Germain Edgar Degas was born in Paris on July 19, 1834. He was the son of a wealthy banker, and his parents didn't object when he decided on a career as an artist.

From the start, Degas was determined to follow in the footsteps of his idol, the painter Jean Auguste Dominique Ingres. Ingres was known for his beautifully drawn portraits and historical scenes. Degas had once met the great man, and Ingres had advised him, "Draw lines, young man, many lines, from memory or from nature. It is in this way that you will become a good painter."

In 1855, Degas enrolled in the École des Beaux-Arts to study with a student of Ingres', Louis Lamothe. Not long after that, he traveled to Italy, where he could study the paintings of the Renaissance masters first-hand. He made copies of the masters' works, and he painted historical pictures of his own. By the time he returned to Paris in 1859, he was already one of the most accomplished draftsmen of his time.

For a while, he continued to paint historical pictures and portraits. But he became more and more disinterested with these subjects. In Paris, he came in contact with intellectuals and with other artists who were dissatisfied with the old, formal art style. They encouraged him to try his hand at painting scenes from everyday life.

Gradually, his work took on a more modern look. He began to use fresher, more vivid colors and quicker brushstrokes. And most of his subjects came from the world around him—the ballet, the theater, horse races, and cafés. He also began to study other art forms. Japanese prints were then popular in Paris, and Degas noted how these prints placed their subjects on a flat plane, with very little depth. The subjects became elements in a design. He also began to study photography, which was just developing at that time. Photographs caught their subjects in unposed gestures, just as they were for a fleeting moment of time.

Degas began to use some of these ideas in his paintings. He composed his pictures from unusual angles—a ballet seen from a theater balcony or from the orchestra pit, for example. Seen from these angles, some of the dancers' heads or legs might be obscured. In other paintings, the subjects were shown walking right off the edge of the canvas. This shocked some art critics. But to Degas, the design of the picture was most important. He arranged his subjects for the most effective design.

He also began to experiment with new colors and materials. Most of the impressionists were interested in studying the effects of natural light, and they often took to the field with their paints to work outdoors. But painting from nature didn't interest Degas. In fact, he once advised another artist to work from memory alone, so that "you reproduce only what has struck you, that is, the essential." Instead, Degas portrayed many of his subjects in artificial light, especially the dramatic light of the stage. This

French impressionist Edgar Degas was dissatisfied with the formal art style of his day. He used quicker brushstrokes and more vivid colors. He was especially well known for his paintings of ballet dancers. (Left: *Dancers, Pink and Green.*) Degas exhibited only one of his sculptures, a wax figure of a young dancer dressed in a real skirt and slippers. After his death, this sculpture was cast in bronze in order to preserve it. (Below: *The Little 14-Year-Old Dancer.*)

called for brilliant colors. And he used a variety of materials to get the effect he wanted —oil paints, pastels, and gouache (opaque watercolors).

Degas also made sculptures, not for exhibit but as a way of studying how the human form was built. He exhibited only one sculpture, a wax figure of a young dancer dressed in a real skirt and slippers.

By the mid-1870's, Degas was no longer submitting his paintings to the Salon, the official exhibit hall for French artists. The Salon wanted nothing to do with such modern works. Instead, he set up a studio in Montmartre, the artists' quarter of Paris, and helped organize the first impressionist exhibit, in 1874. He continued to exhibit with the impressionists until 1886.

But gradually, Degas became more and more withdrawn from society. He never married. And as he grew older, he rarely went out and seldom had visitors. His eyesight began to fail, and he turned increasingly to sculpture. The tone and subjects of his paintings changed, too. He painted many

scenes of women in daily life—combing their hair, trying on a hat, bathing, ironing, and scrubbing laundry. These later paintings are simpler than the earlier ones. There are fewer details, and the masterful arrangements of line and color shine through.

Degas remained a superb draftsman and a student of line throughout his career. But he developed a style that was uniquely his own, unlike that of the old masters or of the other impressionists. He was admired and respected in art circles. Outside those circles, however, he was largely unknown—most of his works were in private collections or in his own studio, where he would constantly rework his paintings. Degas died at the age of 83. And it was only after his death in Paris on September 27, 1917, that the world discovered the treasures he had created.

AN ARTIST WHO PAINTED FOR ART'S SAKE

Like Degas, James Abbott McNeill Whistler came from a well-to-do family. He was born on July 10, 1834, in Lowell, Massachusetts. When he was 9, his father, a railway engineer, was appointed to build a railroad from St. Petersburg (now Leningrad) to Moscow. The family moved to Russia. It was there that Whistler, who had already taken to sketching family members, had his first art lessons. Later, he went to London to stay with a sister who had married an Englishman.

Hard times came to the family in 1849, when Whistler's father died. Whistler returned to the United States and, in 1851, won an appointment to the U.S. Military Academy at West Point. But a military career was not in store for him. His quick wit made him well liked among the cadets but often got him in trouble with his superiors. And while he led his class in drawing, he was near the bottom in every other subject.

By his third year, he had accumulated enough low grades and demerits to get himself expelled. Whistler later jokingly said that he was bounced for one wrong answer on a chemistry test—stating that silicon was a gas. "Had silicon been a gas," he quipped, "I would have been a major general."

Degas painted many scenes of women in daily life—trying on hats, combing their hair, doing chores such as scrubbing laundry and ironing. (Below: *Before a Mirror.*)

From West Point, Whistler took a post as a chartmaker with the U.S. Geodetic and Coastal Survey. There he learned a new artistic technique—etching—that he was to use throughout his life. But he paid more attention to his social life than to his job. And while his charts were accurate and beautifully drawn, he often decorated the borders with sketches and odd designs.

After three months, he resigned the job and sailed for Paris, determined to make a career as an artist. The year was 1855. At first he studied under Charles Gleyre, another follower of Ingres. But he soon decided that he could learn more by sketching the life around him—in the streets and parks of Paris.

He quickly became a familiar figure at the cafés frequented by artists, and he developed a reputation as a wit. During these years Whistler improved both his etching technique and his painting style. His works showed ordinary people in everyday scenes. When he painted from nature, he often painted quickly, trying to catch the mood of the moment. And he applied paint in thin layers to build the tone he wanted.

Whistler's early works were admired by other artists but didn't win approval from the French Salon. In 1859 he went to London, to stay with his sister and her husband. He settled down in Britain for good, although he continued to make frequent trips to Paris.

The British equivalent of the Salon was the Royal Academy. This group gave a slightly warmer reception to Whistler's work. But it rejected his major work of the early 1860's—a painting called *Symphony in White No. 1: The White Girl*. Whistler promptly took the picture to Paris, where it was shown in an exhibit with other impressionist works in 1863.

The painting caused a sensation. It showed a red-haired girl in a white dress, against a background of white draperies. In contrast to the highly polished realistic style then popular, details were sketchy suggestions. Critics were outraged and called the painting unfinished. They also objected that it told no story and presented no moral to the public.

But to Whistler the most important element in a painting was its design. Art, he believed, should exist for its own sake, not to present a moral. To emphasize this, he called his paintings symphonies, nocturnes, harmonies, and arrangements—terms usually used for music. Even in portraits, the design of the canvas took priority. His famous 1872 portrait of his mother, for example, was titled *Arrangement in Gray and Black, No. 1,* (commonly called *Whistler's Mother*). In it, he carefully balanced areas of light and dark to create a design.

Whistler's concern for design even extended to the rooms where his paintings were hung. In one case, he gave a special exhibition in which the gallery walls and the

James Whistler's *The White Girl* caused a sensation because, said critics of his time, it was sketchy and unfinished and told no story. But to Whistler, the most important element in a painting was its design.

uniforms of the attendants matched the colors in the paintings. And when a client bought his painting *Princess of the Land of the Porcelain*, he completely redecorated the client's dining room to suit the picture. The client objected, though, when he painted over the room's expensive leather-covered walls.

Whistler was a genius at creating mood in landscapes. He was especially fond of painting night scenes of river shores, with the water reflecting every point of light. In 1877 the art critic John Ruskin charged that one of these paintings, *Nocturne in Black and Gold: The Falling Rocket*, amounted to "flinging a pot of paint in the public's face." Whistler sued for slander, defending the painting as "an arrangement of line, form, and color." He won the case and was awarded the token amount of one farthing. But the court costs nearly ruined him.

To recover his finances, he traveled to Venice to do a series of etchings. Whistler's etchings were generally better received than his paintings and sold well during his lifetime. He, too, was an admirer of Japanese art. And his etchings showed that like the Japanese, he could capture the mood of a scene with a few quick lines.

Toward the end of his life, Whistler won greater recognition. He became a member of the Royal Society of British Artists and later served as president of the group. But to many people, he was better known as a personality than as a painter. He was the image of the eccentric artist, strolling about in white trousers and bow-topped patent leather shoes. His sarcasm was notorious—to a young artist who claimed to paint only what he saw, Whistler remarked, "Ah, but the shock will come when you see what you paint." A life filled with such remarks led

Even when Whistler painted the famous portrait of his mother, the design of the canvas came first—as can be seen in the carefully balanced areas of light and dark in the background.

Edgar Degas and James Whistler were two of the most controversial artists of their time. Both were creators of new styles. And both were remarkable, sometimes difficult personalities. With this in mind, it's not surprising that the two men were not only friends but also lifelong admirers of each other's work.

The friendship dated from the 1860's when they met in the artists' cafés of Paris. Although Whistler then lived in London, he kept in contact with Degas through letters, and he sometimes visited him in Paris. Whistler also encouraged many British collectors to buy works by Degas, and Degas returned the favor with praise for Whistler's work.

What brought them together was a common belief in the importance of design in art. Both felt that art should do more than just reflect nature—it should reorder the lines and tones of nature to convey an impression. Both were admirers of Japanese and oriental art. Both experimented with new materials and techniques. Both were concerned about how their works were framed and displayed. And while each developed his own style, the two men often influenced each other through their work.

There were major differences between the two, of course—not only in art but in personality. Their self-portraits (*above*) point up some of these differences. Degas was haughty and withdrawn. He chose to show himself dressed as an aristocrat, carrying a top hat and white gloves. Whistler was brash and outgoing, a man who sought fame. He portrayed himself as an eccentric artist, wearing a smock and beret and holding his brushes.

Both men were famous for delivering cutting remarks. But Degas was one of the few people who could make Whistler fall silent. Once, when the American marched into a Paris restaurant dressed to the nines, Degas is reported to have said, "Whistler, you have forgotten your muff."

But their mutual admiration was stronger than these differences. "As far as painting is concerned," Whistler once remarked, "there is only Degas and myself."

him to write a book called *The Gentle Art of Making Enemies,* which was published in 1890.

Still, it was his theories about art that brought him the most renown. He summed up these theories in "The Ten O'Clock" lecture, which he delivered in 1885. The artist's job, he said, was not to represent nature but to choose and group elements of nature for a beautiful effect. Art itself should have no purpose other than beauty.

In 1888, when Whistler was 54, he married Beatrix Godwin. Whistler was devoted to his wife and was grief-stricken when she died in 1896. After that, he found it increasingly difficult to paint.

Whistler died in London on July 17, 1903, at the age of 69. His theories were revolutionary for his time. But it wasn't too long before people began to understand them and to appreciate the beautiful artworks he had created.

MODERN DINOSAURS

Just about everyone has heard of dinosaurs, those mighty reptiles that roamed the Earth's prehistoric swamps millions of years ago. If you've been to a museum of natural history, you may even have seen dinosaur skeletons that were assembled from the fossilized bones of these creatures. But the dinosaurs you see on these pages are a whole new breed. They're modern-day dinosaurs, designed and pieced together from discarded car parts by sculptor Jim Gary.

Gary roams through heaps of twisted metal in the automobile junkyards of New Jersey to find his materials. He doesn't pick up just any car part—he looks for parts with "character" that will fit a design he has in mind. Old oil pans become skulls. Brake shoes help form feet. Leaf springs become ribs. An old car's drive shaft becomes a new dinosaur's neck. The sculptor has even used

the roofs of old Volkswagens to form turtle-like backs for some of his creations.

It can take months or even years to shape the parts and weld them together. Then the new "dinosaur" is painted—often in a startling color, like the hot pink pteranodon shown here.

The dinosaurs have been exhibited in museums from Pittsburgh, Pennsylvania, to Tokyo, Japan. And they always seem to draw a crowd. Many modern sculptors like to use objects they find lying around to create new works of art. But the dinosaurs also make a statement about the importance of recycling: If we continue to waste the Earth's natural resources, they seem to say, we may end up extinct—just like prehistoric dinosaurs.

Perhaps you'd like to try your hand at creating a dinosaur of your own. Look around for interesting objects. Use cans, paperclips, cardboard, paper, fabric, string—your imagination is the only limit.

HAPPY BIRTHDAY

1934   1984

DONALD DUCK

He has starred in more than 150 films, one of which won an Academy Award. His television credits include specials and his own series. His comic strip is carried by 100 foreign and U.S. newspapers, and his comic books are published in 47 lands. All in all, he's one of the most popular and successful entertainers ever. And in 1984, as he celebrated his 50th birthday, everyone agreed that Donald Duck is still a "quack-up."

What makes the dynamic duck so popular? He has certainly got his faults: He's excitable and impatient. He has accidents all the time. He loses his temper, flushes beet-red, and hops up and down with anger. He's a loudmouth (although you can barely understand what he says). And he makes mistakes —big mistakes. In other words, Donald Duck isn't perfect. And this is exactly why people love him so much—he's just like everyone else.

Donald's creator was Walt Disney, who began making animated cartoons in the 1920's. By 1930, Disney had added sound to his cartoons. And sound turned out to be a key factor in Donald Duck's success.

IT STARTED WITH A QUACK

Donald's story begins in the early 1930's, when Disney was auditioning performers to do various animal voices. Among them was a young man named Clarence Nash. He presented a voice described as a cross between a baby goat and a frightened little girl trying to recite ''Mary Had a Little Lamb.'' But to Disney, the voice was pure duck. Nash was hired, and he has provided Donald's voice ever since.

Donald's first cartoon was *The Wise Little Hen,* which was released on June 9, 1934. He played a secondary role: Along with other barnyard animals, he refused to help the hen sow corn—and as a result didn't get to eat any. His second film, a Mickey Mouse cartoon called *Orphan's Benefit,* was released the same year, and in it he was given a much larger speaking (or, more accurately, squawking) role.

From that modest start, it didn't take long for the duck to waddle his way to stardom.

In 1935, he was featured in *Band Concert,* the first color Mickey Mouse cartoon. And by 1936, he was ready to take top billing in a cartoon of his own—*Donald and Pluto.*

As might be expected, the new star soon found romance. In the 1937 cartoon *Don Donald,* he courted a señorita named Donna. She was the model for a new character—Daisy Duck—who was featured in many of Donald's later films. The next year, Donald's three mischievous nephews—Huey, Dewey, and Louie—appeared on the scene. And as the years went by, more fowl characters emerged to round out the Duck family. They included Gyro Gearloose, a wacky inventor, and an uncle, Scrooge McDuck—a jillionaire who liked to spend his free time relaxing in his vast moneybin.

Cartoon shorts weren't enough for this fast-rising duck, however. Before long he was also appearing in full-length feature films—*The Reluctant Dragon* (1941), *Saludos Amigos* (1943), *Fun and Fancy Free* (1947),

Donald Duck's first cartoon was *The Wise Little Hen*, which was released in 1934.

WRITTEN AND ILLUSTRATED BY THE STAFF OF THE WALT DISNEY STUDIOS

Donald soon found romance—in the form of Daisy Duck, who was featured in many of his later films.

and *Melody Time* (1948). *The Three Caballeros* (1945) combined live-action footage and animation, the first film to do so since some experimental films of the 1920's. The duck also became known for a series of safety and education films.

Donald made important contributions to the Allied effort during World War II. Of course, he was drafted into the Army. His draft notice was dated March 24, 1941, and gave his middle name as Fauntleroy. Donald's wartime experiences were recorded in a number of cartoons—*The Vanishing Private, The Old Army Game,* and others. His most famous wartime cartoon was *Der Fuehrer's Face* (1943), which won an Academy Award as best cartoon short subject. And Donald's own feisty face appeared in more than 400 insignias that the Walt Disney Studio designed for the war effort.

Donald's face appeared on a lot of other things as well. As the duck's popularity soared in the 1930's and 1940's, shoppers could buy Donald Duck dolls, Donald Duck balls, Donald Duck bread, Donald Duck orange juice, Donald Duck cookie jars, and Donald Duck lamps. There were even cans of Donald Duck succotash. Today the famous duck is still featured on merchandise that ranges from T-shirts to encyclopedias.

And like many famous film stars, Donald tried his hand at other entertainment fields. In 1935, he began to appear in a comic strip, *Silly Symphony,* with other Disney characters. Three years later he had his own daily strip, and by 1940 Donald Duck comic books were on sale. Over the years he was also featured in many books—including a 256-page biography, *Donald Duck,* published in 1979.

When television came on the scene, Donald was ready. He made his debut in 1954, in a segment of the Disneyland series called "The Donald Duck Story." He also appeared daily on "The Mickey Mouse Club." And in 1960, he was honored by a special show, "This Is Your Life, Donald Duck."

A FABULOUS FIFTIETH

At 50, Donald Duck showed no signs of slowing down. He was still active in television, as host of "Donald Duck Presents" on the Disney cable channel. He continued to greet visitors personally at Disneyland in California, at Walt Disney World in Florida, and at Tokyo Disneyland in Japan. In 1983 he had a major role in a short feature, *Mickey's Christmas Carol*. And during 1984 he was hard at work on his latest film, a short feature based on the life of Christopher Columbus. The lead in this film is played by Mickey Mouse; Donald plays a stalwart crew member.

But Donald still had plenty of time to celebrate his birthday. And what a celebration it was!

A special plane, *Duck One*, carried Donald and Daisy on a four-day coast-to-coast tour. They stopped at fifteen cities for airport birthday celebrations. At Disneyland and at Walt Disney World, Donald starred in special musical variety shows and led parades of costumed characters down Main Street through showers of ticker tape. In California, he visited a Marine base and was named an honorary Marine. In Florida, he led a flock of live ducks to a treat—a birthday cake decorated with peas, corn, and carrot candles. There were special celebrations at Tokyo Disneyland, too.

As the world's most famous duck enters his second half-century, he's still in great demand. Fan mail continues to pour in from people around the world. But success hasn't changed Donald. He's still the same plucky duck—bumbling and hot-tempered but full of charm, ready to take on life against all odds. And as long as he doesn't change, chances are that he'll be just as loved 50 years from now as he is today.

Fifty years after his creation, Donald remains the world's most famous duck.

Susan Saint James and Jane Curtin (best actress, comedy series) in "Kate and Allie."

1984 EMMY AWARDS

CATEGORY	WINNER
Comedy Series	"Cheers"
Actor—comedy series	John Ritter, "Three's Company"
Actress—comedy series	Jane Curtin, "Kate and Allie"
Supporting Actor—comedy series	Pat Harrington, Jr., "One Day at a Time"
Supporting Actress—comedy series	Rhea Perlman, "Cheers"
Drama Series	"Hill Street Blues"
Actor—drama series	Tom Selleck, "Magnum, P.I."
Actress—drama series	Tyne Daly, "Cagney and Lacey"
Supporting Actor—drama series	Bruce Weitz, "Hill Street Blues"
Supporting Actress—drama series	Alfre Woodard, "Hill Street Blues"
Special—drama	"Something About Amelia"
Special—variety, music, or comedy	"The Sixth Annual Kennedy Center Honors: A Celebration of the Performing Arts"

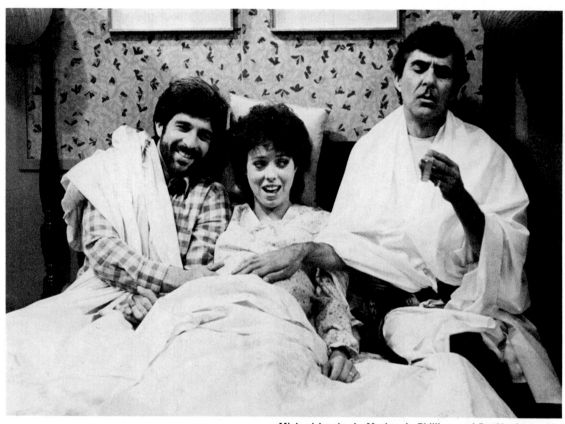

Michael Lembeck, Mackenzie Phillips, and Pat Harrington, Jr.
(best supporting actor, comedy series) in "One Day at a Time."

Sharon Stone and Tom Selleck (best actor, drama series) in "Magnum, P.I."

THE MUSIC SCENE

In every decade, a singing star, musical group, or music style comes along to set the pop scene ablaze. In 1956 it was Elvis Presley. Then in 1964 the Beatles appeared and changed popular music forever. In 1978 disco swept the music world and kept everyone dancing in the clubs.

The 1980's appear to be no different—and so far Michael Jackson has set the tone. His extensive media coverage, the staggering sales of his recordings and video cassettes, his electrifying appearance on rock video programs, and the astronomical box office grosses of the Victory Tour with his brothers all helped to make 1984 Michael Jackson's year . . . and probably the 1980's his decade.

The 25-year-old performer's record-breaking achievements were extraordinary. In 1984 he was nominated for twelve Grammy Awards and actually walked off with eight of them. This accomplishment made him the winner of more Grammys in a single year than any other artist in the 26-year history of the awards. Sales of his *Thriller* album,

Sales of Michael Jackson's *Thriller* album reached 35,000,000 copies in 1984—making it the best-selling album in the history of the record industry.

whose impact had begun to be felt in 1983, reached a record-smashing 35,000,000 discs in 1984. And three smash singles from the album—"Billie Jean," "Beat It," and "Wanna be Startin' Somethin' " were all written by Jackson. As if this weren't enough, Michael (and his brothers) visited the recording studio and came up with the album *Victory*—another best-seller. It provided the public with the hit single "State of Shock."

It was reported that the royalties from albums, video cassettes, and an almost endless array of merchandising tie-ins, plus the reunion Victory Tour with his brothers, would make Michael Jackson worth an incredible $75,000,000!

COMING ON STRONG

If Michael Jackson was the reigning king of the pop music scene, could Prince be far behind in the line of succession? Just about the same age as Jackson, Prince stole the spotlight midway through 1984 with his unconventional singles "When Doves Cry" and "Let's Go Crazy." The young man from Minneapolis also hit number one in the charts with the soundtrack album from his film debut, *Purple Rain*. Prince, who has been described as a combination of Little Richard and Jimi Hendrix, added a new dimension to his explosive personality with the dramatic impact of the film. Autobiographical in nature, *Purple Rain* was one of the top movies of the year. It was hailed by the critics as "the most revolutionary rock film since the Beatles' *Hard Day's Night*."

Bruce Springsteen, a widely heralded American rock star of the 1970's, was just behind Jackson and Prince in popularity and media coverage. Springsteen still maintains a huge following because of his powerhouse stage performances and the brilliance and depth of his songwriting. His popularity was demonstrated in a record-breaking summer tour and new best-sellers. *Born in the U.S.A.* continued his critical examination of the American scene that began two years earlier in his hit album *Nebraska*. Two singles from his new album, "Dancing in the Dark" and "Cover Me," hit the mark with the public and placed on the Top 10 charts.

A VISUAL AND SOUND EXPLOSION

In 1984 it became clear that music videos had changed the record-buying public from listeners to viewers. Singers had to "look hot" as well as "sound hot." Rock films and, in turn, their soundtracks were in great demand. For example, in 1984 teenagers were talking about a new heavy-metal group called Spinal Tap. But there really was no group called Spinal Tap—except in a film and on a soundtrack album. *This Is Spinal Tap,* directed by Rob Reiner (Meathead of the TV series *All in the Family*), was a satirically funny takeoff of heavy-metal music.

Footloose held the honors for being the most popular soundtrack album of the year. The teen-rock musical sold over 5,000,000 copies and yielded two hit singles. Kenny Loggins recorded the title tune, "Footloose," and Deniece Williams hit the charts with "Let's Hear It for the Boy."

The film *Ghostbusters* brought recognition to Ray Parker, Jr., who wrote and recorded the title song, and gained a gold record for his effort. *Eddie and the Cruisers,* a film that didn't do well at the box office in 1983, had a second life on cable television in 1984. The soundtrack also did better the second time around and sold close to a million albums. It proved to be a success for John Cafferty and the Beaver Brown Band, who wrote and performed the musical score, including the single "On the Dark Side."

GIMME A BREAK!

Yet another musical phenomenon swept the country in 1984. Break-dancing—an acrobatic form of dancing that originated in New York City's South Bronx—had everybody leaping, spinning, pushing, and jumping. "Breaking" is part of the "hip hop" black-Hispanic street culture, whose "high priest," Afrika Bambaataa, became its biggest promoter. He founded the Zulu Nation, whose population is made up of "breakers" (dancers), "rappers" (singers), "scratchers" (record spinners), and "burners" (graffiti artists).

But it was the break-dancers who seemed to get most of the attention. The music scene and the media were fascinated by the energy and creativity of the acrobatic dancers, who appeared to spin on every part of their body except their feet.

Break-dancing, an acrobatic form of dancing that originated in New York City's South Bronx, had people spinning on every part of their body except their feet.

The craze swept like a hurricane from coast to coast, and it was responsible for two films. *Beat Street* and *Breakin'* didn't break any box-office records, but they did supply the record-buying public with two eagerly awaited soundtrack albums.

To Harry Belafonte, co-producer of *Beat Street,* "the real story of break-dancing . . . is this protest . . . this folk art that developed under its own steam . . . From the Bronx, this hip hop culture is saying: 'You're not going to be able to forget us. You'll see it on the sides of your subways. You'll see it on the walls of your city. You'll see it in our dancing on every street cor-

Left: Cyndi Lauper projected an image of kookiness and made it big with the album *She's So Unusual*. Right: Britain's Thompson Twins (all three of them) had smash singles with "Hold Me Now" and "Doctor! Doctor!"

ner.' " *Breakin'*, the more popular film, featured fast-paced and eye-catching footwork, and it included in its soundtrack the hit single "There's No Stopping Us" by Ollie and Jerry. That song propelled the album sales of *Breakin'* past the 3,000,000 mark.

A NEW LOOK

Several of the new artists in 1984 were helped by almost continuous exposure on MTV (Music Television), the rock-video cable stations. Brooklyn-born Cyndi Lauper hit the airwaves, and everybody sat up and took notice. Projecting an image of kookiness and flakiness, Lauper scored big with two hit singles, "Girls Just Want to Have Fun" and "Time After Time." She also had a best-selling album with *She's So Unusual*.

One of Britain's hot new exports in 1984 was the Thompson Twins. Despite the name, there were neither Thompsons nor twins in the three-person group. There was, however, one "redhead" (Tom Bailey), one black (Joe Leeway), and one blond (Alannah Currie). This unusual trio produced smash singles with "Hold Me Now" and "Doctor! Doctor!" and a best-selling album, *Into the Gap*. Also on the "newly arrived" list were Patty Smyth of Scandal with the single "The Warrior," and Huey Lewis and the News who hit the big time with *Sports*, a platinum album.

THE BRITISH INVASION

The Thompson Twins weren't the only British musical artists to make their mark on North American audiences in 1984. Culture Club and Eurythmics were two groups whose popularity continued throughout the year. South London's Boy George probably caused the biggest sensation. With his feminine outfits, braided hair, and a face made up with mascara, rouge, and lipstick, Boy George and his Culture Club hit the charts in a big way. *Colour by Numbers* and its singles "Miss Me Blind" and "Karma Chameleon" all proved to be favorites with fans old and new.

Red-headed Annie Lennox of Eurythmics was not nearly as eccentric looking as Boy George. While she did sport an orange crew-cut and mannish, gray suits, she and the group also possessed a musically intriguing sound that lent itself well to *Touch,* and the single "Here Comes the Rain Again."

Twenty-seven-year-old Billy Idol, a British rocker with a style between heavy metal and punk, bombarded the music charts with *Rebel Yell,* his second solo album, and "Eyes Without a Face." Yes, the legendary British progressive rock group of the 1970's, which has undergone many changes in personnel, made a triumphal return to the charts with *90125.* The new-wave Pretenders underwent several changes also and, led by American-born Chrissie Hynde, made a comeback with *Learning to Crawl.*

After suffering a musical slump in the early 1980's, British-born Elton John reappeared on the scene. Minus his trademark glasses, but wearing a black, broad-brimmed, flat-top hat, John enjoyed hit singles in "I Guess That's Why They Call it the Blues" and "Sad Songs (Say So Much)." He made the charts with *Breaking Hearts,* also the title of his 1984 tour.

Britain also supplied us with Duran Duran and "The Reflex," from *Seven and the Ragged Tiger;* John Waite with "Missing You" from his Top 10 album *No Brakes;* and Joe Jackson and his album *Body and Soul.*

GROWN-UP POP

Elvis Costello, once known as the bad boy of rock, seemed to have become a probing commentator on the ills of contemporary life in *Goodbye Cruel World.* In Costello's work, many listeners heard a movement toward "grown-up pop." This term also applies to the "adult contemporary" artistry of Billy Joel ("Leave a Tender Moment Alone") and Neil Diamond ("Turn Around"). Record companies and radio stations also seemed to have taken a liking to the more mellow music

of the Tin Pan Alley era. Toni Tennille, following in the footsteps of Linda Ronstadt and Carly Simon, recorded an album of George Gershwin, Cole Porter, and Duke Ellington standards in *More Than You Know.*

Julio Iglesias, who has been called the Spanish Frank Sinatra, has proven to be an enormously popular entertainer. Iglesias, who records in six languages, has reportedly earned more than 200 gold and platinum records throughout the world. With his Latin charm, Iglesias was on the charts before the end of 1984 with *"To All the Girls I've Loved Before"* (a duet with Willie Nelson), and "All of You" (a duet with Diana Ross). He also recorded the hit album *1100 Bel Air Place.*

Tina Turner hit the charts with the single "What's Love Got to Do With It" and the album *Private Dancer.*

The Everly Brothers reunited after a ten-year split, recorded a new album, and once again appeared on the charts.

The real Frank Sinatra also decided to stand up and be counted. He returned to the recording studio after an absence of several years and cut an album of standard ballads. Titled *L.A. Is My Lady,* the album was produced by the award-winning Quincy Jones, the man responsible for many of Michael Jackson's recordings.

CHARTMAKERS . . . OLD AND NEW

The heavy-metal sound was featured on the charts with Quiet Riot and *Metal Health;* Scorpions with *Love at First Sting;* Judas Priest and *Defenders of the Faith;* Motley Crue with *Shout at the Devil;* Def Leppard and *Pyromania;* and Van Halen with *1984* and the hit single "Jump."

Softer sounds were represented on the charts by Teddy Pendergrass, who made a comeback with *Love Language.* He was joined on the charts by the Pointer Sisters with *Break Out* and the singles "Jump (For My Love)" and "Automatic"; Kool & the Gang with *In the Heart;* and superstar Lionel Richie, whose *Can't Slow Down* album

yielded numerous smash singles. "Stuck on You" was the latest best-seller for the multi-award-winning Richie.

One of the most exciting new developments of the year in the music scene was the rise on the charts of the high-voltage Tina Turner. After trying for eight long years as a solo performer to get a hit on the charts, she finally succeeded with a number-one single, "What's Love Got to Do With It," and the smash album *Private Dancer.*

And after a ten-year split, the Everly Brothers finally got back together, recorded a new album, and once again appeared on the charts. Phil and Don Everly held their public reunion in London and went on to record *EB'84* as their comeback album. The opening song on the album, "On the Wings of a Nightingale," was written by Paul McCartney, who, as a fan of the Everly Brothers, was greatly influenced by their music back in the 1960's.

A new name that popped up on the Top 10 lists belonged to John Rockwell. Before it was discovered that he was the son of Berry

1984 GRAMMY AWARDS

Record of the Year	"Beat It"	Michael Jackson, artist
Album of the Year	*Thriller*	Michael Jackson, artist
Song of the Year	"Every Breath You Take"	Sting, songwriter
New Artist of the Year		Culture Club
Pop Vocal Performance—female	"What a Feeling"	Irene Cara, artist
Pop Vocal Performance—male	*Thriller*	Michael Jackson, artist
Pop Vocal Performance—group	"Every Breath You Take"	The Police, artists
Rock Vocal Performance—female	"Love Is a Battlefield"	Pat Benatar, artist
Rock Vocal Performance—male	"Beat It"	Michael Jackson, artist
Rock Vocal Performance—group	*Synchronicity*	The Police, artists
Country Vocal Performance—female	"A Little Good News"	Anne Murray, artist
Country Vocal Performance—male	"I.O.U."	Lee Greenwood, artist
Country Vocal Performance—group	*The Closer You Get . . .*	Alabama, artists
Rhythm and Blues Vocal Performance—female	*Chaka Khan*	Chaka Khan, artist
Rhythm and Blues Vocal Performance—male	"Billie Jean"	Michael Jackson, artist
Rhythm and Blues Vocal Performance—group	"Ain't Nobody"	Rufus and Chaka Khan, artists
Original Score for a Motion Picture	*Flashdance*	Various composers
Score for an Original Cast Show	*Cats*	Andrew Lloyd Webber, producer
Classical Album	*Mahler: Symphony No. 9 in D Major*	Sir Georg Solti conducting the Chicago Symphony Orchestra
Recording for Children	*E.T. the Extra-Terrestrial*	Michael Jackson, artist

Gordy, Jr., founder of Motown Records, Rockwell had a big hit with "Somebody's Watching Me."

GOING SOLO

During 1984, a number of lead singers embarked on solo ventures while continuing to record and perform with their groups. Steve Perry of Journey made the Top 10 with "Oh, Sherrie" and the album *Street Talk*. Drummer and lead singer Phil Collins of Genesis continued his solo career with the single "Take a Look at Me Now," from the album *Against All Odds*. Christine McVie became the last member of Fleetwood Mac to produce a solo album and a hot single, "Got a Hold on Me." In the permanent break-up department, Roger Waters left Pink Floyd and debuted with *The Pros and Cons of Hitch Hiking*. And Peter Wolf of the J. Geils Band ended sixteen years of togetherness and scored solo with *Lights Out*.

ARNOLD SHAW
Author, *A Dictionary of American Pop/Rock* and *Honkers and Shouters*

Canadian Anne Murray walked off with a 1984 Grammy in the Country Vocal category, for "A Little Good News."

THE PIED PIPER OF POP

On a hot summer night in July, 1984, some 45,000 people crammed into Arrowhead Stadium in Kansas City, Missouri. Teenagers, toddlers, grandparents, and people from all walks of life waited excitedly, their eyes on a huge stage that had been erected in the field.

Finally the stadium lights dimmed—and the stage seemed to explode with color, smoke, and light. From the midst of the explosion emerged a group of men, dressed in glittering costumes. But all eyes were on one of them—a slight figure in a silver sequined jacket.

This was 25-year-old Michael Jackson, on the opening night of the four-month Victory Tour he made with his brothers Jermaine, Marlon, Tito, and Randy. (Brother Jackie was kept off stage by a knee operation.) All the Jacksons are talented rock performers. But Michael has become a phenomenon—a pop star who rivals (and perhaps surpasses) Elvis Presley and the Beatles in popularity.

Michael's album *Thriller* has sold more than 35,000,000 copies worldwide—more than any other album in history. He was nominated for a record twelve Grammy awards in 1984 and walked off with a record eight. Michael Jackson posters, dolls, and biographies are sellouts. And everywhere you look, you see fans adopting his unique style, wearing flashy padded jackets and a single glove.

But what is Michael Jackson really like? On stage, he's all confidence and grace, melting his audiences and keeping them in perfect control. Off stage, he's a mystery. He rarely grants interviews. He's seldom seen in public without a blanket of security guards. At press conferences he hides behind dark glasses and lets others do the talking. When he's not performing, he spends most of his time on the secluded estate near Los Angeles that he shares with his parents and his brothers and sisters. If he ventures out, he's screened by the tinted windows of his Rolls Royce.

Friends say that Michael isn't cold and aloof—he's just painfully shy. Born on August 29, 1958, he grew up in a poor section of Gary, Indiana. Michael was the sixth of nine children in his family. His father, once a guitar player, worked in a steel mill.

It all sounds pretty ordinary—but Michael's life wasn't ordinary for very long. Before he even started school, he was singing with his older brothers—Jackie, Tito, Marlon, and Jermaine. Encouraged by their parents, the boys put together an act and chose a name, the Jackson Five. First they won a local talent contest. Then, when Michael was 5, they began playing in nightclubs. Soon they were on the road, traveling by van from one show to the next. They appeared at the famous Apollo Theater, in New York City. And in 1969, they landed a recording contract with a major studio. Jackson Five hits like "A-B-C," "I Want You Back," and "I'll Be There" started topping the charts.

The Jackson Five continued to record hit after hit, and Michael recorded a few singles, such as "Ben," on his own. Then, in 1975, Jermaine left to pursue a solo career. But younger brother Randy joined the group, and they continued to perform as the Jacksons. They starred in their own television show. And in 1978, Michael made his first solo album, *Off the Wall,* and started skyrocketing to stardom.

What accounts for Michael's enormous popularity? He's a supremely talented singer and dancer, for one thing. But his appeal seems to go beyond his talent. Some people think that his shyness has a lot to do with his popularity. Despite his razzle-dazzle performances, he has a wispy, childlike quality. He comes across as a sensitive person who could be easily hurt. Another factor in his appeal may be his way of life. Unlike many stars, Michael doesn't smoke, drink, or swear. He's a vegetarian. He's deeply religious. And parts of his lifestyle seem to be straight out of a storybook.

Each of his trademark single gloves, for example, is hand embroidered with 1,200 rhinestones. His home looks like a castle. One room is filled with video games. Another room is lined with gold and platinum records. There's a movie theater with 32 red velvet seats. Still another room is a recreation of the Disneyland ride "Pirates of the Caribbean," with mechanical figures.

Michael has his own popcorn cart, his own ice-cream machine, and a "bar" that's actually an old-fashioned soda fountain. He keeps a whole zoo of pets, including a boa constrictor, a llama, exotic birds, and two deer. Sometimes he can be seen riding around the parklike grounds of his estate on a motor scooter or in an electric car.

But the fans who each day keep watch outside the gates of the estate rarely see the star. And the mystery around him has given rise to lots of rumors—that he has had extensive surgery to improve his looks, for example. (Michael's friends and family say that he did have his nose shaped, but that's all.)

Even without gossip, Michael Jackson always seems to be in the news. Early in 1984, when he was burned while filming a television commercial, fans kept a vigil outside the hospital where he was treated. Not long after that, President Ronald Reagan personally handed him an award for helping in a campaign against drinking and driving. Then came summer—and the fabulous thirteen-city Victory Tour. Even at $30 a ticket, it was a sellout everywhere.

The Jacksons say the tour marked the last time that the brothers will appear together. And Michael may branch out in new directions. He's already made top-selling videos of his songs and appeared in the film *The Wiz,* and he says he'd like to star in a movie version of *Peter Pan.* But one thing seems certain—the world will be hearing more from Michael Jackson in the future.

Pop star Michael Jackson (shown here with Quincy Jones) walked off with a record eight Grammy awards in 1984.

FACES, PLACES, EVENTS

"Where's the beef?" When **Clara Peller,** a tiny gravel-voiced grandmother, growled out that question in a TV commercial for a hamburger chain, she became an instant celebrity. A former beautician who lives in Chicago, Peller has been making commercials for about ten years. As a result of the hamburger ad, she now appears on T-shirts, buttons, posters—there's even a Clara Peller doll. And her famous question is quoted by politicians, TV stars, and people everywhere.

Babar, the famous elephant of children's books, celebrated his 54th birthday in 1984. The event was marked by an exhibition of original Babar watercolors and drawings, which toured the United States. Babar was invented by Jean de Brunhoff, a French artist, to illustrate bedtime stories for his children. Once published, the tales proved popular with children all over the world. And they're still as well-loved as ever.

At 50, actress **Shirley MacLaine** had a lot to celebrate. She had won an Academy Award as best actress for the film *Terms of Endearment*. Her book *Out on a Limb* was a best-seller. And she was starring in a Broadway stage review that was a smash hit. MacLaine's star status began in 1954, when as an understudy she took over the leading role in the Broadway show *The Pajama Game*. Her credits since then include well over two dozen film roles, as well as stage and TV appearances.

The new **Dallas Museum of Art** opened in January, 1984. Designed by Edward Larrabee Barnes, the huge, contemporary limestone building cost more than $50,000,000. It is designed so that soft, indirect light illuminates the artworks inside. The museum is the centerpiece of a new Arts District that will include a concert hall and other buildings. Officials hope the district will bring new life to the center of Dallas. Several other U.S.cities, including Atlanta, have also built new museums in recent years.

Straight out of a fairy tale, this **gold-domed palace** is said to be the largest royal residence in the world. It is the home of the Sultan of Brunei, a country about the size of the state of Delaware. The palace was completed in early 1984, just as Brunei gained independence from Britain. It has 1,788 rooms—all air-conditioned, of course. The main banquet hall can seat 4,000 people, and the underground garage holds 800 cars. The 300-acre landscaped site includes gardens, a polo field, and several miles of paved roads. This incredible palace cost about $300,000,000 to build, but the Sultan wasn't worried about the money. "Brunei is very wealthy," he observed.

Kit Williams' first book, *Masquerade,* set off a worldwide search for a jeweled hare that the artist and author had buried in his native Britain. In 1984, Williams published a second book, called . . . well, that's the puzzle. Clues to the book's title can be found in the story and illustrations. Readers who guess it are to send in their answers without using written words (Williams suggests knitting or photography as a way of depicting the title). The answer he judges most creative will be rewarded with a mahogany bee box—containing the only titled copy of the book and a queen bee made of 24-carat gold.

In 1984, the Senegalese poet and statesman **Léopold S. Senghor** became the first black ever admitted to the French Academy. The Academy's 40 lifetime members, called the immortals, are charged with preserving the French language and culture. Senghor, 77, is renowned as the author of poetry in French, English, and his native language, Serer. He also served as president of Senegal, a former French colony, from its independence in 1960 to his retirement in 1981.

What's the only country that is crossed by both the equator and the Tropic of Capricorn? If you can answer that, you can move ahead in **Trivial Pursuit,** the hottest board game of 1984. The game was invented by two Canadian journalists who were bored with Scrabble. It relies on players' ability to answer some 6,000 questions on trivia—bits of otherwise useless information. Now the game is selling by the million in Canada, the United States, and other countries. There are six editions of the game, books telling how to win, and a children's version, Trivia Adventure. (If you didn't guess it, the country is Brazil.)

FUN TO READ

A Medieval Feast *tells the story of a meal fit for a king. Colorful pictures show each step in the preparation of the feast—servants sprucing up the castle for the king's visit, hunting parties gathering food, cooks preparing fancy dishes with such names as Cockentrice and Pudding de Swan Neck. Finally the meal is served, and it lasts all day. This beautiful book was written and illustrated by Aliki.*

In Search of
the Golden Kingdom

When Jacques Cartier set sail from France in 1534, he hoped to find a shortcut to the fabled riches of Asia. It was a lust for gold, silver, and precious jewels that prompted the French King Francis I to send Cartier to the northern reaches of the newly discovered North American continent. Somewhere in the maze of rivers and inlets that crisscrossed the dense woodlands of North America, there must be a passage to the golden-domed temples and palaces of Cathay and Cipango—as China and Japan were then known. So went the popular thinking among navigators and explorers of that day.

With his two ships, Cartier prowled about the coast of present-day Newfoundland and the Gulf of St. Lawrence. The French navigator established friendly relations with local Indians, charted the waters between Newfoundland and the Gaspé Peninsula, and searched for the elusive northwest passage. It was a fool's errand, as disappointed explorers who came before and after him discovered. There was no northwest passage to Asia. But gold and precious treasures there might be in the northern kingdoms of the Iroquois Indians. And so Cartier planted the royal standard of King Francis on Gaspé, and he staked a claim for France to all the surrounding territory.

When he planted the flag and erected a cross that day in 1534, Cartier set in motion events that would make part of Canada a French possession for over 200 years. In 1984, the 450th anniversary of that memorable first voyage by Cartier was celebrated, and summer-long festivities were held throughout Canada's French-speaking province of Quebec.

The highlight was a great seafaring festival held in Quebec City, which from June 23 to August 24 became the sailing capital of the world. In June, a dazzling armada of Tall Ships—magnificent full-rigged sailing vessels—paraded past the city. Throughout the summer there was a series of international sailing competitions, capped by a 3,000-mile (4,800-kilometer) transatlantic race from Quebec to St.-Malo, France, the birthplace of Jacques Cartier. Some 50 sailing boats from all over the world took part in the Transat TAG Quebec–St.-Malo sailing race.

Cartier himself surely would have been pleased by this spectacular array of nautical events, for above all he was a man of the sea. Born around 1491 (the exact date is not known) in the French port town of St.-Malo, he became a seafarer at an early age. On fishing and trading voyages he learned the art of navigation; by the time he was in his mid-

20's he had earned a reputation as a first-rate navigator. Not much is known about Cartier's early years. But there is evidence that he may have accompanied the explorer Verrazano on an expedition to North American waters in 1524, and on another voyage to the northeastern coast of South America in 1528.

So when he set off in 1534 on the first of his three voyages to Canada, Cartier was an experienced seaman. During the first voyage, friendly Indians told Cartier about the kingdom of the Saguenay, where gold and silver were plentiful. Cartier returned to France with this information and persuaded King Francis to send him back the following year with a larger expedition.

In 1535 he returned to North America with three ships, the *Grande Hermine,* the *Petite Hermine,* and the *Emérillon.* On this voyage, Cartier sailed up the St. Lawrence River (which he named in honor of the saint whose feast day occurred on the day his ships arrived at the mouth of the river). He went as far as the present cities of Quebec and Montreal and explored the Saguenay River. Despite more Indian tales of gold and silver to be found farther inland, no such treasures were discovered. Having climbed and named Mount Royal (the future site of Montreal), Cartier wintered near the great Indian village of Stadacona (now Quebec). The winter was harsh, and the dreaded disease scurvy ravaged the French seamen.

Cartier lost so many men that he had to abandon one of his ships on the return voyage to France. From the King's point of view, the expedition had been a failure—no gold and no northwest passage. Still, the Indian stories of great riches in the Saguenay kingdom kept interest in the region alive. Six years later, in 1541, Cartier was sent back to North America as captain and pilot of an expedition headed by a French nobleman named Sieur de Roberval.

Cartier left France with five ships in May, 1541—with Roberval and another three ships following a year later. Cartier's instructions were to set up a permanent settlement in Canada and use it as a base for conquering the supposedly gold-rich kingdom of the Saguenay. The French built a fort at Cap Rouge, near the present city of Quebec, and spent the winter there. A search for the mythical kingdom of the Saguenay proved fruitless. But Cartier and his men did find deposits of quartz and mica, which they mistook for precious gems. To the king of France they reported that they had discovered "veins of mineral matter that show like gold and silver" and "stones like diamonds, the most fair, polished and excellently cut that it is possible for a man to see."

With barrels of fool's gold (iron pyrites) and false gems crammed into the holds of his ships, Cartier began the return voyage to France in the spring of 1542. En route he met Sieur de Roberval's fleet off the coast of Newfoundland. Roberval wanted Cartier to return to Cap Rouge, but the navigator refused his superior's orders and sailed back to France. A member of Roberval's party believed that Cartier and his men wanted "all the glory of the discovery of these parts" for themselves.

Whatever his motive, Cartier found himself in hot water back in France. He had disobeyed the orders of a superior and could have been severely punished. But because of his previous services, the king pardoned him and he was allowed to continue his career as a trader and navigator. This he did until his death in 1557.

No doubt Cartier was bitterly disappointed and frustrated by his failure to find either a short sea route to Asia or the golden kingdom of the Saguenay. But his fragile Cap Rouge settlement, though it lasted only a short time, established France's claim to Canada.

During his first voyage to Canada, Cartier had befriended an Indian chief named Donnacona, who ruled over a tribe of Huron-Iroquois Indians. Cartier brought two of Donnacona's young sons back to France, to learn the white man's ways and language. When Cartier returned to Canada on his second expedition, the Indian youngsters served as translators. In the following fictionalized account, we retrace the course of that eventful second voyage of exploration —as seen through the eyes of Jacques Cartier and his Indian guides.

The storm came upon them suddenly, whipping the North Atlantic into a churning, foaming frenzy. Howling wind gusts tore at canvas sails, and at times the savage wind seemed strong enough to rip the heavy oak masts from the decks of the three French ships.

On the *Grande Hermine,* a sturdy carrack and the flagship of the little fleet, strong-limbed sailors fought their way through rain and wind to check the rigging that secured the swaying masts. From his vantage point on the poop deck, a tall, bearded man with a prominent nose, high cheekbones, and deep-set eyes bellowed orders through a speaking trumpet.

"Boatswain, get your men aloft," shouted Jacques Cartier, captain-general and navigator of the fleet. "Lower your topsail and trim foresails."

"Aye, aye, sir," snapped the boatswain, "but I fear sending my men up to the main top in this gale . . ."

Cartier interrupted him brusquely. "It's either risk the men or lose the ship—if we don't take in sail, the ship may swamp. Now see to it quickly, man."

Brushing spray and rain from his leathery face, the boatswain touched his cap in salute. Then he turned and shouted commands that sent seamen climbing the slippery rigging to the yardarms high above the rolling deck.

Looking out through the mist, Cartier could see the *Grande Hermine*'s sisterships—the *Petite Hermine* and the *Emérillon.* They were heaving and swaying as the high waves buffeted their stubby hulls, tossed about on the stormy sea as if they were pieces of driftwood.

Suddenly the Frenchman heard a shrill cry for help. It came from just below, on the main deck. Clutching a handrail to keep his balance, Cartier peered below. Although fog and rain clouded his eyes, he could make out two small shapes huddled between the main hatch and the ship's longboat—which had come loose from its moorings.

"Help, please, somebody help," came the boyish cry again.

Cartier knew the sound of that voice. It was Deerfoot, one of the Indian princes he had taken back to France on his earlier voyage. Wrapping his cloak tightly about him, Cartier clambered down the ladder to the main deck and moved swiftly toward the swaying longboat. Others had heard the shouts, and several sailors were rushing to help.

Cartier pushed his way through the seamen and saw at once what had happened. Little Bear, the younger of the two Indian boys, was wedged between the boat and the hatch, his cloak entangled under the keel. Deerfoot, his older brother, was trying to pull him free.

"Here, you men, grab hold of the boat and get it back on the chocks," barked Cartier. As the sailors pushed the boat back, the navigator reached between them and deftly plucked Little Bear from the space between the boat and the hatch.

Deerfoot scampered out after him. Cartier gathered the trem-

bling boys under his cloak and guided them gently toward the captain's cabin in the sterncastle.

"Summon the ship's doctor," he called to the boatswain as he entered the cabin.

Moments later Dr. Courbeau and first mate Dubois arrived. Cartier instructed the doctor to check Little Bear's injuries.

"It's nothing serious," said the doctor after looking over Little Bear's arm. "Just a few cuts and bruises. I'll put a salve on it, and if the swelling gets worse I'll cut it and let out the bad blood."

Little Bear winced at this suggestion. "Please, sir," he said to Cartier, "we have our own Indian remedies. My brother can take care of me."

Deerfoot nodded his head in agreement. "It's true, sir. I will use a medicine made from the bark of a tree. My father and his father before him used it to heal their wounds after a battle."

"Ridiculous," snorted Dr. Courbeau. "Indian remedies indeed! Put the boy in my care, Captain, and I'll show you how to heal him properly."

Cartier stroked his beard, then looked at the boys with a fatherly smile. They were both dressed in European clothes—jackets with puffed sleeves, and breeches joined to knee-high stockings. Except for their copper-brown skin color and Indian headbands, they looked every bit like young European gentlemen.

"That's all right, doctor," Cartier said. "They've survived so far without the benefit of our European medicines. Let them see to their own wounds."

Courbeau grunted and stood aside. Then Cartier became stern-faced. He looked hard at the two Indian boys. Deerfoot was nearly 13 years old, lean and muscular and quickly growing into manhood. His younger brother Little Bear was only 10 and still a bit pudgy, with a cheerful moon face. Both had long black hair, for they were not yet old enough to wear the warrior's scalplock.

"Now, boys," the navigator said firmly. "I gave you orders to stay below deck during the storm. Why did you disobey me?"

Both boys lowered their heads. It was Little Bear who finally spoke up, in the school French he had been taught while in Paris. "We meant no disrespect, sir. But we've never seen a storm at sea, and . . . well . . . it was so exciting."

Dubois, the mate, laughed. "Aye, unless you get swept overboard—then you'll think otherwise."

Cartier held back a smile. He liked these boys for their high spirits—and he remembered how he had disobeyed his own father's wishes to go off to sea when he was only a lad.

"Very well," he said at last. "I'll not punish you this time. But if ever again you disobey an order I give you, you'll regret it."

Leaving Little Bear in the care of his older brother, Cartier and Dubois returned on deck. The wind had begun to die down, and the sea appeared to be growing calmer.

"I believe we've seen the worst of this storm, Captain," Dubois observed.

Cartier nodded. "So it would seem. And if I've reckoned correctly, we should be in sight of Newfoundland in a matter of days."

Overhead, a slender ray of sun broke through the leaden blanket of storm clouds. Off in the distance a rainbow was visible.

"There's a good sign," said Dubois.

"Aye, perhaps that rainbow will lead us to a pot of gold," remarked Cartier, "or better yet, to the golden kingdom of the Saguenay our little Indian friends have told us about."

Cartier's calculations were correct. Two days later, the little flotilla arrived off the rugged coast of Newfoundland. It was now early August in the year 1535, and Cartier spent the following weeks exploring the waters to the west and south of Newfoundland. Making his way along the barren coast of the mainland, Cartier's sharp eyes searched for a sea-lane that might lead them to Asia.

Along the way, they saw fish of every kind, as well as great whales and seacows. "Aren't they magnificent?" exclaimed Deerfoot, as they passed a school of whales one bright afternoon. "Wouldn't your chief, the king of France, like to have one of those instead of some little nuggets of shiny metal?"

Laughing heartily, Cartier replied, "No, my boy, I think not. From what I know of King Francis, he would much prefer a hundred barrels of gold to a thousand of whale oil."

Actually, Cartier recognized the value of the whales and other sealife. There was a rich harvest of fish and whale oil and bone to be reaped here. But he knew that like other European kings,

Francis cared only for the treasures of the land and not those of the sea. They must find kingdoms like those the Spaniards had conquered in Mexico and Peru, where, it was said, the very streets were paved with gold.

But no great cities came into view; only tiny Indian villages and endless stretches of woodland. As summer gave way to the first days of autumn, the ships came to the mouth of the great river. Deerfoot told the Frenchmen that this was the river of the Hochelaga.

"If you follow it," said the young Indian, "you will come to the land we call Canada. There you will find the kingdom of Hochelaga and the kingdom of the Saguenay."

Early in September they landed on the Gaspé Peninsula, near where he had stopped the previous year. With a party of armed soldiers and his two Indian guides, Cartier went ashore. The cross he had planted still stood. The Frenchmen gathered around it, bowed their heads, and gave thanks for their safe passage across the Atlantic.

Deerfoot and Little Bear were overjoyed at being back in their homeland. Off came their European clothes and on went their buckskin suits. Heavy leather shoes were replaced by soft-soled moccasins.

Before long, the French were greeted by a party of Iroquois Indians. They carried belts of wampum whose beads spelled out messages for the Indian princes and the French seafarers.

"My father Chief Donnacona bids you welcome," explained Deerfoot as he pointed to the designs on the wampum belts. "He and my people await you at Stadacona, our main village. My brother is to return with the warriors who delivered these belts. I will stay with you and guide your ships up the great river."

So Little Bear, his arm nearly healed, went by land to Stadacona. And Cartier and his three ships, guided by Deerfoot, made a leisurely passage up the river Cartier named the St. Lawrence.

In the last week of September, the French expedition arrived at a point where the river narrowed between frowning cliffs. On one of these stood the great Iroquois village of Stadacona. Approaching the mountaintop fortress, Cartier and his comrades saw Indian men spearing fish and building canoes. As soon as the Indians caught sight of the ships, a great shout went up. Soon hundreds of men, women, and children were streaming down the mountainside, chanting and shaking rattles in a sign of welcome. In return, trumpeters on the ship sounded flourishes.

As soon as his sailors had moored their vessels, Cartier led his men ashore. To impress the Indians, he had his gunners fire cannons in salute. Then the Frenchmen marched up the hill toward the Indian town. Drummers led the way, followed by helmeted soldiers wearing armor breastplates and carrying heavy muskets. Behind them came the ships' crews, decked out in their best clothes and holding banners aloft.

Like other Iroquois towns, Stadacona was protected by a moat and a stockade of tall wooden stakes. As the Europeans marched through the gates, they could see streets lined with longhouses, whose walls and rounded roofs were made of elm bark. This distinctive type of dwelling was the reason why the Iroquois called themselves "the people of the longhouse."

In front of the council lodge in the center of the town stood a group of older men, who wore gaily decorated buckskin shirts and leggings. Their faces and exposed forearms were covered with tattoos. Some of these were elaborate designs, while others were recognizable animal shapes—turtles, deer, bears—that were the symbols of different clans. These were the sachems, or tribal chiefs, and they looked both fierce and majestic.

Even before the procession reached the council lodge, Deerfoot darted ahead. A tall, imposing man with a feathered headdress stepped forward to embrace him. Cartier recognized him immediately as Chief Donnacona. With Deerfoot and Little Bear at his side, Donnacona greeted the Frenchmen.

"You are welcome to remain in our village as long as it pleases you," he declared, his words being translated by Deerfoot. "Stay with us in peace, brothers. Together we will hunt deer in the forest and snare fish from the great river."

Cartier bowed and replied, "We come here in peace, great chief. We wish to learn your ways and to teach you ours. I thank you for trusting us with your sons, who have served us well as guides and now make it possible for us to talk to each other."

Then they exchanged gifts. Cartier gave Donnacona a steel-headed axe and a large brass kettle. The chief presented the Frenchman with a fringed buckskin shirt and a ball-headed Iroquois war club with a beautifully carved maplewood handle.

When the formalities were over, Donnacona exclaimed, "Come now, set down your kettles"—the traditional invitation to visitors to join them in a meal. After they had eaten their fill of venison, steamed fish, corn, dried nuts, and berries, the Frenchmen were taken to a part of the village where lodges had been built to house them.

"We seem to have made a good impression on these savages," remarked Dr. Courbeau as he stood with Cartier in front of the longhouse reserved for the ships' officers.

"You should not be so quick to put them down as savages, doctor," snapped Cartier. "They are a proud and clever people, and better suited to survive in this wilderness than we are."

Dr. Courbeau frowned, pointing to a group of women chatting as they carried heavy baskets filled with corn to where other women cooked the kernels in earthenware pots. "See the way they work their women like pack animals. They are no better than slaves."

Cartier smiled. "You are wrong my dear fellow. As I learned on my earlier voyage, it's the women who own the fields, the houses—everything. Why, they even pick the sachems who sit in the tribal council. In truth, they have more power than our own women."

The navigator looked out beyond the village walls. "But

enough about Indian customs. Being friendly to them is a practical matter. Somewhere out there is a great kingdom with riches beyond our wildest dreams. My two Indian boys assure me it is so, and I believe them. With the help of these people, we will find that kingdom and make France richer than Spain.''

In another part of the village, Chief Donnacona spoke to his sons Deerfoot and Little Bear. They sat on an elevated platform covered with reed mats in one of the half-dozen two-family chambers that formed a longhouse. A passageway separated their living area from the one opposite, and in the center aisle a fire was burning brightly.

"We must find a way to keep these white faces from going farther up the river," Donnacona said in a somber voice.

Deerfoot looked puzzled. "But, Father, it was you who told us to make up stories about towns where there are longhouses filled with gold and silver.''

"Yes, that's true," Little Bear chimed in, giggling and clutching at his father's sleeve. "And we spoke with such straight faces that they believed every word.''

"You are right, my sons," Donnacona agreed, his lips parting in a smile. "I made you tell those tales so the white faces would come back to our land.''

He pointed to the steel knives and hatchets that lay at his feet. "These tools are better than our own. They will make life easier for our people, and that's why I want these strangers to stay. I do not want the other tribes to have these things. Now help me think of a way to discourage the white faces from leaving.''

For a few moments they sat quietly, deep in thought. All at once Deerfoot's eyes brightened. "I have an idea, Father," he blurted. Then he leaned over and whispered it in the chief's ear.

The following evening, the French were invited to a ceremonial dance in their honor. Every Indian in the village turned out, many shaking rattles made from turtle shells or tree bark. Most of the men had stripped to the waist, painting their faces and chests with vivid splashes of colored dyes made from berries. In the growing darkness, with just a sliver of moon and the bobbing tongues of flame from the great bonfire to light the scene, the ceremony had an eerie quality.

Cartier and his men stood off to the side, fascinated by the spectacle but not knowing quite what to make of it. The Indian warriors stomped and gyrated as they danced around the fire, their scalplocks and painted faces making them look all the more ferocious as they swung their heavy war clubs overhead. The village women stood back, wailing and chanting as they shook their rattles and beat sticks together in a steady clatter.

Many of the Frenchmen felt uneasy in the midst of all this sound and fury. Even Cartier, who had seen similar rituals on his first voyage, was edgy.

Suddenly there was shouting from the other end of the village. Several warriors dashed past the fire and began speaking hurriedly to Chief Donnacona and the other sachems. The mass of

dancing warriors stopped and rushed to one side. The women shrank back, as if frightened by some evil force.

Out of the shadows now came six strange-looking creatures. From afar they seemed half-man and half-animal—their bodies were covered with fur, and long horns sprouted from their heads. A few of the French soldiers nervously fingered their muskets while others quietly drew swords from their scabbards.

Cartier waved his hand to reassure his men. "Don't be alarmed," he told them, walking through their ranks. "It is only part of the ceremony. Keep together and do not act afraid."

As the strange-looking newcomers came closer, it was obvious that they were only men dressed in animal skins. Their faces were painted pitch black to make them look more fearsome, and a few wore grotesque masks with great bulging eyes.

Deerfoot rushed up to Cartier, a frightened expression on his face, and grabbed the Frenchman's arm. "You see these devils," the young Indian said excitedly. "They have been sent by the god Cudouagny, who lives in the mountains near the great village of Hochelaga. He has sent these terrible demons to warn you that you will be in great danger if you leave our village and go farther along the river."

Cartier laughed. "Well now, it is very kind of your god Cudouagny to be so concerned about our well being. But our God, whose great churches you have seen in France, will protect us and keep us from harm."

Deerfoot looked dejected. "But sir, you don't understand. It will be bitter cold, and the ice and snow will cover even the highest mountain. You will not be able to survive."

"Our faith will keep us warm," said Cartier with a smile, and his men—now reassured that the devilish creatures were merely Indians in animal getup—laughed heartily.

"You must not mock the demons," said Deerfoot in obvious annoyance. "They will be angry."

"Demons, are they," Cartier responded. "I'm not so sure." The French explorer had been watching one of the "demons" with special interest. He was smaller than the others, and he jumped up and down with more gusto than they did.

Without warning, Cartier grabbed the "demon" by the arm. "Well, what have we here? It seems I've seen these bruises before." And with that, he tore the face mask off the "demon." Before him, looking very sheepish, stood Little Bear.

Cartier pointed a scolding finger at the little Indian prince. "You should have remembered to cover those marks on your arm, my young friend. Now enough of this nonsense. We will not be discouraged from our task by any more of these tricks. You have promised to lead us to Saguenay, and we will hold you to your word."

Reluctantly, Donnacona allowed the Frenchmen to continue up the river. With a party of Indians including Deerfoot, Cartier left Stadacona with the bark *Emérillon* and two longboats in mid-September. Several weeks of sailing brought them to the great Iroquois town of Hochelaga, which stood amidst wide fields used for farming. Three stockade walls surrounded the village, which had over 50 large longhouses. The Frenchmen were warmly greeted by the Indians of Hochelaga, who offered them lodging and prepared great feasts in their honor. Because these Indians had seen no white men before, they thought them to have godlike powers. For several days after their arrival at Hochelaga, the Indians brought their sick and lame to be healed by the Frenchmen. Dr. Courbeau wanted to prescribe some of his European medicines, but Cartier thought it best to merely place his hands on the ailing Indians and read a few passages from the Bible.

Cartier finally persuaded the Indians—who were as intent on keeping him in their village as Donnacona had been to keep him at Stadacona—to let him climb a nearby mountain. With one of the Hochelaga chiefs, Deerfoot, and a small party of Indians and French sailors, Cartier ascended the mountain—which he named Mont Real (Mount Royal). He hoped that from its peak he would see the golden kingdom of Saguenay. The view from the summit was indeed magnificent. The St. Lawrence stretched as far as the eye could see, and there were majestic mountains looming over fertile valleys. But no great kingdom was visible.

Disappointed again, Cartier showed the Hochelaga chief a dagger with a copper hilt and asked, "Do you know of a place where we might find metal such as this?"

The Indian chief's reply was translated by Deerfoot. "He says there are great quantities of this metal to be found . . ."

Before Deerfoot could finish, the Hochelaga chief reached out and touched a silver captain's whistle Cartier wore around his neck. He turned to Deerfoot and spoke excitedly.

"Yes, and metal such as that," Deerfoot continued, pointing to the gleaming whistle.

"Silver—and copper," mused Cartier, his own eyes wide with exhilaration. "But where—ask him where, and how far."

Once more Deerfoot translated the chief's words. "He says you must travel far up the Ottawa River," referring to a waterway that branched off from the St. Lawrence. "It is at least three moons distance by boat."

"Three moons! That means three months," Cartier sighed. With winter nearly upon them, the Frenchman knew he dared not risk men and ships traveling that far along an uncharted waterway. Wisely, he turned his ships around and headed back to Stadacona.

He arrived there to find that disaster had struck. Scurvy, the scourge of seafarers, was sweeping through the ranks of the Frenchmen. The dreaded disease had struck down nearly half his men, with more showing the telltale symptoms every day.

"This is the worst outbreak I have seen in all my years as a physician," reported Dr. Courbeau, who appeared worn and haggard from long days and sleepless nights of treating the sick.

Cartier inspected the longhouses where his men were quartered. Some of the men showed the early signs of the disease—swollen gums that bled at the slightest touch. Their skin color had become ashen and their movement sluggish. Others were in the later stages, when teeth drop from rotted gums, and legs become swollen and movement difficult.

Cartier paused before a familiar figure. It was first mate Dubois. His eyes were glazed and feverish, and there were large dark spots on his legs and thighs. He lay moaning softly and didn't seem to recognize his captain.

"Poor fellow," sighed Cartier. Then, turning to Dr. Courbeau, he asked, "Can you do nothing for him?"

"I've done my best," replied the doctor dejectedly. "I can do no more than cut his gums to let out the bad blood. But I'm afraid he's too far gone."

Angrily, Cartier blurted, "You should have taken better precautions, doctor."

The physician shrugged. "I gave them extra rations of beer, for the yeast is known to protect against the disease. But alas, it hasn't helped much."

In the days that followed, a dozen of the ailing seamen died. The others grew sicker, and it seemed to the despairing Cartier that all his men would perish.

Then, one cold winter afternoon, as Cartier was conferring with Dr. Courbeau, Deerfoot and Little Bear approached holding jugs containing a foul-smelling liquid.

"What have you there?" asked a puzzled Cartier.

Deerfoot spoke up. "We have brought you an Iroquois medicine that will cure your men of the terrible sickness."

"You must make them drink it, and they will get well," said Little Bear.

Cartier put his face close to the jugs and recoiled at the odor.

"By God, I fear this cure may be worse than the disease. What is this stuff?"

"We make it from the buds and bark of spruce trees," Deerfoot explained. "Believe me, sir, it will work for your people as it has for ours."

But Dr. Courbeau thought otherwise. "Tree bark! Spruce buds! Why this is outrageous. I cannot permit you . . ."

Cartier interrupted him. "I command this expedition, doctor, and I will make the decision. Our European methods have failed, so let us try theirs."

With the help of those men who were still strong enough to work, Cartier made the scurvy-ridden sailors drink the unpleasant brew. To his surprise and that of Dr. Courbeau, the Indian remedy worked. Men who were barely able to move gradually regained the use of their legs and arms. The swelling of the gums was reduced, and the ugly spots began to fade. Even first mate Dubois, who had hovered near death, miraculously survived. Dr. Courbeau was so impressed that he asked Deerfoot and Little Bear to give him the formula for the medicine.

Winter finally gave way to spring. As the ice began to melt on the St. Lawrence, Cartier made preparations to return to France. Despite his failure to find Saguenay, he was determined to get backing from the French king for yet another expedition.

Deerfoot and Little Bear felt guilty because their tall tales had sent Cartier on a wild-goose chase. They told their father, Chief Donnacona, they wanted to admit to the French leader that they had lied.

The chief smiled. "He will pay you no heed, my sons, for he wants to believe such a kingdom exists."

But the Indian princes were firm, and later that day they went to see Cartier down by the river, where his ships were being refitted. Deerfoot spoke, while Donnacona and Little Bear stood by. "Sir, my brother and I want to tell you that all those stories about the kingdom of the Saguenay were untrue. We know of no such place with the shiny metal that you seek."

For a moment Cartier looked puzzled. Then his eyes narrowed and his mouth curled in a frown. "You are trying to deceive me, my little friend, because you want me to stay with your people when I return and not go farther up the great river. But I am not so easily fooled. I know the kingdom you spoke of is real. I feel it in my bones—and I will find it. Now I must see to my ships."

As the Indians watched Cartier giving orders to his men, Donnacona put his arms around the shoulders of Deerfoot and Little Bear and quietly remarked, "You see, my sons, it is as I said it would be. Our white friend is a captive of his dreams, and it is foolish to try to destroy those dreams. Better that we tell him what he wishes to hear so we may keep his friendship."

Even as the Iroquois chief spoke, Cartier stood by the riverbank looking up the St. Lawrence, while visions of the golden kingdom he sought danced across his mind.

HENRY I. KURTZ
Author, *John and Sebastian Cabot*

POETRY

OVER HILL, OVER DALE

Over hill, over dale,
Thorough bush, thorough brier,
Over park, over pale,
Thorough flood, thorough fire!
I do wander everywhere,
Swifter than the moon's sphere;
And I serve the fairy queen,
To dew her orbs upon the green;
The cowslips tall her pensioners be;
In their gold coats spots you see;
Those be rubies, fairy favours,
In those freckles live their savours:
I must go seek some dewdrops here,
And hang a pearl in every cowslip's ear.

WILLIAM SHAKESPEARE (1564–1616)

THE YEAR

Answer July—
Where is the Bee—
Where is the Blush—
Where is the Hay?

Ah, said July—
Where is the Seed—
Where is the Bud—
Where is the May—
Answer Thee—Me—

Nay—said the May—
Show me the Snow—
Show me the Bells—
Show me the Jay!

Quibbled the Jay—
Where be the Maize—
Where be the Haze—
Where be the Bur?
Here—said the Year—

EMILY DICKINSON (1830–1886)

THE TEAPOT DRAGON

There's a dragon on our teapot,
  With a long and crinkly tail,
His claws are like a pincer-bug,
  His wings are like a sail;

His tongue is always sticking out,
  And so I used to think
He must be very hungry, or
  He wanted tea to drink.

But once when Mother wasn't round
  I dipped my fingers in,
And when I pulled them out I found
  I'd blistered all the skin.

Now when I see the dragon crawl
  Around our china pot,
I know he's burned his tongue because
  The water is so hot.

RUPERT SARGENT HOLLAND (1878–1952)

THE WIND

I saw you toss the kites on high
And blow the birds about the sky;
And all around I heard you pass,
Like ladies' skirts across the grass—
  O wind, a-blowing all day long,
  O wind, that sings so loud a song!

I saw the different things you did,
But always you yourself you hid.
I felt you push, I heard you call,
I could not see yourself at all—
  O wind, a-blowing all day long,
  O wind, that sings so loud a song!

O you that are so strong and cold,
O blower, are you young or old?
Are you a beast of field and tree,
Or just a stronger child than me?
  O wind, a-blowing all day long,
  O wind, that sings so loud a song!

ROBERT LOUIS STEVENSON (1850–1894)

TWILIGHT AT SEA

The twilight hours, like birds, flew by,
  As lightly and as free,
Ten thousand stars were in the sky,
  Ten thousand on the sea;
For every wave, with dimpled face,
  That leaped upon the air,
Had caught a star in its embrace,
  And held it trembling there.

AMELIA COPPUCK WELBY (dates unknown)

PARADOXES

A pin has a head, but has no hair;
A clock has a face, but no mouth there;
Needles have eyes, but they cannot see;
A fly has a trunk without lock or key;
A timepiece may lose, but cannot win;
A cornfield dimples without a chin;
A hill has no leg, but has a foot;
A wine-glass a stem, but not a root;
Rivers run, though they have no feet;
A saw has teeth, but it does not eat;
Ash-trees have keys, yet never a lock;
And baby crows, without being a cock.

CHRISTINA ROSSETTI (1830–1894)

A MOONLIGHT NIGHT

When the moon has colored half the house,
With the North Star at its height and the South Star setting,
I can feel the first motions of the warm air of spring
In the singing of an insect at my green-silk window.

LIU FANG-P'ING (8th–9th century)

THE CROCUS

The golden crocus reaches up
To catch a sunbeam in her cup.

WALTER CRANE (1845–1915)

THE FROG

What a wonderful bird the frog are!
When he stand he sit almost;
When he hop, he fly almost;
He ain't got no sense hardly;
He ain't got no tail hardly either.
When he sit, he sit on what he ain't got almost.

UNKNOWN

A CHIMNEY

Black within and red without,
With four corners round about.

UNKNOWN

METHUSELAH

Methuselah ate what he found on his plate,
And never, as people do now,
Did he note the amount of the calory count;
He ate it because it was chow.
He wasn't disturbed as at dinner he sat,
Devouring a roast or a pie,
To think it was lacking in granular fat
Or a couple of vitamins shy.
He cheerfully chewed each species of food,
Unmindful of troubles or fears
Lest his health might be hurt
By some fancy dessert;
And he lived over nine hundred years.

UNKOWN

POWDERY HEAVEN

Clouds
    fly gracefully over rolling hills
    yet prance under the mystical heavens
    and dance in the beautiful skies.
Like
    a puffy cottonball high overhead,
    a silky powderpuff drifting slowly by
    or a fluffy pillow waltzing in the whistling wind
Showing
    mercy to all but the wind.

MICHAEL WOLTERBEEK
age 12
Oklahoma City, Oklahoma

WINTER BEAUTY

Winter snow falls
Like little cotton balls.
It whispers with the wind
As it falls on my chin.
The snow flies free,
and settles on a tree.
Look on the ground
There is snow all around.
And I hope it stays
For several days.

AMY FRAILEY
age 8
King of Prussia, Pennsylvania

HUSH!

Silent snowflakes
    Falling gently.
      Graceful,
as a field of milkweeds
      swaying
in a soft evening breeze.
      Snow;
gently gleaming,
      disappears
into the desolate night.

MELISSA REECE
age 16
Morristown, New Jersey

A CERTAIN PLACE

In my uncle's cornfield
On a cloudless dry day
When the sun lowers behind the hill
Then a crow squawks away
And field mice rattle between corn stems.

With me and my brother,
Chucking corncobs at each other,
Aiming only at what we can hear.

CHRIS LEWANDOWSKI
age 12
Renton, Washington

HAIL

The hail fell
like little white flowers
in the field,
dotting the green grass
and red tulips.

ANEEMA VAN GROENOU
age 9
Hayward, California

MIST

The mist of the drizzle
Has settled,
Motionless,
Transforming the glare
Of lone lamps
Into a fairyland blur.

A hushed sheet,
By which
Withered grasses tremble,
Cattails pose,
And fragile wisps of willow
Pause.

JENNIFER HEUER
age 14
Grand Rapids, Michigan

RAIN

The rain comes
slowly at
first,
Then comes
faster
and
faster
until it
starts to
pour.
People out
on the
street are
hurrying for
shelter.
So get out
your
umbrellas
so you
don't get
wet!

SUSAN WALMSLEY
age 10
Montgomery, Massachusetts

FOREST KINGDOM

The lake shone like
a silver goblet,
The swans glided through,
stately as princes,
The willows and pines dipped and bent
Like bowing servants in the forest Kingdom.

DIANE BOUDREAU
age 12
South Hadley, Massachusetts

PLANTS

Seed
Small, flat
Growing, sprouting, changing
Fruits, vegetables, shrubs, flowers
Growing, blossoming, producing
Green, leafy
Plants

TODD KEITH
age 8
Evanston, Illinois

MY SHOPPING POEM

Pick a trolley
Pull it out
Fruit and vegetables
All laid out.
Talk to the manager
With a great smile
And say,
Where are the cabbages?
Down the aisle.
Get some toothpaste,
Some soap as well.
What about a doughnut?
They're all right
Just take
A big big bite.

HOLLY BRYANT
age 8
Maidenhead, England

THE NIGHTINGALE

A long time ago, in ancient days, the emperor of China lived in the most magnificent castle in the world. It was made entirely of fine porcelain and was so fragile that you had to be really careful about touching it. Surrounding the castle were lush gardens containing gorgeous flowers. And attached to the flowers were tiny golden bells that tinkled as you walked past.

The emperor's gardens reached so far that even the gardener didn't know where they ended. But if you kept on walking, there was the loveliest forest with tall trees and meandering streams. The forest went all the way down to the sea, which was deep and blue. Great ships would sail right in under the branches of the trees. And in those branches lived a nightingale that sang so gloriously that even the busy fisherman, who was out at night drawing in his net, would stop for a few moments and listen to the bird. "Oh, how beautiful it sounds!" he would say each evening.

From all over the world, travelers came to the emperor's land and greatly admired it. But when they heard the song of the nightingale, they all said, "That is really the best!" When the travelers returned home, they told all about their adventures. And learned men wrote many books about the castle and the gardens—and about the wondrous nightingale in the forest by the deep sea.

Eventually, one of the books reached the emperor. He sat in his gold chair reading it, his head nodding continually because it pleased him to hear the magnificent descriptions of his castle and gardens. *"But the nightingale is really the best of all!"* was also written there.

"What in the world?" said the emperor. "The nightingale? I don't know anything at all about that! Is there such a bird here in my empire, even in my own garden? I've never heard of it! I have to read about it in a book!"

And then he called his chamberlain, who was so grand that when anyone of lower rank dared to speak to him or ask about anything, his only answer was "P," and that doesn't mean a thing!

"There is supposed to be a highly remarkable bird here called a nightingale," said the emperor. "It is said to be the very best thing in my great empire! Why hasn't anyone said anything to me about it?"

"Why, I've never before heard it mentioned," said the chamberlain. "It has never been presented at court!"

"I want it to come here this evening and sing for me!" said the emperor. "The whole world knows what I have—and I do not!"

"I have never before heard it mentioned," repeated the chamberlain. "I shall search for it, and I shall find it!"

But where was the nightingale to be found? The chamberlain ran up and down all the stairs, through the halls and corridors. None of the many people he met had ever heard of the nightingale. So the chamberlain ran back to the emperor and said that it was probably a fable made up by those people who wrote books. "Your Imperial Majesty should not believe what is written in a book! It is invention and sorcery!"

"But the book in which I read it," said the emperor, "was sent to me from the mighty emperor of Japan, and so it can't be false. I want to hear the nightingale! It shall be here this evening! And if it doesn't come, the whole court will be thumped on their tummies after they have eaten their dinner!"

"P!" said the chamberlain, and he ran back up and down the stairs, through all the halls and corridors. And half the court ran along with him because they didn't want to be thumped on the tummy. Again he asked about the remarkable nightingale that the whole world knew about except the people at the castle.

Finally they met a poor little girl in the kitchen. She said, "Oh heavens, the nightingale! I know it well. Every evening, I hear it sing. Its song is so beautiful that it brings tears to my eyes."

"Little kitchen maid," said the chamberlain, "I shall get you a permanent position in the kitchen and permission to watch the emperor eating if you can lead us to the nightingale. It has been summoned to appear this evening!"

And so they all set out for the forest where the nightingale usually sang. As they were going along, a cow started mooing.

"Oh!" said the courtiers. "There we have it! There is certainly a remarkable force in such a tiny animal. I'm quite sure I've heard it before!"

"No, those are the cows mooing!" said the little kitchen maid. "We're still a long way from the nightingale's place."

Then the frogs started croaking in the pond.

"Delightful!" said the Chinese imperial chaplain. "Now I hear it! It's just like tiny church bells."

"No, no, those are the frogs!" said the little kitchen maid. "But I think we'll hear the nightingale soon."

Then the nightingale started to sing.

"That's it!" said the little girl. "Listen! Listen! And there it sits!" And she pointed to a little brown bird up in the branches.

"Is it possible?" said the chamberlain. "I never imagined it like this! How ordinary it looks! It has probably lost its color from the sight of so many distinguished people."

"Little nightingale," shouted the kitchen maid quite loudly. "Our gracious emperor would so like you to sing for him."

"With the greatest of pleasure," said the nightingale, and it began to sing its delightful song.

"It sounds just like glass bells," said the chamberlain. "And look at that tiny throat. How it vibrates. It's remarkable that we've never heard it before. It will be a great success at court!"

"Shall I sing once more for the emperor?" asked the nightingale, who thought the emperor was there.

"My fine little nightingale," said the chamberlain, "it gives me great pleasure to summon you to a court celebration this evening, where you will enchant his High Imperial Grace with your charming song!"

"My song sounds best out in nature," said the nightingale, but it followed them when it heard that it was the emperor's wish.

The palace had been thoroughly polished up. The porcelain walls and floors gleamed from the light of many thousands of gold lamps. The loveliest flowers, which could tinkle like bells, were arranged in the halls. In fact, there was such a draft from all the running around that the bells kept tinkling and drowned out everything else.

In the middle of the great hall, where the emperor sat, a gold perch had been placed for the nightingale to sit on. The whole court was there, and the little kitchen maid had been given permission to stand behind the door, for now she had the title of Real Kitchen Maid. They were all wearing their most splendid clothes, and they all looked at the little brown bird that was about to sing for the emperor.

And the nightingale sang so delightfully that tears came to the emperor's eyes and rolled down his cheeks. Then the nightingale sang even more beautifully. It went straight to the heart. And the emperor was so happy that he said the nightingale was to have his gold slipper to wear around its neck. But the nightingale said no, thank you, it had already been rewarded enough.

"I have seen tears in the emperor's eyes. For me that is the richest treasure, for an emperor's tears have a wondrous power." And then it sang again with its sweet and glorious voice.

And the ladies of the court were so enchanted that they put water in their mouths so they could gurgle whenever anyone spoke to them. They thought they were nightingales, too. Even the lackeys and chambermaids let it be known that they were also satisfied—and that is saying a lot, for they're the hardest of all to please. The nightingale had really been a success!

The nightingale was now to remain forever at the castle. It would have its own cage and be free to take a walk outside twice each day and once at night. Twelve servants would walk along with it, each one holding a silken ribbon attached to the nightingale's legs. As you can imagine, the nightingale found no pleasure at all in those walks!

Meanwhile, the whole city talked about the remarkable bird. Whenever two people met, the first merely said "Night!" and the other said "Gale!" And then they sighed and understood each other. Indeed, eleven grocers' children were named after the nightingale, but not one of them could sing a note.

One day a small package was delivered to the emperor. On the outside was written "Nightingale."

"This must be a new book about our famous bird," said the emperor. But it was no book. It was a little artificial nightingale made to resemble the real one—except that it was encrusted with diamonds, rubies, and sapphires. And when the artificial bird was wound up, it could sing one of the tunes the real bird sang, and its tail bobbed up and down and glittered with silver and gold. Around its neck hung a ribbon, with a card attached to it that read: "The Emperor of Japan's jeweled nightingale is poor compared to the Emperor of China's real nightingale."

"It is lovely!" everyone said. And the person who had delivered the jeweled bird was immediately granted the title of Chief Imperial Nightingale Bringer.

"Now the two must sing together! What a duet that will be!" And so they had to sing together—but it didn't go well at all. The real nightingale sang in its natural way, but the artificial bird worked with mechanical wheels. "It's not to be blamed," said the music master. "It keeps time perfectly and quite according to my school of music!" Then the artificial bird had to sing alone. It was as much of a success as the real one. Besides that, it was so much nicer to look at!

Thirty-three times the jeweled nightingale sang the same tune, and still it wasn't tired. The people would have liked to have heard it again, but the emperor thought the real nightingale should also sing a little. But where was it? No one had noticed that it had flown out the open window, away to its green forest.

"What is this all about?" asked the emperor. And the courtiers used harsh words and said that the nightingale was a most ungrateful bird. "But we have the best bird right here!" they said, and then the jeweled bird had to sing again. That was the thirty-fourth time they had heard the same tune, but they still wanted to hear it again. And the music master praised the bird tremendously. He even assured them that it was better than the real nightingale, not only on the outside but inside as well.

"For you see, my lords and ladies, and Your Emperorship above all, with the real nightingale you never know what to expect. But with the artificial bird everything is definite! That is how it will be, and no other way! And it can be opened up to show human ingenuity—how the wheels are arranged, how they operate, and how each mechanical thing leads to another!"

"Those are our thoughts precisely!" the lords and ladies said. And on the following Sunday, the music master was allowed to show the bird to the people outside the court. They were also going to hear it sing, said the emperor. And they saw it and they heard it and they loved it. But the poor fisherman who had heard the real nightingale sing said, "It sounds pretty enough, and it looks all right too. But something is missing. I don't know what it is."

From then on, the jeweled bird was always at the emperor's side. It had its place on a silk cushion close to the emperor's bed. In title it had risen to High Imperial Bedside Table Singer, and in rank to number one on the left, for the emperor thought that the side where the heart is was the most distinguished. And even the heart of an emperor is on the left side. The music master wrote a twenty-five-volume work about the jeweled bird. It was very scholarly and very long and very difficult. But all the people said they had read and understood it, for otherwise they would have been thought stupid and thumped on the tummy.

It went on like this for a whole year. But one evening, as the artificial bird was singing away and the emperor was lying in bed listening to it, something went *snap* inside the bird. Something had broken with a *Whirrrrrr!* All the wheels spun around, and then the music stopped.

The emperor sprang out of bed and immediately had his personal physician summoned. But how could *he* help? Then they fetched the royal watchmaker, and after much talk he put the bird more or less in order. But the watchmaker said it must be used very sparingly because the cogs were so very worn. What a great woe! Only once a year did they dare to let the artificial bird sing, and even that was hard on it.

Five years passed. Then a great sorrow fell upon the land—the emperor was very ill and, it was said, would not live. A new emperor had already been chosen, and the people stood out in the street and asked the chamberlain how their emperor was.

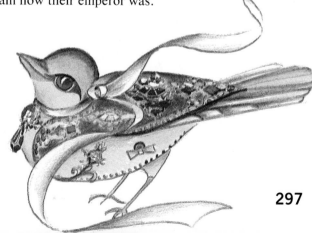

"P!" he said and shook his head.

Cold and pale, the emperor lay in his magnificent room. In all the halls and corridors, cloths had been put down to deaden the sound of footsteps, and so it was quiet, very quiet. The emperor lay in his great bed with the long velvet curtains and the heavy gold tassels. High above him a window was open, and the moon shone in on the emperor and the jeweled bird.

The poor emperor could hardly breathe. It was as though something were sitting on his chest. He opened his eyes and he saw that it was Death who was sitting on his chest. And then Death began to speak . . .

"Music, music," cried the emperor. "Please, let me hear music. I do not want to hear what Death has to say," the emperor groaned and covered his ears. "Oh, sing! Sing! You blessed little gold bird. I've given you so many precious things. I myself hung my gold slipper around your neck. Sing! Oh, sing!"

But the bird stood still. There was no one to wind it up, and it couldn't sing otherwise. Just at that moment, however, the loveliest song could be heard. It was the little living nightingale, sitting on a branch outside the window. It had heard the emperor's cries and had come to sing for him. And as it sang, the blood started to flow faster in the emperor's weak limbs, and Death himself listened and said, "Keep on, little nightingale, keep on!"

The nightingale kept on singing its beautiful song. And Death was so enchanted that he forgot why he was with the emperor and drifted like a cold, white mist out the window.

"Thank you, thank you!" said the emperor. "You wonderful little bird. You have removed Death from my heart! How can I reward you?"

"You have rewarded me," said the nightingale, "I received the tears from your eyes the first time I sang. I'll never forget that. Those are the jewels that do a singer's heart good. But sleep now, and get well and strong. I shall sing for you."

And it sang, and the emperor fell into a sweet sleep.

The next morning, the sun was shining in through the windows when the emperor awoke, strengthened and well. None of his servants had yet appeared, for they thought he was dead. But the nightingale still sat there and sang.

"You must always stay with me!" said the emperor. "You shall sing only when you want to, and I shall break the jeweled bird into a thousand pieces."

"Don't do that," said the nightingale. "It has done what good it could. Keep it as before. I cannot live at the palace, but let me come when I want to myself. Then in the evening, I'll sit on the branch there by the window and sing for you, so that you can be happy and thoughtful as well."

And then the nightingale flew away.

The servants came in to see their dead emperor. Yes, there they stood. And the emperor said, "Good morning!"

LOOKING AT BOOKS

The Little Mermaid

This book retells Hans Christian Andersen's classic tale of a mermaid who longs to become human. One night, when the stormy sea capsizes a ship, the mermaid saves one of the sailors —a handsome prince. She carries him to shore, lays him on the white sand, then disappears before he revives. When a witch offers the mermaid the chance to become human and win the prince's love, she leaves her mer-family and sacrifices her beautiful voice. In 1984, in recognition of the enchanting illustrations by Laszlo Gal, this book was awarded a children's literature prize by the Canada Council.

THE GLORIOUS FLIGHT

This tale begins in Cambrai, France, in the year 1901. Louis Blériot is taking his family for a ride in their new car. As they drive through the city, they hear a loud *clacketa! clacketa!* They look up and see a great white airship—the first airship ever seen over the city. Blériot is overwhelmed. He has only one wish: to build his own flying machine. Blériot builds machine after machine, but each of his attempts to fly ends in disaster. Years pass and, finally, he is successful. To show the world what his wonderful new airplane can do, Blériot announces that he will attempt a flight never before made. On July 25, 1909, he flies to Dover, England, and he becomes the first person to cross the English Channel in an airplane. *The Glorious Flight,* written and illustrated by Alice and Martin Provensen, is based on the true story of French aviator Louis Blériot. The book won the 1984 Caldecott Medal, as the best children's picture book.

Dear Mr. Henshaw

Leigh Botts was in the second grade when he first wrote to his favorite author, Boyd Henshaw. And he has continued to write at least one fan letter a year. Now in the sixth grade, Leigh has moved with his mother to a new town and is having problems as the "new kid" at school. When his teacher assigns an author report, Leigh writes to Mr. Henshaw, asking lots of questions. He is surprised when Mr. Henshaw answers with questions of his own: Who are you? What is your family like? Do you have any pets? What bothers you? What do you wish? Leigh's answers reveal interesting and amusing details about his home and school life. One of the book's highlights occurs when Leigh rigs up an alarm system to catch the thief who steals all the "good stuff" from his lunchbag. This book, written by Beverly Cleary, received the 1984 John Newbery Medal, the highest American award for a book for young people.

The Rose in My Garden

This charming book was written by Arnold Lobel and illustrated by Anita Lobel. As the story begins, a single rose is shown in a garden. A bee falls asleep in the center of the blossom. As you turn the pages, more and more of the garden comes into view. There are hollyhocks, marigolds, zinnias, daisies, bluebells, and many other colorful flowers. Soon a snail appears in the garden, followed by a butterfly, a hummingbird, and other small creatures. Then a frightened little mouse runs into the garden, with a big cat right behind it. As the cat chases the mouse it causes all sorts of havoc. Even the sleeping bee is disturbed—with very unpleasant consequences for the cat!

You're The Detective!

Here are 24 solve-them-yourself picture mysteries, created by Lawrence Treat and illustrated by Kathleen Borowik. Did a thief steal Mr. Bigbelly Bewilliger's watch? Where did Angus Wallamilletti bury his collection of gold coins? Who stole the money from Izzy the Cider Man? To solve these and the other mysteries in the book you must look closely at the clues in the pictures. There are three kinds of clues: Some pictures have objects that shouldn't be there. In other pictures, there are broken objects. And in still other pictures, objects are missing. For instance, in "International Crisis," why are there so few chocolates in the dish on the rolling server? The book ends with a chapter describing the various things that a young detective ought to know, particularly "being able to observe well and keep a cool head."

BOOK OF RIDDLES

What has "long legs, short thighs, bald head, and bullet eyes?"
If you look at the illustration above, the answer is clear: a frog.
This book by Monika Beisner presents 101 old and new riddles
that will test your wit and imagination. Some of the riddles are
illustrated with detailed pictures that contain clues. But you'll
have to work harder to solve other riddles, such as: "What is it
that leaps and runs and has no feet?" "What runs around the
garden without moving?" "What is it that has teeth and can't
eat?" If you can guess the answers to these, you're ready to
tackle the tricky riddles in this delightful book.

Sherlock Holmes is the best-known detective in fiction. He made his creator, the British author Sir Arthur Conan Doyle (1859–1930), famous. And in 1984, the 125th anniversary of Doyle's birth, Holmes was just as popular as ever. But one person never cared for Holmes—and that was Doyle himself.

Doyle was a doctor who began writing to fill out the small income from his practice. His first Holmes story, A Study in Scarlet, was published in 1887. Within just a few years, his detective tales had become so popular that he gave up medicine. But Doyle also wrote other stories, including historical novels such as The White Company (1890). He preferred these writings to the Holmes tales, and by 1893 he was thoroughly sick of his master detective. So he killed Holmes off by having him drowned, along with his arch-enemy Moriarty, in The Final Problem. The public outcry, however, was so great that Doyle brought Holmes back in The Hound of the Baskervilles (1902).

In all, the detective was featured in 60 stories. But Doyle's interests continued to range far and wide. In 1902 he was knighted for works he had written defending Britain's role in the Boer War. He also became interested in spiritualism, the belief that the living can communicate with the dead. He spent his last years writing and lecturing on this subject.

Today Doyle's other writings are largely forgotten. It is Holmes—the pipe-smoking, violin-playing genius of London's Baker Street—who lives on. An adaptation of one of the best-known Sherlock Holmes stories follows.

THE RED-HEADED LEAGUE

I called upon my friend, Mr. Sherlock Holmes, one Saturday in autumn. He was deep in conversation with a stout, florid-faced gentleman, with fiery red hair.

"You could not possibly have come at a better time, my dear Watson," Holmes said, cordially. "Mr. Jabez Wilson here has been telling me a story that sounds most unique. Perhaps, Mr. Wilson, you would be kind enough to repeat your story so my friend Dr. Watson may hear it."

The client then pulled a dirty, wrinkled newspaper from the inside pocket of his coat, opened it up, and flattened it out upon his knee. As he glanced down at the advertisement column, I tried to learn more about the man from his dress and appearance —as my friend Holmes was so famous for doing.

I did not gain very much, however, by my inspection. Our visitor seemed to be an average British tradesman. He wore baggy gray check trousers, a black, unbuttoned coat, a drab waistcoat, and a heavy watch chain from which dangled an odd bit of square metal. A frayed top hat and a faded brown overcoat with a wrinkled velvet collar lay upon a chair beside him. The only remarkable thing about the man was his blazing red hair.

Sherlock Holmes noticed my inspection, and he shook his head at me with a smile. "Beyond the obvious facts that he has at some time done manual labor, that he has been in China, and that he has done a considerable amount of writing lately, I can deduce nothing else," he said.

Mr. Jabez Wilson looked up, startled. "How did you know all that, Mr. Holmes? How did you know, for example, that I did manual labor. For it's true; I began as a ship's carpenter."

"Your hands, my dear sir. Your right hand is about a size larger than your left. You have worked with it, and the muscles are more developed."

"Well, the writing then?"

"Your coat sleeves tell it all. What else can be indicated by that right cuff so very shiny for five inches, and the left with the smooth patch near the elbow where you rest it upon the desk."

"And China?"

"The fish that is tattooed on your right wrist could only have been done in China. I have made a study of tattoo marks, and that trick of staining the fish scales a delicate pink is quite peculiar to China. And when I also see a Chinese coin hanging from your watch chain, the matter becomes even more simple."

Mr. Jabez Wilson laughed. "Well, I never!" said he. "I thought at first that you had done something clever, but I see now that there was nothing to it, after all."

"I begin to think, Watson," said Holmes, "that I make a mistake in explaining my logic. My poor little reputation, such as it is, will suffer if I am so candid. Have you yet found the advertisement, Mr. Wilson?"

"Yes, I have got it now," he answered. "Here it is. This is what began it all. You just read it for yourself, sir."

I took the paper from him and read as follows:

TO THE RED-HEADED LEAGUE: Pertaining to the bequest of the late Ezekiah Hopkins, there is now another vacancy open that entitles a member of the League to a salary of four pounds a week for light labor. All red-headed men who are sound in body and mind, and above the age of 21, are eligible. Apply in person today only, at 11:00, to Duncan Ross, at the offices of the League, 7 Pope's Court, Fleet Street.

"What on earth does this mean?" I asked after I had twice read the extraordinary announcement.

"It is a little off the beaten track, isn't it," said Holmes. "Now, Mr. Wilson, tell us all about yourself, your household, and the effect this advertisement had upon your fortunes."

"Well, it is just as I have been telling you, Mr. Holmes. I have a small pawnbroker's business at Coburg Square, where I live. It's not a very large business, and of late it has not done more than just give me a living. I have only one assistant—and I would have a hard time paying him but for the fact that he is willing to work for half wages, in order to learn the business."

"What is the name of this obliging youth?" asked Holmes.

"His name is Vincent Spaulding, and he's not such a youth, either. It's hard to say his age. But I should not wish for a smarter assistant. And I know very well that he could better himself and earn twice what I am able to pay him. But after all, if he is satisfied, why should I put ideas in his head?"

"Why indeed? You seem most fortunate in having an employee who will take less than the full market price. It is not a common experience in this age. I think your assistant is as remarkable as your advertisement."

"Oh, he has his faults, too," said Mr. Wilson. "Never was there such a fellow for photography. Snapping away with a camera when he ought to be improving his mind, and then diving down into the cellar to develop his pictures. That is his main fault. But on the whole, he's a good worker."

"He is still with you, I presume?"

"Yes, sir. That's all I have in the house, for I am a widower and never had any family. I live very quietly, sir. Then one morning, just two months ago, Spaulding came down to the office with this very paper in his hand. He said, 'Oh, Mr. Wilson, I wish that I was a red-headed man. Here's another vacancy on the League of Red-headed Men, and it's worth a small fortune to any man who gets it. I understand that there are more vacancies than there are men, and the trustees are at their wits' end wondering what to do with the money.'

" 'Why, what is this League, then?' I asked. You see, Mr. Holmes, I am a very stay-at-home man, and so I don't know much of what is going on outside. At any rate, Spaulding seemed very surprised that I had never heard of the League. He said I was eligible for one of the vacancies, and they were worth a few hundred pounds a year. He said the work was slight and need not interfere very much with one's other occupations. Well, you can imagine that made me prick up my ears. My business had not been too good for some years, and an extra couple of hundred pounds would have come in handy. So I asked Spaulding to tell me all about it.

" 'Well,' said he, showing me the advertisement, 'as you can see, there is the address where you should apply for the particulars. As far as I have heard, the league was founded by an American millionaire who was himself red-headed, and he had a great sympathy for all red-headed men. So when he died, he left his enormous fortune in the hands of trustees, with instructions to provide easy jobs for men whose hair was red.'

" 'But,' said I, 'there would be millions of red-headed men who would apply.'

" 'Not so many as you might think,' he answered. 'You see, it is confined to Londoners (this American had started from London when he was young). And I have heard it is no use applying if your hair is light red, or dark red, or anything but real bright, blazing, fiery red—like yours.'

"Now, gentlemen, as you can see, my hair is of a very rich red tint, so it seemed to me that I stood as good a chance as any of getting the vacancy. And since Spaulding seemed to know so much about it, I ordered him to shut up for the day and to come with me right away.

"Mr. Holmes, I never hope to see such a sight as that again. Fleet Street was choked with red-headed folk. I should not have thought there were so many in the whole country as were brought together by that single advertisement. Every shade of color they were—straw, lemon, orange, brick, Irish-setter, liver, clay. But as Spaulding said, there were not many who had my vivid, flame-colored tint.

"Somehow Spaulding pushed and pulled and butted until he got us through the crowd and right up the steps that led to the office. There was nothing in the office but a couple of wooden chairs and a table, behind which sat Mr. Duncan Ross, a small man with a head that was even redder than mine. He said a few words to each candidate as he came up, and then he always managed to find some fault that would disqualify them. But when our turn came, the little man was much more favorable to me than to any of the others.

"He looked at me and said, 'You have every requirement. I cannot recall when I have seen anything so fine.' He took a step backward, cocked his head to one side, and gazed at my hair until I felt quite bashful. Then suddenly he plunged forward, shook my hand, and congratulated me warmly on my success.

" 'It would be wrong to hesitate,' said he. 'You will, however, excuse me for taking an obvious precaution.' With that he seized my hair in both his hands and tugged until I yelled with pain. 'There is water in your eyes,' said he, as he released me. 'I see all is as it should be. But we have to be careful, for we have twice been deceived by wigs and once by paint. Well, Mr. Wilson, when shall you be able to enter upon your new duties?'

"Mr. Duncan Ross then proceeded to tell me about the job. 'You would be paid four pounds a week. The hours would be from ten to two each day, and you have to be in the office the whole time. If you leave, you lose the position forever. And your job would be to copy *The Encyclopedia Britannica.* Can you be ready tomorrow?'

" 'Certainly,' I answered.

" 'Then, good-bye, Mr. Wilson, and let me congratulate you once more on the important position that you have been lucky enough to gain.' He bowed me out of the room and I went home with my assistant, very pleased at my own good fortune.

"The following morning I returned to Pope's Court. The table was set out ready for me, and Mr. Ross was there to see that I got to work. He started me off on the letter A, and then left me. But he would drop in from time to time. At two o'clock he bade me good day, complimented me upon the amount that I had written, and locked the door of the office after me.

"This went on day after day, and on Saturday Mr. Ross plunked down four pounds for my week's work. It was the same the next week and the week after. Eight weeks passed like this, and I had written about Abbots and Archery and Armor and Architecture. I hoped that I might get on to the B's before very long. And then suddenly the whole business came to an end."

"To an end?" said Holmes.

"Yes, sir. Just this morning. I went to work as usual at ten o'clock, but the door was locked. This little square of cardboard was tacked to the middle of it. Read it for yourself."

The white card read: "The Red-headed League Is Dissolved."

"Pray, what steps did you take when you found the card upon the door?" questioned Holmes.

"I was staggered, sir. I did not know what to do. Finally, I went to the landlord, who lives on the ground floor. I asked him if he could tell me what had become of the Red-headed League. He said he had never heard of any such group. Then I asked him who Mr. Duncan Ross was. He answered that the name was new to him.

" 'Well,' said I, 'who is the gentleman in room number 4?'

" 'What, the red-headed man?'

" 'Yes.'

" 'Oh,' said he, 'his name is William Morris. He is a lawyer, and he was using my room temporarily until his new offices were ready. He moved out yesterday.'

"At that point, Mr. Holmes, I went home and asked the advice of my assistant. But he could not help me. Since I did not want to lose such a job without a struggle, and as I had heard that you were good enough to give advice to poor folk, I came right away to you."

"And you did very wisely," said Holmes. "Your case is a remarkable one, and I shall be happy to look into it. From what you have told me I think that graver issues hang from it than might at first appear."

"Grave enough!" said Mr. Wilson. "Why, I have lost four pounds a week."

"As far as you are personally concerned," said Holmes, "I do not see that you have any grievance against this extraordinary League. On the contrary, you are richer by some thirty pounds, to say nothing of the knowledge you have gained on every subject that comes under the letter A. You have lost nothing."

"No, sir. But I want to find out about them and what their object was in playing this prank—if it was a prank—upon me."

"We shall try to clear up these points for you. First, one or two questions, Mr. Wilson. This assistant of yours who first called your attention to the advertisement—how long had he been with you when he showed you the advertisement?"

"About a month."

"Was he your only applicant?"

"No, I had a dozen."

"Why did you pick him?"

"Because he was handy and would come cheap."

"What is he like, this Vincent Spaulding?"

"Small, stout, quick in his ways, no hair on his face though he's about thirty. Has a white splash of acid upon his forehead."

Holmes sat up in his chair in considerable excitement. "Have you ever observed that his ears are pierced for earrings?"

"Yes, sir. He told me that a gypsy had done it for him when he was a lad."

"Hum! I thought as much," said Holmes, sinking back in deep thought. "He is still with you?"

"Oh yes, sir."

"That will do, Mr. Wilson. I shall contact you soon."

"Well, Watson," said Holmes, when our visitor had left us. "What do you make of it all?"

"I make nothing of it," I answered frankly. "It is a most mysterious business."

"As a rule," said Holmes, "the more bizarre a thing is, the less mysterious it proves to be. It is the commonplace, featureless crime that is really puzzling. But I must be quick over this matter."

"What are you going to do, then?" I asked.

"To smoke," he answered. "It is quite a three-pipe problem, and I beg you not to speak to me for fifty minutes." He curled himself up in his chair, with his thin knees drawn up to his hawk-like nose. And there he sat with his eyes closed and his black clay pipe thrusting out like the bill of some strange bird. I had come to the conclusion that he was asleep, and indeed was nodding off myself, when he suddenly sprang out of his chair with the gesture of a man who has made up his mind, and put his pipe down upon the mantelpiece.

"Watson, could your patients spare you for a few hours? I want to see where Mr. Wilson and his assistant live and work."

We traveled by the Underground to Coburg Square. It was a pokey, little, shabby place, where four lines of dingy two-storied brick houses looked out onto lawns of weedy grass. Upon a corner house, three gilt balls and a brown board with "Jabez Wilson" in white letters announced the place where our red-headed client carried on his business.

Sherlock Holmes stopped in front of the house and looked it all over. Then he walked slowly up the street, and then down again. Finally he returned to the pawnbroker's, and, having thumped vigorously upon the pavement with his stick two or three times, he went up to the door and knocked. It was instantly opened by a bright-looking, clean-shaven fellow, who asked him to step in.

"Thank you," said Holmes. "I only wished to ask you how you would go from here to the Strand."

"Third right, fourth left," answered the assistant, and promptly closed the door.

"Smart fellow, that," observed Holmes, as we walked away. "I have known something of him before."

"Evidently Mr. Wilson's assistant counts for a good deal in this mystery of the Red-headed League," said I. "I am sure you asked for directions merely to have a look at him."

"Not him, but the knees of his trousers," said Holmes.

"And what did you see?"

"What I expected to see."

"Why did you thump on the pavement?"

"My dear doctor, this is a time for observation, not for talk. We are spies in an enemy's country. We know something of Coburg Square. Let us now explore the street behind it."

The road in which we found ourselves as we turned the corner presented as great a contrast to Coburg Square as the front of a picture does to the back. It was one of the main districts of the city. Carriages filled the roadway, and pedestrians lined the street.

"Let me see," said Holmes, standing at the corner and glancing at the line of fine shops and stately business offices. "I should like to remember the order of the buildings here. It is a hobby of mine to have an exact knowledge of London. There is the tobacconist, the little newspaper shop, the Coburg branch of the City and Suburban Bank, the Vegetarian Restaurant, and McFarlane's carriage-building depot. And now, doctor, we've done our work. A sandwich and a cup of coffee, and then it's home. I have business to do that will take some hours. This affair at Coburg Square is serious."

"Why serious?"

"A major crime is being planned. I have every reason to believe that we shall be in time to stop it. But today being Saturday rather complicates matters. I shall need your help tonight.

Come to Baker Street at ten. And, I say, doctor, there may be some danger, so kindly put your army revolver in your pocket.''

When I entered 221B Baker Street that night, I found Holmes in animated conversation with two men.

''Ha! Our party is complete,'' said Holmes, buttoning up his jacket and taking his heavy hunting crop from the rack. ''Watson, you know Mr. Jones of Scotland Yard. Let me introduce you to Mr. Merryweather, who will join us in tonight's adventure.''

''I hope a wild goose chase may not prove to be the end of our adventure,'' observed Mr. Merryweather gloomily.

''You may have confidence in Mr. Holmes, sir,'' said the police agent loftily. ''He has his own little methods that are, if he won't mind my saying so, just a little fantastic. But he has the makings of a detective in him. It is not too much to say that once or twice he has been more nearly correct than the official force.''

''Oh, if you say so, Mr. Jones, it is all right,'' said the stranger. ''Still, I miss my card game. It is the first Saturday night in twenty-seven years that I have not had my game.''

''I think you will find,'' said Holmes, ''that you will play for higher stakes tonight than you have ever done before, and that the play will be more exciting. For you, Mr. Merryweather, the stakes will be some 30,000 pounds. And for you, Jones, it will be the man upon whom you wish to lay your hands.''

''John Clay—murderer, thief, and forger. He's a young man, Mr. Merryweather, but he is at the head of his profession. I would rather have my bracelets on him than on any criminal in London. He's a remarkable man, is young Clay. His brain is as cunning as his fingers, and though we see signs of him at every turn, we never know where to find the man himself. I've been on his track for years and have not set eyes on him yet.''

''I hope I may have the pleasure of introducing you tonight,'' said Holmes. ''I've also had one or two little turns with Mr. John Clay, and I agree with you that he is at the head of his profession. Well, it's quite time that we started. If you two will take the first hansom, Watson and I will follow in the second.''

As we got closer to our destination, Holmes remarked, ''This fellow Merryweather is a bank director and personally interested in the matter. I thought it as well to have Jones with us also. He is not a bad fellow, though an absolute imbecile in his profession. But he has one positive virtue. He is as brave as a bulldog, and as tenacious as a lobster if he gets his claws upon anyone.''

We soon reached the same crowded district in which we had found ourselves in the morning. Our cabs were dismissed, and following Mr. Merryweather we passed down a narrow alleyway and through a side door that he opened for us. Within, there was a small corridor that ended in a massive iron gate. This also was opened, and we made our way down a flight of winding stone steps. This terminated at another formidable gate. Mr. Merryweather stopped to light a lantern and then led us down a dark, earth-smelling passage into a huge vault or cellar. Piled all around were crates and massive boxes.

"You are not very vulnerable from above," Holmes remarked, as he held up the lantern and gazed about him.

"Nor from below," said Mr. Merryweather, striking his stick upon the stone floor. "Why, dear me, it sounds quite hollow!" he remarked, looking up in surprise.

"I really must ask you to be a little quieter," said Holmes severely. "You may have harmed the success of our expedition. Please sit down on one of those boxes and do not interfere."

Mr. Merryweather perched himself upon a crate, with a very injured expression upon his face. Meanwhile, Holmes fell upon his knees to the floor and, with the lantern and a magnifying lens, began minutely to examine the cracks between the stones.

He stood up and remarked, "We have at least an hour before us, for they can hardly take any steps until the good pawnbroker is safely in bed. Then they will not waste a minute, for the sooner they do their work, the longer time they will have for their escape. We are at present, doctor, in the cellar of one of London's principal banks. Mr. Merryweather is the president, and he will explain to you why a daring criminal might take a considerable interest in this cellar at present."

"It is our French gold," whispered the director. "We have had several warnings that an attempt might be made upon it."

"Your French gold?"

"Yes. Several months ago, we increased our reserves and borrowed 30,000 napoleons from the Bank of France. It has become known that we have not yet unpacked the money and that it is still in our cellar—in these very crates and boxes."

Holmes interrupted, "It is now time to make our plans. First, Mr. Merryweather, we must put the screen over that lantern."

"And sit in the dark?"

"I am afraid so. We cannot risk the presence of a light. I shall stand behind this crate, and you conceal yourselves behind those. Then when I flash the light upon them, close in quickly. If they fire, Watson, have no compunction about shooting them."

I placed my revolver upon the top of the wooden case behind which I crouched. Holmes shot the slide across the front of the lantern and left us in pitch darkness. The smell of hot metal remained to assure us that the lantern was still there, ready to flash out at a moment's notice.

"They have but one retreat," whispered Holmes. "That is back through the house into Coburg Square. I hope you have done what I asked you, Jones?"

"I have an inspector and two officers at the front door."

"Then we have stopped all the holes. And now we must wait."

Time seemed to drag. My limbs were weary and stiff, yet my nerves were worked up to the highest pitch of tension. From my position I could look over the crate. Suddenly my eyes caught the glint of a light coming from the stone floor.

At first it was but a spark upon the pavement. Then it lengthened out until it became a yellow line. And then, without any warning, a gash seemed to open and a hand appeared, which felt about in the center of the little area of light. For a minute, the hand protruded out of the floor. Then it was withdrawn as suddenly as it had appeared, and all was dark again except for the single spark that marked a chink between the stones.

Its disappearance, however, was but momentary. With a grinding sound, one of the broad, white stones turned over upon its side and left a square, gaping hole through which streamed the light of a lantern. Over the edge there peeped a clean-cut, boyish face. It looked keenly about and then, with a hand on either side of the hole, drew itself shoulder high and waist high, until one knee rested upon the edge. In another instant he was out of the hole, and was hauling after him a companion, lithe and small like himself, with a pale face and a shock of very red hair.

At that moment, Sherlock Holmes sprang out and seized the intruder by the collar. His companion dived down the hole, and I heard the tearing sound of cloth as Jones grabbed at his coat. The lantern flashed on and caught the barrel of a revolver in its light. But Holmes' hunting crop came down on the man's wrist, and the pistol clinked upon the floor.

"It's no use, John Clay," said Holmes, blandly.

"So I see," the other answered, with the utmost coolness. "I fancy that my pal is all right, although I see you have got his coattails."

"Our men are waiting for him at the door," said Holmes.

"Oh, indeed! You seem to have done the thing very completely. I must compliment you."

"And I you," Holmes answered. "Your red-headed idea was very new and most effective."

John Clay then made a sweeping bow to the three of us and walked off in the custody of the detective.

In the wee hours of the morning, as we sat over a glass of whiskey and soda in Baker Street, Holmes explained the case. "You see, Watson, it was perfectly obvious from the first that the only possible object of this rather fantastic business of the Red-headed League must be to get the pawnbroker out of the way for a number of hours every day. And from the time I heard of the assistant working for half wages, it was obvious to me that he had some strong motive for accepting the position."

"But how could you guess what the motive was?"

"Well, the pawnbroker's business was a small one, and there was nothing in his house that could account for such an elaborate scheme. It must, then, be something out of the house. What could it be? I thought of the assistant's fondness for photography and his habit of vanishing into the cellar. The cellar! There was the end of this tangled clue. Then I made inquiries about this mysterious assistant and soon realized I was dealing with one of the coolest and most daring criminals in London. He was doing something in the cellar—something that took many hours a day for months on end. I could think of nothing except that he was digging a tunnel to some other building.

"That's how far I had gotten when we went to visit the scene of action. I surprised you by thumping upon the pavement with my stick. I was trying to find out whether the cellar stretched out in front of the house or behind. It was not in front. Then I rang the bell and, as I hoped, the assistant answered it. We had had some skirmishes in the past, but had never set eyes upon each other before. I hardly looked at his face. His knees were what I wanted to see. You must yourself have noticed how worn, wrinkled, and stained they were. They spoke of those hours of burrowing. The only remaining point was what they were burrowing for. I walked around the corner, saw that the bank abutted on your friend's premises, and felt that I had solved the problem."

"And how could you tell that they would make their attempt tonight?" I asked.

"Well, when they closed their League offices, that was a sign that they no longer cared about Mr. Jabez Wilson's presence—in other words, that they had completed their tunnel. But it was essential that they should use it soon, as it might be discovered or the gold might be removed. Saturday would suit them better than any other day, as the bank was closed and it would give them more time for their escape. For all these reasons, I expected them to come tonight."

"You reasoned it out beautifully," I exclaimed.

"It saved me from boredom," Holmes answered, yawning. "Alas! I already feel it closing in upon me. My life is spent in one long effort to escape from the commonplaces of existence. These little problems help me to do so!"

THE NEW BOOK OF KNOWLEDGE
1985

The following articles are from the 1985 edition of *The New Book of Knowledge*. They are included here to help you keep your encyclopedia up to date.

LIES

"I never lie." Would you say that this statement about yourself is true or false? Most people are tempted to answer "true." But if they did, it would probably be a lie. The truth is that very few of us go through life without ever telling a lie.

▶ BIG AND LITTLE LIES

People believe some lies are only "little white lies," while others are big lies. Whether a lie is big or small depends on many things. One way to judge a lie is by the harm it causes.

For example, imagine that Jenny and her mother are going shopping. Jenny is often late, and she is late again today. She is still in the house when her mother goes outside. When Jenny runs after her, her mother asks, "Did you check to make sure the front door was locked?" The truth is that Jenny was in such a rush she did not check the lock. If she tells the truth, her mother might get angry. So Jenny decides to answer "Yes."

Would you say that this was a big lie or a little one? What if the shopping trip took only 15 minutes, and no one entered the house while Jenny and her mother were gone? Some people (especially Jenny) might say that this was only a little lie because it did not cause any harm.

What if the shopping took several hours and a robber entered the house through the unlocked door? Jenny's lie would have caused a serious problem, and almost everyone (even Jenny) would say it was a big lie.

Another way to judge lies is according to whether or not the person telling the lie knew it was a lie when he or she said it. For example, Jenny knew she had not checked the lock on the door. Since she lied on purpose, that could be considered a big lie.

These are two of the ways that can help a person judge how serious a lie is.

▶ WHY DO PEOPLE LIE?

Some people tell lies to avoid being punished for something. Often they lie because they want to cover up some mistake they have made. Jenny lied to avoid being scolded or punished by her mother for not checking the lock. The polite "social lies" people tell in order to avoid being disliked often cause harm. Suppose you compliment a friend on her unflattering new outfit. She might then wear the outfit to a big party and get a reputation for having poor taste.

Another reason people lie is to make themselves seem better than they really are. For example, some boys at school are talking about a video game. Jeff is new at the school and he wants the boys to like him, so he lies and says that he has gotten a very high score on the game. By lying about how good he is, Jeff hopes to make the boys want him as a friend.

Some people lie in an effort to help solve their problems. But usually lying just causes more problems.

▶ THE BAD EFFECTS OF LYING

People who tell lies can create trouble for themselves and other people. Suppose the other boys do not believe Jeff and ask him to play the game to prove he is really as good at it as he says he is. If he fails to live up to his big claims, it will be very embarrassing for him. Some of the boys might call him a liar and not want him as a friend.

Jenny's mother was counting on Jenny to tell the truth. Making certain the front door is locked is usually very important. When her mother discovers that Jenny lied, she might decide that Jenny cannot be trusted. Her mother might think she has to treat Jenny like a small child who cannot be trusted to take on grown-up responsibilities.

Being trusted by people and having good friends is very important. When people lie, especially if they do it repeatedly, they get a reputation for being untrustworthy. Once they have that reputation, it is very hard for them to win back other people's trust.

Even people who are basically honest sometimes tell a lie. Although telling the truth is better than lying, the fact that a person occasionally tells a little lie does not mean that the person is completely bad. But people who intentionally tell big lies, and who lie often, cause great harm to themselves and to others.

JERALD M. JELLISON
University of Southern California
Author, *I'm Sorry I Didn't Mean To and Other Lies We Love to Tell*

LIE DETECTION

People usually feel bad when they tell a lie. That bad feeling is called guilt. The fact that people usually have these feelings when they lie causes small changes in their bodies. If these small body changes can be accurately measured, they can sometimes help to determine if a person is lying.

When you tell a lie, you often get excited. Often your heart will begin to beat a little faster, the blood will move through your body with more force, and you will begin to breathe more quickly. These small body changes can be measured with a **polygraph** —the recording instrument sometimes called a lie detector.

Here is how a polygraph is used. Let us say Marilyn has been trained to operate a polygraph. She has taken special classes and has had hundreds of hours of practice using the polygraph under the guidance of a more experienced teacher. Marilyn is going to test Jack, who has been accused of robbing a store but who insists that he was somewhere else at the time of the crime.

Marilyn begins by placing some thin electrical wires on Jack's body. The wires do not hurt Jack because they have only a tiny amount of electricity running through them. They are connected to the polygraph, which measures and records on paper the changes in Jack's heart rate, blood pressure, and breathing as he is being tested. The poly-graph may also record changes in the activity of the sweat pores in Jack's hand or changes in the movements of his muscles.

The first questions Marilyn asks are simple ones. ("What is your name?" "What day is this?") These questions are called control questions. They give an indication of Jack's normal body activity when he is not lying. Then the important questions are asked. ("Where were you on the night of the robbery?" "Did you rob the store?") If the polygraph records a big increase in Jack's excitement when he is answering the important questions, it may mean that he is lying.

We can only say that the person *may* be lying because polygraphs are not completely accurate. Polygraphs are so sensitive that they sometimes measure body changes a person might feel even when telling the truth. This is especially so when the operator has not been trained to ask the right kinds of questions in the right way. Another problem is that people can sometimes learn to make their bodies react in ways that fool the polygraph. Because polygraphs are not completely accurate, the results of a polygraph test usually cannot be used in court to definitely prove whether a person lied or committed a crime.

JERALD M. JELLISON
Professor of Psychology
University of Southern California

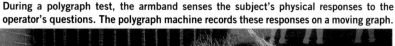

During a polygraph test, the armband senses the subject's physical responses to the operator's questions. The polygraph machine records these responses on a moving graph.

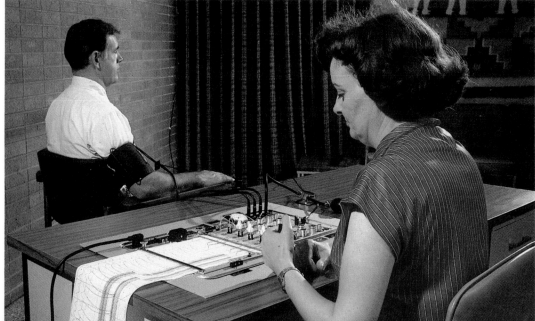

TOLKIEN, J. R. R. (1892–1973)

Although J. R. R. Tolkien was a professor at England's Oxford University and a respected scholar of medieval literature, he is best known as the author of the fantasy novel *The Hobbit* and the triology *The Lord of the Rings*.

John Ronald Reuel Tolkien was born on January 3, 1892, in Bloemfontein, South Africa, where his father was a bank manager. The South African climate proved damaging to young Ronald's health, so his mother took him on a vacation to England in 1895. Soon after arriving, she learned that her husband had died suddenly in Africa. She decided to remain in England, settling in Sarehole, a village outside Birmingham. It was here that Tolkien developed the deep love for English country life that appears so strongly in his stories.

Tolkien had a skill for languages; he even made up his own private words and alphabet in a language he called "Naffarin." While a student at King Edward's School in Birmingham, he excelled in Latin, Greek, German, and Middle English. His skill with words earned him a scholarship to Oxford, where he majored in philology, the study of language. He studied the great medieval literatures in Old English, Old Norse, and Finnish —such poems as *Beowulf, The Elder Edda,* and *The Kalevala*. These gave him the background for his own writings, in which he created a world with its own languages.

Tolkien graduated in June, 1915, and because World War I had begun, enlisted in the army. Before going to France as a signal officer, he married his childhood sweetheart, Edith Bratt. During the war, Tolkien contracted trench fever, remaining ill for nearly a year. His stay in the hospital may have saved his life (most of his friends died in the war); it certainly gave him the time to begin his first important work, *The Book of Lost Tales* (later renamed *The Silmarillion*). After the war, Tolkien returned to Oxford, becoming, in 1925, professor of Anglo-Saxon.

Although he was outwardly a popular lecturer and scholar, Tolkien's inner life was filled with stories. Borrowing material from the unfinished manuscript of *The Silmarillion*, he began telling his children tales about a funny little creature named Bilbo Baggins, who found a magic ring that made its wearer invisible. These stories became *The Hobbit* (1937). Later he invented the evil Sauron, who had made the ring but lost it many years before. Sauron wanted it back, knowing it would give him power to control the entire world. Bilbo's nephew, Frodo, who inherited the ring, learned he must destroy it in the volcanic fires of Mount Doom. His efforts to do so are told in three novels, together called *The Lord of the Rings* (1954–55). The three are *The Fellowship of the Ring, The Two Towers,* and *The Return of the King*.

Tolkien retired from Oxford in 1959, devoting his last years to work on *The Silmarillion*—a task he was unable to finish before his death on September 2, 1973. The novel was edited by his son Christopher and published in 1977. Tolkien remains one of the most beloved and widely read authors in the world.

RANDEL HELMS
Author, *Tolkien's World*

In this excerpt from *The Hobbit*, Bilbo Baggins is lost in the Goblin caves under the Misty Mountains. Trying to find a way out, he stumbles onto Gollum's lair.

Deep down here by the dark water lived old Gollum, a small slimy creature. I don't know where he came from, nor who or what he was. He was Gollum—as dark as darkness, except for two big round pale eyes in his thin face. He had a little boat, and he rowed about quite quietly on the lake; for lake it was, wide and deep and deadly cold. He paddled it with large feet dangling over the side, but never a ripple did he make. Not he. He was looking out of his pale lamp-like eyes for blind fish, which he grabbed with his long fingers as quick as thinking. He liked meat too, Goblin he thought good, when he could get it; but he took care they never found him out. He just throttled them from behind, if they ever came down alone anywhere near the edge of the water, while he was prowling about. They very seldom did, for they had a feeling that something unpleasant was lurking down there, down at the very roots of the mountain. They had come on the lake, when they were tunnelling down long ago, and they found they could go no further; so there their road ended in that direction, and there was no reason to go that way—unless the Great Goblin sent them. Sometimes he took a fancy for fish from the lake, and sometimes neither goblin nor fish came back.

Actually Gollum lived on a slimy island of rock in the middle of the lake. He was watching Bilbo now from the distance with his pale eyes like telescopes. Bilbo could not see him, but he was wondering a lot about Bilbo, for he could see that he was no goblin at all.

Gollum got into his boat and shot off from the island, while Bilbo was sitting on the brink altogether flummoxed and at the end of his way and his wits. Suddenly up came Gollum and whispered and hissed:

"Bless us and splash us, my preciousss! I guess it's a choice feast; at least a tasty morsel it'd make us, gollum!" And when he said *gollum* he made a horrible swallowing noise in his throat. That is how he got his name, though he always called himself 'my precious'.

The hobbit jumped nearly out of his skin when the hiss came in his ears, and he suddenly saw the pale eyes sticking out at him.

"Who are you?" he said, thrusting his dagger in front of him.

"What iss he, my preciouss?" whispered Gollum (who always spoke to himself through never having anyone else to speak to). This is what he had come to find out, for he was not really very hungry at the moment, only curious; otherwise he would have grabbed first and whispered afterwards.

"I am Mr. Bilbo Baggins. I have lost the dwarves and I have lost the wizard, and I don't know where I am; and I don't want to know, if only I can get away."

"What's he got in his handses?" said Gollum, looking at the sword, which he did not quite like.

"A sword, a blade which came out of Gondolin!"

"Sssss" said Gollum, and became quite polite. "Praps ye sits here and chats with it a bitsy, my preciouss. It like riddles, praps it does, does, it?" He was anxious to appear friendly, at any rate for the moment, and until he found out more about the sword and the hobbit, whether he was quite alone really, whether he was good to eat, and whether Gollum was really hungry. Riddles were all he could think of. Asking them and sometimes guessing them, had been the only game he had ever played with other funny creatures sitting in their holes in the long, long ago, before he lost all his friends and was driven away, alone, and crept down, down, into the dark under the mountains.

"Very well," said Bilbo, who was anxious to agree, until he found out more about the creature,

The evil Gollum is a "small slimy creature . . . as dark as darkness, except for two big round pale eyes . . ."

whether he was quite alone, whether he was fierce or hungry, and whether he was a friend of the goblins.

"You ask first," he said, because he had not had time to think of a riddle.

So Gollum hissed:

What has roots as nobody sees,
Is taller than trees
Up, up it goes,
And yet never grows?

"Easy!" said Bilbo. "Mountain, I suppose."

"Does it guess easy? It must have a competition with us, my preciouss! If precious asks, and it doesn't answer, we eats it, my preciousss. If it asks us, and we doesn't answer, then we does what it wants, eh? We shows it the way out, yes!"

Most Hispanic Americans are Roman Catholic. Early Spanish settlers in the United States set up missions to convert the Indians and to serve as parish churches.

HISPANIC AMERICANS

In many parts of the United States, Spanish is heard almost as often as English. It is the language favored by some 16,000,000 Hispanic Americans (also called Latinos), the fastest growing minority in the nation.

Hispanic Americans are residents of the United States who were born in Spanish-speaking lands or whose ancestors migrated from Spanish-speaking lands. They make up 6½ percent of the population. Their customs, music, food, and the lilting sounds of their rapid conversation are worked into the fabric of such widely scattered cities as Los Angeles, New York, Miami, Chicago, Denver, Philadelphia, and San Antonio.

Most English-speaking Americans think of their Hispanic neighbors as one group. But there are several distinct groups among them. More than half the Hispanic population is of Mexican origin. Puerto Ricans on the mainland of the United States number about 2,000,000. Close to 1,000,000 Cubans have moved to the United States since the 1950's. More than 3,000,000 Spanish-speaking Americans came from other countries in Central and South America, while a small percentage trace their lineage to Spain.

Unlike most groups that have immigrated to the United States, Hispanic Americans stem from a great variety of ethnic and racial stocks. Their language and their most common religion (Roman Catholic) come from Spain, as a result of Spain's conquest of vast areas of the Americas. But other aspects of their heritage spring from different cultures of the American continent and of Africa. The African influence came from the importation of African slaves into the Spanish colonies.

In recent years the Hispanic population has increased dramatically and has fanned out through the United States. And it is expected to keep on growing. In addition, the poverty and instability that plague much of Latin America continue to propel thousands of people toward the United States by every means of transportation available. Some even arrive on foot across the Rio Grande, the river that separates the United States and Mexico.

▶ THE FIRST HISPANIC AMERICANS

The Rio Grande (Spanish for "great river") has played a major role in the history of Hispanic Americans. It was on the banks of the Rio Grande in 1598 that the Spanish explorer Don Juan de Oñate—leader of an expedition of 400 men, women, and children —took possession of a territory he called New Mexico. These daring pioneers had journeyed north from Mexico to settle the new lands. Some 250 years later, at the end of the Mexican War, a defeated Mexico ceded the vast region to the United States. Today it consists of the states of Texas, California, New Mexico, and Arizona and sections of Colorado, Utah, and Nevada.

The descendants of the early Spanish settlers taught newly arrived English-speaking settlers techniques of irrigation and mining, how to tame wild horses, and how best to raise cattle in what was often a harsh environment. They gave the English language such words as *rodeo, stampede, corral, canyon, mesa,* and *adobe*. But they came to be a barely tolerated minority in what was once their own land. At the same time, the Rio Grande became the border between the two countries—a frontier destined to be crossed by ever-increasing numbers of immigrants.

From Mexico to the United States

Even today, descendants of the early Spanish settlers live in the state of New Mexico, where they have kept the language, customs, and crafts of their ancestors. But as soon as the border between the United States and Mexico was established, a new trickle of Mexican workers started making its way north to find jobs in the United States. By the early 1900's, hundreds of thousands were crossing the Rio Grande to work for the railroads, mines, and huge farms and ranches that were changing the landscape of the Southwest.

At first, most newly arrived Mexicans worked as migrants, following railroad lines or a succession of crops. They lived in crowded camps or trailers with other Mexicans, and they moved on when the work was completed. After years on the road, a family was often happy to leave the migrant stream and settle in a city. The Mexican American population remained concentrated in Texas, New Mexico, Arizona, Colorado, and California. Los Angeles became home to more people of Mexican descent than any other place except Mexico City.

The Spanish-speaking neighborhoods that developed in cities were known as *barrios*. There, Mexican families lived and worked, apart from the rest of the townspeople. The prejudice that had hounded them as migrants had followed them into the cities. Signs reading "No admittance to Negroes, Mexicans, or dogs" were common.

World War II opened up new opportunities in the armed forces and in war production plants. The status of Mexican Americans began to change. In the mid-1960's the civil rights movement awakened the nation to injustices in many parts of society. Mexican Americans were ready to join the fight for equal rights. Their struggle for equality and justice became known as *Movimiento Chicano,* the "Chicano Movement." ("Chicano," from the Spanish word *mejicanos,* was a term that had once been considered degrading.) During the same years, a strike by California grape workers was organized by the labor union leader Cesar Chavez, himself a former field hand. It dramatized the bad conditions of migrant workers and brought the history of Mexican Americans before the entire nation.

Illegal Immigrants

Even as Mexican Americans were entering the mainstream of American life, a constant flow of new, poor immigrants continued to cross the Rio Grande. Those who have entered the United States from Mexico since the 1960's have done so mostly without legal papers. They are illegal, or undocumented, aliens, caught in a conflict between the lure of the United States job market and the country's laws.

Under the immigration law of 1965, only 120,000 people a year are allowed into the United States from countries in the Western Hemisphere. This figure falls far short of the number that want to enter. Thus untold numbers of people enter the country by a wide variety of illegal means—by stowing away on a boat, by hiding in the trunk of a car, by walking or by swimming across the Rio Grande. The purpose of the Simpson-Mazzoli bill, which was approved by the Senate in 1983 and the House of Representatives in 1984, was to control the flow of undocumented immigrants and to legalize the status of those already in the United States.

▶ EXILES FROM CUBA

On rare occasions, U.S. immigration requirements are lifted to allow entry of a group of people thought to be in special need

In the 1960's, Cesar Chavez (*seated*) organized farm workers into a union to improve their working conditions. Many of the workers were Mexican Americans.

Thousands of Cubans who opposed the regime of Fidel Castro have fled to the United States, often suffering great hardships on the journey.

of shelter in the United States. This has been the case for hundreds of thousands of Cubans who have fled the Marxist regime of President Fidel Castro since the 1950's. A great many arrived from 1965 to 1973, the years of the Freedom Airlift. During this time American planes took thousands of Cubans to join relatives already living in the United States, mostly in Miami. Once there, the exiles received assistance in finding homes and jobs.

The exiles were a cross section of the Cuban population, wealthy as well as poor. They included many trained, middle class people. Because of their determination and high level of skills, they were able to achieve a high standard of living that is in marked contrast to that of other Spanish-speaking Americans.

At first the exiles remained in Miami, sure that the Castro regime would be overthrown and that they could then go back to Cuba. As years passed and the dream of quick return proved false, many put down new roots in New Jersey, New York, and California. But the Miami area remains home to more than half the Cuban American community.

▶ IMMIGRATION FROM PUERTO RICO

Just as Cubans outnumber other Hispanics in Miami, so Puerto Ricans dominate the Latin scene in New York. Puerto Rico is a territory of the United States, acquired in 1898 at the close of the Spanish American War. Its people are therefore U.S. citizens, free to travel to any of the states whenever they wish. Since the mid-1940's, when airlines began low-cost flights to Puerto Rico, hundreds of thousands of people have left their sunny but poor land to try their luck in the job markets of the eastern United States. Many shuttle back and forth, maintaining ties in both worlds.

Most of the Puerto Ricans who migrated to the mainland were rural people, used to farm work and village life in a warm climate. In New York and other eastern cities, they found employment in restaurants and hotels, small factories, hospitals—low paying, low prestige jobs that barely allowed them to pay the rent or buy warm clothes. They were met with the same hostility that most newcomers face. Added to this was prejudice against them as a people of mixed European, African, and Indian heritage.

Today a growing Puerto Rican middle class has carved out a secure place for itself. Public hostility seems to have lessened, and Spanish has become an accepted language in New York and other cities where Puerto Ricans have settled. But at the same time, many Puerto Ricans still live in substandard housing and survive on low incomes or meager state aid.

▶ OTHER HISPANIC COMMUNITIES

The three major groups—Mexican Americans, Cubans, and Puerto Ricans—tend to overshadow the many smaller communities that share the Spanish language. The 3,000,000 people defined by the Census Bureau as "other Spanish" trace their heritage to Spain and to every country, large and small, in Central and South America. They come from teeming cities and farming villages, from fishing ports and the highlands of the Andes. Among them are many people seeking shelter from extreme political disorder and repression. But the greatest number are escaping poverty, hoping to find an opportunity to improve their lot and give their children a better chance for the future.

▶ COMMON LINKS

Despite their different backgrounds, the various Hispanic groups have much in common. The major link is language and, more than any other U.S. immigrants, they have managed to preserve it. They have even succeeded in promoting Spanish to the status of an official second language in many parts of the country. Several states require bilingual instructions on election ballots and on signs in hospitals, public transportation, and municipal offices.

Another common trait is love of family. Parents, grandparents, aunts, uncles, cousins and godparents form a support system for each individual.

Religion plays a vital role in Hispanic neighborhoods. The Roman Catholic Church commands the largest allegiance, and Protestant churches also claim large followings. The Roman Catholic Church has increased the number of Spanish-speaking priests in the United States and provides needed social services.

Unique holiday traditions brighten even the poorest Hispanic homes. For example, *El Día de Los Reyes*—Three Kings Day, on January 6—is considered as important as Christmas. Children and adults take part in pageants that tell the story of the kings who journeyed to see the infant Jesus. On *El Día de los Muertos*—All Souls' Day, November 2—families take symbolic gifts to the cemeteries where loved ones are buried. A girl's 16th birthday is celebrated with a special Mass and a party.

Certain foods are popular among all Hispanics—rice and beans, for example, and *flan,* a custardlike dessert. Such staples of Mexican cooking as tortillas, tacos, and enchiladas have been adopted by the entire nation. And the lively sounds of Latin music can be heard everywhere in the United States.

▶ COMMON PROBLEMS

Most Hispanic Americans are plagued by similar problems. Poor jobs, inferior housing, not enough schooling, and lingering discrimination are facts of life for far too many. For many years their problems—and even their presence—were ignored by most of the nation. In recent years the English-speaking majority has begun to notice the problems of Hispanic Americans and to make up for past injustice.

Hispanic communities have organized such groups as the League of United Latin-American Citizens, the National Hispanic Leadership Conference, the National Council of La Raza, and others. These organiza-

Hispanic Americans keep up many of their cultural traditions. Here, children in colorful costumes take part in a street festival in New York City.

tions hope to achieve such important goals as improved education, an end to discrimination in employment and law enforcement, and increased participation in local, state, and national elections.

Until recently there was little contact among the different Spanish-speaking groups. Even now, individuals tend to identify themselves by their particular family lineage rather than as Hispanics. Since the 1960's, however, community leaders have recognized their common aims and problems. They have realized what effective power there is in acting jointly.

Measures such as civil rights legislation and court decisions outlawing segregation in schools have been taken primarily to protect black Americans. But these measures have helped improve the lot of all minorities. A vital step for the Hispanic community was the passage of the Bilingual Education Act in 1968. This law makes funds available for teaching in both English and Spanish (or another language), so that children can be taught in their native tongue while learning English.

Other measures, such as expanded higher education facilities and open admissions policies, have made it possible for thousands of Hispanics to attend college. As they move into positions of responsibility in business, government, and the professions, they become models for younger people struggling to break out of the cycle of poverty.

ALBERTA EISEMAN
Author, *Mañana Is Now*

GREENAWAY, KATE
(1846–1901)

Beautiful children, dressed in the charming style of the early 19th century, with long flowing dresses, ribbons and bows, pinafores and hats, buttoned trousers and ruffled shirts —these are the boys and girls drawn by the author-illustrator Kate Greenaway. The children in her pictures were delicate and graceful, pure and innocent. The people of Kate Greenaway's day fell in love with them, and the drawings continue to have appeal today.

Catherine Greenaway, always called Kate, was born in London, England, on March 17, 1846. Her mother was a shopkeeper, her father a well-known wood engraver. She showed a talent for drawing, and at age 12 she began formal art training.

Kate Greenaway began her publishing career designing greeting cards and illustrating the works of other writers. In 1878 the color printer Edmund Evans published a collection of her drawings accompanied by verses she had written, titled *Under the Window.* It was an immediate success, and an estimated 250,000 copies were sold. Later books for which she supplied both text and illustrations included *Language of Flowers* (1884), *Marigold Garden* (1885), and *A Apple Pie* (1886). In 1880 she did the drawings for *The Queen of the Pirate Isle,* by the American author Bret Harte. And in 1888 she illustrated the popular tale by Robert Browning, *The Pied Piper of Hamelin.*

The charm of Greenaway's drawings caught the fancy of the public. Her style influenced the fashion world of her day, and her illustrations were used on such items as greeting cards, china, buttons, embroidery patterns, dolls, and even wallpaper. During the 1890's, three exhibitions of her work were held at the Fine Art Society in London, and she was elected a member of the Royal Institute of Painters in Watercolors in 1898.

Kate Greenaway, the shy lover of children, never married and died childless on November 6, 1901. But her quaint, fanciful illustrations helped to change the appearance of children's books, making them more entertaining and enjoyable.

SUSAN RUTH THOMSON
Author, *A Catalogue of the Kate Greenaway Collection, Rare Book Room, Detroit Public Library*

Kate Greenaway's *Under the Window* has delighted young readers for more than 100 years.

Left: *Freedom of Speech* is from a Norman Rockwell series of paintings celebrating democracy. Right: *Breaking Home Ties*, like all the artist's covers for the *Saturday Evening Post*, tells a story about ordinary people in everyday life.

ROCKWELL, NORMAN (1894–1978)

Norman Rockwell was a leading American illustrator whose professional career spanned more than 60 years. Most famous for the hundreds of covers he painted for the *Saturday Evening Post*, Rockwell specialized in lifelike portrayals of ordinary Americans in everyday situations. His accurate powers of observation and gentle humor gave point to his work.

Rockwell was born in New York City on February 3, 1894. He was the son of a businessman who liked to read the works of Charles Dickens to his children, and his grandfather had been an unsuccessful artist. Rockwell showed an early talent for drawing and painting. While still attending the Art Students League in New York City, he became a commercial artist. In 1916 his work began to appear in the *Saturday Evening Post*, and from that time on he was counted among the first rank of American illustrators.

Rockwell's early cover paintings often featured children, elderly people, and dogs in amusing situations. He continued to draw and paint similar subjects throughout his career. During World War I, he served in the Navy but continued to work for the *Post* and other clients. In the 1920's he made a number of trips to Europe and was briefly influenced by modern art. He quickly returned to his realistic style, but he continued to admire Picasso and other modern artists.

Rockwell reached new heights during World War II when his famous series of paintings *The Four Freedoms* (1943), celebrating democracy, toured the country. From that time until the early 1960's, he was at the peak of his talent. The best paintings of those years, such as *Breaking Home Ties* (1954) and *Marriage License* (1955), are important contributions to the tradition of realist painting in America.

Rockwell's later paintings show well-drawn characters in detailed settings—often in corners of his beloved New England. Many of these paintings recorded an America that was vanishing even as he portrayed it on canvas. It was part of his genius that he gave his vast audience a link with the past at a time when the world was changing rapidly. Yet he did this without losing sight of the everyday events of modern life.

In the last years of his life, Rockwell traveled all over the world, from Mexico to Mongolia, painting wherever he went. But his roots remained in the northeastern United States. He died in Stockbridge, Massachusetts, in 1978.

CHRISTOPHER FINCH
Author, *Norman Rockwell's America*

FLORENCE

Travelers who love art and culture are always fascinated by their first glimpse of Florence (Firenze, in Italian). The city is the capital of Firenze province and the region of Tuscany in central Italy. The hills that surround the city are dotted with elegant villas, or country estates, and vineyards that produce the wine of Tuscany. From these hills a visitor can see the soaring towers, spires, and domes of the city itself.

Much of Florence looks just as it did 500 years ago during the period called the Renaissance, when the arts flourished in great splendor. Florence has always been a relatively small city. Its present population is about 450,000, and during the height of the Renaissance there were only about 90,000 people. Nevertheless, Florence played a vital role in the history of art, architecture, philosophy, literature, and science. It also was a leader in promoting free trade, commerce, banking, and a republican form of government.

▶ **A WALK THROUGH THE CITY**

Florence was the first city in Europe to have paved streets and sidewalks. Appropriately, the best way to experience the city is by foot, strolling down the narrow alleyways and cobblestone streets. A first stop might be the Ponte Vecchio, the oldest bridge across the Arno River. The bridge dates from the 14th century and houses many shops that specialize in fine gold jewelry. *Palazzi* (palaces), *piazze* (open squares), churches, statues, museums, and art galleries are some of the other sights awaiting the visitor.

From the Ponte Vecchio, one can walk to the spacious Piazza della Signoria to see the proud Palazzo Vecchio. Built in the 13th century and the traditional seat of the city's government, the palace is now the town hall. Nearby, in the Piazza del Duomo, is Florence cathedral, called the Duomo, topped by a mighty cupola (dome). Alongside the cathedral is a magnificent campanile (bell tower), which rises to a height of 84 meters (276 feet). Across from the Duomo is the eight-sided Baptistery of San Giovanni, which dates from the 6th to the 12th century, and is considered the oldest building in Florence. It is noted for its sculptured bronze doors. The city has dozens of museums and

Florence cathedral, known as the Duomo, and its campanile (bell tower) dominate the city's skyline. In the background are the hills that surround Florence.

art galleries, which house world-renowned art treasures. Among them are the Uffizi; the Pitti Palace, which was the residence of the king of Italy when Florence was briefly the capital; the Bargello; and the Academy, which contains the city's best-known statue, the colossal *David* of Michelangelo.

At midday a visitor can follow the example of the Florentines and have pasta (noodles) and grilled veal at a typical restaurant called a *trattoria*. After lunch, Florentines usually take a nap before resuming the late afternoon's activities. Around four in the afternoon, the streets are suddenly filled with people taking a *passeggiata,* a leisurely stroll, to meet friends and see the latest fashions in the city's famous clothing and leather goods shops.

▶ HISTORY

The Etruscans were the first known settlers in the region. In about 59 B.C. the Romans established a colony that they called Florentia. They were followed by Byzantine and Germanic invaders. Because of its excellent location in the heart of Italy, Florence became a crossroads for trade. By the 12th century the Florentines had established a highly developed form of city government called the Commune. Rules for the conduct of trade and finance were carefully organized. All citizens had to belong to one of the trade guilds that dominated the growing economy. The most powerful of these guilds were those that controlled the wool-making shops and directed the sales of Florence's famous wool products to markets far away.

The decline of the Commune and centuries of political strife did not affect the Florentine talent for business. The first commercial banks in Western Europe began in Florence, and the gold florin became the standard coin accepted throughout Europe. This tremendous prosperity was temporarily halted by the bubonic plague, the Black Death. The plague swept through much of Europe in the 14th century and killed over half the population of Florence.

The Renaissance. The word "renaissance" means "rebirth." Florence was the cradle for the rebirth of philosophy, literature, and art, based on classical (Greek and Roman) ideals, that took place in Italy between the 1300's and 1600's. During this period the Florentine Dante Alighieri completed one of the world's masterpieces, the epic poem *The Divine Comedy*. The poet Petrarch wrote his famous sonnets. Giovanni Boccaccio wrote a series of 100 tales called *The Decameron,* which vividly described the horrors of the plague. And Niccolò Machiavelli set down in his book *The Prince* rules on how to govern.

Florence also produced many of the great painters and sculptors of the Renaissance. Giotto di Bondone, who designed the cathedral campanile, is considered the father of Renaissance art. The painters Masaccio, Fra Angelico, and Sandro Botticelli made Florence their home. Lorenzo Ghiberti cast several of the great bronze doors of the Baptistery of San Giovanni. Filippo Brunelleschi designed the dome of the cathedral. The sculptor Luca della Robbia worked in terra cotta (fired clay). Donatello created the first classic statues since the fall of ancient Rome. Leonardo da Vinci, Michelangelo Buonarroti, and Raphael produced paintings and sculptures that displayed heroic power and served later artists as perfect models.

Between the 15th and 18th centuries, Florence was ruled chiefly by the Medici family. The Medicis gained their power and fortune from banking and used their wealth to donate art to the city. The most famous member of the family was Lorenzo, called the Magnificent, who ruled from 1469 to 1492. This was the city's golden age. Lorenzo was both a poet and a tyrant.

Florence took part in the struggle for the independence and re-unification of Italy in the 19th century. It was the capital of the kingdom of Italy from 1865 to 1870. During World War II, Florence was damaged by bombing, but most of the city's treasures were spared. In 1966, the flooding of the Arno River damaged many works of art. During the 1970's and 1980's, the city had a great growth in population, and special measures had to be taken to preserve the historical center of the city. Today, long after its period of glory, millions of people visit the city each year to experience its art, which reflects the greatness of the human spirit.

PHILIP ELIASOPH
Fairfield University

329

ETIQUETTE

Have you ever stopped to consider why you share your belongings with others? Or why you say "please" when you ask for something and "thank you" when someone does something for you? This kind of behavior is designed to help people get along with one another. It is also intended to prevent people from hurting one another's feelings.

Etiquette is the set of rules that guide how people behave toward one another. Actually, people follow not one but several codes of etiquette. Most people are concerned with a social code of behavior—that is, with how people treat one another in daily life. There is also military etiquette, the special set of rules that people in the military follow. Protocol is yet another kind of etiquette. It is used by government officials and diplomats.

Etiquette also varies from culture to culture. In some countries, people greet each other by shaking hands. In other countries they bow in greeting. In many countries a host goes through a doorway after a guest as a sign of courtesy. But in some parts of the world, the host goes ahead of guests as a sort of honorary form of protection for them.

Even at a very young age, children begin to learn the rules of etiquette. These rules, which may vary from country to country, are based on consideration of others.

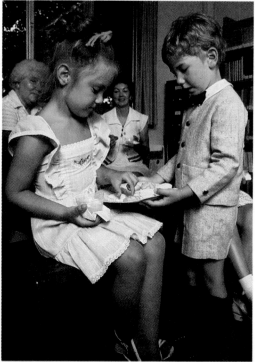

▶ THE HISTORY OF ETIQUETTE

The first etiquette rules probably came about when people began to band together to hunt and to protect one another. If nothing else, these prehistoric people needed rules about sharing the food they had gathered. As people began to live together in larger, more complex groups, they created more rules to help them get along with one another. Eventually, etiquette became a strict set of rules about social behavior.

People have learned about etiquette from their families and also by reading etiquette books. Such books have been written at least since the days of the Roman Empire, and children have often been their target. Throughout history, as many etiquette books have been written for children as for adults. And even the books written for adults have contained lots of advice on how to teach manners to children.

From the 1500's through the early 1900's, children also learned etiquette at school, along with other subjects such as history and geography. Most reading primers consisted of verses and advice on correct behavior. Children were advised on such points as the proper way of kneeling before their teachers, the value of remaining silent until spoken to, and the folly of using a dinner knife as a toothpick.

Over the years, people were expected to follow an increasingly complicated set of rules. Many of the rules seem silly today. For example, in Western countries in the 1800's, a young man could not speak to a young woman he knew until she had first acknowledged him. Little girls curtsied and little boys bowed when introduced to someone. Not many years ago, when a young man and a young woman went out on a date, she was expected to sit quietly in the car while he walked around it to open her door and help her out.

▶ ETIQUETTE TODAY

Since the 1960's, manners have become much more relaxed. Etiquette today is based on treating everyone with the same degree of kindness and consideration, and it consists mostly of common sense. It is helpful, though, to know some rules about how to

RULES for BEHAVIOUR, 1787

CHILDREN'S BEHAVIOUR at the TABLE

COME NOT to the Table without having your Hands and Face washed, and your Head combed.

Ask not for any Thing, but tarry until it be offered thee.

Find no fault with any Thing that is given thee.

If thou wantest any Thing from the Servants, call to them softly.

Make not a Noise with thy Tongue, Mouth, Lips or Breath, in eating or drinking.

Take not Salt with a greasy Knife.

Spit not, cough not, nor blow thy Nose at the Table, if it may be avoided; but if there be necessity, do it aside, and without much Noise.

Stuff not thy Mouth so as to fill thy Cheeks, be content with smaller Mouthfuls.

Blow not thy Meat, but with Patience wait until it be cool.

Smell not of thy Meat, nor put it to thy Nose; turn it not the other Side upward to view it upon thy Plate.

Throw not any Thing under the Table.

Spit not forth any Thing that is not convenient to be swallowed, as the Stones of Plumbs, Cherries, or such like; but with thy left Hand, neatly move them to the Side of thy Plate.

Foul not the Napkin all over, but at one Corner only.

Stare not in the Face of any one, especially thy Superiours, at the Table.

Pick not thy Teeth at the Table, unless holding up thy Napkin before thy Mouth with thine other Hand.

Drink not nor speak with any Thing in thy Mouth.

When thou risest from the Table, having made a Bow at the Side of the Table where thou sattest, withdraw.

From *A Little Pretty Pocket-Book* first printed by John Newbery, London, 1774; first American edition issued by Isaiah Thomas, Worcester, Mass., 1789. Reprinted at the press of The *Virginia Gazette*, Williamsburg, copyright D. Adair, 1949.

Left: According to these 18th-century rules, children should not ask for anything at the table or complain about the food. Above: As part of a course in today's etiquette, a boy learns to select and order from a menu.

behave in certain situations—if only because this makes life more comfortable for you.

Greetings and Introductions

When you meet someone you have not seen for a while, it is polite to say hello. Young people often greet each other casually and always use first names with one another. Greetings to adults are more formal. As a sign of respect, stand up when you greet someone older and call the person by name. Young people do not usually call adults by their first names until the adults have asked them to do so.

It is easy to make an introduction if you remember that it is merely a polite way of making two people known to each other. Young people are usually introduced to older people—"Mrs. McKay, this is Mary Jones" —rather than the other way around. If you are at a party and have not been introduced to everyone, it is quite proper for you to introduce yourself to someone else. When you meet people for the first time, it is polite to shake hands with them.

Table Manners

Probably more has been written about table manners than any other area of etiquette. Almost all the rules are designed to make eating pleasant. There are far more rules than can be listed here, but the basics of good table manners are easy to learn.

To begin with, meals are a special time to sit down and talk with family and friends. They are meant to be quiet lulls in the day. Because of this, the dinner hour is not the time to act rowdy, talk loudly, or argue with anyone. The days are long past when children did not speak at the dinner table except when spoken to. But certain topics of conversation are still ruled out. As a general rule, do not discuss anything that will ruin anyone's appetite. This rules out, for example, what you dissected in science class and any descriptions of serious injury or illness.

There are lots of rules about how to eat specific foods. But you need only a few guidelines to get along well. Learn to hold and use a knife, fork, and spoon correctly. Never use your fingers to push food onto

Above: "Which fork do I use first?" At a modern American etiquette school, a teacher explains the fine points of table settings and menus. Right: Dance classes are often a part of the curriculum in such a school. Dancing is not an essential part of etiquette, but it is a good way to practice social skills.

your fork or spoon. (Certain foods, such as olives, celery, and corn on the cob, may be picked up with your fingers.) Eat quietly and always keep your mouth closed when chewing food. Posture is important, too—no one wants to watch someone slouched over a dinner plate. It is polite to wait for your host or hostess to begin before you start to eat.

At a restaurant or at someone's home, you may encounter a food you have never seen before, and you may have no idea about how to go about eating it. You can do one of two things when this happens. You can say, "Oh, I've never eaten this before. Can you tell me about it?" Or you can wait and watch your hosts eat the food and do what they do.

A formal table setting may have more knives, forks, and spoons than you are used to. If you do not know which one to use for which course, follow this rule: Start from the outside and work in. A soup spoon, for example, is placed outside the dinner fork because soup is served before the main course.

If you must leave the table for any reason during a meal, ask to be excused. Finally, when a dish or a meal has been particularly good, do not forget to compliment the cook. Especially at home, people too often take meals for granted.

Telephone Manners

Good telephone manners also help life run smoothly. Remember that the only impression callers have of you is made by your voice. Try to speak in a normal, pleasant tone.

If the caller asks to speak to a family member who is home, say, "Just one minute, please, I'll call her to the phone." If the person is not home, offer to take a message. Make sure you write down a correctly spelled name and a number. Do not forget to give the message to the person who got the call.

Be thoughtful about when and how long you use the phone. Do not let friends call late at night or during dinner. Do not tie up the phone for hours, especially if someone is waiting for a call or planning to use the phone.

Visiting

When you visit someone, you are a guest. This means that you are extended various small courtesies, but it also means that you have some responsibilities.

When you arrive at someone's house, take a few minutes to greet other family members. Grandparents and other elderly people especially appreciate a few minutes' attention. Ask them how they are feeling or comment on something they are doing.

As a guest your role is to be more a follower than a leader. Your host will suggest activities, and unless you hate the suggestion, you should try to go along with it. Wait until food and drinks are offered to you—do not ask for them except in an emergency.

Finally, do not outstay your welcome. If you have been invited for a Saturday afternoon swim, do not stay on until someone has to invite you to dinner. Realize that your friend may have other plans, and leave an hour or so after the swim. This will help ensure that you will be a welcome guest the next time you visit.

Making Guests Comfortable

"The shoe is on the other foot" when a friend visits as your guest. Then you must do everything possible to make your guest feel comfortable. The key to this is to anticipate your guest's needs.

If someone is visiting overnight or for several days, explain the routine of the household. That way your guest will feel comfortable and will know what is expected. Make a special effort to take your guest's needs into account. Maybe you never eat lunch on Saturdays, for example. Keep in mind that your guest will be hungry, and offer lunch.

Take special care to share things with your guest and to give him or her special treatment—the best seat for watching television, the first turn at a new piece of sports equipment. Try to suggest activities that you know your guest will enjoy. Finally, when your guest is leaving and thanks you for the visit, thank her or him for coming.

Parties

Party manners are not very different from the manners you use when you visit someone's home, but they are sometimes a bit more formal and festive. Since you are not the only guest at a party, it is important to go along with the crowd. Act enthusiastic about all the planned activities.

When you arrive, greet your host and any adults who are there to help with the party. When you leave, say good-bye to these same people and thank them for giving the party or for helping. Offer to help the host—or just lend a hand if you see that something needs doing. A particular kindness at a party is to talk to someone who is shy or a stranger. This frees the host from one responsibility and is also a kindness to the other person.

Thank-You Notes

Another important area of etiquette is correspondence—writing letters. About the only letters that young people must regularly write are thank-you notes. When someone gives you a gift, you should send a handwritten note of thanks. A thank-you note need not be long, but it should be sincere and specific. Mention the gift by name. You might describe something you particularly like about it—its color or its shape—or how you will use it. On the other hand, if you really do not like the gift and probably will not use it, a more general note may help hide this fact.

Manners at Home and in Public

If you remember to be thoughtful and considerate toward other people, you will behave properly wherever you are—at school, in restaurants, on buses, and in theaters, as well as at home.

At a theater you should walk quietly to your seat. If you have to pass in front of people, excuse yourself and be careful not to step on their toes. Avoid talking, rattling candy papers, pushing on the seat in front of you, or bobbing your head from side to side. These things spoil the show for other people.

At a fast-food restaurant, you should eat as politely as you would at any restaurant or at someone's home. In many of these restaurants, you are expected to clear your table and throw out your food wrappers when you are done. Wherever you may be, littering the ground with papers or soda cans is inconsiderate to everyone around you.

As you can see, there are many different kinds of situations where knowing how to act is helpful. Most situations, though, can be handled by following one simple guideline: Treat others as you would like to be treated. That and "please" and "thank you" will get you through almost any awkward moment.

MARJABELLE YOUNG STEWART
Author, *Stand Up, Shake Hands,*
Say "How Do You Do"

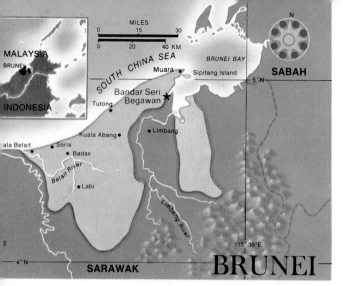

BRUNEI

BRUNEI

The Sultanate of Brunei, a tiny nation rich in oil and natural gas, has one of the world's highest incomes per person. It is made up of two small unconnected territories on the northwest coast of the island of Borneo. Except for its coastline, Brunei is surrounded by the Malaysian state of Sarawak.

▶ THE PEOPLE AND THE ECONOMY

About half the population is Malay; another one fourth is Chinese. The rest of the population includes various native groups, Americans, Europeans, Australians, and guest workers from elsewhere in Asia. About 75 percent of the people live in the capital city or in towns and villages along the coast. Islam is the official religion of Brunei, although other religions are permitted. Islamic laws are strictly enforced for all Muslims.

Commercial oil production in Brunei began in 1929. Petroleum products now make up almost 99 percent of Brunei's exports and account for more than 75 percent of the country's wealth. Money from oil has been invested abroad. Because of its oil wealth, the country has not developed agriculture or consumer industries. Most foodstuffs and consumer goods are imported. But the government has recently supported the development of local agriculture, and in 1982 it bought an Australian ranch—larger than Brunei itself—to provide beef and dairy products.

▶ THE LAND

The two separate parts of Brunei are divided by the Limbang River valley, in Sarawak. The capital, Bandar Seri Begawan, is located near the mouth of the Brunei River in the western (and larger) part of the country. Brunei has a tropical climate with high temperatures, high humidity, and heavy rainfall. Dense forests cover 70 percent of the country.

▶ HISTORY AND GOVERNMENT

Brunei gained independence from the Javanese kingdom of Madjapahit in the 1400's. By the 1500's the sultan of Brunei controlled an empire that extended almost to Manila in the Philippines. Brunei declined rapidly in size and power from the 1600's onward. At the request of the sultan, Brunei was placed under British protection in 1888. Brunei remained under British protection until it regained full independence on January 1, 1984. Because of its concern about defense, Brunei had wanted to remain under British protection. Independence came chiefly at British insistence.

Brunei's first constitution, adopted in 1959, was suspended after an attempted revolution in 1962. The elected councils provided for in the constitution have remained suspended since that time except for a brief period during 1965–68. Sultan Muda Hassanal Bolkiah came to power when his father gave up the throne in 1967. His cabinet is dominated by the royal family, which has been reluctant to share political power.

ROBERT O. TILMAN
North Carolina State University

FACTS AND FIGURES

BRUNEI DARUSSALAM (Brunei, Abode of Peace) is the official name of the country.

CAPITAL: Bandar Seri Begawan.

LOCATION: Northwest coast of Borneo on the South China Sea. **Latitude**—4° 2′N to 5° 3′N. **Longitude**—114°E to 115° 22′E.

AREA: 5,765 km² (2,226 sq mi).

POPULATION: 200,000 (estimate).

LANGUAGES: Malay, Chinese, English.

GOVERNMENT: Islamic Sultanate. **Head of government**—sultan. **International co-operation**—Commonwealth of Nations, Association of Southeast Asian Nations (ASEAN).

ECONOMY: Agricultural products—rice, vegetables, sago (palm starch), tapioca, coconuts, pineapples, pepper, spices. **Industries and products**—oil, liquefied natural gas, liquefied propane, fishing, rubber, forest products. **Chief mineral**—oil. **Chief exports**—oil and oil products. **Chief imports**—machinery and transportation equipment, consumer goods, foodstuffs. **Monetary unit**—Brunei dollar.

POE, EDGAR ALLAN
(1809–1849)

Edgar Allan Poe, who became one of America's most famous poets and short-story writers, was born in Boston, Massachusetts, on January 19, 1809. His parents were actors. Edgar's father deserted his family, and his mother died in 1811. John and Frances Allan of Richmond, Virginia, took Edgar into their home.

Edgar received his early schooling in Richmond. In 1815 he went to England with the Allans and attended boarding schools there before returning to Richmond in 1820. In 1826 he entered the University of Virginia. He was an honors student, but gambling debts forced him to drop out in less than a year.

Penniless, Poe enlisted in the army. He was discharged in 1829 so that he could enter West Point Military Academy. His first volume of poetry, *Tamerlane and Other Poems,* had been published in 1827. Two years later, *Al Aaraaf, Tamerlane, and Minor Poems* was issued. Unable to persuade John Allan to agree to his resignation from West Point so that he could pursue a literary career, Poe deliberately neglected his duties and was dismissed in 1831.

Poe married his cousin, Virginia Clemm, in 1836. He worked as an editor and critic for the *Southern Literary Messenger* in Richmond and was able to increase the magazine's circulation from 500 to 3,500. He later worked for magazines in Philadelphia and New York City.

Poe's contribution to the development of the modern short story was significant. His tales are filled with strange events, but Poe insisted that they were expressions of reality. He believed that a story should work toward a single effect. Among his best-known stories are *The Fall of the House of Usher, The Gold Bug,* and *The Masque of the Red Death.* In *The Purloined Letter* and *Murders in the Rue Morgue,* Poe invented the detective story. The character of the brilliant Auguste Dupin, who solved mysteries by his intellectual genius, was a model for later fictional detectives.

Poe's last volume of poetry, *The Raven and Other Poems,* appeared in 1845. He continued to write, but in 1847 his wife's death from tuberculosis was a severe blow. The cause of his own death, on October 7, 1849, is unknown.

Reviewed by ERWIN HESTER
East Carolina University

In "Eldorado," Poe is saying that hope and something to strive for prevent despair.

ELDORADO

Gayly bedight,
A gallant knight,
In sunshine and in shadow,
Had journeyed long,
Singing a song,
In search of Eldorado.

But he grew old,
This knight so bold,
And o'er his heart a shadow
Fell as he found
No spot of ground
That looked like Eldorado.

And, as his strength
Failed him at length,
He met a pilgrim shadow:
"Shadow," said he,
"Where can it be,
This land of Eldorado?"

"Over the Mountains
Of the Moon,
Down the Valley of the Shadow,
Ride, boldly ride,"
The shade replied,
"If you seek for Eldorado!"

HOLOCAUST

The Holocaust is the name given to the mass murder of 6,000,000 Jewish people in Europe during World War II. The word "holocaust" originally meant "widespread destruction by fire," and this, too, occurred in the period from 1933 to 1945. Jewish homes, businesses, and houses of worship were all destroyed in an effort to annihilate (wipe out) the entire Jewish population.

Adolf Hitler

This nearly complete extinction of the European Jews was planned and carried out by Adolf Hitler, who became chancellor of Germany on January 30, 1933. During the twelve years he was in power, Hitler also caused the murder of his political opponents, people who were mentally or physically handicapped, and others labeled "unworthy of life." Hitler believed that all these people stood in the way of his vision of a new German Reich (empire) of only Aryan (purely Nordic) peoples.

When Hitler first attempted to gain control of the government by force, in 1923, he was sent to prison. There he wrote *Mein Kampf* ("My Struggle"), which clearly stated his beliefs about the Jews and his program to destroy them. A worldwide depression gave Hitler a second chance to gain power and to put his program into effect. Many Germans had lost their jobs. They were ready to listen to a powerful speaker like Hitler, whose slogan was "Germany above all else."

In February, 1933, a fire set by the Nazis destroyed the Reichstag, the German parliament building. In the confusion that followed, Hitler convinced German president Paul von Hindenberg to sign a decree canceling all individual and civil liberties. Now Hitler's party, the National Socialist German Workers Party (Nazis), could take away people's money and personal possessions, open mail, listen in on telephone conversations, and enter homes without a warrant.

In 1934, President von Hindenberg died, and Hitler became *führer,* or absolute dictator, of Germany.

The Nuremberg Laws. In 1935, passage of the Nuremberg Laws deprived Jews of German citizenship, calling them subjects instead.

Other laws barred Jews from public office and most professions and prohibited them from associating with non-Jews. Jewish children were not allowed to study in public schools. Non-Jewish shops had signs that read "Jews not admitted." By 1939, Jews were being forced to wear yellow stars of David as identity badges.

Kristallnacht. On November 7, 1938, a young Jewish refugee in Paris shot and killed Ernst vom Rath, the third secretary of the German embassy. This act provided an excuse for what the Nazis called "spontaneous demonstrations"—which they had actually planned weeks in advance. On the night of November 9, storm troopers illegally entered and destroyed Jewish homes, stores, and synagogues. The destruction in broken glass alone was so great that the incident became known as *Kristallnacht* ("the night of broken glass").

World War II

On September 1, 1939, Hitler's army invaded Poland. This marked the beginning of World War II. Germany then easily defeated France, Belgium, Denmark, Yugoslavia, the Netherlands, and Norway. By the middle of 1940, most of Europe was under the domination of Adolf Hitler and Nazi Germany.

The Ghettos. Hitler established ghettos in many Polish cities. These were small sections of a city where Jews were forced to live in very cramped quarters, with little or no food, electricity, water, or heat.

One of the most famous of the ghettos was in the city of Warsaw. Almost 500,000 people were squeezed into an area that usually housed 10,000. Hunger, disease, and cold killed thousands of them. Others were shot down in the streets, so that by 1943 their number was reduced to about 70,000.

The "Final Solution." In 1942 the Nazis began a program for the complete physical destruction of the Jews. Concentration camps, which had earlier served as labor camps, now became death centers.

The true purpose of the camps was hidden. A sign reading *Arbeit Macht Frei* ("Work will make you free") hung on the gate of the worst camp, Auschwitz. Some

During the Holocaust, many Jews were forced to leave their homes and move into ghettos. Many more were sent to concentration camps, which few survived.

camps had factories, where prisoners were forced to work. Those who were unable to work were gassed. The doors of the gas chambers were labeled "showers." But the showers sprayed poison gas, not water.

Resistance. Although the Jews were weak and unarmed, and they received little help from non-Jews, they resisted in many ways. Some could resist only by remaining human in spite of the inhuman behavior around them. In ghettos and camps they shared their bread and helped those who were sicker than they. They celebrated their holidays in secret. They made heroic efforts to survive.

Resistance in the ghettos and camps was almost physically impossible. The prisoners were weak and had no weapons. It was also very hard for them to believe that genocide —the deliberate destruction of an entire people—could take place in the modern world.

Nevertheless, there were rebellions at Auschwitz, Treblinka, and other camps. At Sobibor, where 250,000 Jews were murdered, a rebellion in October, 1943, finally forced the Nazis to close the camp. Some of those who escaped from the camps fought the Nazis from hiding places in the forests.

The most famous uprising was in the Warsaw ghetto. This courageous resistance was accomplished with only a few homemade weapons. It lasted for 28 days—longer than the armed resistance of Poland's entire army in 1939. When the ghetto was finally destroyed, almost no one was left alive in it.

The Survivors

Finally, in 1945, the Allied armies entered Germany and freed the remaining death camps. During the war the Nazis had kept the activities in the camps as secret as possible, so that Allied soldiers were unprepared for the horrors they uncovered when they entered Auschwitz, Treblinka, Dachau, and other camps. After the war, Nazi leaders were tried for their crimes at a series of trials in Nuremberg, Germany. But punishing the criminals did not wipe out the memory of their crimes.

The Jewish people, especially, have not forgotten the Holocaust. Since the end of World War II, Jews have tried to understand what happened to them and to make non-Jews understand, too. A vast number of books have been written on the Holocaust, and the survivors have met at reunions to share their memories. Memorials to the 6,000,000 victims of the Holocaust have been established all over the world, bearing the message to Jews and non-Jews alike— that such a thing must never be allowed to happen again.

BEA STADTLER
Author, *The Holocaust: A History of Courage and Resistance*

HEALTH

Most people have a good idea of what is meant by "health." But it is difficult to define "health" exactly. The simplest and most traditional definition is that health is the absence of disease. Other definitions emphasize the positive aspects of health, describing it, for example, as the proper working of the body and mind. Still other definitions of health include the idea of well-being. For example, the World Health Organization, a branch of the United Nations, has said that health is "physical, mental, and social well-being, and not merely the absence of disease." But no matter how "health" is defined, keeping the body well is the foundation of good health.

▶ KEEPING THE BODY WELL

To a large extent each person must protect his or her own good health. Sometimes poor health cannot be avoided, but there are many things that you can do, or not do, that will guard your health.

Diet

Proper care of the body begins with a good diet. Food provides the body's energy, and the body needs to take in the proper amount of food. Food energy is measured in Calories. If you take in the proper number of Calories, you will stay at a healthy weight. If you take in too many Calories, you will store the excess as fat. If you take in too few Calories, your weight will go down. If you are seriously overweight or underweight, a number of your body systems may begin to work poorly. In many parts of the world, people do not get enough food to eat, and this results in much disease and disability, especially among children.

In addition to Calories, the body must also take in certain nutrients. These include proteins, which are used to build body structures and run the chemical machinery of the body, and carbohydrates and fats, which are most important as sources of energy. Other important nutrients are vitamins and certain minerals. It is best to get vitamins and minerals from nutritious foods. Some health experts believe that taking additional vitamins, perhaps in the form of pills, can be helpful; others disagree. It is also best to eat a variety of foods. Fad diets and weight-loss diets based on only a few foods rarely provide a good balance of nutrients.

Fiber, or roughage, is found in vegetables,

Much of our good health depends on our own good habits. Getting regular exercise and eating properly balanced meals are two important means of establishing good health.

fruits, and whole grains. Fiber is not a nutrient, but it appears to be important in preventing some intestinal diseases and other health problems.

Water is essential to life. You need more on hot days and when you exercise. If you are basically in good health, you should drink fluids whenever you are thirsty. But drinking large quantities of water beyond your normal needs will not make you any healthier.

Avoiding certain substances in your diet may also help protect your health. For example, avoiding sugar helps prevent cavities in your teeth. (On the other hand, it is not true that chocolate and greasy foods cause acne.) For another example, heart disease is associated with cholesterol (a fatlike substance) and saturated fats—both of which are found in meat, milk fat, and eggs. Most young people do not need to completely avoid food containing cholesterol and saturated fats. But some older people might do well to exclude them from their diet.

Exercise

Regular exercise is very important to good health. Exercise helps keep the muscles in good tone, it helps keep bones strong, and it helps the lungs, heart, and blood vessels work well. Exercise has beneficial effects on the way fats and carbohydrates are used by the body. In general the human body seems to work best when it gets regular exercise. However, if you are not used to a lot of exercise, you should be careful when beginning an exercise program. Suddenly increasing the amount of exercise that you get can be harmful. You should increase your amount of exercise only gradually. People who have not exercised much should consult a physician before planning vigorous exercise.

▶ SLEEP

During each 24-hour period your body needs a number of hours of total rest. No one has yet found out all the changes that take place in the body during the hours of sleep. But it is thought that this is the time in which the cells of the body recover from the work of the day and build up supplies of energy for the next period of activity. Boys and girls of elementary- and high-school ages should have from eight to ten hours of sleep each night.

▶ AVOIDING HAZARDS

Avoiding tobacco is one of the most important single things you can do for your health. Cigarette smoking is the main cause

Regular rest and sleep are necessary to the maintenance of health, as is cleanliness, which helps prevent the spread of some infectious diseases.

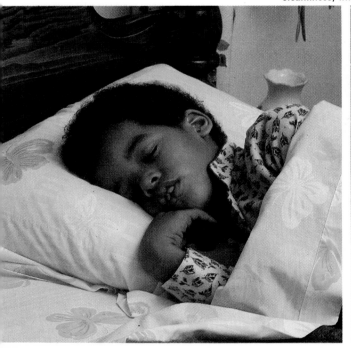

of lung cancer. Tobacco use also contributes to cancer of the mouth, larynx, and esophagus. Smoking is also the main cause of emphysema, a chronic lung disease that causes severe shortness of breath; emphysema can be fatal. Smoking contributes to heart disease and hardening of the arteries. Smoking during pregnancy is associated with miscarriage, premature delivery, and small babies.

Another common substance that can be harmful to your health is alcohol. The brain, the heart, the nerves, and the digestive system—especially the liver—can all be seriously damaged because of heavy drinking. Half of all fatal highway crashes are related to drinking. This is because alcohol can harm a driver's perception, co-ordination, and judgment. Under any circumstances, whether you are driving or not, alcoholic beverages should be used with intelligence and moderation.

Alcohol is only one of many hazardous drugs. The illicit or improper use of narcotics, amphetamines, cocaine, marijuana, LSD, PCP, tranquilizers, and some other drugs can damage your physical and mental health.

Prevention of accidents is another impor-

A child at an immunization clinic receives an injection. Immunization is commonly used to protect people against smallpox, polio, diphtheria, and many other diseases.

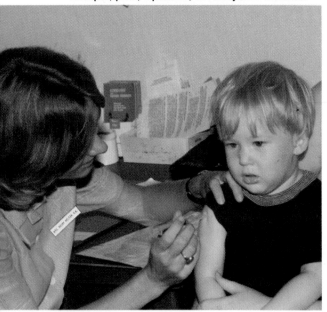

tant part of health. We owe it to ourselves to be sure stairs are safe, floors and bathtubs are not slippery, electrical appliances are used properly, poisonous substances are out of reach of children, and in general that our homes are safe. Driving carefully is even more important. Traffic accidents are one of the most common causes of death in Canada and the United States. Seat belts do save lives; be sure to wear your seat belt whenever you ride in a car.

▶ PREVENTING DISEASES

There are many measures that can prevent certain contagious diseases. One of these measures is **immunization.** Most people in North America have been immunized against diphtheria, whooping cough, and tetanus. Most young people have been immunized with vaccines against measles, mumps, German measles (rubella), and polio. Influenza and pneumonia vaccines are recommended for older people and for people in poor health. Other preventive measures, such as vaccine against typhoid or medication to prevent malaria, are appropriate for people living or traveling in parts of the world where these diseases are common.

There are many infectious diseases for which there are no vaccines. But these diseases can often be avoided through simple precautions. Handwashing and general cleanliness help stop the spread of some of these diseases. For example, people seem to catch colds by getting cold viruses on their hands and then touching their noses or eyes. Other illnesses—such as chicken pox, influenza, and tuberculosis—are spread by the breathing of the sick person. Many diseases such as food poisoning can be prevented if food handlers wash their hands and prepare food properly.

Proper care can help prevent many dental problems. Cavities can be prevented by avoiding sweets, flossing and brushing your teeth regularly, and applying fluoride to your teeth (many toothpastes and some drinking water contain fluoride). Gum disease, the most important cause of tooth loss in adults, may also be prevented by regular flossing and brushing.

Finally, regular checkups and screening

by doctors, dentists, and school health personnel can identify diseases and other problems at an early stage, when they are easier to treat.

▶ MENTAL HEALTH

People who are mentally healthy are generally happy and confident about their lives. They approach life realistically; they can accept some failure as well as success; and they have good relationships with other people. Mentally healthy people understand themselves, and they like themselves.

Mentally healthy people realize that it is sometimes normal to feel angry, depressed, hateful, frightened, jealous, and so on. But they learn to control their actions. Mentally healthy people learn to express their bad feelings in ways that are not harmful. And good feelings, such as love, joy, pleasure, and generosity, are more important in their lives than bad feelings.

Mental health and physical health are closely related. They are both parts of a person's well-being. They can affect one another. For example, many doctors have found that a person often recovers from a sickness more quickly if he or she is confident that recovery will come soon. Furthermore, people who are under great mental stress may be more prone to getting physical ailments.

▶ PUBLIC HEALTH

An individual person can do a lot to protect his or her health. But many health hazards, from air pollution to drunk drivers, are not avoidable by our own actions. Some of these can be controlled by society as a whole. Local, provincial, state, and national governments and international organizations (such as the World Health Organization) all work to protect our health.

Public health efforts have helped check many infectious diseases. These efforts include special handling of sewage in water treatment plants, inspection of food processing plants and restaurants, and enforcement of milk pasteurization laws. Public health clinics also test for contagious diseases. Government agencies keep track of epidemics and make vaccines available for immunization programs.

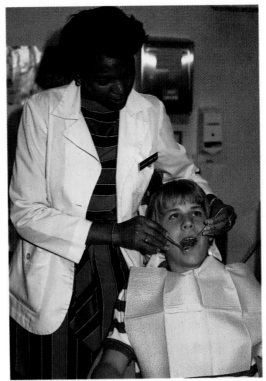

A dentist examines a young man's teeth. Regular checkups by dentists and doctors can detect health problems at an early stage, when they are easier to treat.

In the United States the federal government has been involved in ensuring the purity of food since 1906. Federal law prohibits the use in foods of any additive found to cause cancer in animals. The United States Environmental Protection Agency sets standards for air and water quality and regulates the use and disposal of toxic (poisonous) chemicals. Toxic substances and other hazards that people face at places of work are regulated by the Occupational Safety and Health Administration. Traffic laws are usually controlled by state and local governments, and so is the age at which people may buy alcohol. The Federal Trade Commission requires health warnings on cigarette packages and advertising.

These government agencies, of course, have not eliminated the hazards they are intended to control. But without these agencies, our environment would be much less healthful.

JEAN R. PASCOE, M.D.
Internist

together properly, the result is a "bad bite," called **malocclusion.** Malocclusion may lead to inefficient chewing. The teeth are also more easily injured and more likely to decay.

An **orthodontist** is a dental specialist who straightens teeth, bringing them into line to form an attractive and effective bite. The tools, or "hardware," used by the orthodontist include a variety of wires and elastics, commonly called **braces.** These are attached to the teeth to make the teeth move in a very slow, controlled way.

▶ **WHAT CAUSES MALOCCLUSION?**

The main cause of bad bites seems to be heredity. If you inherit large teeth from one parent and a small jaw from the other, you may have dental problems: Your teeth may be too large to fit comfortably in your jaw and may be crowded and out of line.

If you have missing teeth, the neighboring teeth move into the gap, forcing the whole bite out of line. Malocclusion can also be caused by habits like thumb sucking and tongue thrusting (a forward movement of the tongue during swallowing).

▶ **DIAGNOSING THE PROBLEM**

Usually a family dentist is the first to spot the need for orthodontic treatment. The dentist may find crowded or crooked teeth, a crossbite (when upper teeth fit inside the lower ones instead of fitting over them), or a jaw that protrudes (sticks out) far beyond the other jaw. A protruding upper jaw, producing "buck teeth," is the most common orthodontic problem.

The orthodontist uses a variety of diagnostic tools, including a panoramic X ray that shows all the teeth in the jaws on one film, X rays of the skull, and plaster models of the teeth and jaws. The orthodontist's aim is to bring the teeth into an efficient arrangement and to produce a pleasing appearance of the teeth, jaws, and face.

▶ **ORTHODONTIC TREATMENT**

Generally, orthodontic treatment starts when the patient is 12 or 13 years old. Teenagers may complain about having to wear braces at a time when they are adjusting to so many other changes and are also concerned about their appearance. But the treat-

Orthodontic treatment results in straight teeth and a healthy "bite" for many teenagers. And that is something to smile about!

ORTHODONTICS

A gleaming smile can be a person's most striking feature. But for millions of young people, a smile means a gleam of metal because they are wearing braces to straighten their teeth.

Human teeth are engineered for cutting, tearing, and grinding food. They work best when they are evenly spaced and the upper teeth mesh smoothly with the lower ones. When teeth are crowded or out of line, or when the upper and lower teeth do not fit

ment works best if it is done while the jaws are still growing. Although the majority of braces are worn by teenagers, many adults have orthodontic treatment to correct malocclusions and to improve their appearance.

Most of the work of moving the teeth is done by braces. Braces are brackets attached to the teeth with wires and rubber bands that exert carefully controlled pressure. Sometimes the brackets are fastened to metal bands that clamp around the tooth, but today high-strength adhesives are often used to bond the brackets directly to the tooth.

Teeth are anchored sturdily in the jawbone by their roots, but under the steady pull of the wires and bands, the teeth and roots slide slowly. When the teeth reach their new, straightened positions, the jawbone fills in solidly around the roots, anchoring teeth and roots firmly in place.

While that anchoring is going on, the patient wears a removable **retainer** made of wire and plastic or a **positioner**—a plastic mold into which the teeth fit. If the upper jaw protrudes, the orthodontist may prescribe wearing **headgear** to hold back the upper jaw while the lower jaw grows into line.

The whole process of straightening the teeth takes an average of about two years. In adults, bone does not repair itself as rapidly as in young people, so orthodontic treatment usually takes longer.

People who wear braces need to be especially careful about keeping the teeth clean. Food particles tend to get caught on the brackets and bands and may cause decay if they are not removed promptly. Often people who wear braces have to give up chewing gum and eating some favorite foods, like corn on the cob, that might damage the wires or brackets.

▶ **ORTHODONTICS IN PRACTICE**

Attempts to straighten teeth date back to ancient Greece. But orthodontics did not become a real science until the late 1800's, in the United States. In the 1880's, Dr. J. N. Farrar made a study of how forces actually move teeth and he earned the title "Father of Scientific Orthodontics." Another important pioneer was Edward Angle, who developed a classification of kinds of malocclusion, which orthodontists still use.

Today orthodontists are highly trained specialists. In the United States, for example, orthodontists have five to eight years of training in college and dental school. They have two or three more years of specialized study in orthodontics and may have a year of training in a hospital as well.

Research in orthodontics includes a focus on the use of new materials and techniques to make braces more effective, less noticeable, and easier to wear. Recent developments include the use of removable appliances made of wire and plastic, rather than braces that stay fixed to the teeth for years. Some orthodontists are now using techniques of **lingual orthodontics,** in which braces are fastened to the insides of the teeth. Researchers are also studying the use of tiny electric currents to stimulate the bone and speed up the tooth-moving process.

ALVIN SILVERSTEIN
VIRGINIA SILVERSTEIN
Co-authors, *So You're Getting Braces*

ORTHODONTIC DEVICES

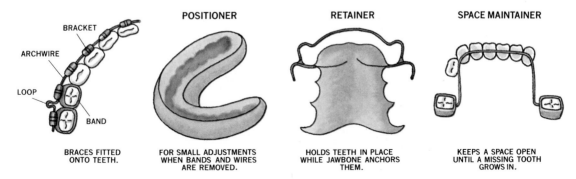

BRACKET
ARCHWIRE
LOOP
BAND
BRACES FITTED ONTO TEETH.

POSITIONER
FOR SMALL ADJUSTMENTS WHEN BANDS AND WIRES ARE REMOVED.

RETAINER
HOLDS TEETH IN PLACE WHILE JAWBONE ANCHORS THEM.

SPACE MAINTAINER
KEEPS A SPACE OPEN UNTIL A MISSING TOOTH GROWS IN.

Shoppers may buy fresh fruits and vegetables already sorted and packaged in a supermarket (*left*) or directly from the grower at an outdoor market (*right*).

FOOD SHOPPING

Choosing the right foods is among the most important decisions consumers face. About one fourth of the average American family's income is spent on food. But deciding what to buy for dinner is becoming increasingly complicated.

A century ago most people shopped at their local general store. It carried a limited selection of necessities, such as flour, sugar, and rice. The average supermarket today carries more than 13,000 different items. There are dozens of brands of ice cream, butter, and breakfast cereal, for example. How is a shopper to sort it all out and get the best value?

Less than half a century ago, many people shopped for food at specialty stores—at a butcher's for meat, a baker's for bread, and so on. Today we can buy nearly everything we need at "one stop" supermarkets, which carry a wide variety of food products and household goods. Small neighborhood stores still exist, mainly in large cities. Items may cost more in a smaller store, but these stores sometimes offer their customers more personal service and greater convenience.

The average shopper has changed, too. Not long ago, women did almost all the family food shopping. Today men do nearly 30 percent of the shopping in the United States. This has caused great changes in how foods and household products are advertised. No longer is there a "typical housewife."

▶ WISE SHOPPING

Whether you shop in a large supermarket or a small country store, it is important to plan ahead carefully to get the most for your money. Make a detailed list of necessities, and do not go shopping when you are hungry. Supermarkets are designed to appeal to "impulse shoppers." That is why candies, soda, and other snack foods are often displayed invitingly at the ends of aisles and near the checkout counter.

So-called "convenience foods," such as frozen dinners and premixed salad dressings, are aimed at busy shoppers who do not want to take the time to prepare something from scratch. These foods are much more expensive than foods you prepare yourself. For example, a bottle of a brand-name salad dressing may cost twice as much as a dressing you can make yourself with ordinary wine vinegar, herbs, and vegetable oil. Pancake mix is nothing more than a blend of flour, baking powder, and salt that you can mix yourself at much less expense.

You can also save money by watching supermarket advertisements in newspapers. These list sales and offer coupons for certain products. If one of your favorite meats is on sale, for example, you can save money by buying a large quantity of it and freezing some for later use. Food companies often offer coupons for discounts on new products in order to get customers to try them.

Two new developments in the grocery industry are generic foods and bulk foods. Generic foods are sold in plain boxes without brand names and fancy color designs. A box of breakfast cereal may say simply "wheat flakes." These products are usually less expensive than brand-name products, and in some cases the quality is the same. But it is best if you compare for yourself.

A new sales technique that has become popular is called "bulk food sales." Certain foods, such as rice, flour, and cereals, are sold in open barrels. Shoppers scoop out as much as they want and pay according to weight. Bulk foods may be a bargain because you are not paying for the packaging, which sometimes costs as much as the food it holds. But it is wise to make a quality comparison for yourself. Also, make sure the food in the barrels is clean and fresh.

Reading the Label

Whether food is sold in barrels, generic cans, or brand-name packages, the U.S. Government requires that all food packages contain a list of ingredients in order of their predominance in the product. For example, many canned fruits and boxed cereals have an extremely high sugar content. If you are concerned about eating too much sugar, read the labels carefully and choose the product that shows sugar farthest down in the list of ingredients.

Canned foods often carry a manufacturer's grading on the label, ranging from fancy (best) to standard (lowest). Select the grade that best suits your purposes. Standard does not necessarily mean that the food is not healthful. It may only be made from smaller or less perfectly shaped fruits or vegetables. These may be just right for making a pie or stew, for example, even though they do not look as nice as higher-grade foods.

When selecting canned goods, never buy cans that have swelled ends. The swelled ends may be caused by gas-producing bacteria, which may be harmful. However, a small dent in the can does not affect the quality of its contents.

When buying frozen foods, select only those packages that are solid and not soft. Softness means that the food has thawed. Frozen foods cannot be stored indefinitely. They should be consumed within several months, or they will begin to dry out.

Adding up the Bill

On the supermarket shelf, prices of goods are often listed "3 for $1" or "5 for $1.99." In some states, markets are required to post the unit price—that is, the price for one item in a package. It is helpful to bring a pocket calculator to the store to quickly compare prices. Some markets also list the price per pound, which is the best means of comparison among foods.

Another general rule is that the larger the package, the lower the price per pound. If you use certain foods often, it is more economical to buy large quantities and store them.

Many supermarkets now have computerized checkout systems. The computer reads a series of numbers and lines on the boxes and cans—the "universal price code" (UPC)—and adds up the bill automatically. These systems are fast, but they are not foolproof. Watch the screen carefully to make sure that the price shown is the same price that was listed on the shelf. It is difficult for the consumer to read the codes themselves, because different products have different markings.

▶ MEAT, POULTRY, FISH, AND EGGS

Meat is among the most expensive parts of a meal, so it should be chosen wisely. The four major types of meat are beef, pork, lamb, and veal. The variety meats, which are less expensive, include liver, heart, tongue, and kidney.

THINGS TO LOOK FOR IN BUYING FRUITS AND VEGETABLES

APPLES—Good color usually indicates full flavor. Learn to know the kinds you like best for cooking and eating raw by buying small samples first.

ASPARAGUS—Tight buds; tender, firm stalks. Stalks with very little white are more tender. Use asparagus soon, as it toughens quickly.

BERRIES—Bright color; plump and solid. Avoid stained containers.

BROCCOLI, BRUSSELS SPROUTS, AND CAULIFLOWER—Flower clusters on broccoli and cauliflower should be tight and close together. Broccoli should be dark green, brussels sprouts firm and solid. Smudgy, dirty spots may indicate insects.

CABBAGE AND HEAD LETTUCE—Choose heads heavy for size. Avoid cabbage with wormholes and lettuce that is discolored, faded, or limp.

CELERY—Brittle, crisp stalks; green leaves.

CUCUMBERS—Choose long, slender, firm cucumbers. May be dark or medium green. Yellowed ones are undesirable.

MELONS—Stem scar should be smooth and rather soft. Fruity odor indicates ripeness. Honeydews are ripe when outside has creamy to yellowish color and is smooth and velvety to touch. Unripe honeydews are whitish green. Ripe watermelons have some yellow on one side. When they are white or pale green on one side, they are not ripe.

ONIONS—Hard but not dried out. No sprouts growing. Avoid onions with wet necks.

ORANGES, GRAPEFRUITS, AND LEMONS—Heavy weight for size. Smoother skins usually indicate more juice. Avoid citrus fruits showing withered, sunken, or soft areas.

PEACHES—Firm, smooth, and unspotted skin showing no green color.

PEAS AND LIMA BEANS—Pods should be well-filled but not bulging. Avoid dry, spotted, or flabby pods.

POTATOES—Firm; few eyes and no sprouts.

ROOT VEGETABLES (Carrots, Turnips, Beets, Parsnips, etc.)—Should be smooth and firm. Avoid oversize vegetables, as they may be woody and tough. Bright orange carrots may contain more vitamin A than paler ones.

SPINACH—Crisp, glossy, dark green leaves.

STRING BEANS—Crisp with small seeds. Avoid beans with dry-looking pods.

TOMATOES—Smooth skins. Firm and not overripe.

The U.S. Government grades meat according to quality. The grade appears in purple on most cuts of meat. Although prime meat is the most expensive, it is not the most healthful. Prime meat contains a good deal of fat, which makes it tender but also high in calories and cholesterol. The less fatty meats, such as shoulder and brisket, can be delicious when cooked slowly for a long time to soften the tough meat fibers. Look for meat that has a bright, shiny color.

Poultry is among the best food bargains. It contains little fat (most fat is in the skin). Poultry is sold in parts or whole. You can save money by buying a whole chicken rather than boned chicken breasts, for example, which may cost twice as much. The bones and neck can be used for soup.

Fish has become more expensive as people consume more of this healthful food, but it is still generally cheaper than meat. Fish is available fresh, frozen, and canned. Fresh is preferable. When buying whole fish, look for those with clear eyes, red color under the gills, and no fishy odor. Any fish that has an odor is not fresh.

Eggs are sold by the dozen in packages marked with the grade—AA, A, B, or C— and the size. Freshness is more important than size, and there is no difference between white and brown eggs. Inspect all the eggs in a carton to make sure there are no hairline cracks in the shells. When you crack open a fresh egg, its yolk will be in the center of the surrounding white, pushed up into a high dome shape. In old eggs the white becomes thin and the yolk flattens.

▶ FRUITS AND VEGETABLES

When buying fresh produce, look for products that are in season. They will be fresher and usually less expensive. Choose fruits and vegetables that are firm and crisp, with good coloring and no wilting or decaying. Buy only what you can consume in several days, unless you plan to make a dish and freeze it. (The above chart tells you what to look for when you are buying fruits and vegetables.)

Many fruits that come from other countries out of season have been sprayed with pesticides or waxed to preserve their color. Wash all produce thoroughly before eating it.

BRYAN MILLER
Food reporter, *The New York Times*

Sugaring Off, painted when Grandma Moses was 83 years old, shows people collecting sap from sugar maple trees and boiling it down to make maple syrup and maple candy.

MOSES, GRANDMA (1860–1961)

The artist Grandma Moses became famous for her simple, bright, cheerful paintings of American farm life. Her full name was Anna Mary Robertson Moses. But she was known to everyone as Grandma Moses because she did not begin to paint seriously until she was in her seventies.

Anna Mary Robertson was born on September 7, 1860, on a farm in Greenwich, New York. She was one of ten children. Life on the farm was hard, and Anna had little schooling. Her days were filled with farm chores—feeding the animals, gathering eggs, making soap, and dipping candles. But she often found time to make pictures. Because she had no proper paints, she used house paint, scraps of colored paper, the juice of wild berries, and even laundry bluing for her colors.

Soon, however, she became too busy to draw or paint. At the age of 12, she went to work as a servant for a family nearby. She worked for other people for many years. Then, when she was 27, she married Thomas Moses, a farmer. And they began raising a family of their own. They moved to a farm near Staunton, Vermont, and later to another at Eagle Bridge, New York. Thomas Moses died there in 1927.

As she grew older, Anna Moses could no longer do heavy farm work. She took up needlework, but her hands became too stiff to continue. Then, in her seventies, she began to paint in oils. Her pictures showed things she remembered from her childhood—farm scenes, small villages, picnics, ice-skating, bringing home the Christmas tree. The forms were simple, and the colors cheerful.

Grandma Moses had a remarkable memory for detail, and her pictures made a record of a way of life that was passing away. People everywhere loved these happy scenes of life in days gone by. Soon her paintings were shown in art galleries, and she became the "grand old lady of American art." She continued to paint almost until her death, on December 13, 1961, at the age of 101.

Reviewed by JANE KALLIR
Author, *Grandma Moses: The Artist Behind the Myth*

CHILD ABUSE

Child abuse is the mistreatment of infants, children, and adolescents by their parents or other caretakers. Countless numbers of children are abused around the world every day. It is estimated that in the United States, one in every 100 children is abused or neglected, and that 2,000 of these children die each year. Children of any age can be victims of child abuse. Those below the age of 3 are at the greatest risk.

Cases of child abuse often go unreported. Sometimes abused children say nothing because they feel that they are the cause of problems in the family and deserve to be punished. Other children feel that they should suffer in silence, to get their parents' love. But child abuse is not the fault of the child, nor does the child deserve punishment. Recently enormous interest in preventing child abuse has developed, and more cases are being reported.

▶ TYPES AND CAUSES OF CHILD ABUSE

Child abuse can be mild or severe. It may consist of any of the following types of abuse or a combination of several types.

Physical abuse is intentional injury. The child may have bruises, burns, broken bones, or injuries to the head. The term "battered child" describes a child with many such injuries in different parts of the body.

Sexual abuse is the sexual molestation of a child by an older person. There is increasing awareness of this problem. In most cases the molesters are friends, neighbors, or relatives of the child.

Nutritional deprivation occurs when food or drink is not given to children, so that they do not grow and thrive properly.

Emotional deprivation occurs when a child is constantly rejected and "picked on." The child feels threatened and does not get the love and understanding that she or he deserves to get.

Parental neglect refers to situations in which parents do not give their children the right food, clothing, shelter, medical care, and protection from accidents.

Adults who abuse children come from all parts of society—from different ethnic, geographic, religious, educational, and economic groups. It is hard to understand why these adults use violence against children or why they fail to love and protect them.

Many of these adults were abused as children themselves. They are immature, unstable, lonely, and feel unloved. They cannot control their violent outbursts, and they repeat what was done to them in the past. They may want to give the love that they did not get as children but they are unable to do so.

Adults who abuse children often treat one child as a favorite and think of another as "bad." Eventually the child thought of as bad does something wrong out of frustration. The child is hoping for love instead of punishment. But the parents use this to convince themselves that they were right all along.

Certain situations increase the risk of child abuse. These situations are unemployed parents, financial difficulty, a poor relationship between the parents, parents who drink too much alcohol or who use drugs, and single parents who are overwhelmed by their responsibilities. These problems cause stress and tension, which is sometimes expressed in neglect or violence toward the children.

▶ TREATMENT

Every state in the United States has laws that require doctors, nurses, and social workers to report suspected cases of child abuse. Other people may report child abuse, too. If they wish, they may do so without giving their names. If children are victims of child abuse or witness another child being abused, they should tell an adult they can trust—a family member, a teacher, a school guidance counselor, or a neighbor.

Children's protective services and family courts are available to help abused children and their families. In cases of severe abuse, a child may be temporarily removed from the home for safety and psychological help.

Parents who abuse children need help, too. They can get it through individual and group therapy, which can give support and teach them to be better parents. There are also self-help groups for these parents, such as Parents Anonymous.

SUBHASH C. INAMDAR, M.D.
New York University School of Medicine

SARLA INAMDAR, M.D.
New York Medical College

INTERNATIONAL STATISTICAL SUPPLEMENT

Independent Nations of the World

The United States

Senate

House of Representatives

Cabinet

Supreme Court

State Governors

Canada and Its Provinces and Territories

INDEPENDENT NATIONS OF THE WORLD

NATION	CAPITAL	AREA (in sq mi)	POPULATION (estimate)	GOVERNMENT
Afghanistan	Kabul	250,000	17,200,000	Babrak Karmal—president
Albania	Tirana	11,100	2,900,000	Enver Hoxha—communist party secretary Adil Carcani—premier
Algeria	Algiers	919,593	20,500,000	Chadli Benjedid—president
Angola	Luanda	481,351	8,500,000	José Eduardo dos Santos—president
Antigua and Barbuda	St. John's	171	78,000	Vere Bird—prime minister
Argentina	Buenos Aires	1,068,297	30,000,000	Raúl Alfonsín—president
Australia	Canberra	2,967,895	15,400,000	Robert Hawke—prime minister
Austria	Vienna	32,374	7,600,000	Rudolf Kirchschläger—president Fred Sinowatz—chancellor
Bahamas	Nassau	5,380	220,000	Lynden O. Pindling—prime minister
Bahrain	Manama	240	400,000	Isa ibn Sulman al-Khalifa—head of government
Bangladesh	Dhaka	55,598	95,000,000	Hussain Mohammed Ershad—president
Barbados	Bridgetown	168	250,000	J. M. G. Adams—prime minister
Belgium	Brussels	11,781	9,900,000	Baudouin I—king Wilfried Martens—premier
Belize	Belmopan	8,867	160,000	Manuel Esquivel—prime minister
Benin (Dahomey)	Porto-Novo	43,483	3,800,000	Mathieu Kerekou—president
Bhutan	Thimbu	18,147	1,400,000	Jigme Singye Wangchuk—king
Bolivia	La Paz Sucre	424,163	6,100,000	Hernán Siles Zuazo—president
Botswana	Gaborone	231,804	1,000,000	Quett Masire—president
Brazil	Brasília	3,286,478	130,000,000	João Figueiredo—president
Brunei Darussalam	Bandar Seri Begawan	2,226	200,000	Sultan Muda Hassanal Bolkiah—head of state
Bulgaria	Sofia	42,823	9,100,000	Todor Zhivkov—communist party secretary Grisha Filipov—premier
Burkina Faso (Upper Volta)	Ouagadougou	105,869	6,400,000	Thomas Sankara—head of government
Burma	Rangoon	261,218	35,500,000	U San Yu—president U Maung Maung Kha—prime minister
Burundi	Bujumbura	10,747	4,500,000	Jean-Baptiste Bagaza—president
Cambodia (Kampuchea)	Pnompenh	69,898	7,000,000	Heng Samrin—communist party secretary
Cameroon	Yaoundé	183,569	9,400,000	Paul Biya—president
Canada	Ottawa	3,851,809	25,000,000	Martin Brian Mulroney—prime minister
Cape Verde	Praia	1,557	340,000	Aristides Pereira—president

NATION	CAPITAL	AREA (in sq mi)	POPULATION (estimate)	GOVERNMENT
Central African Republic	Bangui	240,535	2,500,000	André Kolingba—head of state
Chad	N'Djemena	495,754	4,800,000	Hissen Habré—president
Chile	Santiago	292,257	11,800,000	Augusto Pinochet Ugarte—president
China	Peking	3,705,390	1,040,000,000	Deng Xiaoping—paramount leader Hu Yaobang—communist party secretary Zhao Ziyang—premier
Colombia	Bogotá	439,736	28,000,000	Belisario Betancur Cuartas—president
Comoros	Moroni	838	420,000	Ahmed Abdallah—president
Congo	Brazzaville	132,047	1,700,000	Denis Sassou-Nguessou—president
Costa Rica	San José	19,575	2,400,000	Luis Alberto Monge—president
Cuba	Havana	44,218	10,000,000	Fidel Castro—president
Cyprus	Nicosia	3,572	660,000	Spyros Kyprianou—president
Czechoslovakia	Prague	49,370	15,500,000	Gustáv Husák—communist party secretary and president Lubomir Štrougal—premier
Denmark	Copenhagen	16,629	5,100,000	Margrethe II—queen Poul Schlüter—premier
Djibouti	Djibouti	8,494	330,000	Hassan Gouled Aptidon—president
Dominica	Roseau	290	85,000	Mary Eugenia Charles—prime minister
Dominican Republic	Santo Domingo	18,816	6,000,000	Salvador Jorge Blanco—president
Ecuador	Quito	109,483	8,500,000	León Febres Cordero Rivadeneira—president
Egypt	Cairo	386,660	45,200,000	Muhammad Hosni Mubarak—president Kamal Hasan Ali—premier
El Salvador	San Salvador	8,124	5,200,000	José Napoleón Duarte—president
Equatorial Guinea	Malabo	10,831	380,000	Obiang Nguema Mbasogo—president
Ethiopia	Addis Ababa	471,777	34,000,000	Mengistu Haile Mariam—head of state
Fiji	Suva	7,055	670,000	Ratu Sir Kamisese Mara—prime minister
Finland	Helsinki	130,120	4,900,000	Mauno Koivisto—president Kalevi Sorsa—premier
France	Paris	211,207	54,700,000	François Mitterrand—president Laurent Fabius—premier
Gabon	Libreville	103,346	1,100,000	Omar Bongo—president
Gambia	Banjul	4,361	700,000	Sir Dauda K. Jawara—president
Germany (East)	East Berlin	41,768	16,900,000	Erich Honecker—communist party secretary Willi Stoph—premier
Germany (West)	Bonn	95,976	61,700,000	Richard von Weizsäcker—president Helmut Kohl—chancellor
Ghana	Accra	92,099	12,700,000	Jerry Rawlings—head of state
Greece	Athens	50,944	9,800,000	Constantine Caramanlis—president Andreas Papandreou—premier
Grenada	St. George's	133	110,000	Herbert A. Blaize—prime minister

NATION	CAPITAL	AREA (in sq mi)	POPULATION (estimate)	GOVERNMENT
Guatemala	Guatemala City	42,042	7,600,000	Oscar Humberto Mejía Victores—president
Guinea	Conakry	94,926	5,300,000	Lansana Conté—president
Guinea-Bissau	Bissau	13,948	900,000	João Bernardo Vieira—head of government
Guyana	Georgetown	83,000	900,000	Forbes Burnham—president
Haiti	Port-au-Prince	10,714	5,200,000	Jean-Claude Duvalier—president
Honduras	Tegucigalpa	43,277	4,100,000	Roberto Suazo Córdova—president
Hungary	Budapest	35,919	10,700,000	János Kádár—communist party secretary György Lazar—premier
Iceland	Reykjavik	39,768	240,000	Vigdis Finnbogadottir—president Steingrimur Hermannsson—prime minister
India	New Delhi	1,269,340	735,000,000	Zail Singh—president Rajiv Gandhi—prime minister
Indonesia	Jakarta	735,358	157,000,000	Suharto—president
Iran	Teheran	636,294	42,000,000	Ruhollah Khomeini—religious leader Hojatolislam Ali Khamenei—president Mir Hussein Moussavi—premier
Iraq	Baghdad	167,925	14,700,000	Saddam Hussein—president
Ireland	Dublin	27,136	3,500,000	Patrick Hillery—president Garret FitzGerald—prime minister
Israel	Jerusalem	8,019	4,100,000	Chaim Herzog—president Shimon Peres—prime minister
Italy	Rome	116,303	57,000,000	Alessandro Pertini—president Bettino Craxi—premier
Ivory Coast	Yamoussoukro	124,503	9,200,000	Félix Houphouët-Boigny—president
Jamaica	Kingston	4,244	2,300,000	Edward P. G. Seaga—prime minister
Japan	Tokyo	143,751	119,500,000	Hirohito—emperor Yasuhiro Nakasone—premier
Jordan	Amman	37,738	3,500,000	Hussein I—king Ahmed Majid Obeidat—premier
Kenya	Nairobi	224,959	19,000,000	Daniel arap Moi—president
Kiribati	Tarawa	264	60,000	Ieremia Tabai—president
Korea (North)	Pyongyang	46,540	19,200,000	Kim Il Sung—president Kang Sang-san—premier
Korea (South)	Seoul	38,025	40,000,000	Chun Doo Hwan—president Chin lee Chong—premier
Kuwait	Kuwait	6,880	1,700,000	Jaber al-Ahmed al-Sabah—head of state
Laos	Vientiane	91,429	4,200,000	Souphanouvong—president Kaysone Phomvihan—premier
Lebanon	Beirut	4,015	3,000,000	Amin Gemayel—president Rashid Karami—premier

NATION	CAPITAL	AREA (in sq mi)	POPULATION (estimate)	GOVERNMENT
Lesotho	Maseru	11,720	1,500,000	Moshoeshoe II—king Leabua Jonathan—prime minister
Liberia	Monrovia	43,000	2,100,000	Samuel K. Doe—president
Libya	Tripoli	679,362	3,400,000	Muammar el-Qaddafi—head of state
Liechtenstein	Vaduz	61	26,000	Francis Joseph II—prince
Luxembourg	Luxembourg	999	370,000	Jean—grand duke Jacques Santer—premier
Madagascar	Antananarivo	226,657	9,400,000	Didier Ratsiraka—president
Malawi	Lilongwe	45,747	6,500,000	H. Kamuzu Banda—president
Malaysia	Kuala Lumpur	127,317	14,800,000	Sultan Mahmood Iskandar—king Mahathir Mohammad—prime minister
Maldives	Male	115	170,000	Maumoon Abdul Gayoom—president
Mali	Bamako	478,765	7,600,000	Moussa Traoré—president
Malta	Valletta	122	380,000	Agatha Barbara—president Dom Mintoff—prime minister
Mauritania	Nouakchott	397,954	1,800,000	Maouya Ould Sidi Ahmed Taya—president
Mauritius	Port Louis	790	1,000,000	Aneerood Jugnauth—prime minister
Mexico	Mexico City	761,602	75,000,000	Miguel de la Madrid Hurtado—president
Monaco	Monaco-Ville	0.6	27,000	Rainier III—prince
Mongolia	Ulan Bator	604,248	1,800,000	Dzhambiin Batmunkh—communist party secretary
Morocco	Rabat	172,413	21,000,000	Hassan II—king Mohammad Karim Lamrani—premier
Mozambique	Maputo	309,494	13,300,000	Samora Machel—president
Nauru	Yaren District	8	8,000	Hammer DeRoburt—president
Nepal	Katmandu	54,362	15,800,000	Birendra Bir Bikram Shah Deva—king Lokendra Bahadur Chand—prime minister
Netherlands	Amsterdam	15,770	14,400,000	Beatrix—queen Ruud Lubbers—premier
New Zealand	Wellington	103,736	3,300,000	David Lange—prime minister
Nicaragua	Managua	50,193	3,100,000	Daniel Ortega Saavedra—president
Niger	Niamey	489,190	5,800,000	Seyni Kountche—head of government
Nigeria	Lagos	356,667	89,000,000	Mohammed Buhari—head of government
Norway	Oslo	125,181	4,100,000	Olav V—king Kaare Willoch—premier
Oman	Muscat	82,030	1,100,000	Qabus ibn Said—sultan
Pakistan	Islamabad	310,404	90,000,000	Mohammed Zia ul-Haq—president
Panama	Panama City	29,761	2,100,000	Nicolás Ardito Barletta Vallarina—president

NATION	CAPITAL	AREA (in sq mi)	POPULATION (estimate)	GOVERNMENT
Papua New Guinea	Port Moresby	178,260	3,200,000	Michael Somare—prime minister
Paraguay	Asunción	157,047	3,500,000	Alfredo Stroessner—president
Peru	Lima	496,222	18,800,000	Fernando Belaúnde Terry—president
Philippines	Manila	115,830	52,000,000	Ferdinand E. Marcos—president Cesar Virata—premier
Poland	Warsaw	120,725	36,800,000	Wojciech Jaruzelski—communist party secretary and premier
Portugal	Lisbon	35,553	10,100,000	António Ramalho Eanes—president Mário Soares—premier
Qatar	Doha	4,247	280,000	Khalifa ibn Hamad al-Thani—head of government
Rumania	Bucharest	91,700	22,600,000	Nicolae Ceauşescu—communist party secretary Constantin Dascalescu—premier
Rwanda	Kigali	10,169	5,700,000	Juvénal Habyarimana—president
St. Christopher and Nevis	Basseterre	105	45,000	Kennedy Simmonds—prime minister
St. Lucia	Castries	238	130,000	John Compton—prime minister
St. Vincent and the Grenadines	Kingstown	150	125,000	James Mitchell—prime minister
São Tomé and Príncipe	São Tomé	372	92,000	Manuel Pinto da Costa—president
Saudi Arabia	Riyadh	830,000	10,500,000	Fahd ibn Abdul-Aziz—king
Senegal	Dakar	75,750	6,400,000	Abdou Diouf—president
Seychelles	Victoria	107	65,000	France Albert René—president
Sierra Leone	Freetown	27,700	3,700,000	Siaka P. Stevens—president
Singapore	Singapore	224	2,500,000	C. V. Devan Nair—president Lee Kuan Yew—prime minister
Solomon Islands	Honiara	10,983	260,000	Solomon Mamaloni—prime minister
Somalia	Mogadishu	246,200	5,300,000	Mohammed Siad Barre—president
South Africa	Pretoria Cape Town Bloemfontein	471,444	31,000,000	Pieter W. Botha—president
Spain	Madrid	194,897	38,200,000	Juan Carlos I—king Felipe González Márquez—premier
Sri Lanka (Ceylon)	Colombo	25,332	15,500,000	Junius R. Jayewardene—president Ranasinghe Premadasa—prime minister
Sudan	Khartoum	967,500	20,600,000	Gaafar al-Numeiry—president
Surinam	Paramaribo	63,037	400,000	Dési Bouterse—military leader
Swaziland	Mbabane	6,704	600,000	Ntombi Thwala—queen mother
Sweden	Stockholm	173,731	8,300,000	Carl XVI Gustaf—king Olof Palme—premier

NATION	CAPITAL	AREA (in sq mi)	POPULATION (estimate)	GOVERNMENT
Switzerland	Bern	15,941	6,500,000	Kurt Furgler—president
Syria	Damascus	71,498	9,700,000	Hafez al-Assad—president Abdel Raouf al-Kassem—premier
Taiwan	Taipei	13,885	18,800,000	Chiang Ching-kuo—president Yu Kuo-hua—premier
Tanzania	Dar es Salaam	364,898	20,400,000	Julius K. Nyerere—president
Thailand	Bangkok	198,457	49,500,000	Bhumibol Adulyadej—king Prem Tinsulanonda—premier
Togo	Lomé	21,622	2,800,000	Gnassingbe Eyadema—president
Tonga	Nuku'alofa	270	100,000	Taufa'ahau Tupou IV—king Prince Tu'ipelehake—prime minister
Trinidad & Tobago	Port of Spain	1,980	1,200,000	Sir Ellis Clarke—president George Chambers—prime minister
Tunisia	Tunis	63,170	7,000,000	Habib Bourguiba—president
Turkey	Ankara	301,381	47,300,000	Kenan Evren—president Turgut Ozal—prime minister
Tuvalu	Funafuti	10	8,000	Tomasi Puapua—prime minister
Uganda	Kampala	91,134	14,700,000	Milton Obote—president
U.S.S.R.	Moscow	8,649,512	272,500,000	Konstantin U. Chernenko—communist party secretary and president Nikolai A. Tikhonov—premier
United Arab Emirates	Abu Dhabi	32,278	1,200,000	Zayd ibn Sultan al-Nuhayan—president
United Kingdom	London	94,226	55,700,000	Elizabeth II—queen Margaret Thatcher—prime minister
United States	Washington, D.C.	3,618,467	236,500,000	Ronald W. Reagan—president George H. Bush—vice-president
Uruguay	Montevideo	68,037	3,000,000	Julio María Sanguinetti—president-elect
Vanuatu	Vila	5,700	130,000	Walter Lini—prime minister
Venezuela	Caracas	352,143	16,400,000	Jaime Lusinchi—president-elect
Vietnam	Hanoi	128,402	57,200,000	Le Duan—communist party secretary Pham Van Dong—premier
Western Samoa	Apia	1,097	160,000	Malietoa Tanumafili II—head of state
Yemen (Aden)	Madinat al-Shaab	128,559	2,200,000	Ali Nasser Mohammed—president
Yemen (Sana)	Sana	75,290	6,200,000	Ali Abdullah Saleh al-Hasani—president
Yugoslavia	Belgrade	98,766	23,000,000	Veselin Djuranović—president Milka Planinc—premier
Zaïre	Kinshasa	905,565	31,000,000	Mobutu Sese Seko—president
Zambia	Lusaka	290,585	6,300,000	Kenneth D. Kaunda—president
Zimbabwe	Harare	150,333	7,800,000	Canaan Banana—president Robert Mugabe—prime minister

THE CONGRESS OF THE UNITED STATES

UNITED STATES SENATE

(53 Republicans, 47 Democrats)

Alabama
Howell Heflin (D)**
Jeremiah Denton (R)

Alaska
Ted Stevens (R)**
Frank H. Murkowski (R)

Arizona
Barry Goldwater (R)
Dennis DeConcini (D)

Arkansas
Dale Bumpers (D)
David Pryor (D)**

California
Alan Cranston (D)
Pete Wilson (R)

Colorado
Gary Hart (D)
William L. Armstrong (R)**

Connecticut
Lowell P. Weicker, Jr. (R)
Christopher J. Dodd (D)

Delaware
William V. Roth, Jr. (R)
Joseph R. Biden, Jr. (D)**

Florida
Lawton Chiles (D)
Paula Hawkins (R)

Georgia
Sam Nunn (D)**
Mack Mattingly (R)

Hawaii
Daniel K. Inouye (D)
Spark M. Matsunaga (D)

Idaho
James A. McClure (R)**
Steven D. Symms (R)

Illinois
Alan J. Dixon (D)
Paul Simon (D)*

Indiana
Richard G. Lugar (R)
Dan Quayle (R)

Iowa
Charles E. Grassley (R)
Tom Harkin (D)*

Kansas
Robert Dole (R)
Nancy Landon Kassebaum (R)**

Kentucky
Wendell H. Ford (D)
Mitch McConnell (R)*

Louisiana
Russell B. Long (D)
J. Bennett Johnston (D)**

Maine
William S. Cohen (R)**
George J. Mitchell (D)

Maryland
Charles M. Mathias, Jr. (R)
Paul S. Sarbanes (D)

Massachusetts
Edward M. Kennedy (D)
John F. Kerry (D)*

Michigan
Donald W. Riegle, Jr. (D)
Carl Levin (D)**

Minnesota
David F. Durenberger (R)
Rudy Boschwitz (R)**

Mississippi
John C. Stennis (D)
Thad Cochran (R)**

Missouri
Thomas F. Eagleton (D)
John C. Danforth (R)

Montana
John Melcher (D)
Max Baucus (D)**

Nebraska
Edward Zorinsky (D)
J. James Exon (D)**

Nevada
Paul Laxalt (R)
Chic Hecht (R)

New Hampshire
Gordon J. Humphrey (R)**
Warren Rudman (R)

New Jersey
Bill Bradley (D)**
Frank R. Lautenberg (D)

New Mexico
Pete V. Domenici (R)**
Jeff Bingaman (D)

New York
Daniel P. Moynihan (D)
Alfonse M. D'Amato (R)

North Carolina
Jesse Helms (R)**
John P. East (R)

North Dakota
Quentin N. Burdick (D)
Mark Andrews (R)

Ohio
John Glenn (D)
Howard M. Metzenbaum (D)

Oklahoma
David L. Boren (D)**
Don Nickles (R)

Oregon
Mark O. Hatfield (R)**
Bob Packwood (R)

Pennsylvania
John Heinz (R)
Arlen Specter (R)

Rhode Island
Claiborne Pell (D)**
John H. Chafee (R)

South Carolina
Strom Thurmond (R)**
Ernest F. Hollings (D)

South Dakota
Larry Pressler (R)**
James Abdnor (R)

Tennessee
Jim Sasser (D)
Albert Gore, Jr. (D)*

Texas
Lloyd Bentsen (D)
Phil Gramm (R)*

Utah
Jake Garn (R)
Orrin G. Hatch (R)

Vermont
Robert T. Stafford (R)
Patrick J. Leahy (D)

Virginia
John W. Warner (R)**
Paul S. Trible, Jr. (R)

Washington
Slade Gorton (R)
Daniel J. Evans (R)

West Virginia
Robert C. Byrd (D)
John D. Rockefeller IV (D)*

Wisconsin
William Proxmire (D)
Bob Kasten (R)

Wyoming
Malcolm Wallop (R)
Alan K. Simpson (R)**

(R) Republican
(D) Democrat

*elected in 1984
**re-elected in 1984

UNITED STATES HOUSE OF REPRESENTATIVES

(252 Democrats, 182 Republicans, 1 Vacancy)

Alabama
1. H. L. Callahan (R)*
2. W. L. Dickinson (R)
3. W. Nichols (D)
4. T. Bevill (D)
5. R. Flippo (D)
6. B. Erdreich (D)
7. R. Shelby (D)

Alaska
D. Young (R)

Arizona
1. J. McCain (R)
2. M. K. Udall (D)
3. B. Stump (R)
4. E. Rudd (R)
5. J. Kolbe (R)*

Arkansas
1. W. V. Alexander, Jr. (D)
2. T. Robinson (D)*
3. J. P. Hammerschmidt (R)
4. B. Anthony, Jr. (D)

California
1. D. H. Bosco (D)
2. G. Chappie (R)
3. R. Matsui (D)
4. V. Fazio (D)
5. S. Burton (D)
6. B. Boxer (D)
7. G. Miller (D)
8. R. V. Dellums (D)
9. F. H. Stark, Jr. (D)
10. D. Edwards (D)
11. T. Lantos (D)
12. E. Zschau (R)
13. N. Y. Mineta (D)
14. N. Shumway (R)
15. T. Coelho (D)
16. L. E. Panetta (D)
17. C. Pashayan, Jr. (R)
18. R. Lehman (D)
19. R. J. Lagomarsino (R)
20. W. M. Thomas (R)
21. B. Fiedler (R)
22. C. J. Moorhead (R)
23. A. C. Beilenson (D)
24. H. A. Waxman (D)
25. E. R. Roybal (D)
26. H. L. Berman (D)
27. M. Levine (D)
28. J. Dixon (D)
29. A. F. Hawkins (D)
30. M. G. Martinez (D)
31. M. Dymally (D)
32. G. M. Anderson (D)
33. D. Dreier (R)
34. E. E. Torres (D)
35. J. Lewis (R)
36. G. E. Brown, Jr. (D)
37. A. McCandless (R)
38. R. K. Dornan (R)*
39. W. Dannemeyer (R)
40. R. E. Badham (R)
41. B. Lowery (R)
42. D. Lungren (R)
43. R. C. Packard (R)
44. J. Bates (D)
45. D. Hunter (R)

Colorado
1. P. Schroeder (D)
2. T. E. Wirth (D)
3. M. L. Strang (R)*
4. H. Brown (R)
5. K. Kramer (R)
6. D. L. Schaefer (R)

Connecticut
1. B. B. Kennelly (D)
2. S. Gejdenson (D)
3. B. A. Morrison (D)
4. S. B. McKinney (R)
5. J. G. Rowland (R)*
6. N. L. Johnson (R)

Delaware
T. R. Carper (D)

Florida
1. E. Hutto (D)
2. D. Fuqua (D)
3. C. E. Bennett (D)
4. W. V. Chappell, Jr. (D)
5. B. McCollum (R)
6. B. MacKay (D)
7. S. M. Gibbons (D)
8. C. W. B. Young (R)
9. M. Bilirakis (R)
10. A. Ireland (R)
11. B. Nelson (D)
12. T. Lewis (R)
13. C. Mack (R)
14. D. Mica (D)
15. E. C. Shaw, Jr. (R)
16. L. Smith (D)
17. W. Lehman (D)
18. C. Pepper (D)
19. D. B. Fascell (D)

Georgia
1. L. Thomas (D)
2. C. Hatcher (D)
3. R. Ray (D)
4. P. Swindall (R)*
5. W. Fowler, Jr. (D)
6. N. Gingrich (R)
7. G. Darden (D)
8. J. R. Rowland (D)
9. E. L. Jenkins (D)
10. D. D. Barnard, Jr. (D)

Hawaii
1. C. Heftel (D)
2. D. K. Akaka (D)

Idaho
1. L. Craig (R)
2. R. Stallings (D)*

Illinois
1. C. A. Hayes (D)
2. G. Savage (D)
3. M. A. Russo (D)
4. G. M. O'Brien (R)
5. W. O. Lipinski (D)
6. H. J. Hyde (R)
7. C. Collins (D)
8. D. Rostenkowski (D)
9. S. R. Yates (D)
10. J. Porter (R)
11. F. Annunzio (D)
12. P. M. Crane (R)
13. H. W. Fawell (R)*
14. J. E. Grotberg (R)*
15. E. R. Madigan (R)
16. L. Martin (R)
17. L. Evans (D)
18. R. H. Michel (R)
19. T. L. Bruce (D)*
20. R. J. Durbin (D)
21. M. Price (D)
22. K. J. Gray (D)*

Indiana
1. P. J. Visclosky (D)*
2. P. R. Sharp (D)
3. J. Hiler (R)
4. D. Coats (R)
5. E. H. Hillis (R)
6. D. Burton (R)
7. J. T. Myers (R)
8. vacancy
9. L. H. Hamilton (D)
10. A. Jacobs, Jr. (D)

Iowa
1. J. A. S. Leach (R)
2. T. Tauke (R)
3. C. Evans (R)
4. N. Smith (D)
5. J. R. Lightfoot (R)*
6. B. W. Bedell (D)

Kansas
1. P. Roberts (R)
2. J. Slattery (D)
3. J. Meyers (R)*
4. D. Glickman (D)
5. R. Whittaker (R)

Kentucky
1. C. Hubbard, Jr. (D)
2. W. H. Natcher (D)
3. R. L. Mazzoli (D)
4. G. Snyder (R)
5. H. Rogers (R)
6. L. Hopkins (R)
7. C. C. Perkins (D)*

Louisiana
1. R. L. Livingston, Jr. (R)
2. L. Boggs (D)
3. W. J. Tauzin (D)
4. B. Roemer (D)
5. J. Huckaby (D)
6. W. H. Moore (R)
7. J. B. Breaux (D)
8. G. W. Long (D)

Maine
1. J. R. McKernan, Jr. (R)
2. O. Snowe (R)

Maryland
1. R. Dyson (D)
2. H. Delich Bentley (R)*
3. B. A. Mikulski (D)
4. M. S. Holt (R)
5. S. Hoyer (D)
6. B. Byron (D)
7. P. J. Mitchell (D)
8. M. Barnes (D)

Massachusetts
1. S. O. Conte (R)
2. E. P. Boland (D)
3. J. D. Early (D)
4. B. Frank (D)
5. C. G. Atkins (D)*
6. N. Mavroules (D)
7. E. J. Markey (D)
8. T. P. O'Neill, Jr. (D)
9. J. J. Moakley (D)
10. G. E. Studds (D)
11. B. Donnelly (D)

Michigan
1. J. Conyers, Jr. (D)
2. C. D. Pursell (R)
3. H. Wolpe (D)
4. M. Siljander (R)
5. P. B. Henry (R)*
6. B. Carr (D)
7. D. E. Kildee (D)
8. B. Traxler (D)
9. G. A. Vander Jagt (R)
10. B. Schuette (R)*
11. R. Davis (R)
12. D. E. Bonior (D)
13. G. Crockett, Jr. (D)
14. D. Hertel (D)
15. W. D. Ford (D)
16. J. D. Dingell (D)
17. S. Levin (D)
18. W. S. Broomfield (R)

Minnesota
1. T. J. Penny (D)
2. V. Weber (R)
3. B. Frenzel (R)
4. B. F. Vento (D)
5. M. Sabo (D)
6. G. Sikorski (D)
7. A. Strangeland (R)
8. J. L. Oberstar (D)

Mississippi
1. J. L. Whitten (D)
2. W. Franklin (R)
3. G. V. Montgomery (D)

4. W. Dowdy (D)
5. T. Lott (R)

Missouri
1. W. L. Clay (D)
2. R. A. Young (D)
3. R. A. Gephardt (D)
4. I. Skelton (D)
5. A. Wheat (D)
6. E. T. Coleman (R)
7. G. Taylor (R)
8. B. Emerson (R)
9. H. L. Volkmer (D)

Montana
1. P. Williams (D)
2. R. Marlenee (R)

Nebraska
1. D. Bereuter (R)
2. H. Daub (R)
3. V. Smith (R)

Nevada
1. H. Reid (D)
2. B. Vucanovich (R)

New Hampshire
1. R. C. Smith (R)*
2. J. Gregg (R)

New Jersey
1. J. J. Florio (D)
2. W. J. Hughes (D)
3. J. J. Howard (D)
4. C. Smith (R)
5. M. Roukema (R)
6. B. J. Dwyer (D)
7. M. J. Rinaldo (R)
8. R. A. Roe (D)
9. R. G. Torricelli (D)
10. P. W. Rodino, Jr. (D)
11. D. A. Gallo (R)*
12. J. A. Courter (R)
13. H. J. Saxton (R)*
14. F. Guarini (D)

New Mexico
1. M. Lujan, Jr. (R)
2. J. Skeen (R)
3. B. Richardson (D)

New York
1. W. Carney (R)
2. T. J. Downey (D)
3. R. J. Mrazek (D)
4. N. F. Lent (R)
5. R. McGrath (R)
6. J. P. Addabbo (D)
7. G. Ackerman (D)
8. J. H. Scheuer (D)
9. T. J. Manton (D)*
10. C. E. Schumer (D)
11. E. Towns (D)
12. M. R. Owens (D)
13. S. J. Solarz (D)
14. G. V. Molinari (R)
15. B. Green (R)
16. C. B. Rangel (D)
17. T. Weiss (D)

18. R. Garcia (D)
19. M. Biaggi (D)
20. J. D. DioGuardi (R)*
21. H. Fish, Jr. (R)
22. B. A. Gilman (R)
23. S. S. Stratton (D)
24. G. Solomon (R)
25. S. L. Boehlert (R)
26. D. Martin (R)
27. G. C. Wortley (R)
28. M. F. McHugh (D)
29. F. Horton (R)
30. F. J. Eckert (R)*
31. J. F. Kemp (R)
32. J. J. LaFalce (D)
33. H. J. Nowak (D)
34. S. Lundine (D)

North Carolina
1. W. B. Jones (D)
2. I. T. Valentine, Jr. (D)
3. C. O. Whitley, Sr. (D)
4. W. W. Cobey, Jr. (R)*
5. S. L. Neal (D)
6. H. Coble (R)*
7. C. Rose (D)
8. W. G. Hefner (D)
9. J. A. McMillan (R)*
10. J. T. Broyhill (R)
11. W. M. Hendon (R)*

North Dakota
B. Dorgan (D)

Ohio
1. T. A. Luken (D)
2. W. D. Gradison, Jr. (R)
3. T. Hall (D)
4. M. Oxley (R)
5. D. L. Latta (R)
6. B. McEwen (R)
7. M. DeWine (R)
8. T. N. Kindness (R)
9. M. Kaptur (D)
10. C. E. Miller (R)
11. D. E. Eckart (D)
12. J. R. Kasich (R)
13. D. J. Pease (D)
14. J. F. Seiberling (D)
15. C. P. Wylie (R)
16. R. Regula (R)
17. J. A. Traficant, Jr. (D)*
18. D. Applegate (D)
19. E. F. Feighan (D)
20. M. R. Oakar (D)
21. L. Stokes (D)

Oklahoma
1. J. R. Jones (D)
2. M. Synar (D)
3. W. W. Watkins (D)
4. D. McCurdy (D)
5. M. Edwards (R)
6. G. English (D)

Oregon
1. L. AuCoin (D)
2. R. F. Smith (R)
3. R. Wyden (D)
4. J. Weaver (D)
5. D. Smith (R)

Pennsylvania
1. T. Foglietta (D)
2. W. Gray (D)
3. R. A. Borski, Jr. (D)
4. J. P. Kolter (D)
5. R. T. Schulze (R)
6. G. Yatron (D)
7. R. W. Edgar (D)
8. P. H. Kostmayer (D)
9. B. Shuster (R)
10. J. M. McDade (R)
11. P. E. Kanjorski (D)*
12. J. P. Murtha (D)
13. L. Coughlin (R)
14. W. Coyne (D)
15. D. Ritter (R)
16. R. S. Walker (R)
17. G. W. Gekas (R)
18. D. Walgren (D)
19. W. F. Goodling (R)
20. J. M. Gaydos (D)
21. T. J. Ridge (R)
22. A. J. Murphy (D)
23. W. Clinger, Jr. (R)

Rhode Island
1. F. J. St. Germain (D)
2. C. Schneider (R)

South Carolina
1. T. Hartnett (R)
2. F. D. Spence (R)
3. B. C. Derrick, Jr. (D)
4. C. Campbell, Jr. (R)
5. J. Spratt (D)
6. R. Tallon (D)

South Dakota
T. A. Daschle (D)

Tennessee
1. J. H. Quillen (R)
2. J. J. Duncan (R)
3. M. Lloyd (D)
4. J. Cooper (D)
5. W. H. Boner (D)
6. B. Gordon (D)*
7. D. Sundquist (R)
8. E. Jones (D)
9. H. E. Ford (D)

Texas
1. S. B. Hall, Jr. (D)
2. C. Wilson (D)
3. S. Bartlett (R)
4. R. Hall (D)
5. J. Bryant (D)
6. J. Barton (R)*
7. B. Archer (R)
8. J. Fields (R)
9. J. Brooks (D)
10. J. J. Pickle (D)
11. J. M. Leath (D)
12. J. C. Wright, Jr. (D)
13. B. Boulter (R)*
14. M. Sweeney (R)*
15. E. de la Garza (D)
16. R. Coleman (D)
17. C. Stenholm (D)

18. M. Leland (D)
19. L. Combest (R)*
20. H. B. Gonzalez (D)
21. T. Loeffler (R)
22. T. DeLay (R)*
23. A. G. Bustamente (D)*
24. M. Frost (D)
25. M. Andrews (D)
26. R. Armey (R)*
27. S. P. Ortiz (D)

Utah
1. J. Hansen (R)
2. D. S. Monson (R)*
3. H. C. Neilson (R)

Vermont
J. M. Jeffords (R)

Virginia
1. H. H. Bateman (R)
2. G. W. Whitehurst (R)
3. T. Bliley, Jr. (R)
4. N. Sisisky (D)
5. D. Daniel (D)
6. J. R. Olin (D)
7. D. F. Slaughter (R)*
8. S. Parris (R)
9. F. C. Boucher (D)
10. F. Wolf (R)

Washington
1. J. Miller (R)*
2. A. Swift (D)
3. D. L. Bonker (D)
4. S. Morrison (R)
5. T. S. Foley (D)
6. N. D. Dicks (D)
7. M. Lowry (D)
8. R. Chandler (R)

West Virginia
1. A. B. Mollohan (D)
2. H. O. Staggers, Jr. (D)
3. B. Wise (D)
4. N. J. Rahall (D)

Wisconsin
1. L. Aspin (D)
2. R. W. Kastenmeier (D)
3. S. Gunderson (R)
4. G. D. Kleczka (D)*
5. J. Moody (D)
6. T. E. Petri (R)
7. D. R. Obey (D)
8. T. Roth (R)
9. F. J. Sensenbrenner, Jr. (R)

Wyoming
R. Cheney (R)

*elected in 1984
all others: re-elected in 1984

UNITED STATES SUPREME COURT

Chief Justice: Warren E. Burger (1969)

Associate Justices:
William J. Brennan, Jr. (1956)
Sandra Day O'Connor (1981)
Byron R. White (1962)
Thurgood Marshall (1967)
Harry A. Blackmun (1970)
Lewis F. Powell, Jr. (1971)
William H. Rehnquist (1971)
John Paul Stevens (1975)

UNITED STATES CABINET

Secretary of Agriculture: John R. Block
Attorney General: William French Smith
Secretary of Commerce: Malcolm Baldrige
Secretary of Defense: Caspar W. Weinberger
Secretary of Education: Terrel H. Bell
Secretary of Energy: Donald P. Hodel
Secretary of Health and Human Services:
Margaret M. Heckler
Secretary of Housing and Urban Development:
Samuel R. Pierce, Jr.
Secretary of the Interior: William P. Clark
Secretary of Labor: Raymond J. Donovan
Secretary of State: George P. Shultz
Secretary of Transportation: Elizabeth
Hanford Dole
Secretary of the Treasury: Donald T. Regan

Martha Layne Collins of Kentucky—the only female governor in 1984. (Another woman, Madeleine Kunin, won the Vermont governorship in the 1984 elections and was to begin her term in 1985.)

STATE GOVERNORS

Alabama	George C. Wallace (D)	**Montana**	Ted Schwinden (D)**
Alaska	Bill Sheffield (D)	**Nebraska**	Bob Kerrey (D)
Arizona	Bruce E. Babbitt (D)	**Nevada**	Richard H. Bryan (D)
Arkansas	Bill Clinton (D)**	**New Hampshire**	John H. Sununu (R)**
California	George Deukmejian (R)	**New Jersey**	Thomas H. Kean (R)
Colorado	Richard D. Lamm (D)	**New Mexico**	Toney Anaya (D)
Connecticut	William A. O'Neill (D)	**New York**	Mario M. Cuomo (D)
Delaware	Michael N. Castle (R)*	**North Carolina**	James G. Martin (R)*
Florida	Robert Graham (D)	**North Dakota**	George Sinner (D)*
Georgia	Joe Frank Harris (D)	**Ohio**	Richard F. Celeste (D)
Hawaii	George R. Ariyoshi (D)	**Oklahoma**	George Nigh (D)
Idaho	John V. Evans (D)	**Oregon**	Victor Atiyeh (R)
Illinois	James R. Thompson (R)	**Pennsylvania**	Richard L. Thornburgh (R)
Indiana	Robert D. Orr (R)**	**Rhode Island**	Edward D. DiPriete (R)*
Iowa	Terry Branstad (R)	**South Carolina**	Richard W. Riley (D)
Kansas	John Carlin (D)	**South Dakota**	William J. Janklow (R)
Kentucky	Martha Layne Collins (D)	**Tennessee**	Lamar Alexander (R)
Louisiana	Edwin W. Edward (D)	**Texas**	Mark White (D)
Maine	Joseph E. Brennan (D)	**Utah**	Norman Bangerter (R)*
Maryland	Harry Hughes (D)	**Vermont**	Madeleine Kunin (D)*
Massachusetts	Michael S. Dukakis (D)	**Virginia**	Charles S. Robb (D)
Michigan	James J. Blanchard (D)	**Washington**	Booth Gardner (D)*
Minnesota	Rudy Perpich (D)	**West Virginia**	Arch Moore (R)*
Mississippi	Bill Allain (D)	**Wisconsin**	Anthony S. Earl (D)
Missouri	John Ashcroft (R)*	**Wyoming**	Ed Herschler (D)

*elected in 1984
**re-elected in 1984

CANADA

Capital: Ottawa
Head of State: Queen Elizabeth II
Governor General: Jeanne Sauvé
Prime Minister: Martin Brian Mulroney (Progressive Conservative)
Leader of the Opposition: John Turner (Liberal)
Population: 25,127,900
Area: 3,851,809 sq mi (9,976,185 km²)

PROVINCES AND TERRITORIES

Alberta
Capital: Edmonton
Lieutenant Governor: Frank Lynch-Staunton
Premier: Peter Lougheed (Progressive Conservative)
Leader of the Opposition: Ray Martin (New Democratic Party)
Entered Confederation: Sept. 1, 1905
Population: 2,348,800
Area: 255,285 sq mi (661,188 km²)

British Columbia
Capital: Victoria
Lieutenant Governor: Robert G. Rogers
Premier: William R. Bennett (Social Credit)
Leader of the Opposition: Robert Skelly (New Democratic Party)
Entered Confederation: July 20, 1871
Population: 2,870,800
Area: 366,255 sq mi (948,600 km²)

Manitoba
Capital: Winnipeg
Lieutenant Governor: Pearl McGonigal
Premier: Howard Pawley (New Democratic Party)
Leader of the Opposition: Gary Filmon (Progressive Conservative)
Entered Confederation: July 15, 1870
Population: 1,056,500
Area: 251,000 sq mi (650,090 km²)

New Brunswick
Capital: Fredericton
Lieutenant Governor: George F. G. Stanley
Premier: Richard B. Hatfield (Progressive Conservative)
Leader of the Opposition: Raymond Frenette (Liberal)
Entered Confederation: July 1, 1867
Population: 712,300
Area: 28,354 sq mi (73,436 km²)

Newfoundland
Capital: St. John's
Lieutenant Governor: W. Anthony Paddon
Premier: A. Brian Peckford (Progressive Conservative)
Leader of the Opposition: Leo Barry (Liberal)
Entered Confederation: March 31, 1949
Population: 579,500
Area: 156,185 sq mi (404,517 km²)

Nova Scotia
Capital: Halifax
Lieutenant Governor: John Elvin Shaffner
Premier: John M. Buchanan (Progressive Conservative)
Leader of the Opposition: A. M. (Sandy) Cameron (Liberal)
Entered Confederation: July 1, 1867
Population: 869,900
Area: 21,425 sq mi (55,491 km²)

Ontario
Capital: Toronto
Lieutenant Governor: John Aird
Premier: William G. Davis (Progressive Conservative)
Leader of the Opposition: David Peterson (Liberal)
Entered Confederation: July 1, 1867
Population: 8,937,400
Area: 412,582 sq mi (1,068,582 km²)

Prince Edward Island
Capital: Charlottetown
Lieutenant Governor: J. Aubin Dorion
Premier: James M. Lee (Progressive Conservative)
Leader of the Opposition: Joseph Ghiz (Liberal)
Entered Confederation: July 1, 1873
Population: 125,000
Area: 2,184 sq mi (5,657 km²)

Quebec
Capital: Quebec City
Lieutenant Governor: Giles Lamontagne
Premier: René Lévesque (Parti Québécois)
Leader of the Opposition: Gérard D. Lévesque (Liberal)
Entered Confederation: July 1, 1867
Population: 6,549,000
Area: 594,860 sq mi (1,540,700 km²)

Saskatchewan
Capital: Regina
Lieutenant Governor: F. W. Johnson
Premier: Grant Devine (Progressive Conservative)
Leader of the Opposition: Allan E. Blakeney (New Democratic Party)
Entered Confederation: Sept. 1, 1905
Population: 1,006,200
Area: 251,700 sq mi (651,900 km²)

Northwest Territories
Capital: Yellowknife
Commissioner: John H. Parker
Reconstituted as a territory: September 1, 1905
Population: 49,400
Area: 1,304,896 sq mi (3,379,684 km²)

Yukon Territory
Capital: Whitehorse
Administrator: Douglas Bell
Government Leader: Christopher Pearson
Organized as a territory: June 13, 1898
Population: 21,800
Area: 186,299 sq mi (482,515 km²)

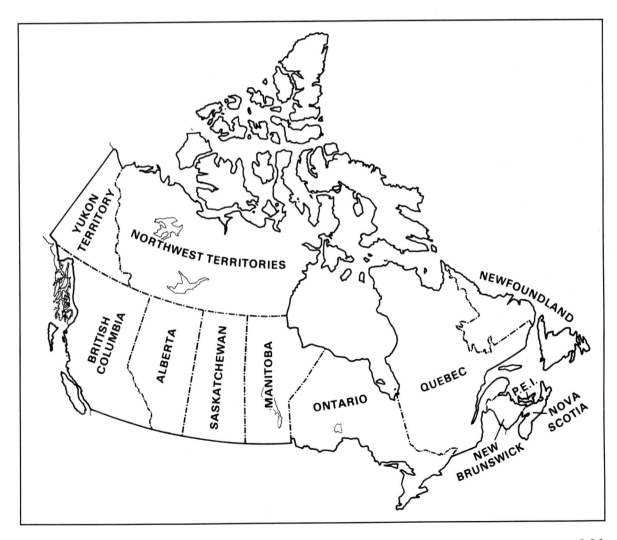

INDEX

C

D

G

Gabon 351
Gadgets, pictures 118–19
Gaines, Rowdy, American athlete 159
Gallup, George H., American developer of public opinion polls 26
Gambia 351
Games 190–93
  Trivial Pursuit, picture 273
Gandhi, Indira, Indian prime minister 33, 56–57
Gandhi, Rajiv, Indian prime minister 33, 56; picture 61
Gardner, Dale A., American astronaut 94
Garneau, Marc, Canadian astronaut 33, 93
Gary, Jim, American sculptor
  dinosaur sculpture 254–55
Gaspé Peninsula, Quebec, Canada 276
Gaynor, Janet, American actress 30
Gemayel, Amin, president of Lebanon 53
  Karami, Rashid, appointment of, as prime minister 21
German Democratic Republic (East Germany) 351
  Olympic Games 153–56
Germany (undivided country before 1945)
  games 192
  giant in folk tale 199
  Holocaust, during World War II 336–37
Germany, Federal Republic of (West Germany) 351
  economic summit meeting, London, England 24
  Olympic Games 156–57, 159, 162
  postage stamp, pictures 132
  Weizsäcker, Richard von, chosen president 23
Gettysburg Address, speech by Abraham Lincoln at Gettysburg, Pennsylvania 209
Ghana 351
  postage stamp, picture 132
Giants 194–99
Gibson, Robert L., American astronaut 92
Giraffe beetle, insect 73
Glenn, John, American astronaut and senator 38
Glorious Flight, The, book by Alice and Martin Provensen, picture 301
Go, game 191
Goat, animal, picture 225
Godes, Mark, American newspaper column writer, picture 228
Golden plover, bird 76
Golden Temple, Amritsar, India, 56; picture 57
Golf, sport 177
Goodman, Robert O., Jr., American Navy pilot 14
Goose, game 193
Gorilla, animal 77–79
Goulet, Michel, Canadian athlete 179
Governors of the states of the United States 359
Grammy Awards, music 267
Grand Canyon, Arizona
  commemorative stamp 133
  legend of the origin of the Grand Canyon 199
Grant, Ulysses S., American general and president 209

Great Britain (United Kingdom of Great Britain and Northern Ireland) 355
  bombing of Brighton hotel 32
  Brunei 334
  Burton, Richard, death of 28
  crown jewels 214
  economic summit meeting, London 24
  French and Indian War 203
  games 192–93
  giants in English legends 196–97
  Greenaway, Kate, author and illustrator 326
  Henry Charles Albert David, Prince, picture 62
  Hong Kong 47–48
  Lebanon, peacekeeping forces in 16, 53
  Libyan embassy incident, London 21
  Marques, sinking of 24
  Mason, James, death of 26
  music 264–65
  Olympic Games 155–56, 158, 162
  postage stamps 133; picture 131
  Priestley, J. B., death of 29
  Red Sea minesweeping operations 55
  Tolkien, J. R. R., writer, 320–21
  War of the Roses 109
  Whistler, James 251–53
  York, Battle of, Ontario, Canada 188–89
Greece 351
  ancient Olympic Games 152
  giants in Greek mythology 195
  Olympic Games 162
  postage stamp, picture 132
  roses in ancient Greek legends 108–09
  superstitions of the ancient Greeks 219
Green, Kerry, American photography program winner, picture 237
Greenaway, Kate, British author and illustrator 326
Greenhouse effect, warming trend caused by carbon dioxide in the atmosphere 111
Greenville, North Carolina
  tornado, picture 19
Grenada 351
  elections 36
  postage stamps, pictures 131, 132
Gretzky, Wayne, Canadian athlete 178–79
Greyhound, dog 74
Gross, Michael, German athlete 159; picture 183
Guam rail, bird, picture 84
Guatemala 352
  Mayan tomb 23; picture 22
Guinea 352
  military coup 20
  Touré, Sékou, death of 19
Guinea-Bissau 352
Gulliver's Travels, book by Jonathan Swift 197–99
Gushiken, Koji, Japanese athlete 160
Gustafson, Tomas, Swedish athlete 155
Guyana 352
Gymnastics, Olympic Games 160, 164

H

I

J

K

L

M

N

O

T

U

Y

Z

ILLUSTRATION CREDITS AND ACKNOWLEDGMENTS

The following list credits or acknowledges, by page, the source of illustrations and text excerpts used in THE NEW BOOK OF KNOWLEDGE ANNUAL. Illustration credits are listed illustration by illustration—left to right, top to bottom. When two or more illustrations appear on one page, their credits are separated by semicolons. When both the photographer or artist and an agency or other source are given for an illustration, they are usually separated by a dash. Excerpts from previously published works are listed by inclusive page numbers.